BADER

THE MAN AND HIS MEN

MICHAEL G. BURNS

CASSELL&CO

ACKNOWLEDGEMENTS

This book took many years to research and is heavily based upon official sources but could not have been written without the help of mumerous publications and persons. For further information upon the many pilots who appear briefly here see *Aces High, Battle of Britain Then and Now* and fine *Bader Wing*. Finally, this book could not have been written without considerable family support Thank you all.

First published by Arms and Armour 1990
This Cassell Military Paperback edition 1998

Reprinted 1998 (three times)
Reprinted 1999
Reprinted 2000 (twice)
Reprinted 2001, 2002

Cassell & Co.
Wellington House, 125 Strand, London WC2R 0BB

British Library Cataloguing in Publication
Data: a catalogue record for this book
is available from the British Library

ISBN 0-304-35052-4

Cover illustrations: Front, *First of the Many*, by Robert Taylor, reproduced by courtesy of The Military Gallery, Bath. This painting is available as a limited-edition print; for a free catalogue detailing this and other prints available write to: The Military Gallery, Queen's Parade Place, Bath BA1 1NN.

Line illustration by the author; line ilustration typesetting and reproduction by Art & Graphics, Edinburgh.

Designed and edited by DAG Publications
Ltd. Designed by David Gibbons; edited by
David Dorrell; Printed and bound in Great Britain by
Cox & Wyman Ltd., Reading, Berks.

CONTENTS

INTRODUCTION

This book treats Douglas Bader as an officer and professional fighting man. It seeks to discern why and how he was such an outstanding air combat tactician, inspired leader and gifted teacher. The contribution made by Bader's education at RAF College Cranwell and his training as an offier and fighter pilot in the early 1930s was paramount to his wartime success. Cranwell encouraged its officers to be innovative and challenging thinkers. The system turned Bader into a total professional.

Bader championed using the fighter wing instead of the squadron or flight to intercept bombers during the Battle of Britain. What is important about wings is not their marginal effect on the 1940 Battle, but what Bader did with the tactical insights he got from leading the Duxford Wing.

Bader analysed and discussed tactics for months. When he led the Tangmere Wing in 1941, he built it from small combat units not massed squadrons, honing timing to stop-watch perfection. With such a flexible force, he controlled a great volume of sky before and during combat defensively and offensively.

This book explores why so many of Bader's pilots became 'greats'. He moulded his squadrons by controlling postings, and by choosing from the squadron pool only the best to fly with him. They learnt by proximity to him. He had a sure eye for pilots who would learn – men like Cork, Donaldson, Crowley-Milling, Johnson, Dundas and Turner, who subsequently developed distinctively as leaders and significantly influenced the tactical employment of fighters and wings.

The small unit Bader developed in 1941 was the legendary 'finger-four' upon which British fighter tactics for the rest of the war were based; the flexible wing he developed in 1941 became the basis of the mid- and late-war fighter and tactical wings; and many pilots who flew with him in 1940 and 1941 became the leading fighter exponents of World War Two. These are the measures of Douglas Bader's greatness as a warrior.

CHAPTER 1

The Making of an Officer

When Douglas Robert Stewart Bader arrived at the Royal Air Force College, Cranwell, in early September 1928, sport and competition dominated his life. Cranwell offered both in abundance, but the College expected more of its young gentlemen, especially the select six who, like Bader, had won a prize cadetship through examination. Cranwell was like a public school and still charged fees to entrants. It was a tough regime, rooted in naval traditions – the site, near Sleaford in Lincolnshire, had been a Royal Naval Air Station – which were perpetuated by its first Commandants, Halahan and Longmore, who were both ex-Royal Navy officers. It was a regime designed to create officers. It provided a rounded training in humanities, engineering, administration, and Service subjects, as well as in flying. The young officers produced by Cranwell were of a very high calibre indeed.

It was largely chance and family that had made getting to Cranwell Douglas Bader's ambition, rather than university at Oxford or Cambridge, or naval college at Dartmouth or a military college at Sandhurst or at Woolwich. His uncle, Cyril Burge, had been a Royal Flying Corps pilot in the Great War, and in the 1920s was adjutant to Cranwell. In the summer before Master Bader had gone to St Edward's public school in Oxford, Uncle Cyril and Aunt Hazel invited him to stay with them at Cranwell.

The boy had been thrilled by the aeroplanes and the flying at Cranwell, but it was the sport and the fitness of the young cadets that he remembered. By the time he was due to think about his life after school, his uncle was personal assistant to the Chief of the Air Staff, Air Chief Marshal Sir Hugh Trenchard. When Douglas expressed his interest in Cranwell, Burge had no doubts that the young man was ideally suited to a career in the Royal Air Force, and encouraged him. His mother thought otherwise – besides, she could not afford the fees. There was nothing for it but a scholarship.

Bader not only excelled at sports; he was obsessed by them, to the detriment of his studies. But the scholarship and a schoolmaster motivated him to cram hard for weeks on end. He could do it – after all, he had won a scholarship from Temple Grove School, Eastbourne, to St Edward's. He also sat the Oxbridge entrance examinations and was offered a place at Oxford University, which he held in reserve.

In June 1928, a letter arrived which gave him the date, time and place for the Civil Service Commissioners' entrance examinations for Cranwell. He duly presented himself in London at Burlington House, off Bond Street. He sat the written examination paper in the morning. The cramming had worked and he found that it was not too hard. After lunch, he faced the impassive board of interviewers. Well primed by his Uncle Cyril on what answers the board liked to hear, he responded to their questions directly, respectfully, trying to avoid sounding too well rehearsed – he thought the Air Force would suit his temperament . . . he preferred team games . . .

The trauma came at the medical examination, for he was failed on high blood pressure. He was told to take it easy for a few weeks and come back. The inactivity and the waiting were excruciating, but it worked well enough to get him through.

Finally, one August morning, he received the OHMS letter informing him that he had won one of the King's cadetships awarded to the top six applicants! In fact, he had come fifth. Bader was delighted. His masters were delighted, but cautioned him to temper his high spirits and remember that he had two years of academic work ahead. Bader thought first and foremost of the sport. Even the yearning to fly had yet to come.

The Cranwell of 1928 was not the impressive edifice familiar today. The buildings of the College were mostly single-storey huts of wood. The architect's plans for the New College were still under discussion, and construction work did not begin until August 1929. One feature was the same: the vast parade ground for drill across which no one dared to walk unless on duty.

Cranwell was an ex-Royal Naval Air Station, and accommodation and facilities had changed little since the war. There were two vast airfields, one to the north and one to south. There were complexes of buildings, with the Electrical and Wireless School for apprentices at the east end and those of the College at the west end. The complexes were joined by the Sleaford Road which ran through the middle of the camp. In between these two complexes, to the south was the Commandant's house and to the north were the Headquarters, Cadet Wing Headquarters, Administration and School blocks, a church and hangars. These hangars included the Flying School's five hangars, known as Flights 'A', 'B', 'C', 'D' and 'E'.

In 1928, the Cadet Wing had two squadrons, 'A' and 'B', each with forty cadets. Bader was placed in 'A' Squadron. The course lasted two years. The First Term began in September and lasted until Christmas, when there was a few days break. The Second Term began early in January, and lasted until late July. The Third and Fourth Terms, comprising the Second Year, covered the same periods.

Each Term's cadets were divided into two sets: one flew while the other did ground school and academic studies, then vice versa. Seniority in the College began at the lower level with the cadets themselves: the Second Year Cadets were considered a rank above First Year Cadets, so had to be saluted by First and Second Termers. The real difference was that Second Year Cadets were flying Service aeroplanes.

Bader's home for his two years at Cranwell was a one-storey hut, of First World War vintage. Each squadron had its own double row of huts connected by covered walkways to the central block which housed the Cadet's Mess, with its ante-room, dining room and billiard room, and utility areas. Each hut accommodated five cadets and a batman who looked after 'his' five cadets.

The dining hall was a long, low, single-storey wooden hut, with four long tables. Dinner was a parade, with a set routine. Flight Cadets were allowed out, after duty, until 23.59 hours. Late return was an offence. Entertainment had to be relatively cheap, as cadets received £4 a month pocket money.

In 1928–30, the Cranwell aeroplanes were the Avro 504N, powered by an 180hp Armstrong Siddeley Lynx radial which gave it a top speed of about 70 knots. The Avro's main advantages were stability and responsiveness. These equipped 'A' and 'C' Flights, the First Year types. For the Second Year, there was the Armstrong Whitworth Atlas with a 400hp Armstrong Siddeley Jaguar radial and 130-knot performance – not an easy aeroplane to master, with some odd stability problems, but a real Service type for those who would go to general-purpose or bomber squadrons. These equipped 'B' and 'D' Flights. There were a few of the fast, streamlined Fairey Foxes in 'E' Flight, and for the fighter squadron nominees, 'F' Flight had Armstrong Whitworth Siskin IIIs.

The Senior NCOs had the greatest responsibility for teaching the Flight Cadets the ways of the Service, instructing them in ground school and on the drill ground, berating them, exemplifying authority and responsibility, inculcating self-respect, self-discipline and self-control. Bader and many others recalled that it was the Senior NCOs who taught the cadets how to become officers.

Each squadron had an NCO drill instructor – a flight sergeant or a sergeant – who was responsible for training cadets to the high standards of drill practised by the Cadet Wing. Before attaining that, cadets would not be allowed to join their squadron on parade. There was a Wing Sergeant Major who was the Senior Drill NCO. He was the final arbiter of a cadet's fitness to join the Wing on parade. Every morning, the two squadrons were called by bugle to the parade ground, and inspected – meticulously, ruthlessly. Each Saturday morning there was the Colour Hoisting Parade.

Drill and flying were the two most important parts of the daily routine. Academic and ground studies were secondary, but not markedly so. Cadets had to undergo a great deal of drill. First, there was basic drill, then arms drill. It took about a month of intensive foot and arms drill every working morning to reach the standard required to perform as a team with the Squadron and the Wing.

A good way of fostering team spirit and formation, drill was an important part of training. It stimulated team work, and required concentration and alertness. It taught cadets all about parading and ceremonials, for they too would have to command and supervise such things one day. Later, as Fourth Termers, cadets had to command the Wing on parade. Bader became under-officer of his 'A' Squadron.

The First Year syllabus emphasized school subjects: mathematics, science, history and English, but Cranwell taught on a gradual basis, and two of the subjects already included Service papers. Science now included aeronautical science, and history included Imperial military geography.

Workshops taught the practice and theory of elementary engineering. They concentrated on aero engines, and the construction and rigging of airframes. An NCO, a flight sergeant, was the instructor.

From the Second Term of First Year, purely Service subjects were introduced and purely academic subjects were dropped. Now, it was navigation, armament, RAF organization, basic accountancy, RAF stores procedures, structure and administration of the RAF Disciplinary Code.

Bader was being given a sound grounding in the subjects which would turn him into an administrator when the time came – dull compared with flying, but vital to the running of the Air Force, and instructors did not let any cadet forget it. At the end of each term there were examinations. Bader was also being given serious education in the technical side of flying an aeroplane, which would be necessary as he moved from aeroplane to aeroplane type and became responsible for a multiplicity of technical matters on squadrons, bases and higher. Poor results in ground school were not treated lightly, even if a cadet were good in the air.

For example, cadets needed accountancy because they would have to administer non-public funds such as clubs and welfare organizations. They needed to know the King's Regulations (KRs), the Air Council Instructions (ACIs), the Manual of Air Force Law and the Air Ministry Orders (AMOs) because they would be called upon to administer discipline for crimes and misdemeanours. All this would be of great assistance in future dealings with the bureaucracy that could enmesh everything military, the famous 'red tape'. It was also essential to know precisely one's own position vis-a-vis officers of the same, junior and senior rank, for there were many rules to trap or thwart the unwary, especially if they happened to be as ebullient as Douglas Bader.

A breadth of interest was expected of cadets, and they were encouraged to join the debating, drama and literary societies, and to use the library of ten thousand volumes. To examine the cadets' research ability, use of the library and ability to write, cadets also had to write two theses: a minor topic at the end of the first year, dealing with a subject chosen from a list of great modern military encounters; and a major topic at the end of the second year, dealing with an aeronautical topic of the cadet's choice.

Cranwell was in many respects a cross between Civil Service staff college, a university, a technical college and a flying school. The end product was a trained, educated, cultured and self-assured individual.

As part of the broadening policy, cadets were encouraged to have a 'wheel' – a motorcycle – as a way of teaching them about internal combustion engines and engineering. Most had single-cylinder 350 or 500cc bikes which cruised at up to 70mph, but some had two-cylinder jobs; Bader owned a flat-twin Douglas. The others had Rudges, Nortons, AJS, BSA and Brough Superiors. An old airship hangar on the North airfield was allocated as a garage where the hard-core of enthusiasts would strip down their engines and reassemble them meticulously. Later, they worked their way on to fine tuning. And then they would try them out on the famous Ancaster straight, or on long and hairy rides through miles of country roads. The late 1920s were halcyon days for motorcycling, with roads threading their way through the country, but traffic was only just beginning to increase, so the bikes were comparatively safe. The risks of accidents to motorcyclists were almost entirely a result of the rider 'overdoing things' . . . consequently, Bader had several.

'Wheels' also gave the cadets the freedom to roam the countryside, to visit the permitted towns (Lincoln was out of bounds except for Fourth Termers – and Sleaford was right out of bounds), as there was limited public transport.

Motor cars were prohibited to Flight Cadets, mainly as they were outside the pockets of most cadets, but Bader's friend John Chance had bought a car and kept it in a barn a mile or so from the College. Bader, Chance and Geoffrey Stephenson made use of it discreetly. One weekend, not long into their first term, an instructor flying overhead spotted them returning to the barn. It was the culmination of a list of misdemeanours and minor offences, high-spirited fun assuredly, but this episode finally provoked the Commandant, Frederick Halahan, to speak to the ring leader – Bader never forgot the short, sharp, stinging words: what the Air Force wanted was 'men, not boys'.

Bader felt humbled, and he knew that he was in danger of being slung out. Within days, he forced himself to change. His remarkable will-power channelled his energies into ground workshops and studying the academic and service subjects that until now had taken second place to sports and flying. His instructors noticed a marked improvement in his performance. The improvement continued. His sport did not suffer, and he played just as hard, and his flying progressed smoothly. He still found time for fun, but there was now less rebellion. The Cranwell system was working.

Bader was already a young man of pronounced preferences, with a will of his own. He did not smoke cigarettes, a habit many of his contemporaries got into, as he did not want to affect his wind. Later, he preferred a pipe, believing that the 'goo' would be caught in the stem and would not dribble down into his lungs and affect his wind. Bader was also teetotal. He felt no need for alcoholic stimulants, preferred outdoor activities and did not want his health affected in any way.

The Cranwell instruction syllabus got cadets into the air as quickly as possible. Within days of arriving, they had a twenty-minute 'Air Experience' flight during which the instructor pointed out the local landmarks and talked the pupil through what he was doing from starting to shut-down.

Bader was placed in 'A' Flight of 'A' Squadron, which flew the Avro 504N. His Flight Commander was Flight Lieutenant Douglas MacFayden, and his instructor was Flying Officer Wilfred Pearson. These two men, the small, calm, precise Pearson, and the elegant, firm, reasonable MacFayden, exerted a powerful influence over the impressionable, ebullient young Flight Cadet. Bader, on the doorstep of manhood, was at the age when a pupil could be moulded in the image of his master. Cranwell picked its instructors for the task of inculcating a special spirit and attitude into its young charges. The instructors were first-rate men, pilots and instructors, the kind of men whom the young tended instinctively to look up to, to emulate.

Bader had his first air experience flight on a mild autumn day, with the countryside still green, on 13 September 1928. He was purely a passive passenger. Bader felt highly self-conscious as he waddled across to the aeroplane in his flying kit for his first flight. The bulky Sidcot suit inhibited his stride and at every step the parachute pack banged against his buttocks. He soon forgot his feelings as Pearson showed him the aeroplane's control surfaces and major components, explained the controls and how and why the machine flew, then enjoined him to get into the rear seat, and strapped him in. Still talking to him, quietly, Pearson got into the front seat and connected the Gosport tube intercommunication system and talked to him through it as he engaged the Hucks starter – a Ford 'T' with a drive belt from its engine which spun the propeller – taxied into wind and effortlessly took off. The instructor continued to talk to the young man, whom he could see leaning over the side enraptured or peering over his shoulders to see the controls, and he kept talking until they had gently settled on to the grass and rolled to a stop. He had no need to ask his pupil what he had thought of the flight for it was plain in his face.

The next day, Bader had his first real lesson – actually two lessons handled as one twenty-minute period. First, Pearson demonstrated the techniques of taxi-ing and handling the Lynx engine to show how to handle the 504 on the ground, a tricky aeroplane to taxi. This was followed by taking off and demonstrating the effect of the controls. Still, Bader was only a passenger, but an actively involved one.

It was during the next lesson, twenty-five minutes of purely straight and level flying, that Bader handled the controls for the first time. When Bader did first take the controls, he was tense, jerky, but Pearson told him to relax. It was not long before the keen, easy reflexes of a natural and superlatively fit athlete produced the smooth movements that signalled to Pearson that he was teaching a boy whose abilities were as great as his own.

Pearson was a naturally gifted pilot, and a sensitive instructor. He taught his pupil to guide his aeroplane, never to force it. He showed Bader how to feel with his hands and feet, to judge by eye and brain, to be at one with the machine and the air. He taught him how to slow his thinking and to anticipate.

Pearson explained to Bader that a 'plane' was the aerofoil, that an 'aeroplane' or 'aircraft' was the whole machine. It was not a 'kite', or a 'ship' or a 'plane'. It was an 'aeroplane' or an 'aircraft'. It was all part of the way that Cranwell taught its Flight Cadets to respect their machines, to think of them clearly and positively.

Completing the basic stage of instruction, the fifth lesson covered aileron drag, the further effect of the controls and introduced stalling, climbing and gliding. It lasted just twenty minutes, and ended the first week of instruction with a taste of things to come.

The next two lessons were handled as one session because they are basic and complementary: getting into the air and getting back to the ground. The pupil flew several short times on this exercise, until mastered sufficiently. However, 'Taking off into wind' and 'Landing and judging distance' became the basic flying exercises, like a chorus in the cadet's logbook, combined with every other sequence in the syllabus.

Before going on, a bit of interest was injected into the flying. The instructor would suddenly slam the throttle shut, and wait for the pupil to react correctly – or not. This taught the pupil the action in case of engine failure during take-off. When the throttle closed and the engine stopped, he should ease the stick forward to get up airspeed, and land straight ahead. Above all, he must not turn back or he would be flying downwind and would stall. From then on, there was always the risk that the instructor would shut the throttle at any moment. For young men of Bader's temperament, this was a challenging possibility.

There were then medium, gliding and steep turns, with and without the engine. The cadet would have three or four hours' flying by now and would be doing complete circuits. After two or three hours' practice, spinning was introduced. At 4,000 feet, the instructor closes the throttle, pulls back the stick, stands her on her tail, everything quiet, pushes the nose back, kicks in hard right rudder, she jerks over . . . two or three turns . . . he centralizes controls, and pulls up her nose – now you do it!

It was as well to teach cadets early that things could go wrong, but that the situation could be retrieved. The biplanes were forgiving, and they could glide, and Lincolnshire is remarkably flat, with many places to put down, even in a hurry. The art of elementary forced landings was practised all over Lincolnshire! After that boost to confidence, the instructor would demonstrate low flying. Other things could go wrong in the air, and fire has always been one of the most feared, hence a lesson was devoted to action to take in case of fire in the air. The cadet by now would be aware of problems and solutions.

The first solo could be a nerve-racking experience, but Bader took to it easily. The Flight Cadet was not told in advance that he was to be tested for going solo, but he was likely to guess what was in the wind. The Flight Commander passed a few comments and told him to take off and fly about. It was as simple and as undramatic as that. It was another way of building confidence, quietly, easily.

On 12 February 1929, after he had been at Cranwell five months and had flown twenty-five times, logging 11 hours and 15 minutes flying time, Pearson took him up as usual. After they had landed, Bader's Flight Commander, Flight Lieutenant Douglas MacFayden, flew with Bader. It lasted just ten minutes. The Flight Cadet had to do all the tricks he had learnt to the satisfaction of both men. It was unexpected, but not entirely mystifying. When Bader and MacFayden landed, the Flight Commander climbed out and made a few low-key comments, then told Bader to take off and fly!

After the solo, flying was divided equally between solo and dual. All elementary lessons were practised repeatedly, and dual was given after every two or three solos to eradicate errors and bad habits, but each flight started and ended with those same refrains:

> 'Take off into wind, medium turns, gliding turns, steep turns with and without engine, climbing turns, spinning, landing and judging distance.'

More advanced lessons were slipped into the dual flights: climbing turns, side-slipping, and taking off and landing cross-wind. It was very useful in the days of lightly loaded biplanes to be able to slip off speed and height on a landing to correct the amount of height and speed in a gliding turn – especially a forced landing. Bader relished the control, the fine touch that gave him mastery of the aeroplane. The real use of landing cross-wind was in making forced landings if the cadet made a mess of an approach.

Once these methods of advanced control had been mastered, the instructors moved the cadets on to advanced forced landings. This was when side-slipping became invaluable and mastery of the cross-wind landing was vital. 'Advanced' meant that an instructor would cut the throttle at some really inconvenient point – just as they had passed the only landing ground within gliding range, and left it on the downwind leg . . . This became part of practically every flight. Cadets became expert at watching out for suitable landing sites as they flew around, and staying conscious of wind direction, speed and height so that they were prepared: it kept them alert. All the factors were beginning slowly to come together. It was excellent training, producing remarkably aware airmen.

The Second Term began gradually enough in Ground School, continuing with the more advanced lessons begun at the end of the First Term. In the air, with some thirty flying hours logged, the pupil would be initiated into gentle aerobatics: loops, half-rolls, then a roll off the top of the loop. When it came to aerobatics, Pearson showed Bader how to relax with the machine, to coax her responses, to think, not to throw the aeroplane around the sky. Manoeuvres had to be smooth and precise. A loop had to be executed with the aeroplane passing right through its own turbulence at the bottom of the loop. In a banked turn, the nose had always to point at the same point on the horizon, neither dipping nor rising nor swaying. Bader found that he revelled in mastering his aeroplane, in feeling her respond, in being precise.

There would also be cross-country flights. The first solo cross-country would involve a fairly short hop to a neighbouring airfield, the strangeness of landing alone at a new airfield, reporting to the Duty Hut, where the Duty Pilot would phone Cranwell to say that the cadet had touched down and would shortly be airborne again. Each stage of the cross-country process was practised in dual meticulously first, with navigation tests at each stage. As progress was made, cadets ventured further.

There was no radio. The map, compass and watch served as instruments, and time between points as the basic method. The route was drawn on the map, prepared with 'way points'. Landmarks would be memorized: railways, junctions, towns, hills. A Course and Distance Calculator (circular slide rule) was used to mark off distance and flying time between the points. A compass course was calculated with estimate of wind speed and direction from the Meteorological Office, and drift off resultant track was corrected by visual reference to way points. This was all within sight of the ground. Bader swiftly became very proficient at cross-country navigation. It put into practice much of what had been learnt in ground school. That had a two-way effect, for Bader redoubled his efforts on the ground, too, now that it was making practical sense.

At the end of the First Year, the ab initio period, all flown on the Avro 504, the cadet was tested by the Senior Flying Instructor in a flight that went through all the parts of the course. If satisfactory, the cadet went on to the next year with Service types. Douglas Bader passed easily. On 8 July 1929, Bader flew with Pearson for the last time, a thirty-minute flight taking in two loops and three forced landings. He now had 25 hours dual and 22 hours 45 minutes solo. Soon, the cadets returned to their families for summer leave.

As in the RAF in general, the afternoons of Saturday and Wednesday were for sports and games. Bader had gone to Cranwell for the sports and the competition. He was not disappointed, nor was Cranwell disappointed in him. As Cranwell had only eighty cadets – compared with the naval and military colleges and universities which had pools of a thousand each – an all-rounder like Bader, who excelled on the rugby field, was a welcome catch for Cranwell. He also boxed at Cranwell. He had twenty fights before he injured a cartilage in his knee playing rugby and that ended his boxing. Only one man beat him, Jock McLean, the Inter-Services Lightheavyweight Champion, with a knock-out, the way Bader himself had won most of his fights.

The important rugby, soccer and cricket matches were those against RMC Sandhurst and RMA Woolwich. In his first term, Bader was selected for the Cranwell Rugby First XV. They beat Woolwich and Sandhurst, the first time they had beaten both in a term. Bader played cricket. He played in Cranwell's First XI, and led the 'A' Squadron First XI in the Second Year Inter-Squadron match – a resounding victory for his team with his own runs being the deciding factor: 194 of the total 227.

The Second Year began in September. The Third Term lasted until December. As a Second Year cadet, Bader was now flying Service types. The Second Year instructors were flight lieutenants and were tough: nose had to be glued to horizon in a turn; had to hit the slipstream every time they came round in a loop; not even the slightest misjudgments of wind speed and direction and height in a landing . . . no over-confidence . . .

The Third Term training sequence was, to begin with, similar to the Avro sequence, getting the cadet used to the new Service aeroplane; concentrating on circuits, turns, advanced forced landings, spins and loops for three or four hours of dual instruction; then an hour of aerobatics: loops, stall turns, slow rolls, low flying. After five to ten hours of dual and a check flight by the Squadron Leader Flying, the cadet went solo. After that, there was the usual rotation of dual and solo sessions.

The Fourth Term began in January, lasting until July. In ground school, the more practical aspects of navigation, aeronautical engineering, stores administration, RAF law, and so on were covered. There were prizes to be won for humanities, aeronautical engineering, Service subjects and mathematics and science, and the final thesis to consider, write and research.

The Fourth Term brought more complicated flying training and ground school. Flying dual and solo in Service types continued, but with a heavy programme of cross-country flights, now further afield, and with bad weather flying included. Pupils also flew the 504 for ten hours' instrument flying, under a hood. The 504s were rigged to make them unstable, so cadets had to learn to distrust their senses and rely on their instruments. At the end of the Fourth Term, cadets had up to 70 hours flying on elementary types, with about 60 hours on Service types.

In June 1930, a Central Flying School instructor tested Bader on the full flying syllabus. The Groves Memorial Prize was awarded at the end of the term for the best all-round pilot of his term. Bader did not win, but he thoroughly enjoyed the competition. The test was taken by CFS instructors: one dual on the 504, one dual on the Service type, one solo on the Service type, then a fifteen-minute aerobatic flight in a sequence which the Cranwell flying instructors had helped the cadet to work out.

The ultimate competition at Cranwell was for the Sword of Honour, awarded to the best all-round cadet: best at flying, ground school, games, drill and discipline. Bader and Patric Coote had become respectively under-officers of 'A' and 'B' Squadrons, and were responsible for many aspects of the cadets' lives. It was another way of grooming the best for excellence. At the end of the Second Year, the Flight Cadets sat their final examinations and submitted their major thesis. The marks for these were the final factor in awarding the Sword of Honour. Coote, a worthy winner, narrowly beat Bader into second place.

The Fourth Term culminated in the Summer Ball, and, before that, of course, on 26 July 1930, the Commissioning and Sword of Honour Parade. Douglas Bader was now a pilot officer. The day before, Flight Cadet Douglas Bader had reported to the Commandant's Office. It was the final review. The Commandant, Arthur Longmore, slipped the confidential report across his desk to Bader, who scanned it swiftly . . . 'plucky, capable, headstrong . . .', and his flying ability was 'above average'. A few words from Longmore, and he was dismissed. It seemed as if the Service had assessed him accurately.

The postings followed. The waiting was frustrating. Bader was certain he would draw a fighter squadron. It was like waiting to see the fixtures pinned up on the school sports notice board to find his name on the team: 'P/O Bader, D. R. S., to 23 Squadron, Kenley'.

CHAPTER 2
An Exclusive Flying Club

Bader took a few weeks' holiday, during which he rode his motorbike down to London and traded it in against a second-hand car, an Austin 7. Bader removed the Cadet's white hat band from his peaked cap and added a pilot officer's single thin ring. He was no longer a cadet. The world was his oyster! On the morning of 25 August 1930, he drove his car through the gates of RAF Station Kenley.

Bader's friend Geoffrey Stephenson also arrived on posting the same day. They were being posted to an exclusive world. Their arrival brought No 23 Squadron's strength to twelve pilots, two over establishment, and seventy-two airmen. Its Adjutant, an important adviser for new pilots in this new yet familiar environment, was Flying Officer A. J. Tunnard. The squadron was commanded by a man to respect, the First World War ace Squadron Leader H. W. Woollett, who had once scored six victories in a single day, 12 April 1918, in a Camel of No 43 Squadron.

Kenley, lying between Croydon and Caterham, was a large grass airfield with hangars on the perimeter and mess and administration buildings, of standard RAF red brick respectability, luxury and impeccable maintenance, astride the main entrance. As Kenley was shared by two fighter squadrons, it had a wing commander as station commander.

Bader roomed in the mess, with Stephenson just down the corridor. Bader liked the life, for there was fun and structure, purpose and fellowship, flying and sport, good living and a Regular commission. RAF officers lived in considerable comfort in bachelor quarters in the mess, with long-serving servants and batmen. A pilot officer was paid 14/6 (72½p) a day, he messed at 3/6 a day and his monthly messing bill averaged between £8 and £15 depending on his consumption of alcohol. Petrol, tobacco, food and drink were cheap.

Each pilot was assigned to a Flight, 'A', 'B' or 'C', under a Flight Commander. Bader was put in 'B' Flight. Seniority was strictly defined. As a flight lieutenant, the Flight Commander was not entitled to the mandatory salute or address as 'sir' accorded to those of senior rank – squadron leader and above. Pilots only addressed their Flight Commander as 'sir' once a day, at the first meeting after Parade when they reported for duty. Thereafter, pilot officers addressed him by his surname, while flying officers might use his Christian name – but new pilot officers used 'sir' throughout the day . . .

One of No 23 Squadron's Flight Commanders was already a household name, a man whose abilities young pilots would hold in awe, and who became a good friend to Douglas Bader. Flight Lieutenant R. L. R. Atcherley had competed in the Schneider Trophy Race held off Spithead on Sunday, 7 September 1929, in a Supermarine S.6 powered by a Rolls-Royce 'R' engine against the Italians' older Macchi M.52bis. His team-mate Waghorn won, but Dick Atcherley missed a pylon and was disqualified, although he established two world speed records in the process. Three months later, after a stint at Central Flying School (CFS), Atcherley had been posted to No 23 Squadron. He left on 8 October 1930 on posting to No 14 (Bomber) Squadron, Amman, Transjordan.

No 23 Squadron had a strength of twelve Gloster Gamecocks, with an immediate reserve of six. It had been the first of five Gamecock squadrons, in May 1926. The Gamecock was a near contemporary of the Gloster Grebe, the Hawker Woodcock and, numerically the most important, the Siskin. No 23 Squadron was also the last Gamecock unit.

Bader was introduced to the Gamecock by his Flight Commander the day after he arrived, and flew one for thirty minutes that morning. The Gamecock was the last in a line of wooden-airframe RAF biplane fighters. It had a relatively short service life, partly because only ninety-nine were built and it had a relatively high attrition rate – twenty-two were lost in either spinning or landing accidents alone. However, the Gamecock had a reputation as a superb aerobatic vehicle.

In August 1930, within days of arriving at Kenley, Bader was selected for the RAF cricket First XI. The cricket season only had a month to run, but in September 1930, when the rugby season began, he was invited to play for the Harlequins. The knee cartilage held and he became one of their centre three-quarters. He rapidly became well-known and respected for his play. Some weeks later, he was selected for the RAF rugby First XV, as fly-half.

Bader had his first experience of simulated warfare in early September. The squadron co-operated with the anti-aircraft defences at RAF Biggin Hill on the 11th, 12th and 14th. Such co-operation was a regular part of a fighter squadron's activities during the period from April to September. However, before Bader could take a full part in the squadron's training for war he had to learn more skills, including air firing, blind-flying and formation flying.

New pilots went to CFS at RAF Wittering for fuller blind-flying tuition using only the 'Turn and Slip', 'Air Speed Indicator', 'Altimeter', 'Compass' and a watch – the 'Basic Six' had yet to come. The course lasted some three months.

Formation flying was a very important part of a fighter pilot's skills. Upon formation depended discipline and cohesion in fighting, for there was no radio, and attacks were carefully orchestrated according to prescribed formulas. Formation flying was taught on the squadron. First, there would be instruction on a two-seater. Then the young pilot would be taken up to formate on his leader. At first, he would find it a little tricky with constant opening and closing of throttle to hold position. The new officers would fly Number 2 or 3 in a 'Vic'. At Number 3, say, the pilot would have to place his aeroplane so as to line up his starboard wing just behind the Number 1's tailplane and parallel with the port wing of the Number 3 on the other side, but making sure that the lateral distance did not overlap the Number 1's port mainplane. The pilot would learn to be smooth with the throttle and controls, to correct with slight movements, as he learned to anticipate.

Having learnt to formate close to the leader, Bader was moved further out in the squadron formation. This made the task more difficult, but Bader relished the demands on his skills. A squadron would fly in formed up flights, and each flight would be of three aeroplanes in a vic. The further from the leader, the greater the lag in responding to a change in position by the leader or his Number 2; it took time for the change to be felt, like a ripple through the formation, then to be implemented – especially if the original change in position was inaccurate and was then being corrected just as the outer men were responding to the first change. All this was exacerbated as an aeroplane would respond slowly to changes of speed if they were to be smooth.

Squadrons would take off and land in formation, which required smooth, integrated flying, especially by the leader, who had to use his throttle smoothly to allow followers ample margin in throttle setting to avoid being caught with too much speed on the point of landing. Flight Commanders had to keep their lateral positions well spaced – if they drifted in they could box in the inner Flight who might be too fast and too high . . . with no room to adjust.

The RAF's policy of gradually introducing officers to authority, and smoothly increasing their skills, was carried through on squadrons. In rotation, Bader would occasionally lead a section, a flight, a squadron, becoming accustomed to the feel of command naturally.

It was easy for the pilots to find their way around the country, map-reading, referring to landmarks, following railways and rivers. There were established routes like the 'Iron Dog', the east-west railway line between Ashford and Tonbridge, which was the bad-weather route that the Imperial Airways pilots followed to find Croydon aerodrome. The Gamecock pilots of No 23 adapted it: taking the second branch line to the right, they flew straight up the valley and there was Croydon dead ahead. From there it was easy to find Kenley. Another route home was to line up the Crystal Palace towers and fly south. If a pilot did get lost, he could land in a field and get directions!

Officers living in the mess had a room to themselves, sparsely furnished, but adequate. Their lives on a squadron were ordered and varied. They were looked after. The 'pampering' these young men received freed them to think only about flying, their jobs. Their social life revolved around their squadron and neighbouring squadrons. As marriage was forbidden until the age of thirty or the rank of squadron leader, girlfriends could not be taken seriously. Life was pleasant, exciting, but could be short.

The Commanding Officer was responsible for all matters of discipline, administered at Orderly Room each morning. No 23 Squadron's Adjutant, Tunnard, was a General Duties Officer who flew with the squadron when possible. Just as in the air, so on the ground young officers were inducted into the ways of responsibility gradually so that it became natural to them. They took turns as Orderly Officer of the day, which involved doing just about everything official for everyone, and presence on all parades. Pilots lived entirely on the base.

For his twenty-first birthday on 21 February 1931, Douglas Bader traded in his Austin 7 for an MG sports car. This was much more in keeping with the image of the young, hot-blooded fighter pilot.

During April 1931, two Flights of No 23 Squadron were re-equipped with the Bristol Bulldog which was faster but less manoeuvrable than the Gamecock. Low aerobatics were strictly forbidden. Pilots ignored the advice. One ignored it and died. One Flight, 'C', retained the Gamecock for aerobatic work – all the other fighter squadrons now had Bulldogs and only No 23 still had any of the agile Gamecocks. Two No 23 Squadron Gamecocks were chosen to fly the combined aerobatics display at the RAF Hendon Pageant in June; the squadron had been picked to perform in June 1929 and June 1930. Squadron Leader Woollett confirmed that 'C' Flight Commander, Flight Lieutenant H. M. A. Day, was to lead the team. Day, who was thirty and had fought as a fighter pilot in the First World War, was an acknowledged aerobatic master, safe, sure and exhilarating to watch. The squadron pilots began practising to try to get selected. One pilot flew himself upside down into the ground. In April, Woollett told Bader that he would be second man with Geoffrey Stephenson as reserve. Bader moved to 'C' Flight. Shortly afterwards Woollett left the squadron. Harry Day became Acting Squadron Leader in the interim.

Pilots were not allowed to aerobat below 500 feet. Bader wanted to and did. He liked to slow roll at 50 feet. This was a court-martial offence. An aeroplane's engine could cut out upside down, and lift could be lost, and thus height . . . Day tolerated spirit and daring in his pilots. He believed that Bader had coolness and judgment and that his escapades were carefully calculated and executed risks.

There were regular exercises by the squadron and Flights throughout the year, and co-operation exercises with other fighter squadrons, ground defences and bomber squadrons. Fighter squadrons were part of the Air Defence net and their pilots had to know their roles: life was far from merely aerobatics and relaxed living, for they had a very serious part to their jobs which they tended to play down and others to glamorize. There were annual Air Defence of Great Britain exercises and squadrons went on a Practice Camp each year to hone the reality of their trade – shooting.

Arriving late, Bader had missed the 1930 Practice Camp and eagerly anticipated the 1931 Camp. It was held over a fortnight, 26 May to 12 June, at RAF Sutton Bridge where the squadron undertook its Annual Air Firing Practice against banner targets and with ciné-guns. The squadron's top air firers were Flying Officer J. McKenna and Pilot Officers G. Stephenson and A. Dobell. Later, on 30 September, the latter two represented the squadron at the Annual Best Firers competition at Sutton Bridge.

It was revealing for the young pilots to practise air-to-air gunnery with a ciné camera. It was also necessary – apart from the safety aspect of live rounds – because of the unreliability of the fighter's Vickers .303-inch machine-guns, adapted infantry weapons which were prone to jamming and consequently were mounted close to the pilot so that he could free a blockage. Also, the Vickers' lethal range was less than 75 yards and the new metal airframes were resistant to it.

The life of a fighter pilot had a serious, hard side that was not reflected in the popular image. No 23 Squadron co-operated with units of the Regular Army and the Territorial Army and units deployed as part of a field formation, like the 1st Anti-Aircraft Battalion, Royal Engineers, and those which operated independently in defence of points which were vulnerable to air attack, like the Royal Artillery or Territorials. On some occasions, they co-operated with several units, particularly during night work, when searchlights were involved as well as guns.

In April 1931, No 23 Squadron resumed co-operation with anti-aircraft gun and searchlight units. The work continued until the end of July when a major affiliation task superseded it. The main anti-aircraft searchlight company with which the squadron worked that year was the 314th, occasionally the 315th and 318th; and the main Royal Artillery anti-aircraft brigades were the 163rd, then the 51st/52nd, while the 1st AA Battalion, Royal Engineers became involved during May. Work was also carried out with the Searchlight Survey Group on 4 and 5 April and the Air Defence Experimental Establishment on 19 May. The work could be very intensive. For instance, during June the squadron co-operated with the 51st/52nd Brigade on the 1st, 7th, 16th and 28th, and the 163rd Brigade on the 6th, 9th, 16th and 28th; and two searchlight companies – sometimes with guns – the 314th on the 7th, 9th, 16th and 30th, and the 315th on the 7th, and also with Territorial Army searchlight units on the 17th.

Guns and fighters were complementary weapons. The task of anti-aircraft artillery was to prevent or impede bomber attacks on Britain. Command of the static defences was a joint Army and RAF responsibility but subject to the overriding control of the RAF which advised on the type and scale of attacks, targets and degree of warning likely. In Gun Defended Areas, strict co-ordination between fighter defences and guns was enforced, fighters operating beyond the Areas or above 10,000 feet.

The squadron provided 'targets' for the guns and searchlights and honed the co-operation between fighters and ground defences which are essential to any air defence system. Pilots took it in turn to consult and liaise with searchlight and gun crews to determine the modes of operation – excellent training for young men like Bader, which stood him in good stead later. Such work cannot be ignored: it is part of the fighter pilot's role and essential to the training and maintenance of air defences. It is a key to understanding the breadth of Bader's assessment of the air defences in 1940.

June was a momentous month for the young Douglas Bader. First, there was the fulfilment of gunnery at the Practice Camp. Then, early in the month, he was again selected to play for the RAF cricket First XI. More importantly, it was confirmed that he would fly at the RAF Display at Hendon, set for the 27th. On the 19th, the weekend before the display, Flight Lieutenant Day, Flying Officer McKenna and Pilot Officers Bader and Stephenson took part in the Andover Air Display, going through their individual display routines in their Gamecocks. After that display, Day decided on his Hendon team: he and Bader were the main pair, with Stephenson as reserve pilot.

The RAF Display at Hendon in 1931 was favoured with a brilliant summer's day. A crowd of 175,000 was inside Hendon aerodrome. Many thousands watched from beyond the perimeter, on the hills and in the fields of the open country round about. Biplanes could be flown so tightly that most performances took place within a few hundred feet of the Royal Box, upon which the flying focused.

There were several Service performances to thrill the crowds. Three Hawker Furies performed formation aerobatics – the first time the Fury had been seen in public – and the Fleet Air Arm's Fairey Flycatchers captivated the crowds with the noise and spectacle of their demonstration. But the professionals reserved their especial accolade for the ten-minute synchronized aerobatic sequence flown by Day and Bader in their Gamecocks. *The Times* declared that they 'provided the most thrilling spectacle ever seen in exhibition flying'.

Day invented five new routines of synchronized aerobatics for that year. In the first, two aircraft dived together, then pulled out in two consecutive loops, three feet between their wing tips, then climbed up again, stall-turned away on either side in a vertical dive, aileron turned inwards so that they faced and crossed each other, wing tip to wing tip, then climbed and rolled off the top of a loop together in opposed directions, dived to either side of the airfield, then turned back and flew fast at each other head-on to start the next routine . . . the next routine involved flying upside down.

Bader was, at twenty-one, a hero and a celebrity in aviation, in sports and in social circles. He was now also on a danger list – the 'Hendon Winners List'. Many of them were killed soon after their victories, aerobatting or flying dangerously, driven to excel themselves repeatedly. Bader was also reaching that dangerous stage when the pilot has enough flying hours to make him confident, but not enough to make him wise, the stage when many fatalities have been seen to occur. Harry Day was well aware of both dangers, and counselled young Bader. On one occasion, on the way back cross-country from a display at Cramlington, Bader broke away from Day and hedge-hopped. Day rebuked him sternly.

The air display season had not ended with Hendon, nor had the squadron's use of the Gamecock. On 22 August, Day, Bader and Flight Lieutenant S. H. V. Harris flew individual and Flight aerobatics in their Gamecocks at the Newcastle Air Display. After that, it was time to relinquish the Gamecocks, and take up the Bulldog as a fighting mount and to begin practising for the next year's aerobatic season.

Bader had many things on his mind now, other than aerobatics. He had begun flying the Bulldog as a 'fighting mount' and was learning how to get the best out of it. His fighter pilot skills were also being developed, as a member of a team and for the promotions examinations. For a fortnight between 4 and 15 August 1931, No 23 Squadron was on attachment to RAF Bircham Newton for affiliation duties with No 207 (Bomber) Squadron. There they practised Fighter Attack sequences against bombers and escorted bomber formations, learning the essentials of their trade. During this period, the squadron also took part in the annual Command Air Exercise, when the Air Force was divided into two and the halves were pitted against each other. Bader was quick to assimilate the lessons, and was being developed by his senior officers.

Bader also had his sporting activities and his future career to consider. The rugby season was coming up, but so were the postings. The 'A' List was posted in the orderly room, the roster of the officers being posted abroad. The RAF might be comparatively small, and there were not many fighter squadrons, but before the Cranwell graduate lay the prospect of Service flying throughout the world. Usually a young officer served a year in a Metropolitian squadron where he would learn the military part of his profession and the more advanced flying techniques, such as blind flying and formation flying, and was then posted to an Empire or Protectorate station. For many this was excitement, but for Bader it might ruin his chance of a cap for England at rugby; but the authorities seemed prepared to postpone sending him overseas.

After the squadron's last Gamecocks were phased out, Bader began to fly the Bulldog, the RAF's new standard day and night fighter. A robust single-bay biplane, armed with two .303-inch machine-guns and powered by a 490hp Bristol Jupiter VIF radial, it remained within the RAF's fighter tradition. It had a modest top speed of 174mph and service ceiling of 27,000 feet. Like the earlier Siskin, the Bulldog had an all-metal airframe and was easy to maintain. It was very manoeuvrable but was not a fine, agile aerobatic mount like the Gamecock. It was, in fact, a serious fighter.

Landing was an unpleasant experience, for the Bulldog was prone to stall on the flare-out, resulting in a broken undercarriage. However, take-off was straightforward, and it climbed away easily, the pilot simply setting the throttle to give an indicated airspeed of 105mph and pulling the control column back. It would climb to 20,000 feet in 14½ minutes.

The aircraft was light and sensitive on the controls for most normal flight manoeuvres, but steep turns at below 130mph needed almost full top rudder to stop the nose from deviating from the horizon. This was a problem of directional stability. There was loss of fine control over the rudder at lower airspeeds. Stalling and spinning characteristics were acceptable.

But the Bulldog had one special quality, the excellent visibility from the cockpit, which was a great boon in aerobatting, giving plenty of sight of partners and easing judgments. If a pilot were to give himself enough sky, he could perform fine aerobatics, using about 200mph in a dive before pulling up in a great sweeping loop.

The Bulldog had two vices which affected the recovery from all manoeuvres: it was slow to respond to the elevator in a dive, and it had exaggerated sink. On No 23 Squadron, it was forbidden to perform any high-loading manoeuvre in which the aeroplane was 'likely to pass below 1,000 feet above the ground'. A climbing turn near the ground had to be made with plenty of speed and power, and pilots were discouraged from rolling the aeroplane below 500 feet because the end of the roll could be over 400 feet lower than the entry . . .

Harry Day counselled caution when aerobatting the Bulldog. He did not want a bunch of over-careful pilots, who would shun risks in combat, but he did want sensible pilots who knew what risks they were running and made every effort to counter them. The Bulldog would sink quicker in a slow roll when inverted, or the engine might stop . . . Fighting Area Regulations forbade aerobatting below 2,000 feet because there had been too many accidents involving low flying.

Bader ignored the advice. During November he went low aerobatting. In fact, he beat up the airfield. Day carpeted him. The lecture stung Bader: 'showing-off'. He began to be more careful. Day went off on leave, still concerned about Bader.

Bader was training hard for rugby. At the end of November, he was selected as fly-half for the Combined Services team against the Springboks. It was the green light that he would make England.

When 'C' Flight's pilots gathered at their Flight office after Parade on Monday morning, 14 December 1931, Harry Day authorized Bader to practise aerobatic sequences near Kenley. As No 23 Squadron's principal aerobatic exponent, Bader was preparing gradually for the 1932 air display season on the Bulldog. He had 32 hours 20 minutes on the Bulldog, and was proficient in all its flying characteristics and fully aerobatic on it. In all, he had 491 hours 50 minutes flying time.

After an hour and a half of throwing the Bulldog around the sky, at a safe height, he landed and strolled over to the Flight office. It was a little after ten o'clock. In the office, he met Flying Officer G. W. Phillips and Stephenson. Phillips was about to fly across to Woodley Aerodrome to lunch with his brother at the Aero Club. He suggested that Bader and Stephenson join him. They agreed with alacrity. It would make a pleasant lunch party, and a pleasant flight on this fine crisp winter's day.

They set course for Reading, enjoying the formation flight and the clear light, glad to be alive, and flying. Presently, they spotted the white Aero Club buildings beyond Reading.

Over lunch the young pilots at Woodley asked Bader about Hendon and aerobatics. He was a hero. After lunch, the three No 23 Squadron pilots took off in line abreast, Bader on the left, Phillips in the centre, Stephenson on the right. As the other two climbed away, Bader held his aeroplane down to build up speed.

Bader felt obliged to make just a small parting salute. It was a matter of courtesy, a thank-you gesture. It would be at low level, his speciality. It was expected of Hendon winners. He had a sense of invulnerability, nearing that magical, dangerous five hundred flying hours.

Bader pulled over to the left in a steep climbing turn, back to the airfield, beginning to dive to gain more speed as he came out of the turn, and crossing the airfield perimeter with the speed nudging 125mph. He would need that speed, not more, not less, for a roll, especially low down.

The Bulldog rocked in some thermals as Bader levelled out, and held her steady, aimed at the centre of the airfield. There was a little knot of spectators watching him from the flight line.

Bader's head was about eighteen feet off the ground – his undercarriage had barely ten feet clearance. That would give him perhaps two feet to play with in a roll. The spectators grinned as they watched the Bulldog, so low that it appeared to be one with its shadow, begin crisply to roll.

Bader eased the control column over to the right and the aeroplane began to revolve in a roll to the right. He kept his eyes on the horizon as it spun evenly in front of him. He knew he had to keep the speed up, for a biplane would lose forward momentum in a roll, and so it would lose height. He applied a little top rudder to keep the nose up as he went into the roll, for if the nose dropped, he would lose height.

The right wingtips reached the vertical. He was clear of the ground by a shaving. He felt the force of gravity pressing him into the right side of the fuselage. He kept the stick over.

Then he was upside down. He knew the feelings. The responses and the timings were automatic. He felt the pressure of his straps on his shoulders and belly as he hung there. His feet were firm on the rudder bar. He kept the stick far enough forward to hold the nose up while the aeroplane was upside down, or he would lose height. He kept the throttle back to hold the torque there and keep the engine still running, or it would cut.

The roll was accurate so far. He felt the pressure shifting to his right side. He was straining to avoid any sink, for it was a vice to which the Bulldog was prone. He had no margin for error.

He began to apply positive top rudder as the aeroplane came out of the roll to prevent the Bulldog losing height. He had to keep the speed up as close as possible to 125mph, but he was losing speed fast. The wings swept round to the vertical, the left wingtips bare feet from the grass.

He felt the slide beginning. He gave more positive top rudder to check it, but the fine control had gone as the speed fell. He needed to apply more . . . There were too many variables, too little time. He held the stick over. He increased engine power. He had no margin for error . . . The wings were rolling past the vertical. The loss of height went on . . . His margin was gone.

The left wingtip brushed the grass. The nose ducked down. The momentum fell, the stability distorted. The wingtip crumpled. In that fraction of time, Douglas Bader lost control of the aeroplane.

The Bulldog went in sideways, propeller and engine tearing loose, bouncing loose, left wing buckling, twisting under the fuselage, right wing collapsing on to the fuselage, upper wing wrenched off the struts – Bader watching it all in slow motion from the open cockpit – fuselage smashing around the startled pilot, strange feelings of utter disorientation, quick sharp smells, noises that were totally unfamiliar yet whose meaning was sickeningly obvious, a trapped feeling in a mass of metal and fabric moving very fast over many feet, slewing, then suddenly stopping and subsiding, chunks of grass and alloy cascading down.

Then there was silence. A feeling of disbelief, a slow observation of where he was, but not understanding.

The young club pilots had begun to run as soon as they saw the wingtip buckle, instinctively.

The pile in the middle of the airfield was still. There was no fire, yet.

When they got to Bader, he was still conscious, but dazed and unaware. The men tore the airframe away from him, and lifted him from the wreckage. The trouser legs of his flying suit were ripped and soaked in blood. A metal bar had gone through one knee. Quick thinking by one of the men saved Bader's life on the spot, for he thrust a thumb into the leg artery, staunching the pumping blood flow. The ambulance arrived. Bader was lifted carefully on to a stretcher. The ambulance drove off, leaving a group of shocked young men gathered around a pile of metal and fabric in the middle of a cold English field, thinking they had watched their hero dying.

Phillips and Stephenson flew back to Kenley with the sad news. That day, No 23 Squadron's Diary noted: 'Pilot Officer D. R. S. Bader posted to Royal Air Force Depot Uxbridge / Supernumerary Non-Effective Sick as a result of Flying Accident at WOODLEY Aerodrome near Reading on 14.12.31.'

Douglas Bader was in intensive care in Reading infirmary for weeks. The crash had seriously injured his legs and one was almost severed. He was in deep physical trauma, semi-conscious. The surgeons amputated one leg in an effort to save his life. Superbly fit, his body sustained the initial shock of the injuries and then the shock of the operation. The other leg had to be amputated to prevent gangrene. His body recoiled from the further shock. Douglas Bader began to die.

On the verge of oblivion, Douglas Bader heard a remark by a nurse: 'Quiet, there's a boy dying in there'. Bader's will galvanized and for the first time since the crash he became aware of the meaning of the pain and the feelings. He began to exert his conscious will. Slowly he began to recover. He took strength with him, for he was never afraid of death again.

In the safety of the shock from the crash, and deep within himself, he had come to terms with the loss of his limbs. Only he was to blame. He set his goals as high as he could. He would get artificial limbs and he would learn to walk. Then, he would go on flying. But for years he had to strive against bouts of deep, grieving depression.

During the high summer of 1932, Bader was staying with Sir Philip Sassoon at Lympne. He was the Under-Secretary of State for Air. He was also Honorary Air Commodore of No 601 (County of London) Squadron, Auxiliary Air Force. Peter Ross, fellow pilot from No 23 Squadron, was with them. The Commanding Officer of No 601 Squadron was Nigel Norman. He suggested to Bader that he fly No 601's 'hack', an Avro 504. Ross acted as guardian. Bader flew over to Kenley, the first time he had been back since his accident.

The flight had a punch line. John Parkes was one of No 601 Squadron's Flight Commanders. The Avro was his responsibility. He wanted to know where it had gone. He asked a sergeant and the sergeant replied: 'Dunno, Sir. Some bloke with no legs took it away.'

The RAF did not agree that Bader could remain in the flying branch of the Service. Although the medical board passed him as A1B except for his legs, and Central Flying School passed him as fully competent as a pilot, there was nothing in King's Regulations that covered his case, and that being so, he could not have a flying job. But he could have a ground job.

Douglas Bader tried a post at RAF Duxford looking after No 19 Squadron's motor transport pool. He disliked it. Six months later, in the summer of 1933, he resigned from the RAF.

Now he had to make a fresh start. It took time and courage to get a job. Bader applied for an interview with the staff manager of the Asiatic Petroleum Company and was pleasantly surprised to learn that they had an Aviation Department, under Walter Hill, which was being expanded. He was offered a post at £200 per annum, and thus began Bader's second career. Shortly afterwards, Asiatic were absorbed by Shell Transport and Trading. During the next few years, he met and made friends with many of the aviation names of the period, including the American, 'Jimmy' Doolittle, with whom he became close. In those years, and with Doolittle, Bader's knowledge of aviation and aeroplanes was widened and deepened, and he did not lose his interest in tactics, especially not when he had a mind as energetic as Doolittle's with which to fence.

PART II

CHAPTER 3
Fighter Command

On 7 February 1940, Flying Officer Douglas Bader reported for flying duty to No 19 Squadron, a Spitfire unit based at RAF Duxford in No 12 Group, RAF Fighter Command. It was not a coincidence that the Commanding Officer was Bader's friend from Cranwell and Kenley, Geoffrey Stephenson, now a squadron leader.

Awakened to the threat to peace by the Munich Crisis of 1938, Bader had written to the Air Ministry asking for flying duties reserve status. He was refused: just as in 1932, there was nothing in King's Regulations that covered the case of a 100 per cent disabled officer who was fully capable of flying. The immediate threat of war was dispelled by Munich, but Bader's ambition to get back to flying did not cease, any more than did Hitler's ambition to seize chunks of Europe.

Following the Munich crisis, the Air Ministry made plans to deploy squadrons to France in order to bring the Royal Air Force's short-range bombers within striking distance of Germany. In January 1939, the Air Ministry announced the formation of the Auxiliary Air Force Reserve to enable ex-RAF personnel to serve with the Auxiliary squadrons in war.

When Germany seized Czechoslovakia, Bader wrote to Air Marshal Sir Charles Portal, the Air Ministry's Air Member for Personnel. Now, however, Geoffrey Stephenson was Portal's personal staff officer. He had some influence and vouched for Bader's qualities as an officer and natural ability as a pilot. Bader habitually went to the top to get his decisions, and was not averse to using his Cranwell connections, for several friends and instructors from the College were now well placed. Cranwell helped in other ways: it had taught him how the Air Force worked, and how to present a case.

The French had asked the British to deploy Hurricane regular squadrons to France. Between 8 and 11 August 1939, more than 1,300 French and British aircraft took part in the annual Home Defence exercises in south-east England. This time, it culminated on the 11th with a practice blackout over London and the south-east. A week later, 200 French aircraft 'attacked' the south of England against RAF fighter defence. The idea of war was being brought home to the people of the Home Counties and London – including Mr Douglas Bader.

On 23 August, all RAF units were ordered to mobilize to war establishment, and the next day the Advanced Air Striking Force (AASF) and Air Component were ordered to mobilize, according to plan. On 31 August, Portal wrote Bader a calculated and well-timed letter: they had no place for him now in peace, but if war were to come, then the Air Force would have him back, provided the medical branch cleared him A1B (full flying category).

Bader began to want war to come. His wife Thelma was totally opposed to his going back into the Air Force. She was not against the Services – after all, her father was a wing commander, and three of her cousins, the Donaldson brothers, were Air Force pilots. No, they had had six good years of marriage, Douglas had a solid career ahead of him in Shell, and had won a long, hard struggle to minimize the loss of his legs and to conquer depression. Her family supported her in her opposition to Douglas's ambition. But the man was intransigent.

Douglas Bader was obsessed. He knew he could still fly, not just well, but better than most. He remembered Philip Sassoon organizing the loan of No 601 Squadron's Avro that afternoon those years ago for himself and Peter Ross – he had proved he could fly then, and CFS at Wittering had confirmed it. Red tape denied him the chance, that was all.

On 1 September, there was complete mobilization of the British Army, Navy and Air Force. The RAF Reserve and Volunteer Reserve and Auxiliary Air Force were called out for permanent service. Next day, the people of south-east England watched the first echelon of the AASF fly to France: ten squadrons with 160 Fairey Battle light bombers – an obsolete aeroplane for an obsolete role.

Now that war had come, Bader was relieved. He took two decisive courses of action. First, he had Shell remove his name from the Reserved Occupation List – he would not bow to arguments that he would have a vital role in the country's air defence by ensuring the supply of aviation fuel. Secondly, he pestered friends and influencers unmercifully at the Air Ministry to get them to honour Portal's pledge – all he asked for was the chance to prove that he could fly operationally, all he wanted was an assessment from CFS.

A month went by, during which the air war became a tentative reality. Bader fretted. Then, Halahan, his commandant from Cranwell, came to his aid. He was now an air vice-marshal involved with ground personnel, but he had influence. He knew Bader's character and abilities. He gave him a written recommendation for the Head of the Air Ministry Medical Board.

Bader went for his medical. The doctors examined him, then he went in to see the wing commander in charge. The officer was reading Halahan's note. He said that Bader was 100 per cent fit – apart from his legs. It was the same verdict that had grounded him in 1932. However, the wing commander said that he agreed with Halahan: Bader was exactly the kind of man the Air Force wanted, and that if he were 100 per cent fit, legs or no legs, he should be given A1B, and sent to CFS for them to decide. The wing commander recommended that he go for assessment at CFS.

Any such assessment had to be in Bader's favour, as he knew the key figures at the School as friends, and they knew his abilities and character. On 14 October, a telegram ended his irrascible waiting. On the 18th, he reported to CFS, which was now at Upavon. The Officer Commanding 'A' Flight of the Refresher Squadron was Squadron Leader Rupert Leigh – another ex-

Cranwell officer, a year below Bader. Wing Commander George Stainforth, of Schneider Trophy fame, was Officer Commanding the Squadron.

The afternoon that Bader arrived, they flew a Harvard. It was strange at first, to be in the air piloting after so long, and to be flying in an all-metal monoplane with an enclosed cockpit and with an engine with more power than a Bulldog's – and a retractable undercarriage. Then, the feel came back, the old contentment. There was just one problem. The Harvard had brake pedals which Bader could not operate. As Service types had handgrip brakes, Leigh simply overlooked the problem, and operated them himself. Leigh had no hesitation in passing Bader fit to fly.

At the end of November, the Air Ministry confirmed that they would honour Portal's commitment: war had come, and the doctors and CFS had passed him fit to fly. He was to be on the Volunteer Reserve, but as a regular officer re-employed in his former rank and seniority. That made him just about the most senior flying officer in the Air Force. First, he had to undergo a full refresher course at CFS, and then he would be posted. For Bader, there was no doubt about what he would fly – fighters. Without legs, he could not see anyone making him pilot of an aeroplane with a crew. More than that: he wanted only fighters.

Leigh had charge of him for the first few weeks. He began to fly on Avro Tutors, perfect little biplanes with more performance than a Gamecock. At 3.30 on the afternoon of 27 November 1939, Douglas Bader went solo in a Tutor (K3242), after just 25 minutes' dual. It was an overcast day, with a 1,500-foot cloud base. Bader slipped away from the traffic around the airfield. He flew around, orientating himself. Then, he pushed the stick over and kicked top rudder . . . 25 minutes later, he was down. Satisfied.

On 4 December, Bader first flew the Fairey Battle. This type was used for familiarization with enclosed cockpit, retractable undercarriage mono-planes, and for experience of handling the Rolls-Royce Merlin engine which the Battle shared with the Hurricane and Spitfire. Compared with the simple routines on the Gamecock and Bulldog, there was a cockpit drill to learn before taxi-ing out, and a multitude of instruments to observe in flight. There were two things in particular that Bader was told to remember: on take-off, do not forget to put the variable-pitch propeller in fine pitch, or you will crash, not fly; and on landing, do not forget to lower the undercarriage, or you will crash, not land.

By now, on the ground, in the mess, he had begun to settle back into Service life. He belonged.

In January 1940, he began to fly Miles Masters. With that type, he *knew* that he was truly destined for single-seaters. Towards the end of January, he flew a Hurricane, with a two-blade fixed-pitch propeller, but a real fighter. The exhilaration he felt on getting into a fighter's cockpit again after eight years was indescribable. It was like strapping on a machine that became an extension of his body. In the air, he was amazed by the Hurricane's performance. On his second flight, he began to explore the fighter's aerobatic ability.

Bader went through the standard refresher course along with other

Regulars of his generation and younger Short Service Officers who had been recalled for duty. He had much to learn of modern equipment and armament. Not only were the aeroplanes enclosed cockpit monoplanes instead of open cockpit biplanes, but flying was far more technical, and gunnery – with eight fast-firing guns instead of two and at twice the airspeed – was more exacting. There had been considerable advances in the 1930s. However, operational techniques – radio transmitting procedures, direction-finding procedures, gunnery – were taught on squadrons. CFS concentrated on flying.

There had been doubt in certain quarters, even at CFS, that Bader could meet the School's stringent requirements. He exceeded them. By the end of January 1940, he had flown 54.15 hours, including 6.20 hours dual, at CFS. The Refresher Squadron instructors announced that they were satisfied with him. The Officer Commanding the squadron, Stainforth, assessed his ability as a pilot as 'Exceptional'.

It was time for a squadron, preferably one whose commanding officer would not be cautious about a limbless fighter pilot. Bader enlisted the Cranwell network again. Geoffrey Stephenson now commanded a squadron, No 19, the first Spitfire unit. Could he help? Stephenson began to pull the necessary strings to get Bader an immediate posting to his unit.

On 3 January 1940, Flying Officer Douglas Bader went home. He put his wife through four days and nights of obsessing about getting back into a squadron, because not until he was operational would he really belong, really believe he had done it. On the morning of 7 February, a knock on the door brought the telegram from the Air Ministry: 'Flying Officer D. R. S. Bader. Posted 19 Squadron, Duxford, w.e.f. February 7th.' His wife packed his kit, and a couple of hours after the telegram arrived, Douglas Bader left for war.

It was the 'Phoney War', and the most bitter winter in memory. Duxford aerodrome had been under snow since the beginning of the month. With the exception of a runway surface test carried out by Flight Lieutenant Wilfred Clouston on 2 January, No 19 Squadron did not fly until the 10th, when the squadron resumed Convoy and Lightship Patrols. With no flying possible, Bader had time to meet old friends on the base. Ironically, No 19 Squadron's motor transport pool at Duxford had been where his RAF career had ended. Now, he found that No 19 Squadron shared the base with No 222 Squadron, a Blenheim fighter unit, commanded by another old friend, Squadron Leader 'Tubby' Mermagen, whom Bader had known when they were young pilot officers.

In the days of inactivity, Bader had time to discuss the state of tactics, to catch up on developments and to absorb information about the Spitfire, which he had yet to fly. No 19 Squadron's Spitfire Mk Is had 1,030hp Rolls-Royce Merlin IIs, which gave a top speed of 362mph. The Spitfire had been designed as a fast-climbing interceptor to counter bomber formations, hence its rate of climb, 2,530 feet a minute, was high, and its ceiling was 31,900 feet. However, it did not need a great radius of action which, with take-off and landing and 15 minutes' combat, was less than 200 miles. It was armed with eight .303-inch machine-guns.

On 13 February, Douglas Bader made his first flight in a Spitfire. A young pilot briefed him, and let him take off, all very matter-of-fact. As was the reaction of most pilots, Bader found taxi-ing to be a trial, with the long nose obscuring everything and the undercarriage feeling far from stable. But once in the air, Bader was impressed by the Spitfire – 'the aeroplane of one's dreams'. It was light on the controls, positive in response, and perfectly harmonized. It had a reserve of speed and power which made aerobatics much safer than on biplanes, although the niceties of manoeuvre might be gone.

Unfortunately, when it came to landing, the technical manuals and the briefing had omitted to tell him that he had to charge up the hydraulic system to take the weight of the undercarriage, before the selector could be moved into the 'Down' position. Bader thought the system was jammed and he tried to call up for assistance on the radio, but the young pilot's briefing about the R/T system had been so complex that Bader had barely understood it, thinking it unnecessary. Now he could not get through on it. It took him many anxious minutes before he managed to free the undercarriage selector, get the wheels down, and land. It was very much on-the-job training.

Bader flew his first two operational sorties on 15 February 1940, flying a Yellow Section Spitfire Mk I (K9825) on two uneventful Lightship Patrols. At 07.45 hours, Red Section took off on the dawn Lightship Patrol, landing back at 09.30 hours. The three pilots of Yellow Section – Flight Lieutenant Lane leading Bader and Sergeant Jennings – set out for the barely overlapping second patrol at 09.25 hours. They were back, cold and hungry, and with nothing to report at 11.00 hours. Red Section flew the third patrol, from 12.15 to 14.05 hours. Lane's Yellow Section took off for the final patrol at 13.45 hours with Bader and Pilot Officer Michael Lyne as his Numbers 2 and 3. They landed back at 15.25 hours.

This was fairly typical of days when there were operations, and there was little significance in the fact that No 19 Squadron flew four 'L/Ship Patrols' that day. These were part of the normal routine of a unit in No 12 Group engaged on the North Sea watch, assisting the Royal Navy in keeping the vital coastal shipping traffic moving by warding off German bombers.

The following day, 16 February, brought the squadron further Lightship Patrols. Bader (L1031) flew one with Red Section from 10.40 to 12.40 hours, with Flight Lieutenant Lane and Squadron Leader Stephenson. Next morning, Geoffrey Stephenson had his squadron aloft for formation practice, and, as the ORB says: 'Various manoeuvres in Air Drill were successfully performed.'

Bader flew no further sorties until 24 February as the weather was very poor. However, on the 21st, the Air Officer Commanding No 12 Group, Air Vice-Marshal Trafford L. Leigh-Mallory, inspected No 19 Squadron, and the squadron demonstrated a quick rearming in 10 minutes 25 seconds. The day had a special significance for Douglas Bader for it was his thirtieth birthday.

On 24 February, the squadron flew three section-strong 'Fishing Fleet Patrols'. Bader (L1031) flew the middle patrol, from 10.15 to 12.25 hours with Squadron Leader Stephenson and Pilot Officer Brinsden as Yellow Section. Bader did not mind the lack of combat, because it was satisfaction to be with fighters and pilots, and to be flying again. What he did mind was the standards of training and skills shown by some of the pilots, those who had come via the late 1930s training schemes who lacked the depth of understanding of the Cranwell officers. Failures in early training would lead to problems in flying and command skills later, just as excellence in Bader's flying and training produced excellence.

On one occasion, returning from patrol, Bader took over the lead of the section when the section leader had got lost. Bader had been map-reading and knew precisely where they were. On another occasion, Bader was tucked in to his leader's wing at very low level when the leader flew close by a hangar, forgetting all about Bader on his wingtip. Bader only just cleared the hangar. It was a clear sign of lack of understanding of what formation flying entailed, and a lack of awareness that stemmed from poor basic training.

It would be too easy to dismiss Bader's attitudes and criticisms as the arrogance of a professional, of an elitist officer. This was not so. Bader saw it as a problem to be understood and solved. Later, when he was a commander himself, Bader was careful to observe the signs of unpreparedness in pilots, and took steps to rectify the problem quickly, sending the pilot off on a course, or returning him to a training school. He was equally tough on entire units, working them hard in the arts of flying as a combat entity, before committing them to action. Otherwise, they would neither survive nor be successful.

The inactivity gave time to hone flying skills and to talk tactics and gunnery. No 19 Squadron's routine was shipping, convoy and lightship patrols, reconnaissance flights off the east coast and interceptions (usually unfruitful or of friendly aircraft), and then practising formations, fighter attacks, co-operation with the Royal Navy, anti-aircraft guns and search-lights. This work was familiar to Bader from his days with No 23 Squadron; although the Sector Station Control of fighters had changed the deployment of fighters considerably, the roles of fighters had not changed substantially. Significantly, as No 19 Squadron was in No 12 Group, it was not aware of the role of radar in its work.

On 28 February, No 19 Squadron's 'A' Flight co-operated with three Vickers Wellington bombers from No 215 Squadron at RAF Bassingbourn: 'Fighter Attacks 3 and 4 and deflection shooting with cine guns were successfully carried out' [ORB]. The following day, the 29th (1940 being a Leap Year), it was 'B' Flight's turn: 'Fighter Attacks 1, 2, 3 and 4 were carried out and cine guns were used' [ORB].

Bader was unimpressed by such demonstrations of skill. He asserted that they were unrealistic, as the Wellingtons flew straight and level – albeit dangerously low sometimes – and no one fired back. He was confident that the lessons of the First World War would still apply. He was sure that Fighter Attack 1 would not work especially: queueing up behind the leader to go in one at a time, fire, then swing away, exposing their vulnerable bellies to the bomber's fire.

Bader advocated far more aggressive tactics than were practised by Fighter Command. He believed in attack with surprise from the sun and swooping from height, not letting the bombers become aware of a whole squadron queueing up. An attacker pressing close from a surprise attack had little to fear, for the deflection problems for a bomber's gunners became acute the closer the attack, while the fighter pilot had an engine and an armoured windscreen in front of him.

Bader had absorbed the writings of the First World War aces, McCudden, Ball, Mannock. Bader, even with only theory to rely on, was dogmatic that the maxims they had propounded still applied: He who has the height, he who has the sun and he who gets in close will win. Bader distrusted the Fighter Attack methods, for they were worked out on the basis of theoretical understandings of the physical laws governing the curves described by a fighter in an attack, and not on practical experience and an understanding of the essence of all tactics, whether on land, on sea or in the air – position.

Bader asserted that the successful fighter pilots of the First World War were those who got in very close before firing. A machine-gun's bullets will produce an oval pattern, with 75 per cent of the bullets in a central circle, and the remaining 25 per cent in upper and lower arcs. The First World War aces waited until the range was short enough for their small bullet groups to be aimed with minimum chance of missing the target. This was not just applied to small, jinking, fleeting targets. Even in a surprise attack from dead astern when the target was flying straight and level at a constant speed, experience had shown that such short range was still necessary. It was also applied successfully when attacking formations of bombers.

Getting in close was not in question: the question was how close. There was a tendency among the pilots of the new monoplanes to regard the teachings of the First World War as outmoded, founding their belief on the great increase in firepower of eight guns which would give a better, large pattern. However, air gunnery had not increased in accuracy in the intervening twenty years. At best, air gunnery was an inexact science; at worst, it was very inaccurate, dependent upon individual skill and aptitude. Therefore, the fighter pilot had to fire the maximum number of rounds at a range at which the number of missing bullets would be the minimum. The greater bullet density of the eight-gun Hurricane and Spitfire over the twin-gun Sopwith Camel was offset by the fact that a modern bomber's airframe would deflect or stop a large proportion of the .303-inch-calibre bullets. A 1940 bomber could sustain a large number of hits without lethal damage – and the longer the range, the fewer the bullets that would hit.

The view of Fighter Command was that the best opening range varied from about 500 yards when attacking a slow bomber with good defensive fire, to about 300 yards when attacking a fast bomber like the Junkers Ju 88. However, the final decision would be left to the pilot in combat. No hard and fast range could be laid down. . .In practice, pilots found that they would have to get within 120 yards to ensure a kill with machine-guns. There was a lot of learning to be done about air gunnery before air tactics could be developed.

In regard to what was to be expected of the fighter squadrons, Fighter Command did not equivocate:

'It is vitally important that the heaviest possible casualties should be inflicted on the first bombing raids to reach this country, even at considerable cost to our fighter defences. The knowledge that a fighter will normally attack at a range at which his fire is most decisive in the overwhelming majority of cases, and that his tactics are such as to make it very difficult to shoot him down before reaching that range, will provide the greatest deterrent to further attacks.'

The kinds of desperate and bloody battles envisaged by such prose were very far from the mind of No 19 Squadron's Diarist as he summarized the month of February 1940:

'With the exception of several bad weather periods, when the work of the squadron was somewhat curtailed, the squadron was moderately active, carrying out quite a number of convoy and lightship patrols, during which several interceptions of friendly aircraft took place, no enemy aircraft being observed.'

It was still the 'Phoney War'.

From 2 March 1940, Brinsden, promoted to flying officer on 27 February 1940, began to lead a section. He led a 25-minute patrol, taking off at 10.20 hours, with Bader (K9836) and Flight Sergeant Unwin. Sections were by no means static and depended upon duty roster. Colours were assigned on the basis that Red was normally first off. Rank did not influence a section's composition, although the senior officer would lead it. For instance, on 16 March, Bader (K9836) flew with Squadron Leader Stephenson as Leader and Sergeant Unwin as Red Section. Then on 17 March, Bader flew with Flying Officer Matheson as Leader and Pilot Officer Michael Lyne as Red Section Number 2. (Michael Lyne took the business of convoy protection a step further in 1941 when he became one of the first to volunteer for service as a pilot with the Merchant Ship Fighter Unit, to be catapulted off merchantmen in an effort to protect Atlantic convoys from German maritime bombers.)

On 28 March, Bader began to lead a section. He (K9825) took off on his first sortie as a section leader at 07.40 hours, with Sergeants Jennings and Coleman tucked in close on his wingtips in formation.

From time to time, the squadron deployed a flight or section to RAF Horsham St Faith. On 31 March, Bader made one of his rare but spectacular mistakes. It was not an uncommon mistake, especially for ex-biplane pilots. He was Section Leader of a detachment at Horsham, detailed for convoy patrol duties. The Section was scrambled to intercept a 'bogey'. The three Spitfires began to roll. Bader's Spitfire (K9858) gathered speed. Bader raised the tail, expecting to lift off within seconds, but the Spitfire, engine racing, just kept going, with no feeling of lifting off. In an instant he realized his error, but it was too late. The perimeter was rushing up. He had forgotten to put the propeller into fine pitch for take-off. The Spitfire crashed off the airfield and slithered to a halt in a field. Bader released himself from the write-off, went back to the dispersal area, and mounted another Spitfire. He joined the other two Spitfires in their orbit over the North Sea a little late.

From 1 April, one Flight of No 19 Squadron was deployed almost daily to Horsham from where it carried out 'several uneventful patrols'. Two weeks later, the Squadron Commander received notification that No 19 was to move to Horsham on 17 April.

Bader did not go with the unit. He remained at RAF Duxford. No 222 Squadron was re-equipping with Spitfires. Squadron Leader H. W. Mermagen wanted a new Flight Commander, one with experience of leading, with background, and with knowledge of the Spitfire. It was natural that his mental filing system should highlight Douglas Bader, for he saw him most days. He asked Bader; if the AOC and Stephenson were to agree, Bader said he would be delighted to serve on No 222 Squadron. Stephenson and Leigh-Mallory agreed swiftly; it was evident to both of them that Bader was ripe for responsibility. The day before No 19 Squadron's move became effective, Douglas Bader was posted to No 222 Squadron as a Flight Commander, with the rank of flight lieutenant.

CHAPTER 4
Operation DYNAMO

Bader took over command of 'A' Flight of No 222 (Natal) Squadron on 17 April 1940. Commanded by Squadron Leader Mermagen, the squadron was based on the other side of RAF Duxford from No 19 Squadron, and like it, flew the Spitfire Mk I. Being a Flight Commander gave Bader real self-esteem. He could now influence tactics. With Mermagen's support, he told his Flight that the Fighter Attacks they had been practising were just that – practice. They would learn other methods.

First of all, he made his pilots practise the prescribed Fighter Attacks, but with a twist. He made each pilot take it in turn to act as the target aeroplane. He told them to observe closely their colleagues' attacks, noting how each came in one after another, line astern, almost predictably, fired and then broke in regulated directions, presenting their bellies as targets. The lesson was obvious: the Fighter Attacks made them vulnerable.

Bader told them they would now use the methods used in the First World War, adapted. The objectives were to surprise the enemy, to bring as many guns to bear as close as possible on the first pass, and not to sacrifice oneself. He showed them how individually to exploit the sun and height to achieve surprise and set up the best attack. Shooting down bombers was not a matter of chivalry. The more were destroyed the better. Therefore, the fighter should get as high as possible in order to swoop on the bombers; it should fly with the sun behind it, in order to be hidden in the sun's glare. The fighter would swoop, take aim, and hack bombers out of the formation.

In the first stage of a combat, each section would act as a unit – three aircraft. They would place themselves up sun. They would attack in line abreast out of the sun. They would select a target and attack from the beam, fire, then break away to the front and below, avoiding the tail gunners. When several sections were available, they would attack in quick succession different parts of the formation. Bader made his men rehearse the individual, pair and section attacks for many hours.

Bader did not neglect fighter-versus-fighter and made his pilots practise against each other. So much of a fighter squadron's activities are like formalized games that Bader had no trouble making the training stimulating and entertaining, with the reward of praise for success. He also led his pilots in formation aerobatics, not expecting them to reach his standards, but expecting them to discover for themselves the full performance range of their fighters and to learn, just like on the drill ground at Cranwell, the joy and the necessity of co-ordination. Bader still revelled in individual aerobatics. It was essential to him to take risks. He would aerobat at low level, illegally. It gave his pilots a good feeling to know that their 'old man' was still a bit of a tearaway.

The squadron undertook air firing at RAF Sutton Bridge. They fired their eight .303-inch machine-guns at a drogue towed behind a slow monoplane. It was real enough, but for all of the pilots it was the most threatening thing that they had ever seen in the air. None of them had ever been in combat. None of them knew definitely what formations the Germans employed. It was still all theory. Bader was not alone in Fighter Command in exploring fighter tactics.

In early May, No 66 Squadron flew into Duxford. Its commander was none other than Rupert Leigh, ex-Cranwell, who had helped to get Bader through the bureaucracy at CFS. He had used his influence now for his own ends and got himself an operational posting.

At mid-morning on 10 May, while Flight Lieutenant Douglas Bader was on readiness with a section, the news broke that the German Blitzkrieg had opened in France. The 'Phoney War' was over. Now, the fighter pilots could use their training, and get at the enemy. They were ecstatic, but, while the panzers rolled into France, nothing happened over southern England, and Bader was stood down at lunch time. In fact, nothing much happened over England for days. The pilots waited for nearly two weeks to be deployed, tense and nervous.

The British Expeditionary Force was being squeezed north into a narrow pocket on the Channel coast behind Dunkirk, but the French main body and some British forces, including the British Air Forces in France, were withdrawing beyond Paris. The bases of the Hurricanes were now in the centre and west of France, too far from the north-eastern front line to cover the British Expeditionary Force. That task now fell to the home-based squadrons of RAF Fighter Command. On 24 May, Operation DYNAMO was put into motion, the evacuation of the British Expeditionary Force and any Allied troops from Dunkirk.

At mid-morning on 22 May, Squadron Leader Mermagen's grey Humber staff car roared up to No 222 Squadron's dispersals and screeched to a halt. 'Tubby' leapt out. The pilots were all looking at him. He shouted: 'We've been posted to Kirton-in-Lindsey. We're to be ready to fly out at 15.00 hours. Better get started.'

There was a stunned silence. Bader, more knowledgeable than the others, filled in the geography for his Flight: 'It's in Lincolnshire. The wrong way. Now get moving!' He held on to his own disappointment.

No 222 Squadron had eighteen Spitfires, including its six reserves, to get to Kirton. It had several lorry loads of personal kit, mechanical equipment and office equipment and files to get there by road. The groundstaff would have to make the journey partly at night in order to be ready for the next morning. At 15.30 hours, the last of the Spitfires was disappearing north.

It was all a great anti-climax after the intensive training, and the expectation. They were being rotated north to fly convoy patrols over the North Sea – Grimsby Sector – routine, dull, uninspiring, waiting at readiness. The official radio and newspaper news from France was optimistic, and the

Hurricanes seemed to be having a great time shooting down Nazi aeroplanes. A young New Zealander whom the newspapers could only call 'Cobber' was making a name. But snatches of news filtered through from time to time from pilot to pilot, some of it interesting, but most of it depressing. The German tactics were excellent, and their aeroplanes were a match for the Hurricanes in France. More than that, the British ground organization seemed to have collapsed and the fighter pilots were faced with fighting a war without proper support.

However, late in the afternoon of 27 May, armour plate for No 222 Squadron's Spitfires arrived. The pilots helped the fitters to bolt it in place behind their seats. It was a sign of the times. The pilots on Nos 1 and 73 Squadrons in France had had it for many weeks. No 222 Squadron knew that they would soon be in combat themselves.

At 03.00 hours on the morning of 28 May, Bader's batman roused him from sleep, and told him that the squadron was to take off for RAF Martlesham Heath in an hour's time. Bader was awake in seconds. Martlesham was in No 11 Group, near Ipswich, Suffolk. The urgency and the location could mean only one thing. He was out of bed, strapping on his legs and donning his clothes and minutes later was rudely awakening the rest of the Flight. He met Mermagen, unshaven, tousled, but well awake. He confirmed Bader's conjectures. They were flying off immediately, not stopping to take personal kit or equipment. They were to rendezvous with other squadrons at Martlesham for a patrol. They were being committed to combat, if only briefly.

Just after dawn on 28 May, No 222 Squadron descended through a thick sea fog to land at Martlesham Heath. No 92 Squadron was already there, with its Spitfires.

Bader was keen to know what was going to happen. While his Spitfire was refuelled, he found No 92 Squadron's Commanding Officer, Bob Tuck, out on the tarmac beside his Spitfire. Bader thought the Acting Squadron Leader looked a bit too raffish, which provoked the worst in Bader. He fixed him with his flint blue eyes and asked bluntly: 'What's the form, old boy?'

It was early in the morning. Tuck was tired after several days of combat. He did not take kindly to this unblooded, obstreperous, swaggering Flight Commander asking belligerent questions. He replied tetchily: 'Haven't a clue. We're all waiting to find out, aren't we?' Then, arrogantly, he added: 'It's all right – we know you're all bloody keen.'

The two individuals stared at each other for a few seconds, until Bader spun on his heels, and stomped off. Tuck fired a parting comment, aimed at Bader's silk cravat: 'By the way . . . old boy . . . I wouldn't fly with that thing round your neck.'

Bader stopped. He looked back over his shoulder: 'Why the hell shouldn't I?'

'Because if you have to jump, it'll catch on something and you'll hang your silly self, that's why.'

Bader was totally unused to such sarcasm from anyone. Words failed him. Tuck and Bader stomped off into the mist in opposite directions.

Orders came through not long after. The three squadrons were to fly a wing patrol over the Dunkirk area, patrolling at 12,000 feet. The wing was to be led by Squadron Leader Tuck at the head of No 92 Squadron.

The wing took off and formed up in squadron formation, and headed for France. Mermagen led No 222 Squadron in two Flights, each of two Sections in stepped-up 'Vics' of three aeroplanes, all formed up in a diamond, with the last aeroplane acting as 'weaver'. Tuck led No 92 Squadron in loose pairs, well spaced. Tuck and his wingman, Bob Holland, had worked out and perfected a system. Holland always followed Tuck's manoeuvres, always knew his intentions and always protected his tail.

Between nine and ten thousand feet there was a layer of light cloud across the Channel. The wing broke through it into brilliant sunlight, and climbed to 12,000 feet. Ahead, through the cloud, there was a tower of heavy black smoke. The oil storage tanks at Dunkirk were burning. It could be seen from the Thames Estuary at that height. Tuck led the squadron towards it. For two hours they patrolled round the pyre, up and down the French coast, above the cloud, but saw nothing. Below the cloud, the German bombers and fighters were working over the beaches, but the fighters had their orders and did not descend.

Mermagen was instructed to land at RAF Manston, on the north-east tip of Kent. There, they were sent north-west to Duxford. Then, they were ordered to fly south to RAF Hornchurch, north of London.

They arrived at Hornchurch to find that it was being used by Nos 54 and 65 Squadrons, which had been engaged over Dunkirk for several days. Nos 41 and 222 Squadrons were the two fresh units being flown in to replace them, while they flew north for rest. Bader looked at the Spitfire pilots with alarm – withdrawn, weary, sometimes unshaven, many with service issue .38 revolvers thrust down their flying boots like desperados. No 222 Squadron began to realize that they were involved in a major operation, and felt the personal impact when they had to borrow kit.

That night in the mess at Hornchurch, Bader grilled Flight Lieutenant 'Prof' Leathart and Flying Officer Allan Deere about their experiences. It came as something of a shock to him to learn that other squadrons had made similar assessments of the Fighter Attacks as he had made. In fact, No 54 Squadron had resolved to abandon them before even seeing combat, but had tried a Number 5 attack on their first squadron interception and had proved it ineffective and lethal for attackers. During the Dunkirk fighting, most squadrons abandoned the Fighter Attack systems.

Next morning, 29 May, No 222 Squadron was roused at 03.30 hours. Bader was told to be ready for take-off at 04.30 hours.

This time they patrolled at 3,000 feet. Poor weather was hindering operations, and a layer of cloud lay at 4,000 feet. The squadron headed out over the Channel east of Dover. Below them the Channel was full of vessels. Bader thought spontaneously that it was 'like the Great West Road on a Bank Holiday Monday!' The burning oil tanks of Dunkirk were visible from miles, even at a height of a mile, even through the fog and rain.

The squadron crossed the French coast at Gravelines and Mermagen wheeled them along the line of the coast towards Dunkirk. There was no time to observe the beaches or the mass of ships off shore, though pilots sneaked amazed glances downwards. They kept their eyes scanning the sky between the ground and cloud for the enemy.

A group of aeroplanes appeared ahead. With a jolt, Bader realized that here at last was the enemy – Messerschmitt Bf 110 twin-engined, two-seat fighters, Goering's vaunted 'Destroyers'. The two formations were closing head-on at about 500mph. The Germans saw the British fighters and broke to their left sharply, out of range of the Spitfires' machine-guns, heading for the cloud, a usual German move when attacked. Mermagen, at the front of No 222 Squadron, hauled his stick back and kicked in top rudder, and opened fire, without much hope. Just as the Bf 110s reached the sanctuary of the cloud, one of them blew out a puff of smoke, then smoke billowed from one of its engines, flames leapt along a wing, and it cartwheeled down, and, as the Spitfires passed by, exploded on the ground a few seconds later.

The rest of the patrol was uneventful. They landed back at Hornchurch, and clustered around Mermagen. He was just as amazed as the rest of them that he had destroyed the Bf 110 at such extreme range, but the squadron was elated: it was its first fighter victory.

Bader was awakened at 03.30 hours the next morning, 30 May. The squadron went to readiness nearly an hour later. The weather remained poor, with low cloud and drizzle, and there was no sign of the enemy throughout the squadron's patrols over Dunkirk. Other squadrons and wings did engage, and there were several hot battles.

The RAF pilots still did not know the true position. The radio and newspapers still told of holding the Germans. In France, the Army thought the RAF had deserted them. Far from the eyes of the troops, British fighters fought off the German bombers and fighters intent on bombing and strafing the beaches at Dunkirk. It was a rift that was not attended to until much later in the war.

All but three of Fighter Command's squadrons were involved at some point in the fighting over Dunkirk. The 2,739 individual fighter sorties flown between 27 May and 4 June express the intensity of operations. The British lost over one hundred fighters and eighty pilots.

British fighters had to maintain a defensive ring around the Dunkirk area and the sea corridor from England to Dunkirk, with a patrol line between Ostend and Boulogne, holding the German aircraft at a distance. Offensive fighting was deeply imbued in the RAF's young fighter pilots, a lesson learnt during the First World War by their fathers. Air defence could not be done flying over the beaches. The fighters could only do their job over and behind the German's front-line – that was why the troops rarely saw the fighters, that and the thick low cloud.

On 31 May, Bader was awake at 03.15 hours, and they were patrolling at 3,000 feet within an hour of the dawn, but there were no enemy aeroplanes about. In the afternoon, Bader had to turn back when his Merlin engine began to run rough. Other squadrons engaged the enemy, but combat seemed to elude No 222 Squadron.

As No 222 Squadron was moved round the forward bases in No 11 Group almost daily for operations – Hornchurch, Gravesend, Manston and Tangmere – there was opportunity to discuss with pilots from other squadrons what they were experiencing, and to exchange tactical information. They were all learning. Douglas Bader noted that the Germans often flew in line abreast.

The Dunkirk days were long and exhausting. They started with a call just after 3.00 a.m. so that pilots could be at readiness before dawn. Readiness ran right through until nightfall at nine or ten o'clock. Over Dunkirk patrols each lasted around two hours on station, plus time to and from station.

No 222 Squadron sometimes flew alone, and sometimes as one of a two-squadron wing, with No 41 Squadron. Mermagen usually led the squadron. Bader led his 'A' Flight behind Mermagen, with his wingman, Pilot Officer Tim Vigors, a native of Tipperary and an old Etonian. They learnt that patrols had continually to change altitude to avoid anti-aircraft fire. They discovered that patrols could not be flown in tight formations for the pilots had to concentrate too hard on avoiding collisions, rather than scanning the sky for the enemy. Tight formations were vulnerable, too, but a loose formation could respond quicker when attacked and when attacking. A separation of five spans, minimum two spans, was advisable.

On 1 June, Bader was awoken at 03.30 hours. The groundcrews had been awake longer, some of them all night, to get twelve Spitfires ready for operations. They would have to work all day, too, rearming, refuelling, maintaining, repairing battle damage.

Bader was now feeling the effects of the constant patrolling, perhaps more than the others for he was older and he had the added strain of artificial legs. He was out on the flight line with the others, shaved, washed and carefully dressed, without an outward sign of discomfort.

The squadron took off in formation and flew over the Channel at 3,000 feet, and set up its patrol pattern: up the coast, and then behind the pyre over Dunkirk, looking for enemy aircraft. There were many about, behaving without cohesion.

Ahead, the squadron saw a formation of bomb-carrying Bf 110s. The Germans saw the Spitfires and turned for home, bombs still aboard, a minor tactical gain for the Spitfires. The Spitfire pilots rammed their throttles to the firewall, and their aeroplanes accelerated. The pilots set their reflector sights and turned their gun switches to 'Fire'. The Spitfires and their pilots did not have identical performance and the squadron formation was soon falling apart.

All pilots were intent on the Bf 110s, but Bader switched his glance to the left and right and behind, like the First World War aces he recalled reading. There, at his nine o'clock and above were two, three, four little grey crosses, diving, then . . . he called the break over the radio. Too late, the Bf 109s were diving through the squadron, guns flashing . . . Bader reacted, hauling on his control column and kicked his rudder hard, and dived to the right in a banking turn after them.

It was surprisingly easy. He selected a Bf 109 which was flying just below

3,000 feet, directly in front of him, heading the same way and at the same speed. Bader aimed and opened fire, with hardly any deflection. The gunfire did not seem to have any effect on the fighter, and nor did the pilot make an evasive move, either startled or a novice. Bader fired again, a flicker of flame became a stream of burning petrol from the tank below the pilot's seat, and the Bf 109 fell out of control.

Bader was exultant. It was his first victory. But, in the same combat, two of his fellow pilots were reported missing.

In the early afternoon, Mermagen led another patrol over Dunkirk, again at low level. Bader spotted a Dornier Do 17 bombing a destroyer about a mile away. He accelerated hard and dived on the German bomber as it turned for the coast. The Germans saw Bader's Spitfire and the rear upper gunner opened fire. Bader fired a short burst at point-blank range, saw the rear gunner's canopy shatter, saw his bullets strike the nose, where the crew were concentrated, then broke off violently just before he rammed the Dornier. The rear gunner stopped firing, probably dead.

Bader had lost speed and position veering off so sharply and by the time he was ready to attack, the bomber was already some distance away. That was why it was important to make the first pass count, because there was so little speed margin. Other Spitfires were already curving in for the kill, so Bader did not pursue the Dornier. Bader learnt from this combat one of the vital lessons of combat: overtake the target smoothly and slowly, decide the point of aim, take careful aim, relax and then open fire. That way his attack would be safer and more lethal.

The Dornier and its new attackers disappeared. Bader looked around him. He was alone. The rest of his squadron had gone. At that moment, the destroyer that had just been bombed opened fire on him. Naval gunners were never reliable in identifying aeroplanes.

On 2 June, from Hornchurch, they were up again at 03.15 hours, breakfasting quickly with stomachs churning, minds a grey blank. It was not common knowledge that a great disaster had befallen the British in France. It was being presented as a 'tactical withdrawal', but to those who had seen the fighting, the reality was different.

Each day, they patrolled. After each patrol, they were debriefed. The lucky ones wrote their combat reports. After that, they grabbed some hot tea and sandwiches, trying to eat them, feeling dog-tired, pent up but let down at the same time. They would wait by their aeroplanes until well past sunset, until they were stood down after 21.00 hours, to take a few hours of deep dreamless sleep or long wakeful minutes until the station batmen called them in the cold grey hours before the dawn when the airfield smelled fresh. Yet, combat still seemed to elude No 222 Squadron.

On 3 June, the Germans on the ground were on the outskirts of Dunkirk, and the Luftwaffe's activity was limited to attacking the huddled masses on the beaches, the long lines of troops standing patiently waiting to embark in the boats that still plied too and fro, defiantly.

That day, Bader heard that Geoffrey Stephenson had been missing since 26 May. He had been shot down by the rear gunner of a Ju 87 when he had apparently made a Fighter Attack Number 2 on it. He had been seen going down over an enemy-held area, but no parachute had been seen. Bader felt a strange lassitude.

The Dunkirk work continued until the morning of 4 June when the last survivors on the beaches surrendered to the Germans in the early hours. On that day No 222 Squadron flew the final patrol over Dunkirk. The evacuation was over. The boats were gone, the beaches returned to the waves.

No 222 Squadron was stood down. Its pilots and groundcrews slept.

The Dunkirk air operations were unique: fighter support for an ill-planned withdrawal against ill-planned German air attacks. There were experiments, and Fighter Command had learnt several lessons. Air Vice-Marshal Park had used offensive wing formations in the closing stages of the fighting, with success. The squadrons had decisively rejected the Fighter Attack systems, but were still exploring new formations and attacks. The Air Ministry Air Tactics Branch was busy collating, assessing and preparing to disseminate to squadrons the information on German tactics and new RAF formations. There was a great deal of work to be done, and no one knew how long it would be before the Germans began an air assault on Britain, followed by invasion.

Douglas Bader had been with No 222 Squadron less than eight weeks, but he had become a combat veteran in that time. It did not change Bader: it confirmed in him several deeply held beliefs on tactics:

> He who has the height, controls the battle;
> He who has the sun, achieves surprise;
> He who goes in close, shoots them down.

The only differences between the Great War and the Hitler War fighters were in the speed of the aeroplanes and the number of the guns – and each factor cancelled out the advantage of the other.

For the great majority of the RAF fighter pilots involved in Operation DYNAMO, this was their first sighting of the enemy. A minority of the pilots tangled with the Bf 109s victoriously, including Bader. The Bf 109 was to be the main opponent of the Spitfires for some time, and fought wherever the Luftwaffe fought. Conceived as a short-range air-superiority fighter to support the German land forces, it was also employed as a bomber escort, bomber interceptor, light bomber and ground-support aircraft. The Bf 109 was blooded during the Spanish Civil War, where the Luftwaffe's fighter pilots learnt the lessons of modern air combat, which gave them a decisive edge over the Allies in 1939–40. In combat there was little to choose between the Bf 109 and the Spitfire and Hurricane. Pilots had to exploit their own mount's merits and the opponent's faults – but in tactical knowledge the Luftwaffe was ahead.

After over a week of intense combat operations, Douglas Bader took Tim Vigors with him for a weekend break, 9 and 10 June, to his wife's family home, the Pantiles. They spent most of their time sleeping, utterly exhausted.

He broke the news to his wife that their friend Geoffrey Stephenson was missing, and might be dead, or at least a prisoner of war, but there was bad news for the family that weekend. The oldest of Thelma Bader's three cousins, Jack, was dead. Squadron Leader J. W. Donaldson, known as 'Baldy' in the Service and 'Jack' to his family, had been Commanding Officer of No 263 Squadron, flying Gloster Gladiator fighters. Along with the Hurricanes of No 46 Squadron, commanded by Squadron Leader Kenneth B. B. Cross, they had gone to Norway to counter the German invasion.

Outnumbered, the British fighters had flown against the Luftwaffe from frozen lakes south of Narvik. When it was evident that no more could be achieved, they were ordered to burn their surviving aircraft and evacuate in the aircraft carrier HMS *Glorious*. The squadron ground crews embarked, but the pilots landed their Hurricanes and Gladiators on *Glorious*, thus proving that Hurricanes could land on carriers – an important proof.

Unfortunately, the German battle-cruisers *Gneisenau* and *Scharnhorst* were at sea and intercepted *Glorious*, sinking her. All the aeroplanes were lost. Of the ship's company and RAF personnel aboard, some 1,400 in all, a scant forty survived the shelling, the sea and the Arctic cold. Among the few survivors were Squadron Leader Cross of No 46 Squadron and Flight Lieutenant 'Jamie' Jameson of No 263 Squadron. Donaldson was not among them. He was awarded a posthumous Distinguished Service Order for his bravery during the campaign in Norway.

Thelma Bader's step-father was a colonel, her father had been a wing commander and all of her three Donaldson cousins were pilots. A few days later, the family learnt that Teddy Donaldson, the middle brother, had also been awarded the DSO, for his services in France. He had been in the thick of the fighting in France as the Commanding Officer of No 151 (Hurricane) Squadron, one of the most effective units. He was now sent to the United States to promote the RAF. Arthur Donaldson, the youngest, also a squadron leader, was one of Central Flying School's select instructors, but was striving hard to get into Fighter Command.

No 222 Squadron retired to RAF Kirton-in-Lindsey to rest after their trial over Dunkirk. In eight days of fighting between 28 May and 4 June 1940, Douglas Bader flew 26 hours 10 minutes. Bader's total time of 767 hours 25 minutes after Dunkirk made him one of the most experienced fighter pilots at that point in the war.

Within 36 hours of the collapse of resistance at Dunkirk, the Germans had started a limited night bomber offensive against the aerodromes and ports of eastern England. The bombers struck on the night of 5/6 June, and nightly thereafter. The formations were small and the damage was light, but it could not be allowed to go unchallenged. The night fighter defences were inadequate and the searchlight and anti-aircraft guns could not be spread too thinly around all the airfields. There was little that could be done.

Late on the evening of 13 June, Bader was scrambled to intercept a raid seen on radar coming in from Germany. The Fighter Controller directed him to patrol the Humber estuary at 12,000 feet. Bader found the same as every other single-seat night fighter pilot. His view from his high-mounted cockpit through the perspex of the tiny canopy was obscured downwards by the long nose and the wings, while the flaring exhausts destroyed his peripheral vision

– the essential component of night vision.

He saw nothing. Below, England was black. The Fighter Controller called him up to instruct him to return as there was rain coming in. Bader turned on to a bearing for home and dropped to low level. The rain by now had become very heavy and he was almost on top of the flarepath at Kirton before he saw it.

Bader swung round the flarepath and made his approach. The conditions were appalling. As he slowed, the rain rippled in streams across his canopy, distorting his vision. Wind began to gust. He saw the first flare, and knew he was too high, too fast; he dropped and saw the second flare wave in yellow spirals past, then he set the Spitfire down just after the third flare, but the wind was strong and she was floating. The tail would not drop. He was too fast. He held the stick back, but he knew it was all too late . . . there were no more flares and nothing he could do. The Spitfire, still travelling fast, went off the end of the flarepath and bounced into an aircraft pen, destroying its undercarriage.

The station fire and rescue services were on the scene in minutes, but not before Mermagen. Bader could have made excuses, but he did not: it was pilot error. Mermagen agreed.

A few days later, the RAF faced the consequences of defeat in France. The few Battles that could still fly returned to England on 15 June, and the last Hurricanes were ordered to fly out on the 18th, when the last squadrons evacuated as the Western France evacuation, Operation ARIEL, was completed.

On 22 June 1940, the pilots of No 222 Squadron were standing around the radio in the mess anteroom after lunch listening to the BBC news broadcast. It was the most important news of the war so far. The reader announced in measured tones that the French Government had capitulated. The news was greeted with silence, until Squadron Leader Mermagen expressed the feelings of everyone in that room: 'Thank God. Now we're on our own!'

CHAPTER 5
Bader's Finest

On 23 June 1940, the Air Officer Commanding No 12 Group, Air Vice-Marshal Trafford Leigh-Mallory, asked to see Bader at his Headquarters at Hucknall. Leigh-Mallory had a problem he wanted Bader to solve. One of his squadrons, No 242 (Canadian) Squadron, had returned from a severe mauling in France barely a week before, leaderless and demoralized. The pilots were Canadians. Experience in the First World War had shown that they were exceptional fighters but that they did not give a damn about the 'old school tie' and were unlikely to bow to any but the best British leader that the Royal Air Force could provide. Leigh-Mallory did not disguise the fact that it was a tough assignment, but he wanted Bader to take command of the squadron. He thought that Bader had the right qualities, the direct manner and the experience to mould No 242 Squadron into a fighting unit. It was based at RAF Coltishall in Norfolk. With a parting 'Good luck', he sent Bader on his way to take command with immediate effect.

Bader returned to Kirton, said goodbye to No 222 Squadron and set off for Coltishall that evening. He left in ebullient mood, delighted to have his own operational squadron. He arrived late at night, tired and irritated by the problem of driving in the black-out. Next morning, 24 June, Acting Squadron Leader Douglas Bader assumed command of No 242 (Canadian) Squadron.

Bader sought out first the Station Commander, Wing Commander Walter 'Bike' Beiseigel, a Regular RAF officer, who gave a dismal view of No 242 Squadron. Then Bader spoke to the Squadron Adjutant, Peter MacDonald. He was a First World War pilot and now the Member of Parliament for the Isle of Wight, but he was in fact a Canadian by birth. 'Boozey Mac' had endeared himself to the young pilots, and had become, as a good squadron adjutant should, the mentor, the confidant, the friend, the counsellor and the organizer for his high-spirited crowd of young pilots. His perceptions and recall of the squadron's activities were now of fundamental importance to Bader in understanding how to tackle No 242 (Canadian) Squadron.

Peter MacDonald filled in the details underlying Leigh-Mallory's warning comments. All of No 242 Squadron's original flying personnel had been Canadians. The squadron had been formed for political reasons, to weld the Commonwealth to the defence of the Motherland. The original Commanding Officer had had a training background, and was well suited to working-up the squadron, and the Flight Commanders had had long and sound service. However, none of them had had any experience of leading a fighting unit.

This had not been a problem during the training stage, nor even during the Dunkirk fighting.

Bader had MacDonald assemble the pilots in his office. It was still early morning. The pilots were scruffy and dressed in an assortment of flying clothing. They looked rough, and anything but tractable. Bader addressed them, firm but friendly, and told them how he believed that the members of a good squadron should behave and dress. Then he asked if anyone had any comments. Silence. Then Stan Turner spoke: 'Horseshit . . . ' Bader was stunned. After a long pause, the pilot drawled: ' . . . Sir.' Indefinably, this respect of senior rank made this totally insubordinate comment acceptable. It cleared the air, too.

There followed a lively exchange of views, beginning with an explanation of why they wore an assortment of clothing (the rest was in France), and ending with a long discussion on the squadron's experience in combat. By the end of half an hour, Douglas Bader had a very clear idea of just who was who in the squadron and just what they had been through and just what they needed to happen, but he had also stamped his own authority over the situation. One thing was clear: these men needed a leader who led from the front.

After talking to MacDonald, Bader spoke to Warrant Officer Bernard West, the squadron's Engineer, who gave him a dismal picture of the stores and equipment situation. Apart from the direct testimony of these two cornerstones of the squadron, Bader could also quickly scan the squadron's records, particularly its Operations Record Book (Form 540) – in effect its diary. No 242 (Canadian) Squadron had formed at RAF Church Fenton in No 13 Group, Fighter Command, on 30 October 1939, the first Canadian squadron to form under the Command of the Air Officer Commanding, Air Vice-Marshal R. E. Saul. On 1 November, the Squadron Commander arrived followed by the two Flight Commanders. On 6 November, the Squadron Adjutant had arrived, Pilot Officer P. D MacDonald, MP. More airmen and pilots arrived throughout the month, until by the 30th, the squadron's strength was twenty-three officers, all Canadians, and 173 airmen. Bader noted particularly the arrival of P. S. Turner on 20 November.

On 27 December, the squadron was told that it would be equipped with Hurricanes. The pilots had been under great pressure to learn the textbook lessons of the trade. Now they were to be placed under similar pressure to learn to fly the tool of their trade, the Hurricane fighter. There was to be no gradual building of confidence, imparting of experience, development of attitudes of the Regular Air Force. Fittingly, the squadron had to wait until the new decade to get its fighters, on 5 January 1940. During January, February and March, the squadron had trained hard in the air by day and night, weather permitting, which was not too often. On 23 March, the ORB recorded:

'SQUADRON BECAME OPERATIONAL BY DAY. This great event in our history took place exactly 20 flying days after receipt of our first Hurricane Aircraft. . . . '

This was very short work, perhaps too short.

On 10 May 1940, the German offensive in France had started. Soon No 242 Squadron was committed to combat. The squadron had suffered its first combat losses on 19 May when two pilots, including a Flight Commander, were killed. On the 22nd, the squadron began operating from Biggin Hill, carrying out patrols over France and Belgium. Next day, four members of the squadron failed to return from a patrol.

From 28 May, No 242 Squadron had begun operating from RAF Manston to cover Operation DYNAMO. That morning, the squadron destroyed two Bf 109s but two No 242 Squadron pilots had fallen, both killed. The following day, the squadron had begun to patrol over Dunkirk. On the 31st, the squadron was ordered to France. Operating as part of No 67 Wing, it was in the thick of the fighting in the west of France. On 13 June, the squadron was ordered to move from Châteaudun to Ancenis in company with No 1 (Hurricane) Squadron.

Bader found that the squadron diary did not really record adequate information about the fighting in France. Peter MacDonald was able to sketch the circumstances. The unit had been forced to make a series of rapid retreating moves. Pilots maintained their own machines and slept under their wings. Orders had been delayed and inexact. MacDonald had found it increasingly difficult to keep the squadron together as it retreated, and to maintain control over the pilots. It had been there, in France, that a commander trained and experienced in leading a fighting formation had been needed. Lacking this, No 242 Squadron had fallen apart. It was hardly the fault of the men elected by the Canadians to lead the unit: they did their best under circumstances which they had had no preparation to meet. The remaining Hurricanes in France were ordered to fly out on 18 June, including No 242's, but most of the ground equipment had to be left behind. The rest of the personnel proceeded by ship.

No 242 Squadron's losses had been heavy. On 18 June, the surviving core of the squadron – Flight Lieutenant Plinston, Pilot Officers Eckford, Latta, McKnight, Crowley-Milling, Turner, Atkinson and Bush – had flown into Tangmere with the squadron's remaining Hurricanes. They had been swiftly refuelled and had then flown on directly to Coltishall. Two days later, the ground contingent from France had arrived there, but without the ground equipment. There they had rejoined the rest of the squadron who had remained in England. Surprisingly, by 22 June, the squadron was again considered to be operational by day and night.

Squadron Leader Douglas Bader took swift action to make sure the squadron knew that he was not a passenger. The weather was fine and dry with good visibility, a perfect day for flying, just as it had been for days. At 14.10 hours on 24 June, he took off in a Hurricane Mk I (P2967). For the next fifty minutes, in a tight, impeccable display, he wrung the performance out of the Hurricane. Knots of pilots and airmen were scattered around the airfield watching. By the time Bader landed, he had made his point: he could fly as well as any of them.

Bader then set about forming a team. He went against the concept of the squadron's establishment by bringing in two proven, Regular, Flight Commanders. The squadron had lost a Flight Commander in France, so as soon as Bader was appointed to command the unit he had asked that Flight Lieutenant G. E. M. Ball be transferred from No 19 Squadron, at nearby Duxford, with whom Bader had flown. Eric Ball assumed command of 'A' Flight at the same time as Bader took over the squadron. As Plinston was being posted to the gunnery school at Sutton Bridge, 'B' Flight also needed a new Flight Commander. Bader asked who was in the Fighter Command pool. He was told that Flight Lieutenant George Powell-Sheddon was available, experienced, but he stuttered. Bader threw the suggestion back, for he would have no one on his radio who stuttered, but the personnel officer gently persisted, saying that it was not a bad stutter and that Powell-Sheddon was about Bader's age, an experienced leader. Then he added slyly that he had been at Cranwell. Bader snapped him up and Powell-Sheddon arrived, to assume command of 'B' Flight on 11 July.

Now, while most of No 242 Squadron's aircrew were Canadians in whom Bader had sufficient confidence, it had four English officers to give it a stiffening of experienced leadership to bring out the best in them: Bader, the two Flight Commanders, Ball and Powell-Sheddon, and, the most senior pilot, Pilot Officer Denis Crowley-Milling, who had been attached to the squadron during the Battle of France. Bader took to the fair-haired Crowley-Milling – 'Crow' – an able fighter pilot who looked younger than his twenty-one years. He was one of the well-trained pre-war Volunteer Reservists, with a sound knowledge of aeroplanes.

Born on 22 March 1919, Crowley-Milling had been educated at Malvern College, Worcester, and had been a Rolls-Royce apprentice since 1937. He had joined the RAF Volunteer Reserve in 1937, and had learnt to fly. He was called up with the Volunteer Reserve. Completing his flying training, he had been attached to No 615 (County of Surrey) Squadron, Auxiliary Air Force, based at Kenley and flying Gladiators. The Auxiliary Air Force was intended to be a second-line of territorial squadrons, but Fighter Command's front-line reserves were limited, so twelve Auxiliary units were re-equipped with either Hurricanes or Spitfires, as front-line reserves. Auxiliary squadrons reached a strength of twenty by 1939.

The expansion of the RAF in the late 1930s had not only depended on having enough aircraft. It was also critical to have sufficient aircrew to fly them and ground personnel to maintain them, minister to the needs of the squadrons and direct the course of the fighting. While aircraft could be replaced fairly rapidly, it took a long time to train combat aircrew and it was essential to have reserves – 150 per cent of front-line strength – to replace combat losses to give stamina to Fighter Command's war effort. Thus, the new RAF Volunteer Reserve was introduced and the Auxiliary Air Force was expanded and modernized.

Crowley-Milling was called up when the Volunteer Reserve was mobilized along with the Auxiliary and Regular Air Force on 23 August 1939. He was posted 'for the duration of hostilities' to No 615 Squadron, which by then was designated as a Hurricane unit, but it was with No 242 Squadron that he had endured the Battle of France.

By the end of June 1940, No 242 Squadron had a complement of twelve Hurricane Mk Is. Its pilots included Pilot Officers Stansfield, Atkinson, Bush, Campbell, Eckford, Grassick, Latta, McKnight, Crowley-Milling and Turner; and Sergeants Armitage, Brimble, Meredith, Porter, Richardson and Terras. Bader knew that the squadron's original pilots and ground crews had been through a very harsh experience during the Dunkirk fighting and in France, but he brought in new blood and he worked the squadron hard. That was the way to restore morale, pride in unit. A good squadron commander could turn a fighter squadron from a mediocre one into a top-line unit in a matter of weeks. That was all they had as they faced the prospect of imminent German invasion in the early summer of 1940.

The squadron flew sector reconnaissances, but for the most part took advantage of the fine weather which continued to the end of the month to practise, long and soundly under Bader's persuasive leadership. On 25 June, the squadron flew twelve hours, twenty-two hours on the 26th, twenty-eight hours on the 27th, thirty-four hours on the 28th and forty-two hours on the 29th.

On 29 June, Bader informed Fighter Command that No 242 Squadron was still non-operational. On 1 July, the squadron remained non-operational except for one hour's readiness at dawn. Nevertheless, Bader worked the men and had them carry out flying training, including cloud-flying and formation training from the 1 to 5 July.

Bader made his pilots fly tight wingtip to wingtip formations, straight and level, then climbs, turns, banks . . . Then he would put them in line astern, and lead them into a loop. It was like the drill at Cranwell, it moulded the team, taught them to trust their fellow pilots, to react instinctively to commands and movements in the formation. It instilled tight, co-ordinated discipline. It was tough work, demanding great concentration, but it produced results. Each pilot began to understand how to get the most out of his aircraft in combat, how to fly as a team, and how to trust his leader.

By the first week of July, Bader was certain that he could declare his pilots operational, but for one thing: if they were to go into action, they would not be able to sustain operations for very long. The squadron's equipment had been lost in France, and had not been replaced. Several tons of maintenance equipment was needed. Warrant Officer West and his groundcrews worked long hours to keep the squadron flying, but he could not prevail upon the Supply Branch at Fighter Command to provide the necessary equipment. There was, of course, a queue.

Nobody who really knew him was surprised that, on 4 July, as the Squadron ORB recorded, Squadron Leader Bader reported to No 12 Group Headquarters and Fighter Command Headquarters that the squadron was '. . . operationally trained by day, so far as pilots were concerned but non-operational as regards equipment'.

In 1940, discipline was strict and one did not complain, especially a new squadron leader to Command Headquarters. However, working on the sound grounding in the acceptance of responsibility and authority he had had at

Cranwell, Bader had learnt at Shell the techniques of line management – delegation and how to go to the top for important decisions. He was unusually skilful in management technique for an Air Force General Duties Officer. This and his strident personality and unequivocal character made him a force that even the Air Force bureaucracy found great difficulty resisting. Quite simply, Bader created a situation that had to be resolved.

A squadron leader equipment officer at Fighter Command Headquarters attempted to talk Bader out of daring to create problems over his squadron's equipment. Bader firmly and politely invited him to do his job or be quiet. It was inevitable that the Commander-in-Chief Fighter Command, Air Marshal Hugh Dowding, should want to see him. Bader presented his case directly and reasonably, without judgment inviting Dowding to understand the facts for himself. Dowding's decisiveness hit even Bader solidly in the solar plexus. Dowding stated that keeping squadrons operational was a priority, sacked the equipment officer and ordered the equipment for No 242 Squadron with immediate effect. Again, Douglas Bader's policy of going to the top had worked. It had a spin-off effect, for it won him renewed respect from his seniors and his squadron.

On 8 July, Air Vice-Marshal Leigh-Mallory, Air Officer Commanding No 12 Group, visited the squadron to assess the situation for himself, and was regaled with a Station Defence exercise. Leigh-Mallory found out what the situation was from Bader, unequivocally, and he agreed with Bader's assessment. On 9 July, the equipment began to arrive. By 12.00 hours, the squadron was fully operational by day.

Until this situation had been resolved, Bader did not lose time and continued to train the squadron, although it had also mounted dawn and dusk readiness. On 6 July, the squadron had 'carried out Air Practice Firing at Sutton Bridge – record scores for Fighter Command'.

Not all fighter pilots were good shots, especially when they were using at high speed and with large deflection angles a battery of eight .303-inch machine-guns capable of firing a total of 8,800 rounds a minute. Deflection depended on range, distance and speed and, surprisingly, deflection as great as three lengths of the target aircraft was often needed. In practice, getting in close astern and aiming carefully was the most satisfactory, but could be risky. 'Hosing' the target was not wise, and a two- or three-second burst was enough, especially as fighters had enough ammunition to fire only ten bursts of two to three seconds. It also helped to be very tightly strapped in with the Sutton harness in order to feel the recoil of the guns.

The reflector sight was a great improvement over the mechanical ring-and-bead sight which the biplane pilot had had to peer down to sight his guns. The reflector sight projected an image of a graticule (crossed lines) upwards on to the rear surface of the armoured windscreen glass in the line of sight of the pilot. Thus, it had the major advantage that the pilot could aim at the target while flying normally, especially as a pilot can be under high G force in combat. Once the range had been adjusted on the sight, the image was immediately available. It was also better in poor light.

Sighting the guns was a vital element in fighter pilot training. Guns were lined up to converge on a selected point at a chosen range. Trials failed to discover a single best pattern and there was much disagreement on the pattern of sighting to be used. The Navy favoured an oval pattern. The Air Force devised a rather complicated 'box' in which the two outer guns were centred horizontally to converge at 400 yards, and the other guns were disposed in opposite pairs alternately elevated and depressed at 200 and 300 yards range: this gave the maximum possible spread from different ranges, and compensated for 'poor shots'. Changing patterns too often on a fighter was not encouraged, as it took time. A Supermarine test pilot, Don Robertson, explained the method of aligning a gun:

> 'The aircraft was jacked up and placed on stands fore and aft with the fuselage datum at the angle it assumed in flight at the expected attack speed. Then, by removing the breech block, a small inverted periscope was inserted to allow the adjuster to see through the barrel to whatever the gun was aimed at and to adjust the mounting to bring the gun into position on the chosen pattern.'

During this period of non-operational flying, three new and rather unusual pilots had been posted to bolster the squadron. On 1 July, Sub-Lieutenants R. J. Cork, RN, and R. E. Gardner, RNVR, and Midshipman R. J. Patterson, reported for duty with No 242 Squadron. Bader warmly welcomed the naval pilots to No 242 Squadron. His respect was partly attributable to his experience at Cranwell of several senior officers, Longmore, Halahan and Evill, who had been First World War naval pilots. The College itself had preserved many naval traditions and phrases.

The Fleet Air Arm's role in the Battle of Britain was small but significant: some fifty-eight naval pilots flew with RAF squadrons on secondment to make up the numbers of RAF pilots. They wore naval uniform, but were subject to RAF discipline as full members of their RAF squadrons. Some were promoted and had RAF pilots under their command. Bader considered the pilots seconded to the Royal Air Force from the Navy to be without exception well trained, highly disciplined and strongly motivated.

Patterson was a youth of nineteen. Gardner and Cork were a couple of years older. Richard Exton Gardner was familiarly known as 'Jimmy'. Unlike the RAF, the Fleet Air Arm – manned between the wars by RAF air and deck crews – had not maintained a volunteer reserve until the late 1930s when volunteer reserve observer officers were trained. They were followed, from February 1939, by a score or so of pilots. With the outbreak of World War Two, thousands volunteered for the RNVR Air Branch.

Richard John Cork was a tall, good-looking, charming young man, with fine eyes and wavy hair. Tough and cheerful, he was an excellent pilot, and Bader often put him in his section of three, along with Willie McKnight. Cork, after completing officer training, was commissioned as an acting sub-lieutenant in the Air Branch, with a seniority date of 1 May 1939. Attached to HMS *President*, he was posted to No 14 Elementary and Reserve Flying Training School (ERFTS) at Gravesend aerodrome, where his flying course began on 21 August 1939. The same day, he was aloft in a Tiger Moth on an 'air experience' flight. After 7 hours and 10 minutes of dual instruction, he went solo in a Tiger Moth (H6447). On 28 October, Cork completed his ab initio flying course, and was posted to No 1 Flying Training School, Netheravon. On 14 March 1940, he was confirmed in the rank of sub-lieutenant (A). He signed out of No 1 FTS, graded 'Average', on 18 March. He wrote with quiet pride in his logbook that day: 'Authorised to wear the flying badge W.E.F. 20/1/40.'

From 21 April until 11 June, Cork was posted to Nos 759 and 760 Squadrons, fighter training and pilot pool units flying Skuas and Gladiators at RNAS Eastleigh and Worthy Down. On 22 April, he had his first flight in a Skua. On 11 June, he signed out, graded, 'Above the Average'.

On 17 June, Cork was attached to HMS *Daedalus*, and posted to No 7 Operational Training Unit, RAF Hawarden, for conversion to Merlin-engined fighters. In ten days, he flew just 23 hours 15 minutes on Spitfires. He signed out on 29 June, but without grading. Cork remained attached to *Daedalus* throughout his secondment to the RAF, the parent unit for FAA pilots. On 1 July, Cork joined No 242 Squadron, RAF, flying Hurricanes from Coltishall. That day he made his first flight in a Hurricane of No 242 Squadron. A few days later, during the gunnery exercises at Sutton Bridge, Cork crashed his Hurricane (P3813). He escaped without injury or reprimand.

On 10 July, No 242 Squadron began to fly operations again – convoy patrols, the staple type for squadrons in this area. Gardner made it a good beginning. He was on a convoy patrol with his section when they engaged enemy bombers over the sea. Gardner latched on to one of the Ju 88s and chased it some 50 miles out to sea before nailing it. Thus he opened the naval pilots' scoring, which was also the first victory for the reconstituted squadron in that sector. Two other bombers were damaged.

Ju 88s were tough, as Gardner's chasing combat illustrates, but the Do 17 in contrast could not take much damage. Early the next morning, 11 July, Bader had an experience that confirmed the Do 17's fragility.

Bader was in the dispersal hut when the RAF Coltishall Operations Room Controller rang him at about 07.00 hours:

'There's a "bandit" flying up the coast from east of Yarmouth towards Cromer at about 1,000 feet. It's terrible weather, but can you get a Section off to intercept it?'

Bader looked out at the weather – low cloud, steady drizzle, and visibility around two to three thousand yards, too poor for anyone to be flying, but it sounded as if the Controller was very sure of his information. Bader responded:

'It's worth a try. I'll go myself. I'll be out of radio contact so I'll fly north, then straight back. No hanging around.'

The Controller gave him more exact details of course, height and bearing and Bader tramped off across the wet grass to his Hurricane, which sat hunched in the drizzle. Shortly he was ascending through the cloud at 700 feet. He was surprised how good the view from the Hurricane was under such conditions. He stayed low until he saw the sea.

The cloud lifted to 1,000 feet over the coast. He flew north up the coast towards Cromer, below the cloud, where the 'bogey' was supposed to be too. Then, surprised, he saw it, barely 400 yards in front of him, a Do 17. Bader had surprised the Germans, too. Flying steady and level, they could not have been expecting a fighter to be up that early, at that level and in those conditions, and it hardly seemed that this particular Dornier would be a decoy.

When he was 250 yards behind the Dornier, Bader adjusted his reflector sight to give a range of 200 yards. Then the rear gunner began to fire at him. The gunfire did not worry him. Bader had learnt from his over-eager attack on the bomber over Dunkirk. Now, with an engine and armoured glass in front of him and his eight machine-guns to the rear gunner's one, he relaxed, took careful aim, got closer, right behind the bomber, and then fired, a short burst. The Hurricane remained solid as the guns fired. He knew his aim was precise, but all the enemy pilot did was to bank steeply to port, still below the cloud. Bader adjusted his aim and fired again. The Dornier had completely reversed course and flew straight, climbing slowly to the cloud, with its rear gunner firing at the Hurricane. The German reached the cloud. Bader chased it in, shooting at it, but it had gone and there was no point in chasing it blindly in clouds.

Back at Coltishall dispersal, he thanked the Controller for accurate instructions but reported that the Dornier had escaped. However, just fifteen minutes later, the Controller telephoned back to say that an Observer Corps post had reported seeing a Dornier crash into the sea off Cromer at the same time as Bader engaged his Do 17.

Later that day, Pilot Officer Bob Grassick crashed his Hurricane, but was uninjured. The weather was still appalling.

No 242 Squadron had been sharing Duxford with No 66 Squadron, commanded by Douglas Bader's friend Rupert Leigh. They co-operated in training when there was little operational activity and weather permitted. On 20 and 24 July, Nos 66 and 242 Squadrons carried out 'wing exercises' [ORB]. One of the standard formations of Fighter Command was the two-squadron wing.

Behind the glamour and excitement or routine of flying, behind the fine living of fighter pilots, lay the tedium and hard work for the squadron commander, the adjutant and the staff of the squadron's headquarters. There was a great deal of work to be done in connection with the posting to the squadron of new pilots. The pilots had to be assessed, and the suitable ones accepted and moulded. Those who did not fit into that particular squadron – for every squadron was like a family with its own character – had to be re-posted. There was now an additional problem to confront: new pilots with inadequate training on fighters.

In one fortnight five pilots joined the squadron, beginning with Pilot Officer J. Benzie, on 11 July, and, on 13 July, Pilot Officer M. K. Brown. Both had been shot down in France and had been recuperating in hospital at Torquay. Benzie had been one of four members of No 242 Squadron who had failed to return to base after a patrol on 23 May. He had been brought down in France, wounded, but he had been fortunate to be recovered by Allied forces and returned to England. He had spent six weeks in Torquay recovering from his wounds.

Bader was not satisfied with the level of experience of some of the new pilots coming from the schools, and not only said so bluntly, but posted them back for further training. It was no slur on the pilots. Pilot Officer Morris-Hart, an RAF Volunteer Reserve pilot, arrived on 18 July. The next day he was on his way to No 5 Operational Training Unit at RAF Aston Down for further training. He was posted back to No 242 Squadron on 12 August, with a higher chance of being successful and surviving.

Most of the pilots needed no further training, and some were brought in to lead. On 20 July, Sergeant Lonsdale arrived from No 46 Squadron, followed next day by Flying Officer G. P. Christie from RAF Heston. Christie was experienced and became a Section Leader, beginning on 1 August, leading Pilot Officer Roy Bush who had fought with No 242 Squadron since France, and the newcomer Sergeant Lonsdale. Bader's choice of Christie was sound and his opinion of him was good. A bare six weeks later, on 3 September and in time for the September battles, Christie was transferred on promotion when Rupert Leigh needed a new Flight Commander for No 66 Squadron, on the other side of RAF Duxford.

On 1 August, one of the pilots whom Bader had his eye on as a likely leader one day, Pilot Officer Stan Turner, 'proceeded on Fighter Course to Northolt' [ORB] to learn fighter tactics. Bader believed in educating pilots appropriately, according to their talents. Next day, appropriately too, Pilot Officer Benzie 'proceeded on Parachute Course to Weeton Preston', while Pilot Officer Noel Stansfield 'proceeded on Navigational Course to St Athan', returning upon its completion on 25 August.

The vagaries of the posting system were baffling, sometimes. On 5 August, Pilot Officer H. N. Tamblyn reported for duty with No 242 Squadron from No 141 Squadron, in place of Sergeant Meredith, who four days later proceeded to No 141 Squadron at RAF Prestwick, for posting. On 10 August, Pilot Officer Atkinson and Sergeant Porter were posted to No 600 Squadron, RAF Manston, and No 615 Squadron respectively, replacing Flying Officers Cave and Gammer who were posted to No 242 Squadron for flying duties. However, although the next day Cave reported for duty at his new squadron, Gammer's posting was cancelled.

Not all postings to training units were for training. On 20 August, Pilot Officer Waterton was posted to No 6 OTU, RAF Sutton Bridge. He was one of the squadron's original 'A' Flight members. His tour was over and his experience was to be used instructing new pilots, which was a common procedure, supposedly under the guise of 'rest'. He would have been well placed to take pertinent observations about the standards of training with him to his new posting.

On 26 August, Pilot Officer K. M. Sclanders reported from No 6 OTU. He was posted to Powell-Sheddon's 'B' Flight, and began flying with the squadron a few days later. However, on 31 August, Pilot Officer Lawrence E. Cryderman – a pre-war jazz band leader – was posted to No 242 Squadron from RAF Andover. He was attached the same day to No 5 OTU, RAF Aston

Down, for training. He returned on 4 September, but was promptly re-attached to No 5 OTU. He did not return to the squadron until 26 September, but then became a very useful member of the squadron.

On 30 July, Squadron Leader Bader felt comfortable enough with his unit's progress to take four days' leave. He returned on 2 August much refreshed. Douglas Bader had brought his wife, Thelma, to live in a public house near RAF Duxford. She was a welcome and supportive guest in the mess. Air Vice-Marshal Sir Dermot Boyle spoke movingly of Thelma Bader's remarkable qualities at the Thanksgiving Service for her life on 5 March 1971, in words that give an impression of the impact she had on the boys who flew under her husband's command on No 242 Squadron:

> ' . . . living amongst those engaged in the critical air battles of the time, she became a continuous source of comfort and encouragement to everyone. Many of the young pilots were a long way from their homeland, some of them were tired and saddened and even disillusioned by the futility of war. She gave so generously of her help and affection at this time, the fact that her anxieties were much greater than theirs tended to be overlooked . . . '

The squadron had to wait through the anti-convoy fighting of July and early August. There were frequent flights and interceptions, few successful, and most of them turned out to be Blenheims. The mainstay were base and convoy patrols. Bader would sometimes fly alone, as on 7 August, when he took off at 16.35 hours in his Hurricane (P3061) on a convoy patrol. He sighted no enemy aeroplanes, and landed at 18.15 hours – a typical sortie of 1 hour 40 minutes. Training and exercises continued. On 18 August, the squadron carred out air-to-air firing practice at Sutton Bridge.

On 20 August, clouds and driving rain almost to ground level made flying senseless, but a Fighter Controller at another base scrambled a section of No 242 Hurricanes to intercept a 'bogey'. The section comprised Pilot Officers Neil Campbell and Denis Crowley-Milling, and Midshipman R. J. Patterson. One of the pilot officers reported seeing another of the section diving out of control from the cloud and crash into the sea five miles north-east of Winterton at 15.30 hours. It was young Patterson, killed, presumed shot down.

Bader was incensed. He had not been at the Duty Centre when the Controller had ordered the section to take off, otherwise he would have stopped it. He drove to the Sector Control Room and berated the man for being a fool to send young men into such dangerous weather. He was the first man that Douglas Bader had lost.

The next day, 21 August, Bader avenged Patterson. The weather had improved only marginally. Bader was leading his Section back over Coltishall after a practice flight. He heard the Controller give a Section of Rupert Leigh's No 66 Squadron a vector to a 'bogey' over Yarmouth at 7,000 feet, on 110 degrees. It was just as likely to be a Blenheim as a Dornier – they had had their fill of friendly interceptions, especially as the Blenheim and Dornier looked similar from many angles. They could not take chances, though.

Bader took the instruction. Leaving his Section he turned south-east and sped the 15 miles to Yarmouth, crossing the coast north of the town four minutes later. The Spitfires had not arrived and he could see no 'bogey' below the cloud. There was an overcast at 8,000 feet. Bader searched through it – fine eyesight is essential for a fighter pilot. There, a few hundred feet above it, Bader made out the unmistakable heron-like plan silhouette of a Do 17, pencil fuselage, heavy wings, twin tails. Bader climbed straight through the thin cloud. The bomber pilot saw him emerge. A gunner began to fire. A chain of aerial grenades whirled past, released from the bomber. The bomber was diving into the overcast.

Bader fired and kept firing, knowing he was damaging the enemy. It slipped past him and into the cloud and he lost it. He dived after it, but it had gone. He orbitted, hopefully then irritably until he knew he had to return to base, angry. He reported failure. However, again, the Observer Corps had seen a Dornier plunge out of the cloud into the sea. He was credited with a bomber destroyed. The Dornier simply could not take punishment.

By the end of August, Bader had moulded No 242 Squadron into a superb fighting unit, aggressive, well trained and highly motivated. But there was no action. On the 23rd, a section of three – Pilot Officers Morris-Hart and Tamblyn led by Flight Lieutenant Powell-Sheddon – flew a base patrol (18.10 to 18.45 hours), without incident. At the same time, the squadrons in No 11 Group were heavily committed. It was typical of the frustration faced by No 12 Group squadrons. Next day, the Battle of Britain entered its third and critical phase, with widespread attacks on No 11 Group fighter airfields inland. Bader was champing at the bit, but all that came were base patrols and unsuccessful interception.

Having waited through the anti-convoy fighting of July and early August, No 242 Squadron now waited through the bombing of No 11 Group's airfields. They waited six days, lounging beside their aeroplanes at readiness, waiting to be scrambled to intervene in the battles over No 11 Group's area. Then at last, on 30 August, the squadron became embroiled in the Battle of Britain.

PART III

CHAPTER 6
The Wing Concept

O n Friday, 30 August, No 242 Squadron moved the hundred miles south-west from RAF Coltishall to RAF Duxford to be nearer to the front line. This meant that it was being controlled by the Duxford Sector Operations Room Controller, Wing Commander A. B. Woodhall. The squadron was at readiness all day. At 16.26 hours, No 242 Squadron was scrambled from Duxford with orders to patrol over RAF North Weald at 15,000 feet, on a vector of 190 degrees. The enemy had a force of over seventy bombers heading that way. As usual, a No 12 Group squadron was to patrol a No 11 Group base while its squadrons were going forward to intercept. Thirteen No 242 Squadron Hurricanes were airborne swiftly and headed for North Weald – not far distant. Bader led as Red 1, with Willie McKnight and Denis Crowley-Milling as Red 2 and 3 at his wingtips.

Fifteen minutes after take-off, No 242 Squadron was in the area specified, at the required height. The sun was to their starboard. Just north of North Weald, the Fighter Controller gave Bader a vector of 340 degrees. Bader altered course. He was not prepared to orbit the airfield at 15,000 feet as No 11 Group wanted. That was no way to defend a target in mobile warfare – a box round the standard. Altitude and position up-sun was the key. He reasoned that the Germans would attack with the sun behind them – from the west. Therefore, he had to be behind the enemy in the sun – some 20 miles behind the enemy. So, Bader used his instructions as information. He climbed his squadron to 4,000 feet above the altitude he had been given, and took his squadron 20 miles to the west, into the sun, behind the raiders.

Within seconds, Powell-Sheddon (Blue 1) spotted three aeroplanes below and to starboard. Bader detached Blue Section's three Hurricanes to investigate. Seconds later, Christie (Green Leader) saw a large formation over Enfield, and he told Bader over the radio. Bader saw them instantly. It was hard not to see them. There were almost a hundred, flying in perfect formation. The Germans were flying east. Bader was flying east with the sun behind him, and was higher than the enemy main formation. He had got it right.

Bader had time to observe the nature of the formation, in order to assess its vulnerabilities. There were over eighty bombers, Heinkel He 111s and a few Dornier Do 17s. They flew in fourteen tight double 'Vics' of six. This was a favourite German formation, and the Hurricanes would have to be careful not to get caught inside the 'Vics'. The 'Vics' were stepped up from 12,000 feet to 14,000 feet. Behind and above the bombers, there were some thirty twin-engined Bf 110 fighter escorts, stepped up from 15,000 to 20,000 feet. There were no single-seat Bf 109s. The Hurricanes were above the bombers but the bombers were screened from attack from above by Bf 110s.

Suddenly as he saw the bomber formation over his country, anger surged up in Bader, really seeing and feeling the meaning of the war for the first time:

'Who the Hell do these Huns think they are, flying like this over OUR country in their bloody bombers covered with Iron Crosses and Swastikas?'

But over the radio, Bader calmly issued his instructions.

Bader had ten Hurricanes now, in three Sections: his Red Section was leading, as usual, followed by Yellow Section and Green Section, then Black Section, the weavers. Bader ordered Flying Officer Christie (Green 1) to take his Green Section down and attack the top of the lowest formation of fighters. The Canadian acknowledged and Green Section's three Hurricanes peeled off in line astern. It was all according to training.

Bader ordered his Flight (Red and Yellow Sections) into line astern and dived. He intended to deliver a simultaneous, standard attack on the middle section of fighters, and break it up. It was a classic 'bounce'.

Green Section had taken the top of the lower formation, as ordered by Bader. This lower formation consisted of four layers and Christie had charged the top layer. He singled out a Bf 110, which broke to starboard, diving. Christie stayed on its tail. He closed in to 50 yards. His thumb pressed the red button on his control column, as his hand moved the control column easily to hold the enemy in the graticule as the hunted and hunter dived. At such a range, although a considerable number of bullets had to be hitting the enemy aeroplane, they might lack the concentration to do fatal damage. The two fighters were at 6,000 feet. Suddenly, oil and petrol spurted from the Bf 110. Its dive became vertical. It did not pull out.

After Green Section had made contact with the lowest fighter formation, the Bf 110s had swiftly dispersed, leaving Pilot Officer Morris-Hart (Green 3) with no Bf 110 to attack. He shifted his attention to the bombers just below. He saw three flying in line astern a thousand feet below him. He set up his attack on the third in the line, but Ball got in an attack quicker so Morris-Hart shifted his attention to the second in line and sent the bomber diving down, with his Hurricane on its tail, but Morris-Hart saw the remaining bomber turn steeply right, so he cut its turn and pumped a long burst into it. It went straight in. The victor broke off, as he now had three Bf 110s on his tail.

Meanwhile, Bader's Red Section had broken into the centre formation, hitting a double 'Vic'. The Bf 110s broke outwards, as was their custom. Three Bf 110s went left, with Willie McKnight chasing them, and three Bf 110s went right, with Bader on their tails. The Bf 110s made fast climbing turns, then stall-turned to get on to the Hurricanes' tails. Bader caught one of them at the top of its climb and pumped three seconds of machine-gun bullets into it at very close range. It exploded in flames. Bader continued his fast climb. A second Bf 110 appeared below and right, just falling into a dive after its stall turn. Bader swung in behind it, got it in his sight at 150 yards, steadied his aim, expecting return fire from the rear gunner at any moment, closed to

100 yards, opened fire, the machine-guns drumming, the cockpit filling with cordite fumes . . . two, three, four seconds . . . Still the rear gunner did not fire. The enemy pilot yo-yoed violently. As he reached the top of the second yo-yo, Bader fired again, into the starboard engine. The wing burst into flames: victory two; but Bader snapped a look in his mirror and saw a Bf 110's nose, and tracer coming towards his Hurricane. He turned to face the Bf 110, who promptly and wisely dug his nose down and dived, losing Bader who tried to follow him, before levelling off at 6,000 feet.

Bader had seen nothing of the rest of the fight after he had made contact, and he could see no bombers. All he saw were Bf 110s. He climbed to 12,000 feet.

After Red Section had hit the formation, on the left two of the Bf 110s had sought to isolate McKnight, but he had closed in on the tail of one of them at 100 yards and sent it diving down out of control. Now McKnight was through to the bombers. He attacked the nearest He 111 from the beam, and knocked out its port engine with an accurate burst of fire. As he broke away, he saw it flick on to its back, belch smoke, then suddenly flare up and dive. McKnight pulled out of his break at around 10,000 feet. A Bf 110 had seen him and now latched on to McKnight, but he turned so effectively that he got on to its tail and fired. The German pilot dived to 1,000 feet, spiralling in very tight, banked turns. McKnight was on its tail all the way. The German rear gunner was firing frantically. McKnight got the shot he wanted at just 30 yards. At that range the Hurricane gun pattern was wide – wingtip to wingtip. Both its engines dead, the German aeroplane smashed into the ground.

Bader's Number 3, Denis Crowley-Milling, attacked a Heinkel from astern with a five-second burst. It went down, slowly. He was just about to follow when tracer whipped past his starboard wing. He broke to port, and shook the attacking Bf 110 off.

Yellow Section attacked next: Flight Lieutenant Eric Ball (Yellow 1), Sub-Lieutenant Dicky Cork (Yellow 2) and Sergeant Lonsdale (Yellow 3). Ball came in from up-sun, diving. He saw a lone He 111, pounced on it and hosed it from 100 yards, setting both its engines on fire. It went down to force-land. Ball looked around him, wary of enemies, but he saw a Bf 110 alone and down-sun. He attacked it from astern, and it too went down. Now Ball dived down into the exposed bomber formations . . .

Lonsdale also saw a lone He 111. He came in from the enemy's rear three-quarters. He opened fire at 300 yards, closing to 50 yards – a burst of no less than ten seconds. He had initially over-estimated his range, as those new to combat were prone to do. The He 111 circled, before crashing.

Cork had joined other Hurricanes in attacking a solitary Bf 110, which went down. But Cork had seen another Bf 110 and broke off to port to attack it from the beam as it passed, with a three-second burst of fire. He gave it another two three-second bursts as he curved in on its path. His bullets smashed the port engine, which began to burn. The German tried to stall-turn out of trouble, but he lost power and control and spun down to explode on impact with the ground.

Black Section – Pilot Officer Noel Stansfield (Black 1) and Sergeant Brimble (Black 2) – was last to dive in to the attack and had gone straight into the bombers. Stansfield launched an attack on a straggling He 111. He made two passes, firing short and effective bursts on each, and receiving return fire from the rear gunner. On the third pass, he silenced the gunner. Ball and Brimble had joined in the attack and the He 111's port engine was smoking and its starboard engine had stopped. The bomber pilot dropped very low, Stansfield following, then saw a civil aerodrome strewn with derelict cars, and belly-landed.

Brimble had left Stansfield to finish off the He 111, and turned to port to see a Bf 110 in a shallow turn, a hundred feet above the ground. Brimble cut in on the Bf 110 from the quarter and fired from 250 yards. There was little room for evasion. The Bf 110 hit the ground. As Brimble turned to find Stansfield to rejoin, he found himself in a head-on charge with a Bf 110. It was 350 yards away. The range was closing rapidly. His guns were set to converge at 400 yards. Over 'open sights', Brimble simply hosed the Bf 110 which passed right through the cone of fire. Brimble could hardly have missed. His fire hit its forward fuselage. The front portion of its canopy and windscreen disintegrated. The aeroplane kicked and bucked, its pilot dead, and it fell away. Brimble broke off as he saw over his shoulder a Bf 110 attacking him. He outstripped the German and headed for home.

The German formation had retreated. The German bombers and fighters were heading for home. The No 242 Squadron pilots in their individual combats at heights from zero to 12,000 feet, looked around for more, but there were none. The whole combat had lasted between five and ten minutes.

Bader was above the area of the battle. A number of pyres marked crashed aeroplanes, but the sky was empty of the enemy. Bader called up Duxford and was told to land. He joined up with Christie and Powell-Sheddon's Blue Section on the way back.

Blue Section had missed the battle. They had seen no action. They were blasphemous.

The 30th August was the first time that Bader led his squadron into battle – against between sixty and one hundred German bombers flying at 17,000 feet in formation near North Weald. The engagement took place just west of Enfield – 15–20 miles up-sun from the target airfield, a very different position from the one the Fighter Controller in No 11 Group had dictated – which would have placed them down-sun and below the Germans. The Hurricanes were perfectly placed right above the bombers and hidden in the glare of the sun. The squadron was back an hour and thirty minutes after take-off. Remarkably, no Hurricane was lost.

When the evening reports were in, No 242 Squadron learned the full measure of its success. No bombs had fallen on RAF North Weald. The squadron had a total claim of twelve 'destroyed'. Bader had shot down two, McKnight three, Turner one, Crowley-Milling one and Ball one. All three men already had considerable combat experience, but a rare talent had been shown by the rawhide, Dicky Cork who scored one Bf 110 in flames and a half share in a He 111 in flames, his first victories. The broken raid had been hit by other Spitfires and Hurricanes which pulled down stragglers like hyenas. The main objectives were achieved – the Germans had been reminded again that their raids would be countered and the raid had been thwarted. For No 242 Squadron, the combat had been essential: the squadron had acted successfully as a fighting unit.

This day (rather unrepresentatively) brought No 242 Squadron's score for the month of August to fourteen enemy aircraft certainly 'destroyed' and five 'probably destroyed'. After the action, the Chief of the Air Staff sent the squadron a signal:

> 'Magnificent Fighting. You are well on top of the enemy and obviously the fine Canadian traditions of the last war are safe in your hands.'

Air Vice-Marshal Leigh-Mallory telephoned Bader to congratulate him on his achievement that day. Bader told him that he had had the height, the sun and surprise, but he had had to detach one section, Blue, and he added: 'If I had had more fighters with me, we would have shot down lots more of them.'

It was a sentiment with which Leigh-Mallory agreed. Although No 242 Squadron had enjoyed the advantage of height and sun, and had dictated the fight, they had been heavily outnumbered. Bader felt that with more fighters he would have been even more successful. Leigh-Mallory agreed. He suggested a wing.

Bader reasoned: several squadrons in No 12 Group were standing by at any one time; why not use them all at once, together? He believed that getting as many fighters above an enemy bomber formation as possible was the essence of fighter-versus-bomber tactics; after the attack had begun, nothing more could be done to co-ordinate the fighters. Usually the German formations assembled over the Pas de Calais at 15,000–17,000 feet before flying over the English Channel. They could be seen on radar. Why, asked Bader, did No 11 Group not call No 12 Group unless they needed help badly? By then, Bader contested, it was too late for No 12 Group's squadrons to get into position to help. Douglas Bader reasoned that No 12 Group was far enough back to allow concentration of force: that should be its role, allowing No 11 Group to climb to height behind the bombers to attack them on their way home.

Less than twenty-four hours after leading his first squadron interception, Bader was told by Leigh-Mallory that he was to start preparing to lead a wing immediately. Next day, Sunday, 1 September, Bader was to take No 242 Squadron down to RAF Duxford and operate from there until further notice (although, officially, the squadron remained based at Coltishall, from where detachments were to operate as required). The Duxford Sector was adjacent to No 11 Group. It was barely 45 miles from Gravesend, over which the German bombers frequently made a turn. Duxford was No 12 Group's front-line station.

The Duxford Station Commander and Sector Fighter Controller was Wing Commander A. B. Woodhall. He was responsible for liaising with No 11 Group's Fighter Control, and for guiding his squadrons over No 11 Group's area. His personality, experience and ability were to be critical factors in

RAF Duxford's fortunes in the next month. A friendship and understanding developed between Woodhall and Bader which helped them to work together. Woodhall was a veteran fighter pilot from World War One. He knew what the fighter leaders were facing. He knew the ways of fighter warfare. He also knew the limitations of the air defence radars, and took account of them. When he spoke to an airborne fighter leader in his calm, deep, measured voice, guiding, not ordering, Woodhall knew that the fighter leader was the only man who could see the enemy.

Duxford was the premier No 12 Group station, and its squadrons were Leigh-Mallory's elite, Nos 19 and 310. He now considered No 242 Squadron one of the elite. No 19 Squadron, with whom Douglas Bader had served earlier in the year, was now commanded by the able Regular Squadron Leader R. Pinkham. It was equipped with Spitfire Mk IBs, which were armed with two 20mm Hispano cannon and four .303-inch machine-guns. No 310 Squadron was a Free Czech unit, the first Czech fighter squadron in the RAF, whose Commanding Officer was Squadron Leader Douglas 'Bill' Blackwood. Like No 242 Squadron, it was equipped with the Hurricane Mk I.

Bader discussed the theory of a wing with Squadron Leaders Blackwood and Pinkham. The squadrons began to fly a wing in practice, to iron out the problems of forming up, control and communications, moving on to tactical deployment. Nos 242 and 310 Squadrons would take off from Duxford and No 19 Squadron from Fowlmere. Bader, Blackwood and Lane would turn on to the vector and climb, coming together as a formation during the climb. It took between four and six minutes for all three squadrons to take off, climb on course and join up.

The two Hurricane squadrons flew in the prescribed Fighter Command wing formation, line astern, No 242 Squadron leading. The Spitfires of No 19 Squadron would act as the 'upper guard' for the Hurricanes, and would therefore fly two, three or four thousand feet above them, on a flank and slightly behind them. The Hurricanes had an advantage in their climbing speed, and had a better machine-gun pattern for dealing with bombers, but the Spitfires had a marginally better performance to tackle fighters. The formation continued its climb for twenty minutes to 20,000 feet, with the Spitfires above at 24,000 feet, over the Thames Estuary, placed so that Bader could manoeuvre them to put the sun behind them.

The control of the wing was in Bader's hands. The Fighter Controller directed Bader. All three squadrons were on the same HF radio frequency. Commands were rehearsed, so that intentions were clear immediately. The Hurricanes were to attack the bombers while the Spitfires were guarding against the top cover Bf 109s; if there were no Bf 109s, the Spitfires would then attack. None of this was a revolution in tactics: the principles and the ideas already existed.

Bader and other junior leaders accused RAF Fighter Command of not passing on to the fighter squadrons in Britain the lessons of combat and tactical information from the fighting over France and off the French and Belgian coasts. However, the Air Ministry's Air Tactics Branch produced a series of Fighter Command Tactical Memoranda for circulation from May

1940 onwards. These reported on the facts of the fighting and made recommendations. Of course, it may have been that these memoranda were slow to circulate to all units, especially squadron leaders preoccupied with training.

It was Fighter Command doctrine that a two-squadron wing, with the second squadron higher and to the beam of the first, was the most successful formation in which to search for bombers. Each was led independently. The leading squadron would attack first, while the second remained in place to cover it. Whatever the strength of a fighter unit, a proportion had always to be detailed for this duty, so the 'upper guard' was supplied by the rear section of each squadron and by the second squadron complete. Fighter Command had issued documents covering the tactical use of two-squadron wings. Park had used two- and four-squadron wings over Dunkirk, when they had had time to form up on the climb from bases in southern England.

A standard patrol formation for a squadron was sections of three in line astern, stepped up, the third section to a flank and the fourth section acting as look-out to the rear. In any formation, the rear units were to be employed solely on look-out duties to try to prevent surprise attack from astern or above. The duty had to be rotated among the sections during a mission, because 'weaving' used up considerably more petrol than normal flying. In combat, a squadron quickly became broken into sections of three; each section then relied on its own Number 3 to protect their tails - the luckless 'Arse-end Charlie'; when the sections then became split up, it was every man for himself.

Search patrols had also been mounted – over France – in flights of five aircraft, each five forming an independent unit under its own leader. The Numbers 4 and 5 provided the look-out by crossing over above the formation in a figure of eight. Two flights of five could be operated together, one flying above and to the flank, each providing its own two-aircraft look-out: more than two flights could be flown, in echelon.

A Fighter Command advisory document of June 1940 summarized the principles of multi-squadron attack:

> 'Upon approaching the enemy bombers, every effort should be made to achieve surprise. If this is successful it may be possible to deliver an attack without interference. The "upper" squadron or unit may be able to draw off their escort and, if necessary, attack them while the "lower" squadron attacks the bombers . . . even a small detachment from our fighters . . . may draw large numbers of them off and so enable the remaining fighters to deliver an attack unmolested. . . .

> 'Always ensure that the upper guard is in position ready to assist before attacking, or that the enemy has no available protection. . . .

> 'Whenever possible, fighters should attack enemy bomber formations in equal numbers by astern or quarter attacks from the same level . . . a short burst of two or three seconds may well be decisive, but in any case this should not be exceeded without breaking away to ensure that an enemy fighter is not on one's tail. If all is well, the attack can be immediately renewed.'

French experience had confirmed that this Fighter Command doctrine of simultaneous attacks against compact sections was most effective. This method distracted the attention of machine-gunners and enabled the fighters to benefit from superiority of fire. The French, however, had actually prohibited attack in line astern, the Fighting Area No 1 Attack, against compact sections. Although simultaneous attacks were successful, Fighter Command still adhered to formalized attack patterns which were rarely practical, as indicated in an advisory document of July 1940:

> 'If interference from enemy fighters can be temporarily neglected, a flight of five aircraft can use the "astern attack from the beam". Aircraft take position in line astern, 800 yards to port of the enemy bomber formation, and ahead and 1,000 feet above. On the order "turn to right in astern. Going down", the flight turns in simultaneously. Nos 1 and 2 deliver a full beam attack, Nos 3 and 4 a quarter attack, and No 5 an astern attack. After the attack, fighters break away to the left and downwards, reform line astern to port of the formation and repeat the manoeuvre.'

Where there were too few fighters to attack the bombers successfully, Fighter Command advocated a series of 'nibbling' attacks, in which fighters individually attacked and broke away and swung back to hold station until they could attack again. This might pick off a few bombers, but the effect could only be slow and cumulative. Bader, on the other hand, advocated diving into the formation with the deliberate intention of causing it to fragment – the so-called "disintegration' tactics. Then, individual bombers could be picked off. It was a blunt instrument, but Bader's record shows that it worked.

Bader was attempting to solve the two main problems in bomber interception, hitting hard but surviving. Hitting hard, he reasoned, could be solved by overwhelming numbers, and using surprise – greater altitude and the sun. However, the major problem in bomber interception was protecting one's tail from escort fighters when attacking. This could only be done effectively by another fighter. It was a problem which Bader fully recognized, as becomes clear. It is central to the reason why the experience of flying wings in September 1940 is important – not to the Battle of Britain, but to the development of fighter tactics for the rest of the war.

Bader asserted that it was pointless protecting airfields by patrolling over them, for another reason. Once the bombers had broken through and were attacking, some of them were bound to succeed. The place to patrol was well forward. The squadrons could then attack the Germans before they crossed the Thames on their bomb runs.

Bader asserted that the only person who could decide how to get a squadron into the right position up-sun was the man leading it. Therefore, the Fighter Controllers – rather than issuing orders as to where and what height the defenders were to patrol – should restrict themselves to giving the fighter leader information about the German raid's height, bearing and numbers. Using that information, the tactical leader in the air was the best person to place his squadrons. Like this, he was convinced that the Duxford Wing could break up raids and destroy large numbers of the enemy.

Bader responded warmly to Leigh-Mallory, in one of those contradictions of Bader's nature: he, the hero, needed his own hero, a trait seen in him from his schooldays forward. Bader believed that Leigh-Mallory was tough and enthusiastic and had a receptive mind, quick to understand and quick to question and probe. Whether the readiness of Leigh-Mallory to accept Bader's views is due to this, or to the fact that Leigh-Mallory had formed similar views and had – which Bader ought not to have known – a political axe to grind.

Leigh-Mallory took Bader's views of the actual engagement and put them into the context of the Group's objectives, as he saw them. He asserted that, as the Germans were sending over not a few bombers but mass formations escorted by even greater numbers of fighters, it was 'wholly inadequate' when No 12 Group was asked to protect No 11 Group's aerodromes to send only one squadron. He argued that several squadrons should be used, operating cohesively. Definite roles should be allocated to the squadrons: Spitfires flying as an 'upper guard' to deal with the fighter escort while Hurricanes attacked and broke up the bomber formations, and – this was an important point to watch in the Wing's actual combats – other fighters went in to destroy stragglers. Wings were not new concepts; 'upper guards' were not new concepts; but the 'disintegration' tactics was a new concept.

At 48 years of age, Trafford Leigh-Mallory had been Air Officer Commanding No 12 Group for three years and he knew his job thoroughly. An old boy of Haileybury public school and a graduate of Magdalene College, Cambridge, he had been trained to think intellectually and historically, which set him apart from his Service-educated peers. He was a reserved, austere man, but he was a man who gave unstinting support to those in whom he believed. Bader was one of those. Leigh-Mallory had wanted a tough nut to lick No 242 Squadron into shape. In Bader, he met a man who not only thought seriously about modifying tactics, but who had the intellectual toughness, the stamina of will, to prosecute his beliefs. Bader had been trained to lead since his schooldays; Cranwell had given him the tools; Shell had given him the experience; and his own personality ensured that whatever he did, he would attract attention. Now he had his own squadron, it seemed so natural and so inevitable that he slipped into the new responsibilities without a doubt. His drive to compete, to be best, to excel, to make his mark now broke through again.

Leigh-Mallory collected at RAF Duxford the premier No 12 Group squadrons. He wanted to keep them together, and not have them squandered reinforcing the front-line No 11 Group. The consequence of a concentration of elites without a major role was inevitable: frustration. It was from this that the 'The Big Wing' controversy originated.

Whereas Park and Dowding had fought with distinction during the First World War as fighter squadron commanders, Leigh-Mallory had fought with distinction as an army co-operation squadron commander. This has often been cited to diminish Leigh-Mallory, but to do so misses important points. He alone had experience of the tactical governance of a major battle. Commanding No 8 Squadron, he oversaw the new tank/aeroplane co-operation techniques which truly changed the role of machines in war. The whole matter hinged upon clear, timely communication between aeroplanes to Control, and Control to tanks. His experiments ran from semaphore to wireless. His despatches reveal his awareness of both the possibilities and limitations of the new technologies, from munitions to wireless telegraphy. Tank/aeroplane co-operation made a great impact during the Battle of Amiens from 8 August 1918. During the Third Army Battle from 21 August 1918, Leigh-Mallory commanded a Wing comprising No 8 Squadron, an R.E.8 unit used for observation, and No 73 Squadron, a Camel unit for anti-tank gun elimination. He had a broader perception than those raised in the pure fighter traditions of the inter-war Royal Air Force. It was the tactical application of the aeroplane that mattered to him, whether fighter or bomber. He thought himself into the minds of the German bomber tacticians.

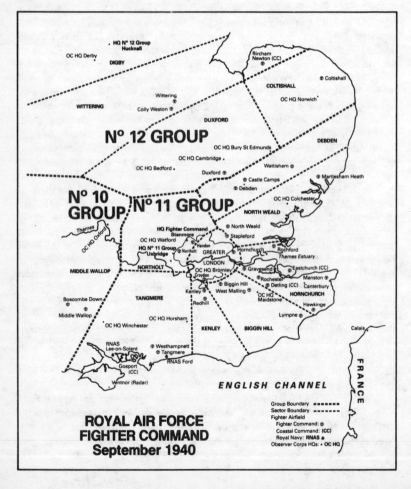

ROYAL AIR FORCE
FIGHTER COMMAND
September 1940

In one evident sense, he was the right man to command No 12 Group. Were the Germans to have invaded and successfully established a beachhead, spreading out into the open country towards the plains north of the Thames, there was only one commander in the RAF who had solid experience of aircraft versus tank – Trafford Leigh-Mallory.

Unfortunately, his experiences of the continual sniping to which army co-operation was subjected by the rest of his Service had led him to regard his fellow commanders with a suspicion often bordering on hostility. His failure on 15 August 1940 against the German raid across the North Sea on the north-east of England wrankled. While No 13 Group had met the raid that was directed at its zone with all available force, Leigh-Mallory had put up initially just one full squadron, No 616, and one Flight of No 73 Squadron. Too many of the bombers had got through to bomb Bridlington and other locations. Leigh-Mallory had got it wrong, yet Park was meeting large formations with small formations of fighters, and Fighter Command Headquarters supported him.

Had he been in No 11 Group, it is unlikely that Bader would have had the time to develop his wing hypothesis in practical terms; and he certainly would not have had the support of the Air Officer Commanding the group. In No 12 Group, there was time to discover if the tactical advantages of greater numbers were enough to outweigh the difficulties of assembling on time in the right place and attacking cohesively, and whether the use of three squadrons actually did do more to ensure a tactical victory.

In 1940 radar was still unreliable, and it was difficult to gauge the height of the formations. Moreover, warning could not be given until the formations were clearly on their way, which might be some time after they began to form up. No 11 Group Fighter Controllers could not call the squadrons off the ground early enough. Therefore, frequently squadrons were not at sufficient altitude to dive on the enemy, or worse, were still in the climb and vulnerable to attack.

A Fighter Command document in June 1940 advised, categorically: 'Fighters in search formation should always patrol higher than the anticipated or reported heights of the enemy if weather conditions permit.'

Fighter Command's Group Controllers normally added height to the reported height of an enemy formation. Unfortunately, Park complained, the Sector Controller then added height, to be sure, and sometimes so did the fighter leader in the air. The result, as Park said, was that enemy formations had frequently slipped in unintercepted at below 15,000 feet, and had bombed successfully. His remarks had most application to No 12 Group squadrons.

Wings were practical for fighters with time to get into position to assault raids, like those in No 12 Group; No 11 Group did not have sufficient warning to form up and climb to an altitude above the enemy's usual attack height. Rarely, however, was the warning available to squadrons during the Battle of Britain adequate to allow this; swift to learn, latterly, the Germans simply adopted the tactic of placing a high cover at 30,000 feet.

☆   ☆   ☆

Fighter Command was entrusted with defending the whole of the United Kingdom from air attack. In the summer of 1940, the Command was divided into four Groups. No 11 Group covered the south-east of England; No 10 Group covered the south-west of England and Wales; No 12 Group covered the Midlands; and No 13 Group covered the north of England and all of Scotland. No 11 Group was the most critical area as it was nearest to and directly faced the Continent. Each group was divided into sectors controlled by the main aerodrome in it.

The Fighter Command system had been developed in the immediate pre-war years to give warning of bomber attacks and to allow co-ordinated control of interceptions. It depended upon a network of communications and a hierarchy of command and control; and it could not function without intelligence input from radar and signals intelligence. It was an archetypal Command, Control, Communications and Intelligence system – the now familiar C_3I. The Germans nearly won the Battle of Britain by disrupting that system. Additional strains, from within, were not desirable.

The system needed tactical intelligence. Fighter Command depended on radar – known originally as Radio Direction-Finding (RDF) – to detect aeroplanes approaching the United Kingdom and the Observer Corps to track their progress once across the coast and behind the radar screen. The Observer Corps was essential to support the radar system, estimating the height, range or speed of formations and gauging strength. There were two types of radar: the Chain Home system which detected medium- to high-level threats; and the Chain Home Low system which covered altitudes below 500 feet. The Chain Home was complete; the Chain Home Low covered all south-eastern areas. The information from the radar stations and Observer Corps Headquarters was passed to Fighter Command's Operational Control Centre where it was assessed before being passed to the Groups.

Control was the key. The brain of the system was Fighter Command Headquarters at Bentley Priory. All information from the radar chains and the Observer Corps was received by the 'filter room', where it was assessed; it was then passed to the adjacent Operations Room where it was turned into a 'plot' on the operations board – a large-scale map of the entire United Kingdom area and its sea approaches. The states of all squadrons in Fighter Command were displayed by a system of lights. Here was the only place where aircraft approaching or flying over the United Kingdom were tracked; here alone the development of the whole battle was seen.

Command was centralized, and reached down a pyramid. Presiding over the Fighter Command Operations Room was the Commander-in-Chief of Fighter Command, Dowding, with the Commander-in-Chief of Anti-Aircraft Command, Pyle, and the Commandant General of the Observer Corps. Liaison officers from Bomber and Coastal Commands, the Royal Navy, the Army and the Secret Security Services were also present. Under Dowding were his group commanders, and under them were their sector commanders, under whom where the squadron commanders.

The information received in the Command Operations Room was assessed swiftly and the appropriate response was determined. The information was passed to the Group Operations Room, presided over by the Air-Officer-Commanding the Group. The room was a smaller version of the Command Operations Room, with a board covering only the Group's area on which the information from Fighter Command was plotted. The information was then passed outwards again to the Sector Operations Rooms.

The Sector Operations Rooms were controlled by the Sector Controller. Squadrons were scrambled according to his instructions. From the Sector Operations Rooms, he guided them towards the enemy by radio. He was responsible for the control of a squadron until the airborne fighter leader saw the enemy. When the enemy was in sight, the fighter leader took control. After the combat, the Controller again took control.

Originally, Sector Controllers had been seconded from the Signals Branch, as they were familiar with radio and communications. However, it was found that fighter pilots, preferably with combat experience, were best for that job. Men too old for combat, or on 'rest', were posted. Usually, they were the Station Commander of the main Sector Station. Generally, in 1940, they were of the rank of squadron leader, sometimes wing commander, an immense burden for such a rank. The Sector Controllers were the final link in the Fighter Command system before reaching the fighter pilots. They frequently had to rely upon instinct.

Communications were vital to the success of the 'Dowding System'. A comprehensive telephone network linked all parts of the Fighter Command system, supported by the Defence Teleprinter Network. Information and orders could be relayed in seconds. Sector Controllers used HF (later VHF) radio to talk to fighter leaders.

The system also needed strategic and logistic intelligence. Fighter Command was fighting the battle on a longer term basis. The Listening Service had already provided Fighter Command with invaluable intelligence. As the entire Luftwaffe order of battle was known and the call-signs of many units had been identified, the likely return route of each formation to its base could be deduced – and it could be intercepted. By intercepting the Germans' wireless signals traffic, the Service discovered information about the timings, size and target of raids, especially when radio direction-finding equipment became available. This was passed within minutes of being intercepted to Dowding. The information assisted in reacting appropriately to bombing raids. The existence of this intelligence was kept secret. In addition, the British had cracked the 'Ultra' code-machine. British monitoring could read the German's Most Secret communications, providing Dowding with intelligence about Luftwaffe High Command decisions and orders. Knowledge of the existence of this intelligence source was confined to Hugh Dowding and Keith Park. With these sources of information, Dowding could form a view of the Germans' prosecution of the aerial assault on Britain.

Radar was secret. Many fighter pilots were not aware of its existence, even though much of the coastal patrolling had to do with protecting the radar stations. To many who knew of it, it remained a mystery, of which expectations were somewhat unrealistic: Bader made this mistake. Radar did not, however, solve all the problems of advance warning. At best, it gave adequate warning. It had technical limitations. In basic terms, the radar set's emitter sent out a radio signal; if this signal struck a solid object, it bounced back and was picked up by the radar set's receiver. By halving the time that the signal took to go out and return, the range of the object could be determined. The bearing could be confirmed by triangulation – two radar sets, some distance apart, picked up the same object. Azimuth (height) posed greater problems as control of the radar beam was still relatively un-developed. Discrimination was a further problem: if several formations of aircraft were detected over the French coast, it was difficult plotting them all, separating them and ultimately determining which was the major raid. Moreover, it was very hard to differentiate between fighters and bombers. In short, warning could only be given when the direction, speed, range and altitude of the main forces were known. The radars looked outwards; once the bombers crossed the coast, the Observer Corps took over.

It is a principle of defence that threats be assessed centrally and that reactions are controlled from a nerve centre. Each component force must confine its actions only to its allotted task. On the other hand in offensive operations, once the battle plan has been decided, each component force must move against its individual objective according to that plan, but be free to exploit local weaknesses. The 1940 battle was defensive.

It is the function of a commander-in-chief to explain to his subordinate commanders the nature of his battle plan and to ensure that they act according to it in co-ordination. It is the function of those subordinate commanders to control their junior commanders; and it is the function of junior commanders to obey, without question. Dowding failed to control the dispute between Leigh-Mallory and Park; and he failed to perceive that Leigh-Mallory did not comprehend the Fighter Command system. Park and Leigh-Mallory failed to work together. Leigh-Mallory failed to work within the Fighter Command system; and he failed to control Bader. Douglas Bader failed to obey without question. In the old adage: 'Shall we court-martial the bugger, sir, or give him a gong?'

Bader has been excused on several occasions by explaining that there was failure on the part of those above him. But it is not necessary for every captain to know the general's battle plan – only to know his role. Bader was a captain.

CHAPTER 7
The Duxford Wing

August 1940 went out with a bang for two of the squadrons which were to form the wing, but the first week of September was mixed for the Duxford squadrons, especially No 19, as they built up towards wing operations. Just as the Friday had been No 242 Squadron's day, so Saturday, 31 August was No 310 (Czech) Squadron's day. There was a great deal of enemy activity over No 11 Group's area between 08.00 and 09.30 hours. Six No 12 Group squadrons were ordered to help: Nos 19, 66, 229, 242, 310 and 611 Squadrons. No 242 Squadron was scrambled three times, but did not find the enemy. Only No 310 Squadron, from Duxford, met the Germans – twice. In the morning, they claimed one Bf 110 'probable', but lost three Hurricanes with one pilot killed and one wounded. That afternoon, they took off again at 13.00 hours with orders to patrol the RAF Hornchurch–RAF North Weald line at 10,000 feet. At 13.15 hours, they saw a force of fifteen Dorniers and a score of Bf 109s. The Germans saw them and turned east. The squadron used rehearsed tactics: both Flights attacking simultaneously from opposite beams. Flight Lieutenant Sinclair led the squadron at the head of 'A' Flight and Flight Lieutenant Jeffries led 'B' Flight.

The Germans were above the British fighters. Sinclair ordered the Hurricanes to climb 2,000 feet. Then, he told Jeffries to take his 'B' Flight to the left of the enemy formation while he took his 'A' Flight down on the starboard. Their dives would continue through and past the formation, before levelling out. In the initial attacks, the Hurricanes managed to drive down bombers, before being set on by the escorting Bf 109s. The battle swiftly broke up into individual dogfights, in which all cohesive action by the attackers was lost – though not by the defenders. The Hurricanes claimed four Dorniers and one Bf 109 'destroyed', but lost two Hurricanes and one of the pilots.

During this period, night activity over No 12 Group was inconsistent and light, but the Group's day fighters could do little at night to counter the bombers, and their main commitment had to remain day work. During the hours of darkness from the night of 30/31 August, heavy bombing raids concentrated on industrial and dock areas on the Mersey and in the Midlands with some attacks on cities and East Anglian airfields. It was heavy on Merseyside during the first week of September, but petered out with poor weather in the second week.

Although the weather was fair and sunny, 1 September was a relatively quiet day after intense activity by the Germans during the night. No 242 Squadron saw no action, but its move had put the squadron in good spirits. However, over at Duxford's satellite, Fowlmere, September opened very badly indeed for No 19 Squadron. This unit had seen too little combat and when it had fought, its cannon had either jammed or malfunctioned. After a boring Sunday, No 19 Squadron flew four squadron patrols on 2 September, a day of poor weather and little German activity. The first, over RAF Debden, was led by Flight Lieutenant Wilfrid Clouston, taking off at 08.00 hours. Pinkham led the other three patrols, all over RAF Duxford, at 12.25, 16.50 and 17.35 hours. No enemy aircraft were seen. It was very dispiriting. Spirits fell even further when, as the squadron ORB records, they were told that 'it was probable squadron would be moved to Digby due to faulty functioning of cannon. Great displeasure.'

On Tuesday, 3 September, the German offensive escalated, and No 12 Group was again called upon to help No 11 Group. Two of the Duxford/ Fowlmere squadrons were in action, but not No 242 Squadron. No 310 Squadron was scrambled from Duxford at 09.28 hours, to intercept a raid coming in to RAF North Weald from the south-east at 20,000 feet. They located the enemy: 150 Dorniers and Bf 110s flying in tight patterns of five bombers in line abreast and five Bf 110s in line abreast. The fight illustrates well the tactical problems faced by 'The Few'. Up sun, 'B' Flight's five Hurricanes climbed above the formation, went into line astern, and attacked the port of the formation. 'A' Flight remained high at 26,000 feet to guard 'B' Flight from attack from above as it engaged – there were more Bf 110s stacked up over the formation. However, as soon as it was apparent that there were no Bf 109s around, 'A' Flight dived to attack out of the sun on the rear of the formation. The Flight Commander, Sinclair, kept his fighters together and climbed after each attack back to 23,000 feet to maintain the advantage. No 310 Squadron performed with textbook smoothness, felling five Bf 110s and one Dornier for the loss of one Hurricane.

At the same time, No 19 Squadron engaged another force just to the south of Colchester. It brought this squadron some measure of compensation. The ORB recorded:

'All available [eight Spitfires] on security patrol over Duxford and Debden led by S/Ldr Pinkham. Advised of enemy aircraft over North Weald and intercepted *after* they had finished bombing. Flying in pairs line astern the Squadron attacked from above and in front. Approximately 60 enemy bombers and 150 fighters. Me 110s on each side of the bombers and one in front about quarter of a mile from the formation. Possibly look-out or navigator though not likely the latter.' [*Author's emphasis*]

It is notable that No 19 Squadron flew in pairs, not threes. Flying Officer Haines shot down one Bf 110, Flight Sergeant Unwin another, and Sub-Lieutenant A. G. Blake, RN, claimed a Bf 110 'probable'.

That evening, there was further good news for the squadron. Pinkham had made representations that their Spitfire Mk IBs should be swapped with eight-gun machines from No 57 Operational Training Unit at RAF Hawarden, and the Commander-in-Chief Fighter Command, Dowding, had approved the idea. The squadron stood down to receive them, and No 611 Squadron from RAF Digby flew in to Fowlmere to stand by in its place. The change-over was swift and smooth. The squadron was operational again on 4 September, making two uneventful patrols, although its ORB stated succinctly that the eight-machine-gun Spitfires were 'wrecks. At least the guns will fire'. In fact, there was little activity anywhere over No 12 Group on the 4th.

Other squadrons were posted into the Duxford Sector, for periods. On 3 September, No 616 Squadron, Auxiliary Air Force, had arrived at Fowlmere alongside No 19 Squadron. It brought with it the real taste of the desperate battles being fought by No 11 Group's squadrons. It had been in the front-line for a fortnight, and was being rotated north to re-form. Posted on 19 August to Kenley, south of London in the heart of No 11 Group, No 616 had faced the campaign of heavy raids on the airfields which had begun on 24 August. On the 25th, they had lost seven Spitfires and two pilots killed and four wounded. Their base was shattered by a bombing raid, and was working at considerably below normal efficiency. On 3 September, the squadron was moved north. It had lost twelve Spitfires and eight pilots – only three of the original pilots were still with the unit!

They might have a different outlook on discipline and appearance, but any question of the Auxiliaries being different from the Regular Air Force in matters of skill or courage had been dispelled; their level of losses was attributable to having had too little combat experience, an all too common factor in the high losses of 'new' No 11 Group squadrons against those of the 'regular' No 11 Group squadrons. Squadron Leader 'Billy' Burton, a Cranwell Sword of Honour Regular, was appointed to command the squadron, to re-form it. He saw that it was no longer capable of operations, so began a training regime to bring it back to fighting strength, but it remained at Fowlmere.

On 4 September, No 73 Squadron from RAF Church Fenton reinforced Duxford. Owing to heavy mist over their base's area, the squadron's eighteen Hurricanes did not arrive until past eleven o'clock. During the day, Squadron Leader Marcus Robinson led twelve of them into the air with orders to patrol over RAF North Weald at 10,000 feet, and later Eastchurch, 'but', commented No 73 Squadron's ORB drily, 'without result as we were too low'. This remark is noteworthy because No 73 was one of the most experienced fighter squadrons, having fought in France since the first week of the war, and it knew the opposition's thinking. No 73 Squadron returned home that evening. They found orders to move permanently next day to RAF Debden in No 11 Group's most northerly Sector. They were needed there rather more urgently than at Duxford.

Thursday, 5 September was very poor for No 19 Squadron. At 09.45 hours, Nos 19 and 310 Squadrons were scrambled to help No 11 Group. No 310 Squadron found no action, called too late to get into position. Ordered to patrol over RAF Hornchurch at 15,000 feet, No 19 Squadron – eleven Spitfire Mk IAs led by Squadron Leader Pinkham and Flying Officer Brinsden – found a force of forty Dorniers in stepped up 'Vics' of five apiece and one hundred Bf 109s in several waves of line-abreast formations slightly higher, over the Medway/Thames Estuary. No 19 Squadron did not have enough height. It was a very fine day, visibility was excellent and No 19 Squadron was clearly visible to the Germans.

According to rehearsed tactics, 'B' Flight went straight in to attack the bombers. 'A' Flight, who had to 'deal with the fighter escort' [ORB], began to turn away and climb into the sun in order to try to get enough height to cover 'B' Flight effectively. As they did so, the Bf 109 top cover dived straight through them and hit 'B' Flight, shooting down P9422 flown by Pinkham and seriously damaging N3286 and P9391 flown by Flying Officer Lawson and Pilot Officer Burgoyne. Sergeant Plzak got a definite Bf 109 and Flying Officer Haines a Bf 110. Burgoyne had got a 'probable' Dornier before he himself was forced out of the fight.

Squadron Leader Pinkham was posted missing after this fight, and Flight Lieutenant Lane led the squadron on a patrol over RAF Stations North Weald and Hornchurch at 20,000 feet, taking off at 12.55 hours, but without seeing any enemy aircraft. Later that day, Pinkham was found dead. This was a further blow to the squadron. However, their loss was mitigated by their satisfaction that it was one of their own number, 'Sandy' Lane, who was promoted to the rank of acting squadron leader and appointed to command No 19 Squadron. Flying Officer Lawson was promoted to acting flight lieutenant and took over Lane's 'A' Flight.

The excellent weather continued on Friday, 6 September. No 242 Squadron and one Flight from each of Nos 19 and 310 Squadrons were ordered to patrol in No 11 Group's area. They found no enemy aeroplanes. However, after several days of practice, all three squadrons were now beginning joint operations. They had the joint take-off down to three minutes. Bader felt that they were ready for operations. Leigh-Mallory gave his blessing. They did not have long to wait.

☆   ☆   ☆

Saturday, 7 September 1940 was significant in two respects. First, the objective of the German air assault was changed from the RAF sector stations and major fighter bases to London – a tactical blunder that gave Fighter Command essential time to make good damage to its control system. Secondly, Bader led the Duxford Wing into action for the first time in the afternoon.

It was a lovely day, warm and sunny, and there had been little activity during the morning. At bases across southern England, fighter pilots sat around in the sun or the shade according to inclination, waiting. Shortly before 17.00 hours, Fighter Command's radars detected over three hundred bombers assembling over the Pas de Calais. In two waves, organized in a number of formations at 20,000 feet, they headed north-west. There was a brisk headwind which delayed them. Their slowness to form up and tardy progress allowed Fighter Command to get its interceptors in place accurately. But the Germans had provided the largest escort formations so far mounted, stepped up to 30,000 feet, a dangerous height for the RAF.

Bader had been fuming at the Controller, demanding activity. At last, at 16.55 hours, Bader was ordered to take his Wing off to patrol RAF North Weald at 10,000 feet – Nos 19, 242 and 310 Squadrons. He was told that there were a hundred enemy aircraft coming in from the east. Bader disobeyed the Controller and climbed to 15,000 feet – well above the height requested: he wanted altitude, for surprise. The Wing arrived over North Weald. Anti-aircraft fire attracted Bader's attention to a pack of enemy bombers some 5,000 feet (a mile) above the Wing, coming in over the Thames Estuary. The bombers were in a large rectangle, in sections of three in 'Vics' in line astern. Bader knew there were escort fighters above that. The Wing had lost all surprise. It was below the bombers. The German high cover was in the sun. This was precisely what Bader had argued should not happen.

Bader told Duxford the position and asked for permission to engage. It was granted. It was 17.10 hours. The Wing had to attack now or not at all. Bader instructed a rapid battle climb in line astern to get to the same level. Full out, the difference in individual pilot skill and aeroplane climbing performance caused the formation to lose cohesion.

The bombers were starting their bombing run on the Thameshaven oil refineries.

Douglas Bader (Red 1) and Dicky Cork (Red 2) arrived first and together, followed by Denis Crowley-Milling (Red 3). The enemy bombers were firing on them as they climbed and the fire became persistent as they launched their attack . . . the enemy top escorts began to pour down on to them from 4,000 feet above. The two Hurricanes began their attack.

Together, Bader and Cork skidded port at the forward beam of the nearest bomber formation and simultaneously opened fire from 100 yards, and held their thumbs on the firing button for 50 yards. Bader pulled up his Hurricane's nose for a quick burst into a Bf 110 in the middle of the formation – it belched smoke. The enemy formation did not break apart, and its return fire was accurate. Bader's aeroplane had already been hit. Now the Bf 109s were among the British fighters. Bader kept checking his rear-view mirror. He saw a Bf 109 behind him. Too late, he broke into a steep diving turn. He felt a thud as a bullet pierced the right side of his cockpit, broke the undercarriage levers, and exploded against the Kigas engine priming pump. But Bader lost the Bf 109. He had a Bf 110 in his sights, now, slightly below, full tail on to him. He fired. The Bf 110 kicked and then went down vertically.

Cork had seen a vulnerable bomber at the end of the formation. He broke to port from Red Section. He fired at the Dornier. Fire seized hold of its port engine. It slipped over and went down vertically. At that instant, shells hit Cork's port wing. He turned hard and dived, losing the Bf 109 that had attacked him but nearly collided head-on with a Bf 110. He took a snap shot, a very good snap shot, and blew the Bf 110's canopy and front cockpit to pieces. As Cork broke over the enemy fighter, he saw two crew bale out. He turned and followed the Bf 110, which fell like a leaf in autumn in a series of stalls. Cork followed the Bf 110 long enough to know it would crash, but too long for safety. A Bf 109 got on to his tail. It fired. A bullet smashed his reflector sight and windscreen. Glass flew into his eyes. He could barely see. He broke away in a half-roll and dive, and lost the Bf 109. He could do no more. He headed back to Duxford.

Crowley-Milling's original attack had been thwarted by a Bf 110 which cut in on him. He banked off hard to port and turned in behind the bombers. But again a Bf 110 diverted him, this time as a target. He held a four-second burst across the engines and fuselage. The port engine smoked, and he saw bullets strike the starboard engine nacelle. He had flown level for too long. The Bf 109 escort had arrived. One latched on to Crowley-Milling and strafed his Hurricane, smashing the radiator, left aileron and rear of the cockpit. He was out of the combat. The Hurricane went into a dive . . .

Ball led Yellow Section into the fray. Watching Bader lead his Section directly on to the bombers, Ball curved his Section to a position two thousand feet above the bombers before attacking. The Section split up swiftly. Lonsdale (Yellow 2) selected a Dornier. He found out how hard Do 17s could be to bring down. From 350 yards to point-blank range, trying to hold his aim against the slipstream, he poured bullets into it. He ran out of ammunition. Other Hurricanes took over the punishment. Ball meanwhile had fired on a Bf 110 but had to break off when he was caught by a Bf 109 from the top cover. He shook free, and chased the enemy south, attacking several other Bf 110s in quick succession. Two began to burn. A Bf 109 cornered him, and he had to end the chase and save himself.

Powell-Sheddon's Blue Section lost sight of Red and Yellow Sections. Then the three Blue Section pilots became separated. Powell-Sheddon climbed past the bombers to 22,000 feet to attack the escort. He blew a Bf 109 off the tail of another Hurricane, but the Hurricane went down trailing smoke. Blue 2, Roy Bush, had to break off his attack on a bomber to deal with Bf 110s, one of which he hit. Blue 3, Hugh Tamblyn, caught a Bf 110 in his gunfire. It exploded. Then he fired on a Bf 109, which went into a dive.

Stan Turner was leading No 242 Squadron's third Section, Green. He attacked a Bf 110 just as the Bf 109 top cover arrived. He broke into a Bf 109, and manoeuvred on to its tail, fired a full burst at it and the Bf 109 dived away. Then he tried to head into the bombers but he was cut off by the Bf 109s every time. His ammunition exhausted, he turned for Duxford. 'Jimmie' Gardner (Green 4) and Mike Stansfield (Black 1) arrived last of No 242 Squadron in the fight. Both of them caught a bomber and claimed to have shot it down, but Gardner's Hurricane was badly damaged by return fire.

Led by Flight Lieutenant Gordon Sinclair (Red 1), No 310 Squadron's eleven Hurricanes followed No 242 Squadron in an untidy climb at full boost. Sinclair saw No 242 Squadron wade into the bombers. He took Red Section in a curving climb into the sun and came in behind a group of Bf 110s astern of the bombers. All three pilots fired at one Bf 110, then swept on. Furst (Red 2) broke off to attack other Bf 110s, damaging one over the Thames Estuary. He trailed a group of bombers near Canterbury. A Bf 109 appeared in front of him from nowhere. He fired. The German baled out. Seda (Red 3) clung to Sinclair in a curving attack across the rear of the bombers. Seda fired accurately on a Bf 110 and Sinclair on two other Bf 110s in succession, before their guns clacked and hissed, empty of rounds. They turned for home.

No 310 Squadron's Yellow Section's three Hurricanes led by Pilot Officer Janouch levelled off at 25,000 feet over Grays Thurrock. They were between the sun and a formation of bombers, but there was a group of escorts blocking their way. They swept in, and all three attacked one Bf 110 which dived away, crippled. Janouch drew his Section into a climb to join another group of Hurricanes. But the main battle had passed by. They were recalled by Duxford Control.

Flight Lieutenant Jeffries climbed his Blue Section in from the sun – and told them to select isolated enemy aircraft. Jeffries himself fired on a Bf 110 but could not bring it in range. Pilot Officer Goth (Blue 2) destroyed a Bf 110's crew area: it went down quickly, but Goth's Hurricane had been hit by return fire. A Bf 110 set upon him. He turned into the attack and hit the port engine which burst into flames. The Bf 110 fell into the sea. His Hurricane's engine was dying. He crash-landed in north-west Essex. Blue 3, Flying Officer Boulton, attacked a Bf 110 without result, then spotted a lone He 111, retreating. He fired carefully into its port engine. It smoked. The He 111 crashed into the sea.

Green Section were the last two Hurricanes in the climb, Pilot Officer Fechtner and Zimprich (Green 1 and 2). They launched their attack right over the bomber's target area. They were too low to use the sun. Fechtner fired into the bombers from below. A Bf 110 caught his eye. He fired at it, and it spun away. Zimprich abandoned his attempt to reach the bombers and hit a Bf 110 from extreme range, and then stalked another Bf 110 which exploded in the air under his fire.

Lowest in the wing formation by some five thousand feet, the eight Spitfires of No 19 Squadron, led by Squadron Leader Lane (Red 1), were the last to attack. When Bader ordered the attack, Lane saw about twenty bombers and fifty escorts flying east at 15,000 feet. They put on full boost to climb to engage. Still in the climb, Lane spotted a Bf 110 and attacked. He followed it down, still firing, past the other seven Spitfires, most of which took shots at the Bf 110. Two Hurricanes joined the chase. They nailed the Bf 110. But No 19 Squadron missed the battle. They arrived too late. Lane and Sergeants Jennings (Red 2) and Lawson (Yellow 1) found the sky empty. Last in the battle climb, Flight Lieutenant Wilfrid Clouston (Blue 1) and Sergeant Steere (Blue 2) arrived too late to intercept the bombers. All returned to base.

However, by luck, three No 19 Squadron pilots had overtaken their colleagues and joined up with Hurricanes which were attacking bombers. All three were successful. Sergeant Unwin (Red 3) climbed to 25,000 feet and joined a group of Hurricanes attacking sixty enemy bombers and fighters. His Spitfire was singled out by Bf 109s, from which he escaped with difficulty, claiming to have inflicted damage. He shadowed some bombers, then attacked stragglers with some success before returning to base. Pilot Officer Cunningham (Yellow 2) shot down a bomber near the Kent Channel coast and Pilot Officer Dolezal (Blue 3) shot a Bf 110 into the sea.

When he landed at base, Bader immediately telephoned the Duxford Operations Room 'in a fury' to know why they had been sent so late – he was told that he was called as soon as No 11 Group had asked for No 12 Group support. This was a major problem for Fighter Command during the Battle of Britain: No 11 Group was too near the enemy, and deployed their own squadrons first, and then asked for No 12 Group to back up their dispositions, a complex procedure. If a ground forces commander were in a similar position of having to send forward contact patrols to meet incursions, he also would back up the base areas, but he would have more time to organize his forces.

All but two of No 242 Squadron's pilots were back by 16.55 hours. Pilot Officer Benzie was reported missing – he was dead. Denis Crowley-Milling's Hurricane had been badly shot up but he managed to crash-land near Chelmsford. He was shaken but unharmed and reported back to Duxford for duty the same day. Dicky Cork had shot down a Dornier and a Bf 110, but his Hurricane was so badly damaged that it was written off. A further five Hurricanes were unserviceable through combat damage, including Bader's which had a cockpit full of bullets and its starboard aileron smashed off.

Bader, Cork, Crowley-Milling and Gardner all had reason to be glad of the toughness of the Hurricane, Crowley-Milling in particular – the shells struck the armour behind his cockpit! Hurricanes had been quickly modified to incorporate an armour shield behind the pilot's body as a defence against surprise attack. Any extra weight was undesirable because it reduced the climb performance. Most pilots would have preferred to have had the performance in a climb, which would have given the chance to climb above the enemy to dominate the action, but were glad enough of the armour! Armour also gave protection in the break away, for it was not always on the attack that fighters were damaged by bombers. The break away after an attack on bombers was far more critical – although only a short moment, it could be fatal. A steep or violent climbing turn gave a bomber's gunner an easy shot – there was a period in which the only relative movement between him and the fighter was that of extending range – tantamount to point-blank aim. The safest method was to break out and down at the maximum speed possible, gradually changing the angle between the bomber's and fighter's flight paths, but this was not always possible, especially when enemy fighters were about.

What was clear from the casualties was that the Spitfires had failed to keep the German escorts off the Hurricanes attacking the bombers. The Hurricanes had been unable to concentrate single-mindedly on their attacks. Only in the absence of escorts, or if they were preoccupied, could the Hurricanes break up and then pick off the bombers with effective attacks. If these conditions did not exist, then 'nibbling' attacks were the most effective – diving into the formation from above and away, or attacking head-on and going straight through. This had been found effective in No 11 Group.

Although this attack was launched from very unfavourable positions and the combat with the bombers had been uncontrolled and inconclusive, the Wing made twenty 'destroyed', five 'probable' and six 'damaged' claims. No 242 Squadron was notably successful, claiming ten 'destroyed', two 'probables' and three 'damaged'. No 19 Squadron claimed five 'destroyed', the rest going to No 310 Squadron. Again, the Duxford squadrons had made over-high claims. The Wing lost four Hurricanes, and one damaged, with one pilot, Benzie, dead and one wounded. 'But,' wrote Bader, 'it was windy work, let there be no mistake.'

The coincidence that the first wing was in combat on the same day as the Germans diverted their attack from bases to London is indeed fortunate: had the Germans still been inflicting damage on the faltering Fighter Command control system, and had the wing failed to intercept a raid on an airfield as too many No 12 Group squadrons had done, the consequences would have been very serious. Bader took a risk, and won, but not because he understood the real tactical situation of the battle of which he was a small but increasingly prominent part.

☆   ☆   ☆

Sunday, 8 September passed quietly, with opportunity for church parade. The weather was cold and cloudy in the morning and the Luftwaffe confined itself to reconnaissance; it did not have the resources to mount such a large scale of raids for two days running. One Flight of No 266 Squadron was now operating from No 242 Squadron's dispersal point, serviced by No 242 Squadron personnel.

By the afternoon, there was a feeling of autumn but it did not last. Monday was again cold and windy, but there was action. Again the Germans sent over two waves of bombers, with heavy fighter escort. Some escorts swept ahead, freelance and dangerous. Others held position over the formations. Others were tied to the bombers, by order – an inflexible position the German fighter pilots resented. The waves followed each other swiftly. The objective was to overwhelm the defenders and go for London and the Hawker assembly plant at Brooklands to destroy one of the Hurricane's production centres. Park intended to meet the raids well forward.

Bader was kept on the ground. As usual, he expressed his resentment to Wing Commander Woodhall, the Sector Commander. In turn, Woodhall, pressed the No 12 Group Fighter Controller. In his turn, he consulted the No 11 Group Fighter Controller. Was the Duxford Wing needed? This all took time. The answer came back to Woodhall.

Eventually, Woodhall ordered Bader's Wing to scramble. Thirty-three Hurricanes and Spitfires took off. Bader went through on the radio to Woodhall and told him he was airborne, and asked for instructions. Woodhall said: 'Will you patrol between North Weald and Hornchurch, angels twenty?'

This was a question, not an order. Woodhall was giving Bader the tactical information: No 11 Group believed that the enemy were threatening the Sector aerodromes at North Weald and Hornchurch, although they might not actually be attacking them; No 11 Group perceived that interceptors would have to be at 20,000 feet in order to intercept. What Bader did with this information reveals his technique.

He intercepted the German bombers on their way in. He climbed his Wing at full power to the south to get between the bombers and the sun – setting in the west, to Bader's right. He believed that the Germans would always come out of the evening sun. He grouped his Wing over Staines, 30 miles west of RAF Hornchurch.

He was only just in time. He had his Wing at 22,000 feet between the sun and the formation of bombers. He saw them at 17.40 hours, 15 miles to his south-west at 22,000 feet – above the height he would have been at had he obeyed instructions. Bader made the Wing climb further while leading it round to head off the bombers.

The enemy were flying in two rectangular formations. The leading formation was about sixty strong. The second formation, about 500 yards behind and 500 feet higher, was also sixty strong.

Bader ordered No 19 Squadron to climb further to cover the Hurricanes' tails. In line astern, Bader turned Nos 242 and 310 Squadrons into the van of the front bomber formation, down sun and a thousand feet below the Hurricanes. Bader climbed hard over the top of the formation. He had identified the leader of the formation who flew slightly in front. He went for him.

Bader wheeled his squadron in to attack from just above the bombers. As he did so, he caught a flicker below the sun – Bf 109s who fell on No 242 Squadron as it turned. The Yellow Section Hurricanes at the rear of the line-astern formation turned towards the attack, and held them off the leaders.

From a thousand feet above the bombers, Bader made a single pass on the leading Dornier. He pulled up below it for another, but saw that the bomber was turning on its back. He went for other targets. He flew below the formation, firing into their vulnerable, blind bellies. Suddenly, their bomb doors opened and bombs cascaded around the Hurricane. Bader veered off. He continued to fire at the bombers, short bursts, to do the maximum damage – and take home wounded crew. Then his ammunition ran out.

As Cork (Red 3) went right, Willie McKnight (Red 2) had veered off from Bader's line of attack and come in on the enemy's left beam. McKnight broke hard left to attack the escorts. He quickly shot one down in flames. He saw two escorts pounding a Hurricane and got between them and dispatched one swiftly. As he opened fire on the second, another got on to his tail and fired. McKnight's port aileron spun off. He dived for the ground . . .

Powell-Sheddon (Blue 1) watched Red Section attack as he struggled to follow the climb. He decided to attack the leading bomber, following Bader, but he overshot. He turned hard. The leader was going down – Bader's attack had been enough. Powell-Sheddon attacked the second leader – this time, his fire had effect. The bomber's port engine burst into flames and the bomber fell away in a curve to port and became a straggler. But return fire severed an aileron control wire and his Hurricane fell out of the sky. He recovered control a few thousand feet from the ground and flew back to base on trim.

Eric Ball (Yellow 1) was behind Bader's Section. Seeing Bader go for the leading bomber and formation, Ball attacked the second formation, 400 yards behind and slightly higher. He lanced through the escorts and made a head-on attack in an attempt to break up the formation. It failed. A Bf 109 was on his tail. He manoeuvred and kept turning, until he was on the Bf 109's tail. He fired a long burst from 300 yards, closing to 100 yards. The Bf 109 disintegrated in a red ball of fire. But Pilot Officer Sclanders (Yellow 2) was also falling out of the sky . . .

Roy Bush (Blue 2) and Hugh Tamblyn (Blue 3) followed behind Powell-Sheddon, attacking the leading bombers. Tamblyn was diverted from his attack on the leading bombers when he saw five Bf 110s swinging around the rear of the bomber formation. As Powell-Sheddon was opening fire, he was set upon by a Bf 109. He outmanoeuvred it. A Bf 110 crossed his sights. He fired. The Bf 110 disintegrated. Another Bf 110 crept up on him, and opened fire. As Powell-Sheddon half-rolled out of trouble, Tamblyn saw what was happening and fired at the Bf 110 on Blue 2's tail. One of Tamblyn's bursts set one of the fighter's Daimler-Benz engines smoking. He left it, and flew round the bombers and fired a sustained burst into a Bf 110 which fell apart in a dive. Powell-Sheddon had recovered from his diving escape too low to rejoin the fast expanding battle.

Displaying great tenacity, Sergeant Richardson (Green 1) succeeded in shooting down a Dornier after three successive lone attacks against heavy counter-fire. Then he was attacked by Bf 109s. His Number 2, John Latta was also heavily engaged with ten Bf 109s. He destroyed one with a long burst – eight seconds – but a bullet from another jammed his port aileron. He left the fight in a hurry.

After Lonsdale had freed himself from the Bf 109s which had attacked the rear of No 242 Squadron as it went in to the attack, he re-assessed. He attacked the rear of the bomber formation, but experienced heavy cross-fire. His Hurricane was badly damaged but he used up all his ammunition before breaking off. With smoke pouring from his engine, his controls blown away, he baled out at 19,000 feet over Caterham.

No 310 Squadron hit the enemy shortly after No 242 Squadron. Flight Lieutenant Gordon Sinclair (Yellow 1), leading, began the attack just as Roy Bush and Powell-Sheddon made for home. He turned the squadron to starboard to attack the bombers, but saw Bf 109s diving on them from their port. He swung on to the opposite tack to observe the Bf 109s. Flying Officer Boulton (Yellow 2) behind him kept on course. Pilot Officer Bergman saw what happened next. Boulton rammed into Sinclair's port wing and rear fuselage. Sinclair's port wing tore off. Boulton's starboard wing folded over his cockpit and his fighter bounced into a bomber. Both aeroplanes burst into flames and exploded. Then Bergman saw Sinclair detach himself from his wrecked fighter, and seconds later, his parachute billowed.

Sinclair's Number 3, Fejar, cut a Bf 110 out of a formation, and sent it down smoking. Then his own right wing leading edge came loose; he could not control his fighter and he left for base. Meanwhile, Bergman had seen a Bf 110 on the tail of a Hurricane. He turned on the Bf 110, opened fire and the other Hurricane flew free. The Bf 110's engines caught fire. Behind them, Hubacek clashed with Bf 109s, then attacked four Bf 110s, shooting the tail off one. Rypl fired successfully on a Bf 109 which was attacking other Hurricanes. Then he chased after the bombers, which were now retiring to France. He ran out of fuel and had to crash-land. Rechka was attacked by three Bf 110s, but he managed to damage one, and broke free. Fechtner and Zimprich (Green 1 and 2) tried to attack the bombers head-on but became separated. Zimprich succeeded in damaging a Bf 110. He and Fechtner, isolated, chased after the bombers. Zimprich forced one to crash-land.

Bader had instructed No 19 Squadron's Spitfires to keep the escort fighters occupied while the Hurricanes went for the bombers. Flight Lieutenant Clouston (Blue 1) led the squadron, nine Spitfires. He put them in a line-astern climb to 23,000 feet to cut off six Bf 110s which were also climbing for height. Two Bf 109s cut across Clouston's sights – he fired and one Bf 109 erupted in flames and the other's engine stopped. But Clouston used all his ammunition; now he was a passenger. His wingmen, Sergeant Steere and Flight Lieutenant Burgoyne (Blue 2 and 3), took over the lead of the attack. Burgoyne got in a steady close burst on one Bf 110 and it went down. Then he flew with the unarmed Clouston to protect him. Steere could not get in range of his target.

Red Section was successful. Flight Lieutenant Lawson (Red 1) and Pilot Officer Cunningham (Red 3) each destroyed Bf 109s in the attack on the top escorts, but Cunningham's controls were damaged and he had to forced-land. Sub-Lieutenant Blake (Red 2) did not fire in this initial attack. Blake followed the bomber formation out over the Channel and sent a He 111 straggler into the sea.

Last to attack of No 19 Squadron, Yellow Section's three Spitfires went first for the Bf 109s but then diverted its attack on the top escort and went for the bombers. Flying Officer Brinsden (Yellow 1) took a high deflection shot at one of a pair of Bf 109s but did not hit it. He saw another Hurricane attacking an He 111 and went in from astern, using all his ammunition. Pilot Officer Vokes (Yellow 2) attacked a straggling bomber. He emptied his ammunition boxes into it. Another Spitfire, Brinsden or Blake, took over the attack. Sergeant Cox (Yellow 3) shot down a Bf 109 in the first clash, but it was a fraught fight, and the Bf 109 had scored several hits.

The statistical result of the Wing combat on 9 September, the second action by the Wing, was a total claim of twenty-one 'destroyed', five 'probables' and two damaged. No 242 Squadron claimed eleven 'destroyed' and eleven 'probables'; No 310 Squadron, four 'destroyed', two 'probables' and one 'damaged'; and No 19 Squadron, six 'destroyed', one 'probable' and one 'damaged'. Four British aircraft were written off and three were damaged. Although Sclanders of No 242 Squadron and Boulton of No 310 Squadron were killed, these were excellent results. They were somewhat far from the actual losses suffered by the Luftwaffe.

Fortunately, the vulnerable points that Bader was supposed to protect were not attacked: RAF Hornchurch and RAF North Weald. If they had been, Park would have had to weigh the results of the German attack against the results of Bader's Wing action – and then weigh the result with the obvious fact that Bader had disobeyed orders. He could have lodged an official complaint, but he did not. Leigh-Mallory was delighted by the results all round. Bader had acted as he knew a good fighter leader should – with initiative, and had won.

☆   ☆   ☆

On Tuesday, 10 September the weather worsened, with rain in the north-west driven by a northerly wind to the south-east and out across the Channel to envelop northern France. There was little sunlight, either, so attacks by the German bombers were unlikely. Squadron Leader Douglas Bader had arranged to visit Air Vice-Marshal Leigh-Mallory, his Group Air Officer Commanding, at Group Headquarters at RAF Hucknall to discuss the wing tactics. They were in general agreement.

Bader said that the enemy had used the same tactics when the Wing intercepted as on the occasions No 242 Squadron had made interceptions. The raids took place in the evening, so the sun was in the west. On the way in the Germans had flown in from the south over the west of London, and thus came in from the sun; on the way home, they had turned and headed south-east. It was therefore a waste of time and forces for the Duxford squadrons to patrol over RAF North Weald and RAF Hornchurch. If he were watching for the enemy who was coming in from the sun over London, he would not be able to see very far because the sunlight would blind him; but if he were looking with the sun, he could see perhaps 50 miles. The patrol line should therefore be south-east of the Thames in the morning, and south-west in the evening, because of the sun. This would place the Duxford squadrons between the sun and the Germans. It would give them the tactical advantage. Controllers should provide height and bearing information and leave the fighter leader to position his fighters and 'sort out the tactics in the air'.

In short, Bader believed: It was pointless protecting airfields by flying over them; the bombers should be caught coming in. It was pointless having a controller on the ground fight the battle: he could not see the enemy. It was pointless using penny-packets to pick off bombers out of a mass enemy formation: the enemy should be overwhelmed and annihilated. It was a temptingly simple and brutal solution that made Park's careful concentration of his squadrons in 'time and space' look like an over-elaborate ballet.

Bader's line of argument had been developing since he and Leigh-Mallory had begun to discuss wings. The more he thought about it, the more he became convinced that it was right. The more he was kept on the ground, the more he resented the lack of action. Now, in conversation with Leigh-Mallory on the 10th, he added a further observation to his argument: he felt sure that the German formations could have been broken up more swiftly and deeply, and more of them shot down, if two further, fresh, squadrons had followed the three-squadron attack. On that basis, Bader said he was convinced that they would have shot down at least twice the number they had on 7 and 9 September.

Leigh-Mallory had already grasped this point and now gave intellectual polish to Bader's gut-thinking. Leigh-Mallory said that the wing had to achieve three main things in order to be successful: neutralize the enemy fighters while the attack on the bombers was made; break up the bomber formation; and then shoot down the bombers. He did not think that these criteria had been met for two main reasons. First, he argued that because the Spitfires had not kept the German escorts off the Hurricanes while they attacked the bombers, the Hurricanes had not been fully effective in breaking up the bomber formation. Secondly, he argued that there were many bombers which became detached from the main formation and that these easy targets had not been shot down because there were no more British fighters to catch them. Clearly, he reasoned, there had been too few British fighters to occupy the escorts and deal with the straggling bombers. Therefore (as his No 12 Group Internal Report on Wings 120/2.5011/1 recorded), he judged by the sizes of enemy formations encountered so far that:

> '. . . at least two Spitfire Squadrons are required to neutralise the enemy fighters [and] at least three Squadrons are required to break up the enemy bomber formations and carry out the main attack on them.'

The repeated 'at least' is worth noting. After the bomber formation had been broken up, one of the fighter squadrons keeping the escorts at bay might be able to descend to pick off straggling bombers.

Leigh-Mallory and Bader were in agreement. Leigh-Mallory gave Bader two more squadrons. So far, there had been nothing particularly unusual about flying wings: the two-squadron search or patrol wing was a standard Fighter Command formation; adding another squadron as top cover had been done before, and was merely prudence. To fly five squadrons as a fighter force was taking things much further. This was a 'Big Wing'.

☆   ☆   ☆

The Duxford squadrons were not the only ones to fly wings, nor was No 12 Group alone in turning to larger formations. No 11 Group was responding to the larger formations of German bombers and fighters. Park was having two squadrons fly together. With the German's target clear – London – and the formations massive, wings could work. Clearly the conflict between Nos 11 and 12 Group did not lie solely in a difference of opinion about the use of large formations of fighters.

Among the first No 11 Group wings to be formed was one based at Debden. Significantly, it was in No 11 Group's most northerly sector, which gave it the greatest distance in which to form up, and 'next door' to the Duxford Wing. Initially, it comprised Nos 17 and 73 Squadrons; within a week, a third squadron was added. The initial discussion at No 11 Group Headquarters took place before Bader and Leigh-Mallory met at Hucknall.

On the evening of 10 September, the Commanding Officers of Nos 17 and 73 Squadrons discussed tactics for operating together. They would take off and join up over Debden, before proceeding to the patrol line. Before each sortie, one squadron would be designated the leader, with its squadron leader assuming overall command. The two-squadron Debden Wing began operations the next day. They were on patrol over the Thames Estuary when they made a successful interception and 'destroyed' five of a formation of Bf 110s. It is doubtful if the result would have been worse if only a squadron had been engaged, or better if three had been engaged. More evidence was needed.

☆   ☆   ☆

On 10 September 1940, Leigh-Mallory allocated Nos 74 (Hurricane) and 611 (Spitfire) Squadrons to Duxford's Wing. No 74 Squadron was to fly in the main body, while No 611 (West Lancashire) Squadron was to pair up with No 19 Squadron to provide top cover. No 74 Squadron was commanded by the strict and successful Squadron Leader A. G. 'Sailor' Malan. No 611 Squadron was commanded by Squadron Leader James McComb, an Auxiliary Air Force pilot. He had joined No 607 (County of Durham) Squadron in 1933. In 1939, he was notified that he was in a 'reserved occupation'; like Bader, he rebelled and had his name removed from the list. He was called up. He was an experienced pilot and leader and rose rapidly to squadron command. His concern for the young and inexperienced pilots posted to his squadron contributed to the survival of many of them – 'Johnnie' Johnson among them.

Room was made for No 74 Squadron in the Duxford Sector by displacing No 616 Squadron. This unit was still re-forming after its trial at Kenley. However, on 7 September, Dowding was forced to categorize his units in order to ensure enough replacement pilots in front-line units. Throughout the Battle of Britain there were never problems with insufficient aircraft; the critical factor was the loss of trained and experienced pilots – that could lose the Battle. Three categories of squadron were now created: 'A' Class which had the full twenty-six pilots; 'B' Class which were brought to full strength to rotate with squadrons in the front-line; and 'C' Class which had a nominal five officers for training. No 616 Squadron became a 'C' Class unit and was moved north. It is germane to ask whether, when No 11 Group was becoming so short of pilots, it was justifiable for No 12 Group to maintain five 'A' Class squadrons – 130 pilots whom Leigh-Mallory had no intention should ever reinforce No 11 Group?

Wednesday, 11 September brought a very cold, boisterous wind. Four of the squadrons were standing by. At 15.20 hours, Squadron Leader Lane led off the Duxford Wing to patrol the North Weald–Hornchurch line at 23,000 feet, a more realistic altitude. Bader and No 242 Squadron did not fly. The Wing comprised Nos 611 and 74 Squadrons and, leading the Wing, a 'composite squadron' formed of one Flight (eight) of Lane's No 19 Squadron and the Flight (six) of No 266 Squadron which was operating from No 242 Squadron's dispersal – a total of thirty-six fighters. The Hurricanes were to go for the bombers, while the Spitfires kept the escort busy.

Twenty minutes later, the Wing Leader, attracted by anti-aircraft fire between Gravesend and London, saw 150 enemy aircraft at 20,000 feet, flying north. There were Do 17s, He 111s and Ju 88s in a tight formation at above 18,000 feet. A force of Bf 110s was behind the bombers. Behind and above at 24,000 feet was an escort formation of Bf 109s. The formation was a mile deep! The preconceived tactics were modified. The fighters would have to rush the bombers head-on, try to achieve the maximum success on the first pass, and then try to pick off stragglers.

'No 19/266 Squadron's' fourteen Spitfires dived head-on in line astern at the leading Heinkels and their Bf 110 close escort. No 74 Squadron dived on the Ju 88s, ignoring the Bf 109s that came chasing down on them. No 611 Squadron divided its attentions between the bombers and fighters. In most cases, the bombers maintained their formation until attacked, then turned south-east for home. Showing their usual respect for the eight guns of the British fighters, the Bf 110s, rather than protect the bombers, formed a circle

– if British fighters tried to break into it, Bf 109s intervened. One Dornier even turned on a Spitfire and damaged it with gunfire badly enough to force it to crash-land. Several pilots were forced to break off their attacks before achieving a result to deal with the Bf 109s, which came down as soon as the bombers were threatened. Nevertheless, the rush had been successful, and bombers fell, and others became separated and were picked off. The 'score' was twelve 'destroyed', fourteen 'probables' and seven 'damaged' for the loss of one pilot killed. The tactical situation appeared to confirm that the discussions between Leigh-Mallory and Bader had been along the right lines: five squadrons were needed.

On 12 September, the weather reduced visibility, with a cold northerly wind, clouds and rain on and off all day. There was little enemy activity, and scant success. On Friday, 13 September No 11 Group coped with what little activity there was, and No 12 Group was not called on to help. There was no action over No 12 Group at all. However, No 302 Squadron, a new Free Polish unit, was posted to the Duxford Sector to replace No 74 Squadron in the Wing.

Saturday, 14 September dawned cloudy but turned into a beautiful morning. Activity rose from midday. The enemy directed his attacks on the East Anglian airfields and coastal towns. The five-squadron Duxford Wing, consisting of Nos 242, 310, 302, 19 and 611 Squadrons, was held in case a big raid came in. This left No 74 Squadron at RAF Coltishall alone to deal with the activity over East Anglia. It was hard pressed. In the morning, Blue Section, led by Flight Lieutenant Mungo-Park, intercepted a Bf 110 raider over the North Sea; at 14.00 hours, Yellow Section caught a Bf 110 and Ju 88 well out over the North Sea, and shot down the bomber; Red Section damaged an He 111 near Lowestoft; and Green Section damaged a Ju 88 near Ipswich. The reason it was hard pressed was that the Duxford Wing was keeping the available resources tied down. It hardly pleased Squadron Leader Malan. It was still very much the same routine of sea and coastal protection as No 12 Group had been flying since the war began, and fortunately never developed into a threat.

No 11 Group's Debden Wing was also now getting into its stride. On the 14th, after two days of inactivity owing to poor weather, the two-squadron Wing was ordered to patrol RAF North Weald at 15,000 feet – the squadron commanders interpreted this as an instruction to patrol forward of this point, as far as north Kent. Tragedy overtook them. They were 'bounced' by a squadron of Spitfires, and lost several Hurricanes.

At Duxford, Bader had been 'straining at the leash' as the clouds of early morning dispersed and a beautiful day for flying developed. At 16.00 hours, Bader led off four squadrons, Nos 242, 310, 19 and 611 – the Poles of No 302 Squadron were not yet ready. The Wing headed for London, hunting, but found no enemy aeroplanes, and returned. Refuelling rapidly, Bader pummelled the Controller to let the Wing off again: he wanted to fly the 'Big Wing'. At 18.00 hours, Bader led off the full five squadrons, as agreed with Leigh-Mallory, to patrol the Debden–North Weald–Hornchurch triangle. It was the first five-squadron wing patrol. They found nothing. However, this was an important dress rehearsal of the five-squadron 'Big Wing'.

CHAPTER 8
The Big Wing

Sunday, 15 September dawned cool and a little misty in the south-east of England but turned into a fine morning. The mist had cleared by 08.00 hours to reveal light cumulus cloud between two and three thousand feet, heavy enough in some areas to produce light showers. With a slight westerly wind shifting to north-west, the visibility improved as the morning wore on from moderate to good.

It was a fine day for the enemy. Park expected them. Fighter Command's radar became active soon after 09.00 hours when enemy patrols were detected off Dover, the Thames Estuary, Harwich, Lympne and Dungeness: they were probing. At about 10.30 hours, the first plots appeared on the No 11 Group board as the German bomber formations assembled over the French coast. There appeared to be several hundred aeroplanes! They were forming up slowly. This gave Park of No 11 Group the chance to organize his defence and put in place Nos 10 and 12 Groups' support for his own deployments.

It was not until just after 11.30 hours that the Luftwaffe's forward formations crossed the English Channel coast. At heights between 15,000 and 26,000 feet, the raids came in at three points: near Ramsgate, between Dover and Folkestone, and a mile north of Dungeness. The Germans were coming in out of the late morning sun. There were 100 bombers of Kampfgeschwader 3 and 300 escort fighters: the Germans were attempting to overwhelm the British defences which they believed already to be fragile.

The Germans were flying in various formations: 'Vics' of three, five or seven aircraft, in rows like a herring-bone, which gave good cross-fire if a British fighter pilot were foolish enough to get into the middle of one. The Bf 110 escorts gave close support to bomber formations on an almost one-to-one basis. The Bf 109s flew above the bombers, as top cover. However, tardy forming up over France led to fighters having to turn back too soon.

They were met by the Spitfires of Nos 72 and 92 Squadrons and the Hurricanes of Nos 253 and 501 Squadrons. Soon, three more Spitfire units attacked over mid-Kent. Between the Medway and south London, the Hurricanes of Nos 229 and 303 Squadrons (the Poles of No 303 charged head-on) made contact. The score of Hurricanes of the Debden Wing (Nos 17 and 73 Squadrons), which had been ordered to scramble at 11.05 hours to patrol Chelmsford at 15,000 feet, hit the bombers over Maidstone, breaking up a formation. Park had set up the interceptions perfectly – a stream of units to harry and break up the Germans, a steady application of force. The raid had spread out. Bombers were straggling out of formation. The Bf 109s, behind and above and beside and below, tried to protect the bombers. But about a hundred bombers continued on towards the south and east of London. There, other fighter squadrons awaited them.

Almost as soon as the German formations left the French coast, No 11 Group Control authorized Duxford Fighter Control to scramble their squadrons. At 11.22 hours, Woodhall scrambled No 242 Squadron, and Nos 19, 302, 310 and 611 Squadrons followed. There was no question this time that they were not being called early enough – but that was because the Germans had formed up slowly, not because No 11 Group had acted 'more promptly'. The fifty-six aircraft of the Wing formed up over Duxford, and flew south in a steady climb. They were to patrol over the Gravesend area – frequently the area of battle.

Bader flew the Wing in a curve to the south-east in order to place it up-sun. This would also give them a stern attack. At 25,000 feet, he levelled off, but the two Spitfire squadrons, Nos 19 and 611, continued to climb until they levelled off above 26,000 feet, as the 'upper guard', up-sun of the Hurricanes. When they encountered the German bombers, the Wing would be in the sun. The Wing had swung in from the south-east to get up-sun and behind the Germans. It was over Hammersmith, in the west of London, before they engaged. The Germans had flown over the heart of the city at 17,000 feet. It might be a perfect tactical situation, but it was leaving things a bit too late.

Now, the Wing was flying north-west, with the noon-day sun on their port rear quarter. At 25,000 feet, No 242 Squadron led followed by No 310 then No 302 Squadrons. Above and to the right was No 19 Squadron at 26,000 feet. Flying behind and to the right of No 19 Squadron, No 611 Squadron's twelve Spitfires were higher still, at nearly 28,000 feet. No 611 Squadron was well positioned, up-sun of the enemy and the Wing. Further into the sun there were about thirty Bf 109s, slightly higher than No 611 Squadron; so long as No 611 Squadron's Spitfires held station, the Bf 109s would not attack the Hurricanes.

The Wing was flying north-west over London. Bader saw two formations of enemy bombers passing several thousand feet below the Wing. Then he saw anti-aircraft shells bursting, pinpointing the enemy, so he turned the Wing. The enemy were 3,000 feet below, down-sun of the Wing. There were three formations of bombers, one for each Hurricane squadron.

Bader was preparing the attack, when he saw Bf 109s coming out of the sun. He alerted the Spitfires which lunged into the Bf 109s. The German fighters were surprised and broke, heading south-east, leaving their bombers.

Bader then had to hold the Wing's attack because other Hurricanes and Spitfires, from No 11 Group, were attacking the German bombers. Bader did not want to risk collisions. He watched the combat below – it was Nos 257 and 504 Squadrons, which had just made a head-on attack on a large formation of bombers. Then, he told his three Hurricane squadrons to fall into line astern, and prepare to attack. As the Sections of the Wing fell down their separate ribbons of sky, the German formations turned south-east.

Bader selected the most westerly of the three enemy formations; Squadron Leader Satchell of No 302 Squadron selected the middle formation;

and Flight Lieutenant Jeffries selected the most easterly formation for his No 310 Squadron.

Coming in from astern of the westerly formation in an almost vertical dive, Bader's leading Red Section went for the last section of three bombers, Neil Campbell for the left-hand bomber, Douglas Bader for the centre one and Dicky Cork for the right-hand machine. The three bombers had lost cohesion when they had turned. Now, the three fighters dived steeply on them. Bader's first burst caused his target's wing to burst into flame. He flashed past, pulled up and attacked a Dornier ahead, but a Spitfire was in his way and he broke off. Bader fired at a few Dorniers in the mêlée but was not sure if he hit any of them as he had constantly to watch out for other fighters; in front of him, a Spitfire smashed into a Dornier and the pair fell earthwards. There were many Spitfires and Hurricanes and many bombers in the same airspace, trying to get in their own attacks – there was no co-ordination, no sequence, fighters jostling to be first. Either the Germans were outnumbered or the British had committed too many fighters: it depends upon how the 'Big Wing' is viewed.

Bader eventually isolated a Dornier which had been crippled. He harried it into the clouds. One of its crew baled out, and became entangled in the tail – not uncommon with Dorniers. Then Bader ran out of ammunition. He headed for home.

Bader's Number 2, Cork, had hit his target effectively in his first pass. He broke downwards and right, then pulled up for height for another pass, but he saw that the bomber's starboard engine was on fire. It was being pursued by four other Hurricanes. He broke downwards to port and joined three Hurricanes in an attack on another Dornier which fell vertically. Bader's Number 3, Neil Campbell, fired into the belly of his target, which gushed smoke, but he lost it in the chaos of the battle.

Leading Yellow Section, Eric Ball attacked a Dornier but the return fire was accurate. His Hurricane began to burn. He killed his engine and crash-landed.

Noel Stansfield at Yellow 2 attacked a Dornier from astern, receiving heavy return fire from the rear gunner until his Brownings silenced him. Stansfield chased the Dornier through clouds. Both engines well alight, it crashed.

Blue Section could claim two bombers 'destroyed', shared with other fighter pilots. Powell-Sheddon (Blue 1) selected a Dornier and attacked repeatedly, with other Hurricanes. One of the bomber's engines caught fire, the crew baled out and it went down in a very steep dive to crash and explode. Hugh Tamblyn (Blue 2) followed his Section Leader, Powell-Sheddon. He selected a Dornier and began attacking. He was joined by five Hurricanes and Spitfires, and all six harried the bomber until its crew jumped. John Latta had fired on several bombers, but made no claims.

Stan Turner and his wingmen Richardson and 'Norrie' Hart went into the fray last of No 242 Squadron. Richardson made no claims, but Turner isolated a bomber, attacked repeatedly, finally going in to 50 yards, and watched the crew bale out. Meanwhile, Hart, the last of No 242's pilots to arrive, had used his head. He had seen that the German bombers were heavily outnumbered and that there were too many fighters in the airspace already. He looked around for other targets. He spotted a Bf 109 flying several thousand feet below – 15,000 feet or so – and continued his dive, on to its tail. The Bf 109 dived for the cloud, but Hart followed and opened fire at 150 yards. A flame gouted from the Bf 109, the cockpit canopy flew into shards, and the engine cowlings sprung. It began to burn. Hart followed it as it broke through the cloud and crashed into the sea.

No 310 Squadron, behind No 242 Squadron, was led by Flight Lieutenant J. Jeffries. He saw the enemy, who were flying north over west London, turn southwards as they were attacked. Jeffries turned No 310 Squadron south and cut the Germans' turn: they were actually parallel with the Germans' leading formation, but above them. Then he ordered the attack. It was just after noon. Jeffries himself set a Dornier's engine aflame – other Hurricanes set upon it and finished it while Jeffries fired on another Dornier whose crew swiftly leapt out near Kingston-on-Thames. Jeffries fired on another Dornier – but as the crew were baling out, a Spitfire crashed into it.

Four other members of No 310 Squadron made claims for shared 'kills'. Jeffries' Number 2, Sergeant Kominek, and three other Hurricanes attacked a single Dornier which made for the clouds. Kominek alone pursued it, and sent it into the ground near Tunbridge Wells. Sergeant Kauchy and two other Hurricanes attacked a Dornier, whose crew baled out over London. Nearby, Sergeant Hubacek knocked out a Dornier's engines. Another Hurricane joined in the attack. The enemy began to fall into a dive. Other fighters attacked. Crewmen baled out. The Dornier crashed south of London. Thirty miles away, Sergeant Puda knocked out a Dornier's engines with one burst. As he came in again, a Spitfire cut across and gave the coup de grâce.

Squadron Leader Satchell, leading the Poles of No 302 Squadron, had selected the middle group of the German formations. From 25,000 feet, he led his squadron down in a very steep dive on to the Dorniers 7,000 feet below. He fired on the left-hand leader when the Dornier filled his sight's graticule. Satchell pulled out of his dive and re-engaged the enemy. The bombers' defensive fire was accurate and he knew his Hurricane had been hit. Now, as he went in on another Dornier, a Bf 109 caught his aircraft. He escaped, but lost his targets. He went after other Dorniers retiring south-east. He thought he damaged one badly enough for it to crash.

Flight Lieutenant Chlopik (Red 1) led his section in on the rear of the formation in a full beam attack from the port – out of the quarter of the sun which was high to the south. His Number 2, Flight Lieutenant Jastrzebski, attacked it from the starboard. The Dornier zigzagged, trying to evade the fighters. The fighters' joint fire brought down the Dornier, whose crew baled out over south-east London. Chlopik veered off and attacked another Dornier which, wounded, was then set upon by Hurricanes and Spitfires. Red 3, Kowalski, attacked a Dornier from under 100 yards, but it vanished into clouds (he optimistically claimed a 'probable').

Czerwinski and Wedzik (Blue 2 and 3) attacked a Dornier on the left of the formation, Wedzik from astern and Czerwinski from below. They set the port engine and wing alight. The bomber turned left in a steep bank. Wedzik lost it. Czerwinski attacked again, but other Hurricanes had made passes at it and the crew were jumping.

Pilot Officer J. Chalupa led Green Section, almost the last to attack. He aimed his attack dive at the leader of the second 'Vic' of the bomber formation. He opened fire in a steep, 400mph dive at 250 yards and closed to a breath-taking 30 yards. The Dornier dived. Chalupa broke to port and downwards as the Dornier dived acutely. Chalupa attacked another Dornier from its rear port quarter, from slightly above at 100 yards. The port engine burst into flames. Crewmen baled out. The bomber began to fall. Another Polish Hurricane sliced off the Dornier's tail with its own wing. This might have been Sergeant Sindak (Yellow 2), attacking last of the Poles: he shot up a Dornier's cockpit but his wing was badly damaged in the engagement, with a leading-edge panel knocked off – which Sindak assumed was the result of return fire from the German gunner. He recorded that another Hurricane finished off the Dornier. Chalupa's Number 2 on this occasion was Palak, who may also have shared in the attack on this particular Dornier with the two other Hurricanes.

The third member of Green Section, Sergeant Paterek (Green 3), selected the port outer bomber in a 'Vic' of five flying at just 5,000 feet. He launched an attack from the beam. He killed the rear gunner, so he came in close and steady and fired a long rip along the fuselage and across the wings. The bomber fell out of control, he reported, straight into the ground.

After sharing in the attack on the Dornier, Palak climbed to try to find the main fight. He was lucky: he saw a Bf 109 which was about to attack another Hurricane. Palak accelerated, turned towards the Bf 109 and fired, two short, closing bursts. He saw pieces spin off the fighter. The German dived away vertically – a common 'Emil' escape manoeuvre, so Palak only claimed a 'probable'. He was the only Duxford Wing Pole to fight with the fighters that morning.

No 19 Squadron was at least two thousand feet above the Hurricane squadrons when Bader attacked. Flight Lieutenant Lawson had the lead, and ordered a line-astern attack on twenty or so Dorniers at about 18,000 feet, with an escort of Bf 109s – they went for both the bombers and the fighters. Squadron Leader Lane and Sub-Lieutenant Blake (Yellow 1 and 2) took on a Dornier, while Pilot Officer Cunningham (Yellow 3) bored in on a Bf 110 escort, sharing it with another Hurricane pilot. Lawson (Red 1) swung round in front of the formation of bombers and made a head-on attack, then came in on its stern, shooting into the rear port Dornier. He veered around again and attacked the same bomber, closing to less than 50 yards. The bomber lost altitude, trailing smoke. His Number 2 attacked but made no firm claims, but his Numbers 3 and 4 (Unwin and Steere) each claimed success over a Bf 109, forming the escort, as did Green 1 and Green 3 (Haines and Cox); three were seen to crash.

Flying behind and to the right of No 19 Squadron, No 611 Squadron's twelve Spitfires were higher still, at nearly 28,000 feet. No 611 Squadron was flying north-west: they were up-sun of the enemy and the Wing, with the sun on their port rear quarter. Further into the sun were about thirty Bf 109s, slightly higher than No 611 Squadron. They did not attack. No 611 Squadron held position, holding the German fighters off the Wing while it attacked. Keeping pace with the fight's movement towards the Channel, Squadron Leader McComb watched the combat develop more than 10,000 feet below him. After about five minutes, he radioed to Bader that he was bringing his Spitfires into the battle too. He ordered his fighters into echelon to his port. Swiftly, the eleven fighters formed up on him, and they dived head-on into ten Dorniers and an escort of Bf 110s. It was over very quickly. The fighters broke the bomber formation, then, with their section formation sundered, the Spitfires chased stragglers to the Channel coast. With certainty, the combined efforts of several No 611 Squadron pilots knocked down two Dorniers – their crews were seen to bale out – while the persistence of another pilot's attack left another Dornier flaming.

Fifty-six fighter pilots had taken off from Duxford and Coltishall. Between them they claimed twenty bombers and six fighters 'destroyed', and eight enemy aircraft 'probably destroyed' and two 'damaged'. Bader's No 242 Squadron alone claimed five Dorniers and one Bf 109, exceeded by No 302 Squadron's claim for eight Dorniers, and followed by No 310 Squadron's four Dorniers, No 611 Squadron's three Dorniers and No 19 Squadron's three Bf 109s and two Bf 110s. Claims were subjected to rigorous inspection; those making the claims did so with total integrity of intention but, when a mass of fighters is attacking a mass of bombers while being pursued by escorts, confusion arises. The total claim by Fighter Command in repulsing this onslaught by one hundred Dornier Do 17s of Kampfgeschwader 3 was unrealistic, and the Duxford Wing's claim was totally inaccurate: in the morning's operations, the Luftwaffe lost fewer than ten bombers, probably only six. At the time, the Duxford's Wing's claim was accepted. It was used to promote the success of the concept of a Wing.

Park was the real victor, for it was he who had deployed the squadrons, and it was he who had seen the value of No 11 and No 12 Group 'Big Wings' on this day. His squadrons had intercepted the Germans all the way from the coast. As the Germans approached London, mass fighter squadrons were waiting. The German bombers jettisoned their bombs and ran for home. The RAF prevented the German bombers from achieving worthwhile results.

Leigh-Mallory's report contrasts with the laconic No 242 Squadron ORB entry for the day: 'Wing composed of Nos 242, 19, 302, 310 and 611 Squadrons. Combat over London in morning . . .'

Leigh-Mallory wrote his report on the morning's combat two days later. It is worth quoting for its neat summary of the events, and for its political highlighting of particular aspects of the fight. It is surprising that he could so accurately quote the number of aircraft involved and the heights they flew at, yet cannot give the time of take-off: the Wing took off at 11.22–11.25, which is hardly 'before noon'. Leigh-Mallory wrote:

' . . . the Wing consisted of five squadrons with 56 aircraft, and took off from Duxford before noon on the 15th September. The three Hurricane squadrons patrolled at 25,000 feet with the two Spitfire squadrons about 2,000 feet above them. They saw about 30 enemy bombers (Dorniers) south of the Estuary flying north-west with a large number of Me.109s protecting them. The leader saw Spitfires and Hurricanes belonging to No 11 Group, engage the enemy and waited to avoid the risk of collision. As the Hurricane squadrons went in to attack the bombers, Me.109s dived towards them out of the sun, but, as the Spitfires turned to attack them, the enemy fighters broke away and climbed towards the south-east, making no further effort to protect their own bombers, who were actually endeavouring to escape towards the west and the south. They did not all, however, manage to save their own skins in their precipitous flight, as the Spitfires were able to destroy a number of them before they got away. In the meantime, the Hurricanes were able to destroy all the Dorniers that they could see and one of the squadrons saw a further small formation of Dorniers, which had no doubt broken away from the main formation in the first attack, and promptly destroyed the lot. One of the Spitfire squadrons, seeing that the enemy fighters were getting out of range, also came down and took part in the destruction of the enemy bombers. In this engagement, the prearranged idea worked perfectly, for there were sufficient numbers of Spitfires to attack the enemy fighters and prevent them from exercising their primary function of protecting their own bombers, which were destroyed by the three Hurricane squadrons at their leisure. The enemy were outnumbered in the action and appeared in the circumstances to be quite helpless.'

Dicky Cork, however, summed up the engagement rather more pungently with a comment on his Combat Report Form F: 'The success of the whole attack was definitely due to the good positioning and perfect timing of the C.O. of 242 Squadron, who was leading the Wing formation.'

☆   ☆   ☆

Both sides prepared for the second round. The Germans had reasoned that after the first wave, the British fighters would need less than an hour to refuel and rearm, more properly, to re-form. Therefore, they planned to send a second wave of bombers close on the heels of the first, to try to catch the RAF on the ground. The mauling that the first wave received contributed to upsetting the German programme. The Germans bombed-up 150 Heinkel He 111s and Dornier Do 17s from Kampfgeschwadern 2, 53 and 76, and elements of Kampfgeschwadern 1, 4 and 26. They assembled three hundred escorts.

Of the Duxford Wing pilots who had made it back to Duxford or Fowlmere, all were back by 13.00 hours. Others reported in by telephone from other airfields such as Detling or Wattisham. Some were refuelling and flying back to their base, but others were not. There was time for a rapid lunch. Another raid from the Luftwaffe was expected. At all bases throughout the southern sectors of Fighter Command, armourers, fitters and riggers worked ceaselessly to have as many fighters as possible ready to counter the German onslaught.

The weather remained fine. The breeze was now north-west, the cumulus lifted to 5,000 feet, with eight-tenths cover. Above that, the sun shone brilliantly from the south-west quarter. That, reasoned Bader, was where the Hun would come from.

It was not until after 14.00 hours that the three major formations of bombers and their escorts approached the English coast. The Germans had made up some of their lost time by forming up much more quickly than they had done in the morning. This gave Park less time to deploy his squadrons and call in Nos 10 and 12 Groups' support.

Just after 14.00 hours, the No 11 Group Controllers alerted their squadrons of an incoming raid. Within minutes, this time, they had passed the alert to No 12 Group Control requesting maximum assistance. No 12 Group alerted Wing Commander Woodhall at Duxford and at about 14.10 hours he scrambled Nos 19, 242, 302 (seven aircraft), 310 and 611 (eight) Squadrons from Duxford and Fowlmere – the Duxford Wing. Bader, Cork and Neil Campbell (Red), Stansfield, Crowley-Milling and Norris-Hart (Yellow), Powell-Sheddon, Turner and Latta (Blue) of No 242 Squadron were airborne at 14.12 hours, followed swiftly by No 310 Squadron, then No 302 Squadron in line astern with Nos 19 and 611 Squadrons climbing into position to their right. The Hurricanes climbed slightly quicker than the Spitfires, which were slightly behind. There were forty-nine fighters. Bader was ordered to fly south to intercept a bomber force of over a hundred aircraft which were crossing into England near Dover. Woodhall asked Bader if he would patrol Canterbury; he left the interpretation of that request to the Wing Leader. Bader climbed hard due south.

Meanwhile, fighters from No 11 Group's Nos 213 and 607 Squadrons hit one of the bomber formations so hard that it turned for home – the news of the morning must have shaken the Germans! The surviving Germans reached southern London at about 15.00 hours. Nearly 150 fighters waited for them.

No 242 Squadron was climbing through the 16,000 feet band. Ahead, Bader saw anti-aircraft shells bursting, and there, at 20,000 feet, he saw the enemy. The Duxford Wing was at a tactical disadvantage. It was exactly the kind of situation Bader deplored; he blamed the late call from No 11 Group Control, but it was the Germans' swiftness to form up and the weaknesses of radar that were to blame.

Bader kept the Wing climbing as fast as possible towards the enemy, but Bf 109s pounced on No 242 Squadron from above and behind. Over the radio, Bader ordered the Spitfire squadrons to attack the bombers while the Hurricanes, this time, took on the fighter escort. They were between Kenley and Maidstone. It was just past 15.00 hours.

Bader himself broke violently, greying out in the turn and nearly colliding with Denis Crowley-Milling, bounced off his slipstream into a spin and recovering at 5,000 feet. He climbed back to the fight. He fired at a bomber, but stalled again and lost more height. Bader was furious, and frankly admitted that his leadership on this occasion was lacking. The Wing, he asserted, had been called late; it was poorly placed, in the climb; the attack had been poorly made; and then he had spun out of the lead!

Dicky Cork captures the mood of the engagement, seen from his cockpit:

'Whilst flying as Red 2 in the leading section of the squadron we sighted the enemy to the south and well above us. We climbed as fast as possible to the attack, but on the way were attacked from above and behind by a number of Me 109s. The order was given on R/T to break formation, so I broke sharply away with an Me on my tail. I was now in a dive and suddenly flew through the second squadron of the Wing formation and lost the enemy machine; at the same time I saw a Do 17 on my starboard, flying N.W. I dived 6,000 ft to attack and fired a long burst at the port engine, which started to smoke. I attacked again on the beam – large pieces of enemy machine flew off and his starboard wing burst into flames near the wing tip. He dived straight into the cloud, heading towards a clear patch, so I waited until he came into the open and fired another burst in a head-on attack and the machine dived into the ground.

'I climbed up 1,000 ft and was attacked by two yellow-nosed Me 109s from above, so I did a steep turn to left and managed to get on the tail of one, fired a very short burst, and then ran out of ammunition. No damage was seen on enemy machine, but as I was being attacked from behind by a second fighter I went into a vertical dive down to 2,000 ft and returned to base. No damage to my own machine.'

Crowley-Milling (Yellow 2) had been startled by Bader's violent manoeuvre across his path, but he got on the tail of a Bf 109 and kept there as the German pilot tried to shake him off, and finally got in a good burst which set the German fighter alight around the cockpit. He watched it crash.

Yellow Leader, Noel Stansfield, actually managed to climb to 21,000 feet. Stansfield attacked a Heinkel which was already being attacked by a pair of Hurricanes. He blew out the bomber's port engine; the other engine was already dead. The Heinkel crash-landed. Norris Hart (Yellow 3) like the third member of Red Section, Neil Campbell, expended all his ammunition but made no claims.

Powell-Sheddon's Blue Section was successful. Blue 3 – John Latta – was set upon by several Bf 109s in that first encounter, but one overshot him, leaving itself vulnerable, and Latta had a straight shot from dead astern at barely 50 yards. The Bf 109 burst into flames and Latta saw it fall through the cloud at 5,000 feet with little appearance of being under control. After that first break to avoid the Bf 109s, Stan Turner (Blue 2) caught a Bf 109 in his sights and it went into a vicious spin. Seconds later, a Bf 109 got Turner's Hurricane in its sights and shells exploded under his tail, hurling him into a spin. He regained control but had lost height – he was below 5,000 feet. He spotted a Dornier, and attacked from the starboard beam with full deflection. He hit the right engine which began to burn. The Dornier swooped down and crashed.

In contrast to Turner's opportunistic attack, Powell-Sheddon's attack on the bombers below was a deliberate choice. In the first contact, he was attacked by a Bf 109 head-on. He fired at it. Then he saw thirty bombers heading north-west for London. They were not being attacked. He broke off from the Bf 109s and dived on the bombers. As he began his attack, the bombers turned south-east. He was between the bombers and the sun, a thousand feet above them. He selected a Dornier which was out of formation, attacking from out of the sun and on the beam. The Dornier disappeared in cloud. He claimed a 'probable'. He turned for home, but suddenly he found himself under fire – bounced by a Bf 109. The controls of the Hurricane were hit. He inverted the aeroplane and dropped out.

Led by Flight Lieutenant Jeffries, No 310 Squadron was behind No 242

Squadron. As they climbed for height, they too were attacked by Bf 109s. Jeffries succeeded in reaching 24,000 feet. A group of the enemy turned west, towards the direction of the sun where Jeffries waited. He let them complete the manoeuvre, then charged them head-on. He hit one. Sergeant Rechka and two other Hurricanes attacked another Heinkel, and saw it crash-land. Sergeant Kauchy and two Spitfires attacked a Dornier which dived through the cloud layer where it was set on by other fighters. Kauchy pursued another bomber out to the coast but lost it in cloud. Squadron Leader Hess and his Number 2, Fejfar, fought with a number of Bf 109s but escaped without damage or claims. They then joined three Hurricanes and two Spitfires in an attack on a group of Dorniers. Stragglers broke from the formation. Fejfar damaged one, then chased another through the cloud layer, eventually seeing it crash-land

No 302 Squadron, led by Squadron Leader Satchell, climbed hard behind Nos 242 and 310 Squadrons as they saw the German bombers high above them. Satchell (Blue 1) was attempting to get into position to attack a formation of bombers when he was attacked from above and behind by a Bf 109. He hauled his Hurricane upwards. The Bf 109 raced past beneath him. Satchell snapped forwards and was on the German's tail. He fired several long bursts. The Bf 109 smoked, rolled on its back and spun into the earth. Satchell's Number 2, Pilch, went for the bombers, joining Chlopik (Red 1). The bombers accelerated for the cover of the cloud. Pilch waited until they came out below. He fired on a Dornier from head-on. A Spitfire made a pass on this Dornier, then Pilch attacked from astern. The Dornier was left burning and losing altitude. Another Dornier emerged. Its rear gunner fired at Pilch. He fired back and the gun fell silent. One of the Dornier's engines smoked. Just then, anti-aircraft guns opened up on the combatants. When they stopped, Pilch attacked again, and the Dornier crashed into the sea. Two pilots had been unlucky for, within minutes of combat commencing, Blue 3 and 4 had been forced out of the fight by mechanical failures without making much impact on the German bombers.

No 302 Squadron's Red Section was led by Chlopik, with his Numbers 2 and 3 Lapka and Kowalski. They were in action swiftly, managing to evade or ignore the Bf 109s, and going for the bombers. Chlopik's initial attacks were joined by Pilch. A few minutes later, he attacked a Dornier which he hit – other pilots saw it disintegrate as it dived. Lapka made a diving beam attack on a Dornier, but his Hurricane sustained damage. His cockpit filled with smoke and he had no option but to bale out. Kowalski attacked a straggling Dornier, going in to barely 30 yards with such effect that the tailplane shattered and the bomber plunged down. Ahead was another Dornier, whose gunner fired at him, damaging his Hurricane, but he attacked the bomber twice until he ran out of ammunition. He held close station on the bomber as it dived down out of control. Meanwhile, Chlopik had been engaging the enemy closely, and had gone in so close that his Hurricane too was hit. He baled out. His parachute failed to open.

It was the job of the Spitfires to keep the escorts off the Hurricanes. Squadron Leader Lane (Red 1) was leading No 19 Squadron. He saw the bomber formation above the Wing, but he was more interested in the fighter escort flying at 30,000 feet – Bf 109s. Lane kept Red Section climbing, reaching nearly 25,000 feet when two pairs of Bf 109s fell on the Section, followed by more on Yellow Section. Lane broke to starboard and tried to get one of the Bf 109s in his sight, but failed. He broke off when he saw some Bf 110s higher up, and climbed to intercept, but a pair of Bf 109s appeared above him and he angled on to the tail of one. As soon as he fired, the German pilot took smart evasive action, manoeuvring and heading for the cloud. Lane caught the Bf 109 in at least part of a five-second burst. The Bf 109 flipped over and continued into the cloud (Lane made a claim for it). Lane saw two formations of bombers to the south. He went after them. He made a head-on pass right through one of the formations, firing. Out of ammunition, he went home. Meanwhile, Lane's Number 3, Sergeant Unwin, had climbed up towards the escorts and engaged a Bf 109 at 25,000 feet. He attacked at point-blank range and the Bf 109 dived away. Unwin followed, but lost the German when his Spitfire's windscreen froze over in the cloud at 6,000 feet. He climbed back to 25,000 feet and chased a pair of Bf 109s which were retreating south-east. Unwin was a fine shot: he picked off one of the Bf 109s, and saw it crash; then he attacked the second, and saw it crash also.

Hearing Bader's order for the Spitfires to attack the bombers, Flight Lieutenant Clouston (Blue 1) led No 19 Squadron's 'B' Flight (Blue and Green Sections) in an attack on a group of Dorniers. Clouston selected a Dornier and set its starboard engine on fire. It dived for cloud. He followed it through. He chased it at less than 5,000 feet out along the Thames, over Southend and Burnham and halfway across the North Sea before the crew finally baled out. Meanwhile, Steere (Blue 2) inflicted serious damage on a Dornier in a determined attack. The crew baled out. Vokes (Green 2) came in to attack just behind Steere, but he was set upon by a Bf 110. It took him several minutes to manoeuvre on to its tail and then he went in to 50 yards. He shot out its starboard engine and sent the enemy fighter down out of control. Haines had followed Vokes's attack on the bombers, but he noticed one Bf 109 dive away from a flight of five Bf 109s in a defensive ring. Suspecting that there was something wrong with it, he followed the Bf 109, and caught it as it levelled out at 15,000 feet. Haines fired down to 50 yards. The Bf 109 exploded. Haines climbed back to 25,000 feet and after a few minutes saw Hurricanes attacking a number of bombers. Nearby, a group of Bf 110 escorts formed a defensive circle as soon as they saw Haines's Spitfire. Haines fired on one of the Bf 110s. The starboard engine stopped. He was experiencing return fire but he was not deterred. 'His' Bf 110 was trying to escape across the Channel. He gave chase, firing. He was not satisfied until he saw it crumple on to a French beach.

Yellow Section of No 19 Squadron did not get near the bombers. They were hit hard from behind by Bf 109s. Sergeant Roden (Yellow 2) was hit immediately. Cunningham broke hard right to try to cover Roden, and Lawson (Yellow Leader) swung left into the Bf 109s. A swift flowing fight developed until the Spitfire pilots broke free. Cunningham saw three Bf 109s retreating east, and joined a Hurricane in a stern attack on them: the

Hurricane attacked one Bf 109, scoring hits, but Cunningham's victim flashed alight and went down burning.

As they climbed west behind No 19 Squadron towards the Bf 109 top cover, No 611 Squadron's eight Spitfires encountered two dozen bombers flying south. They ignored the bombers. They had to protect the rest of the Wing. They began to struggle for altitude. Their Spitfires were old. The Bf 109s remained beyond their reach. Squadron Leader H. E. McComb ordered the Spitfires into right echelon and dived on the Dorniers they had passed. McComb seriously damaged one Dornier and came in again, but diverted to another target as the Dornier was falling away, smoking. Pilot Officer Brown then fired on it. Flight Lieutenant Heather attacked the bomber next to McComb's target (which he saw crashing) and used all his ammunition on it, seriously damaging it; although it still flew, he pressed his claim. He dived for cover when he was attacked by Bf 110s. McComb's Number 2, Williams, had attacked a Heinkel which also took a tremendous amount of punishment, but this one showed no signs of serious damage.

Meanwhile, Brown had been forced out of the fight because his windscreen had become covered in oil from one of the bombers. Heading for cloud, he found an isolated Heinkel. He fired and hit it. The enemy aircraft spiralled. Brown did not follow it down, because he was threatened by Bf 109s. He headed home. He made a claim for the Heinkel. Pilot Officer Lund also attacked a bomber isolated from the group, which was then attacked by a pack of four Spitfires. Lund broke off when he was attacked head-on by a Bf 110: he fired as the German fired, and both aircraft sustained hits. Flight Lieutenant Sadler, along with a Hurricane, attacked a Dornier which headed for the deck. It was not seen to crash but the two pilots pressed a 'shared claim'. In total, No 19 Squadron pilots made claims for two Dorniers, one Heinkel, five Bf 109s and one Bf 110 – nine victories.

Leigh-Mallory wrote his report on the No 12 Group Wing's combat two days later. The blame for the tactical failure of the interception was shifted on to No 11 Group in not calling for No 12 Group's squadrons earlier. In fact, No 11 Group realized that the raid was coming at about 14.00 hours and the 'Duxford Wing' was airborne between 14.12 and 14.15 hours – not 14.30 hours; and it did not intercept until 15.00 hours. Leigh-Mallory wrote:

'The same five squadrons [as in the morning], though with the slightly reduced number of 49 aircraft, took off again in the afternoon at about 14.30 hours. They climbed up through a gap in the clouds, which was 8/10ths at 5,000 feet, the three Hurricane Squadrons in line astern with the two Spitfire Squadrons to the right and slightly above them. They saw AA fire and then a large number of enemy aircraft at 20,000 feet. The leader of the Wing found that he was at a tactical disadvantage as he had not had time to reach his patrol height, with the result that this formation was attacked by Me.109s, as they were trying to get in position. Because of this, the leader of the Wing told the Spitfires to attack the bombers, and the Hurricanes to break up and engage the fighters. The results of the engagement were satisfactory as far as they went, but under the circumstances it was impossible to break up the bomber formation and so achieve the same tactical superiority as in the [morning].'

Tactical success or not, the total victory claim by the Duxford Wing for the afternoon's work amounted to twenty-six 'destroyed', eight 'probables' and one 'damaged'. The individual squadron claims were: No 19 Squadron, nine victories; No 242 Squadron, three Dorniers, one Heinkel and two Bf 109s; No 302 Squadron, three Dorniers; No 310 Squadron, one Dornier, one Heinkel and one Bf 109; and No 611 Squadron, four Dorniers. Other Fighter Command squadrons had intercepted these raids and made claims, not as high as those of the Duxford Wing squadrons, but still high. On the other hand, the Duxford Wing's losses were small. Out of forty-nine pilots committed to action, two were killed, two were wounded. Three aircraft were write-offs, two damaged.

German sources indicate that twenty bombers were lost during the attacks. Fourteen Dorniers were lost, with Kampfgeschwader 76 suffering worst with eight losses. Ten Heinkels fell, six from Kampfgeschwader 53 and others from Kampfgeschwadern 1, 4 and 26. The escorting Bf 109Es of Jagdgeschwadern 26 and 54 suffered moderate losses defending the bombers.

This brought the total German losses for the day to about 55, less than on 'Black Thursday', 15 August, or 18 August – 'The Hardest Day'. German losses were effectively 6 per cent in the morning and 13 per cent in the afternoon, an aggregate of nearly 10 per cent. The British claimed that a total of 185 German aircraft had been brought down – two-thirds of those committed throughout the entire day! The real significance of the scale of losses lay in the proportion of fighters to bombers: the RAF had got to the bombers and thus demonstrated that it was still vigorous and that the cost of bombing would be prohibitive. As a result, the Dorniers and Heinkels were now used for night bombing, and the remaining day raids were entrusted to fast, nimble and resilient Junkers Ju 88s and to fighter-bombers.

The Germans knew that they had lost the day: they had failed to bomb accurately in the morning, and although a majority of their bombers had bombed in the afternoon, the bombing had only a marginal effect; they had heavy losses in bombers and bomber crews; the tactics employed by the escort fighters had failed. This was no shattered foe. The Germans also realized that they had lost the air superiority struggle: contrary to the opinions of Goering, the RAF was clearly still vigorous and had opposed the incursion fiercely, both in the morning and two hours later in the afternoon. The reception given the German bombers over London by the Debden Wing and the Duxford Wing shattered the Luftwaffe crews – told to expect 'the last fifty Spitfires'.

The RAF knew it had won the day; it made heavy (very exaggerated) claims but the significance of the two battles was that force had been applied so successfully that the Germans had been driven from the skies. The Duxford Wing had achieved a notable success against the Luftwaffe, for which no less a person than Leutnant-General Theo Osterkamp, the General of Fighters, is the authority. He told Goering on the 16th at a meeting to discuss the defeat:

'The British are using new tactics. They are using powerful fighter formations to attack in force. Our radio-interception service informs us that they have strict orders to attack only our bombers. Yesterday, their new tactics took us by surprise.'

Clearly, the Germans realized the significance of failing to win the air superiority battle. The invasion of Britain depended upon the Luftwaffe smashing Fighter Command and achieving total air superiority. Without that, the invasion was not viable. Two days later, Hitler postponed Operation SEALION indefinitely. This is the true importance of 15 September 1940, and why it is Battle of Britain Day.

The Duxford Wing first went into action on 7 September; the major battle was fought a week later on 15 September. In the five Wing actions between 7 and 15 September, the Wing's squadrons claimed 145 enemy aircraft 'destroyed', forty 'probables' and eighteen 'damaged'. These were very optimistic figures, even by Fighter Command's rose-tinted standards, but were good for propaganda. The Wing's squadrons had lost six pilots killed or missing and five wounded, and had lost fourteen aircraft. By 21 September, less than a week after the victory of the 15th, the major battles were over, but there was more to come before the weather closed in and the Germans quit the field.

No 242 Squadron's losses had been comparatively light. George Powell-Sheddon, shot down, was admitted immediately to Rye hospital with a dislocated shoulder. He was transferred to the RAF hospital on 20 September. He would be out of action for some time. Bader placed Stan Turner in charge of Powell-Sheddon's Flight as an acting flight lieutenant.

☆   ☆   ☆

After the momentous events of 15 September, the next two days brought an anti-climax for the Wing, along with poor weather. The Wing continued to fly together. In view of the infrequency of raids, it is questionable whether such a concentration of assets was an appropriate reaction to the actual tactical situation, let alone the 'Fighter Command System'. Consider the number of sorties flown by the end of September against the overall results:

At 07.45 hours on Monday, 16 September, a very windy, blustery day, Nos 310, 302 and 19 Squadrons were ordered to patrol the Debden-North Weald line. They did not find the enemy. At 08.45 hours, Nos 242 and 611 Squadrons relieved them. Thirty minutes later, these two squadrons were ordered to return. They had not seen any enemy. There was little offensive action over or near No 12 Group during the day: the weather was not good, and the Luftwaffe was unable to sustain heavy operations for two days in a row; and there was little activity that night. Next day, the 17th, the poor weather of the night only slightly improved. A strong wind blew all day. There were a few localized enemy bombings. The five-squadron No 12 Group Wing was sent aloft, led by Bader to patrol the North Weald area. They saw no enemy aircraft.

The following day, Wednesday, 18 September was very windy but sunny. The No 12 Group Wing was twice ordered to patrol North Weald, at 09.00 and 12.50 hours, but did not see the enemy on either occasion. At 16.16 hours, the Wing was ordered up again: the Hurricane Mk Is of Nos 242, 310 and 302 Squadrons in that order, with the Spitfire Mk IAs of Nos 19 and 611

Squadrons 2,000 feet above and behind as the upper guard. This time, their patrol area was from London to Thameshaven at 24,000 feet, to protect RAF Hornchurch.

The Wing broke through the thin layer of eight-tenths cloud at 6,000 feet. Higher, at 20,000 feet was a 100-foot thick layer of ten-tenths cloud at 20,000 feet. Bader set the Hurricane squadrons at 19,000 to 20,000 feet, just below this layer, with the two Spitfire squadrons above the cloud as the upper guard. In his rear-view mirror, Bader saw one of the Blue Section Hurricanes peel off and dive for home – it was Stan Turner, with engine trouble.

To the south-west, Bader saw anti-aircraft shells bursting above the lower clouds. He turned the Wing north-west. Almost over Gravesend, he found two enemy formations of about thirty bombers flying in 'Vics' of five between 15,000 and 17,000 feet – apparently unescorted. The bombers were clearly visible over and below the cloud layers.

Bader wanted to hit them before they crossed the river. He took No 242 Squadron in a dive from the east to the west, then swung left to attack. He went in too fast, so he had no recourse but to dive into the centre of the formation, opening fire as he dived. He turned hard on to the rear three-quarters of the leading three Ju 88s. He hit the one on the left, which fell away (it crashed). He had succeeded in breaking up the front of the formation. He turned into another group, but got caught in cross-fire and risked collision. Then he ricocheted through a slipsteam, and his Hurricane was wrenched out of control. He spun. He fell 3,000 feet before he recovered. He searched for more bombers. He found a lone Dornier, and attacked. The rear gunner baled out, but his parachute became entangled in the tailplane. The bomber jinked and twisted. Then two more crew baled out. The bomber was out of control, with the rear gunner tied to it by his harness. Bader fired at him, as a mercy, but missed. The Dornier plunged vertically through cloud.

Willie McKnight and Neil Campbell (Red 2 and 3) had attacked with Bader, but Campbell was going too fast and overshot. McKnight shot down one Dornier, its crew baling out, then he and a Spitfire destroyed both engines of a Ju 88, which crashed. Meanwhile, Campbell had found a Ju 88 straggling behind, and shot it down with a two-second burst. A little later, he found another, whose engines he shot out. He spotted a main formation and attacked from below and behind, but, although he damaged a Ju 88, he was beaten off by effective cross-fire which damaged his aeroplane. Shortly after that, he saw a Spitfire attack a Junkers, one of whose engines started to burn. Campbell attacked and the other engine began to burn.

Yellow Leader, Eric Ball, followed Bader's Section in a diving attack from astern on the main bomber formation of Junkers and Dorniers, helping to break up the rest of the formation. Ball turned off, gained height, saw a lone Junkers and attacked, firing from 300 yards in to 100 yards when his windscreen was sprayed with oil and he broke away. He thought his oil tank was punctured so quickly dived down and landed at RAF Gravesend, but his Hurricane was unharmed; it was the Junkers' oil.

Ball's Number 2 attacked, but made no claims. His Number 3, Brimble, attacked a Dornier which was out of formation, and vulnerable. With four three-second bursts, he sent it tumbling to earth. He searched for other targets, but the battle was over.

Hugh Tamblyn had arrived with the first attackers in the middle of the formation. The cross-fire was too accurate for comfort, but he had time to fire a good burst into a Dornier before breaking out of the trap. Back at base, he made no claims, but McKnight confirmed that Tamblyn's shooting had been good as the Dornier had crashed in flames.

'Norrie' Hart was showing strong potential, and a cool mind. He selected a Junkers. He opened fire at just 75 yards, aiming at the crew compartment in the nose. He broke down and away, gained speed and altitude and curved in for another attack. He aimed for the crew again. The cockpit was on fire. Obeying instructions to follow a victim, he saw the Junkers go straight into the ground. Reasoning that the battle was heading for the Channel, he flew south and found another Junkers. It was flying at only 5,000 feet, with its port engine out. Hart accelerated, dropping below the bomber into its blind spot a few hundred feet below, and executed a climbing attack. He opened fire from just 30 yards into the other engine and the cockpit. At that range, the gun alignment gave a very concentrated pattern. The starboard engine stopped. The bomber flipped over and went down.

In the first rush, Sub-Lieutenant 'Jimmie' Gardner led Green Section – Roy Bush and Denis Crowley-Milling – down on to the rear of a box of a dozen bombers. Gardner was going too fast to aim effectively, and broke off his own attack. Bush managed to fire on one bomber, which then fell out of the formation – but he did not get a chance to move in for the kill as a No 19 Squadron Spitfire mistook him for a Hun and clung to his tail, though without firing. Crowley-Milling fired at the bombers, but made no claims. Meanwhile, recovering from the over-enthusiasm of his first attack, Gardner swiftly assessed the situation. He saw a few stragglers around the rear of the formation. Another Hurricane was among them – Bader, having a rough time. Gardner selected a Dornier. He made a quarter attack, setting the port wing and engine alight. The Dornier dived into the Thames Estuary. Then he saw in the distance six, perhaps eight bombers heading for home in an intact formation. He needed full boost to overhaul them. It took him three minutes. They were 10,000 feet high near the Medway/Thames confluence when he caught them. One of the bombers was now trailing – lame duck. Gardner caught it, and fired a burst into its port engine. In textbook fashion, he pulled off and came in on the starboard for the other engine. He tried to damage one of the other bombers, but he ran out of ammunition. He returned home.

Flight Lieutenant Jeffries led No 310 Squadron into the attack after No 242 Squadron. He saw about fifteen Dorniers over south-east London at 19,000 feet. Jeffries led the attack, brought the squadron level with them, but turned too sharply and came too close to the bombers when they turned towards the Hurricanes. He broke away to avoid their fire. He climbed the squadron and swung it in from over and behind the bombers . . . a running chase began. Jeffries crippled one bomber, then moved on to another which he left at the coast with engine trouble. Zimprich expended all his ammunition trying to bring down a Dornier which refused to die. Janouch and Fejfar (Red

1 and 2) attacked the same bomber, and shared in its destruction. Jirovdek (Red 3) and Puda (Green 2) brought down another Dornier. Fechtner fired at a Dornier from extreme range – half a mile – but followed it over the Thames Estuary until he had destroyed both its engines. Yellow Section attacked last, and Bergmann and Prohal each claimed a Dornier. The squadron's total claim was five Dorniers out of fifteen, and several damaged; but, more to the point, they had broken up the formation completely.

No 302 Squadron went in third: Squadron Leader Satchell (Red 1) led Red Section in an attack on one of the formations of bombers. He selected a bomber and fired right in to point-blank range, setting it on fire. His Numbers 2 and 3, Wing Commander Mumler and Flying Officer Kowalski, attacked another bomber which began to disintegrate. Yellow Section followed Red Section: Farmer damaged a Dornier and a Junkers; Laguna's reflector sight malfunctioned and he could not fight; Wedzik and another Hurricane chased a Ju 88 out to sea, damaging it. Green Section broke up an enemy group with its first rush into the centre of the bombers. Persistent attacks by Green Leader, Pilot Officer Pilch, knocked down one Junkers. Green 2, Sergeant Peterek, set a Ju 88 alight. Its crew departed by parachute. Chunks flew off and struck Peterek's Hurricane. His radiator and fuel tank were punctured – leaking coolant and fuel. He stopped his engine and forced-landed. Green 3, Karwowski, repeatedly attacked a group of bombers until he knocked one of them out and down into the sea. The three Blue Section Hurricanes came in from high above the bombers. Blue Leader, Flight Lieutenant Riley, shot down two Ju 88s with surprising speed. Flight Lieutenant Jastrzebski (Blue 2) sprayed several bombers, damaging them. Pilot Officer Wapniarek (Blue 3) damaged one Ju 88 and then sent another down to break up on the sea. The squadron's total claim was five Junkers and two Dorniers, and several damaged, out of thirty bombers; they had shattered the formation, and prevented the bomber attack developing.

When Bader led the three Hurricane squadrons into the attack, No 19 Squadron came through the cloud and followed the Hurricanes. No 611 Squadron remained on patrol above the clouds, and did not engage the enemy. By the time No 19 Squadron attacked, only one of the original two bomber formations was left, twenty Ju 88s and He 111s, and some Bf 110s. Flight Lieutenant Clouston (Blue 1) led the attack. He fastened on to a Ju 88 and used all his ammunition to bring it down. Steere (Blue 2) followed him in and caught an He 111 which tried to escape in the lower cloud layer, and shot it down. Unwin (Blue 3) took out a Bf 110 in his first onslaught. Haines (Green 1) shot a Ju 88 out of formation – which Steere then finished off as it dived away – then engaged a pair of Bf 109s with uncertain results. Green 2 and 3 each claimed an He 111. The four Red Section Hurricanes led by Flight Lieutenant Lawson attacked a group of nine Ju 88s which turned for home. Lawson, Cunningham and Lloyd (Red 1, 2 and 3) jointly claimed one Ju 88 'destroyed'.

No 242 Squadron's ORB recorded that the squadron 'shot down 12 enemy bombers – 12 Group Wing led by Squadron Leader Bader DSO'.

This engagement justified Leigh-Mallory's and Bader's arguments: with sufficient fighters, they could break up bomber formations and then pick off isolated targets, while leaving a strong 'upper guard' still in position, part of which could join in the killing if there were a weak or non-existent enemy top cover. However, as the bombers were unescorted on this occasion, too much cannot be inferred.

☆   ☆   ☆

The next week brought a change in operations. There was little day activity. There had been only sporadic activity on the two nights following 15 September, but from the night of 18/19 September, the Germans renewed their efforts. That night they bombed Merseyside and towns and airfields in East Anglia and Lincolnshire. On the 19th, the raids continued into the daylight hours, with bombing in the mid-west. Cloud over East Anglia allowed 'pop-out' attacks by the enemy but made interception difficult. The next day, there were a few isolated raids over East Anglia during daylight, enough to warrant sending up the No 12 Group Wing for a patrol, but they sighted no enemy aircraft and returned without engagement. The raid on Merseyside that night was lighter and the area was not hit again until the 24th/25th. Although No 12 Group airfields were pestered almost nightly over the next week, the tempo was definitely lessening.

On 19 September, No 616 (South Yorkshire) Squadron, Auxiliary Air Force, joined the Duxford Wing. After being badly mauled on the teeth of the German assault on the No 11 Group airfields in late August, No 616 had spent a few days at Fowlmere alongside No 19 Squadron earlier in the month, before retiring to its peacetime base at Kirton-in-Lindsey to re-form under Squadron Leader 'Billy' Burton as a 'C' Class squadron. He had declared it operational on the 18th. The next morning, the squadron flew down to Fowlmere, alongside No 19 Squadron's Spitfires. Immediately they arrived, the squadron was greeted robustly by both Douglas Bader and 'Woody' Woodhall, the two most important figures in controlling the 'Big Wing'. They had a considerable personal effect on the pilots: they exuded an air of utter confidence in the devastation that their 'Big Wing' would wreak on the Hun. Though there was no action that day, and No 616 Squadron flew back to Kirton-in-Lindsey in the evening, there was no anti-climax. No 616 Squadron was back on most succeeding days, sometimes remaining overnight. There was no action for a week.

Saturday, 21 September was bright and sunny with no cloud, but the No 12 Group Wing waited all day. Breakfast passed, lunch, afternoon tea . . . then at 18.06 hours, the Wing was ordered to patrol over RAF Duxford and RAF Hornchurch. There was no sign of the enemy, and they landed back, disappointed or thankful. The next day, Sunday, was a complete contrast, at least in weather – wet and miserable; there was little activity. On 23 September, greeting a sunny morning, the No 12 Group Wing went up at 09.32 hours and again in the evening at 18.07 hours, but without finding anything of interest to report. On 24 September, after a night of bombing raids against airfields and industrial targets, Fighter Command expected the raids to continue into the day. Taking advantage of the fine morning, the No 12 Group Wing was ordered off at 08.30 hours and again at 11.40 hours, but there was no enemy to be found. On 24/25 September, Merseyside was bombed, and East Anglian airfields were raided and the No 12 Group Wing was ordered to patrol at 09.35 hours, but without meeting the enemy.

On Thursday, 26 September there was a good deal of enthusiasm at Fowlmere, when, as its ORB recorded, No 19 Squadron: 'Received several Spitfire IIs today. Cartridge starters and extra boost.' In theory, these new variants would give the squadron better climb and higher altitude to tackle the Bf 109s.

Over at No 242 Squadron's mess, Laurie Cryderman was welcomed back after his further training at OTU. He was itching to get into action, but Bader would not allow him to fly until he had had a chance to work his way into an operational squadron. Bader did not like to lose pilots unnecessarily.

It was cold, windy and cloudy, not a day for 'Big Wing' actions. The Germans had changed their tactics. They took advantage of the low cloud to send over intruders which struck hard at shipyards and docks at Liverpool, and inaccurately on the Shell oil refinery at Ellesmere Port. The raids escalated during the night, heavily against Liverpool, and a dozen struck Lincolnshire targets. The momentum and direction of the assault changed the next day, Friday, 27 September, with attacks on London and Bristol. It was a cold but sunny day, with medium cloud. The Germans exploited the weather with another change of tactics.

The Germans launched a final fling, even though the SEALION invasion of Britain had been postponed indefinitely. The Germans had two targets: London and the Bristol aircraft factory at Filton. About a hundred bombers, with two hundred fighter escorts, were launched against the former, in two waves. First, Bf 109s were sent over with a few bombers. This was a decoy, intended to make Fighter Command order its interceptors aloft prematurely, and thus be caught on the ground refuelling when the main raid came over. Park saw through the decoy and scrambled a number of No 11 Group squadrons which forced the bombers to jettison their bombs well before they reached London. Park kept his main force in hand. Meanwhile, the German freelance fighters gathered over Kent, waiting for the main force. No 11 Group's squadrons were therefore sent south to meet the German bombers as they approached the coast with inadequate escort. Bader took on the fighters south of London.

The Duxford Wing had taken off at 09.00 hours and had flown an uneventful patrol. The Wing that day comprised four squadrons: Nos 242 and 310 with Hurricanes wedged in below and left of No 19 with Spitfire Mk IAs and IIAs and No 616 with Spitfire Mk IAs.

At 11.42 hours, the Wing was ordered to patrol the London area, in support of No 11 Group squadrons engaged over southern Kent. The Duxford Sector controller informed Bader that there were enemy aeroplanes south-east of the Thames Estuary. Bader led the Wing towards the enemy's supposed position, and searched but without success. He told the Duxford Controller who ordered the Wing home, but Bader insisted upon having another attempt.

He turned the four squadrons south at 23,000 feet, and swung round in a search with the sun behind them. There was a layer of cloud at about 25,000 feet, but visibility was excellent at medium altitude. A few minutes later, he saw the German aeroplanes, Bf 109s orbiting like a cloud of starlings at 20,000 feet to the east of the Dover-Canterbury axis – waiting for the bombers. Bader was well aware that his Wing was deep inside No 11 Group's area.

It was almost exactly noon. The Wing was up-sun and higher. He observed the Bf 109s. There were about a hundred. They had no formation. They had no bombers to escort. They seemed to have no purpose. There was no logical pressure point to attack, no focus. A co-ordinated attack was pointless. He instructed the squadron leaders: 'Break up and attack.' Now, each section aimed for a point in the milling mass of fighters.

Bader's first attack was a success. He pulled round on the tail of a Bf 109, gave it a two-second burst, and the Bf 109 turned over, smoking and dived vertically. Bader cast his eye around for another target. He swung on to the tail of another Bf 109. He gave it a two-second burst. The German half-rolled and dived; Bader followed. The German pulled out for a zoom-climb. Bader hauled back his stick and cut off the German's climb, with a quick burst. With supercharger wide open, he chased the Bf 109 as it fled south. He fired at 400 yards – no result – then a white puff. The Bf 109 slowed. Bader fired a series of 'squirts'. Black smoke billowed from the fighter. Its engine was dead. It was gliding towards the Channel. It was pointless following. Bader had no more ammunition and was low on fuel. He headed for RAF Gravesend.

Bader's Number 2 was Pilot Officer Mike Stansfield. He also chased a Bf 109 to the Channel coast, but lost it. He then came across a stray Junkers Ju 88 – perhaps taking advantage of the cloud for a raid on the coast. He fired at it from 200 yards and took out one of its engines. He bored in again . . . but his guns clacked and hissed. He lost the Junkers in the cloud. Stansfield headed for home.

Eric Ball selected an opponent as he made his dive on the mass of enemy fighters. The German pilot was very experienced. A manoeuvring fight began, with the German closing on Ball and Ball as quickly turning on him. After several minutes, Ball got on to the German's tail long enough to fire a burst at 200 yards but he could not close the distance. Ball nevertheless hit the Bf 109's cockpit area with his gunfire. As he fired, he smelt the sweet smell of petrol fumes mix with the acrid smoke of the guns' cordite. This German or another had hit him in the fuel system. The tank was self-sealing but petrol was splashing on to the burning hot engine. Suddenly, flames licked out of the cowling. Ball cut the throttle and killed the engine. He had seconds to make a decision. He stayed with his Hurricane. He thought he could make Manston, but his glide ended several miles short in a muddy field. He swiftly tumbled out of his Hurricane.

The aggressive Turner was after a kill today, following his disappointment on the 18th and the frustrations of the last week. In the initial attack, he took his Blue Section – himself, Roy Bush and Norris-Hart – in a steep dive, the second last Section of No 242 Squadron. Turner mistimed the dive. None of the pilots managed to steady themselves on a target. They plunged through and below the main Bf 109 formation several thousand feet. They pulled out and began to climb hard. Bush had selected a formation of six Bf 109s a thousand yards above him. He tried to reach the rear one without being seen, but the Bf 109 leader peeled off and fell on him as he was still climbing – a dangerous position. Bush kicked his rudder and stalled into a spinning dive. The Bf 109 followed him. Bush pulled out of the dive and turned, cut the enemy's turn and fired into the Bf 109. The Bf 109 fell apart.

Hugh Tamblyn led No 242 Squadron's last Section, Green, into the attack from 21,000 feet. He selected a tough opponent, who simply accelerated towards the Channel when he saw Tamblyn attack. The German nearly got away. He dived from over twelve thousand to below one hundred feet. Tamblyn's Hurricane's Merlin was at full boost, but he was only just holding on to the German. He was getting in quick bursts, but could see no results until they had crossed the coast, when fluid streamed out of the Bf 109 and it began to slow down. Tamblyn fired a final burst – seven guns empty, one jammed – but the German vanished into the now heavy cloud halfway over the Channel. He could only claim a 'probable'.

Tamblyn's Number 3, John Latta, saw a Bf 109 in a banked turn and closed on it, waited until it levelled out, and fired a burst from astern. The German exploded. The kill was over swiftly and, unlike his colleagues, Latta had not lost height – he was at 18,000 feet south of Canterbury. He took advantage of his altitude to observe: the Germans were everywhere routed and retreating towards the Channel. He saw a group of Bf 109s heading for the coast. He dived on them and arrived fast, but steady, closed to 50 yards behind one and fired. It exploded in a red and yellow ball and Latta had to haul off hard to avoid debris. He was low on ammunition and low on fuel. He needed to land.

Squadron Leader Lane, hearing Bader's order to attack, ordered No 19 Squadron to follow Flight Lieutenant Lawson in a line-astern attack on the main formation of Bf 109s. Eleven Spitfire Mk Is and IIs peeled off, but Lane himself held off above his squadron to observe as 'upper guard'. As the squadron dived, a section of Bf 109s prepared to attack them. Immediately behind Lawson, Sub-Lieutenant Blake (Red 2) saw the Bf 109s and broke out of line in a hard right turn into them. He fired head-on. One of the Bf 109s began to smoke, and promptly headed south. Further back in the line of fighters, Yellow 3 and Green 4 had been shot down as the Bf 109s sliced into the rear of the diving squadron, but Blake's action allowed the first Spitfires to continue to follow their leader in the attack on the group below. Lane, above the diving Spitfires, saw the higher group of Bf 109s curving in on his men, and dived on a pair, firing as he passed them. He tried to pull up and make another pass, but his Spitfire Mk IIA kept diving to 3,000 feet before he could regain control. Above him, his men fought desperately but his aeroplane was clearly not safe. He headed home.

After the British fighters had dropped on the Germans, a massive dogfight, without focus, developed. There was chaos, everyone for himself. The enemy had no bombers to protect, so could simply turn for home. There were aeroplanes everywhere – nearly two hundred. Pilots took snap shots.

Only the experienced, the cool or the lucky shot anyone else down. Most kept turning, climbing, diving, trying to avoid being shot down, trying to flash a shot at a fleeting target, while trying to avoid collision. Then, suddenly, the big bang effect emptied the sky . . . the fighters at over 250mph from 18,000 feet down to roof, tree and wave top level had burst away in all directions, and miles separated individual fighters.

Once distracted from the attack on the main formation, Blake himself had chased the Bf 109 that he had damaged. He caught it and fired again. The enemy tried to skid across right in front of him. He fired again, with deflection. His aim was good. The Bf 109 fell into the sea. Blake saw other Bf 109s speeding south, their propellers almost creasing the waves. Blake manoeuvred over one, and sent the pilot into the sea. As the fight drew to an end, visibility over the Channel coast was already down to about a mile.

In the attacking dive, Lawson had seen Blake in front of him veer off, but he had already selected a Bf 109 in the main formation and carried on. He fired several bursts at it with slight deflection. The Bf 109 lost altitude quickly, heading for France. Lawson followed, firing from astern. It was smoking. It got over half way to France before hitting the sea. Lawson turned for home. Lawson's Number 3, Pilot Officer Bradil (Red 3), arrived next and claimed one Bf 109 'damaged'.

The pilot of the Bf 109 that Sergeant Unwin (Yellow Leader) had attacked had shown skill, courage then desperation. Unwin got on his tail and though the German pilot manoeuvred skilfully and hard, stayed there. But he could not get in a burst for nearly ten minutes. The German was good. But his fuel was getting low. He had to make a run for France. He suddenly levelled out and pulled his throttle back, but Unwin was barely 50 yards behind him, and he fired. He held his thumb on the button for seven seconds and stayed there, but still the German flew on. Unwin fired another long burst. The Bf 109 had slowed down. Unwin swung round to its right and fired from point-blank range into the cockpit and engine. The Bf 109 spun down into the sea.

Sergeant Jenning (Yellow 2) attacked a 'five' of Bf 109s, picking off the right-hand aircraft. His victim fell away to starboard, trailing white vapour. In a series of swift glances, Jenning saw thick black smoke envelop the whole aeroplane, but he could not follow it down because he now had to get free from the other four Bf 109s which attacked him ruthlessly. He arrived back at Duxford sweat-soaked and exhausted, but undamaged.

Sergeant Lloyd (Yellow 4) attacked another formation of Bf 109s, but they formed themselves into a defensive circle. He could not break in without suffering return fire. If he broke away carelessly, he would become a victim. Eventually, he gave up the attempt and dived against the Bf 109s' direction and headed off after other prey.

Green Leader, Sergeant Steere, led his Section on to a formation of eight Bf 109s. Steere opened fire on one Bf 109 from 300 yards, but broke off without seeing any result. However, as his Number 2 – Flying Officer Parrot – thumbed his firing button with the same Bf 109 in his sights, it burst aflame. Parrot chose another Bf 109, and held his guns on it long enough to send it down out of control. Then, he joined a group of No 616 Squadron pilots for a head-on attack . . .

Meanwhile, Green 3, Sergeant Plzak fired into a Bf 109 until they were over the Channel coast, descending. His ammunition was nearly exhausted. Plzak fired a final burst and the Bf 109 burst into flames and cartwheeled into the waves.

No 242 Squadron's Green Leader, John Latta, headed for RAF Gravesend, where he joined Bader and No 66 Squadron for lunch. Bader himself had had two tough kills, and was cock-a-hoop with the apparent success of the interception. Latta's news fuelled his enthusiasm. Latta had had two easy kills. He had kept out of trouble. But after he landed, a rigger inspected Latta's aeroplane and found damage to his tail and one wing. Some of the damage was from debris, perhaps, but some of it from gunfire. He must have come under fire while firing on the first Bf 109, yet – though there were many fighters in the area – he had not been conscious of being under attack himself. The whole fight had been haphazard. The new boy, Flying Officer Homer, at Green 2, was struck out of the fight by Bf 109s and crashed. Several of Bader's best men made no claims. Sergeant Lonsdale (Red 3), Denis Crowley-Milling (Yellow 2), Sergeant Brimble (Yellow 3), a fuming Stan Turner (Blue 1) and 'Norrie' Hart (Blue 3) had all become caught up in the desperate and lonely manoeuvring dogfight over Kent. They had all fired at many Bf 109s in the fray, but did not see results, either too busy protecting themselves or because the Bf 109s went to full throttle and headed home. They had run all over the sky, from Canterbury to mid-Channel. They had run out of ammunition and gone home. Dicky Cork was absent from the lists.

Nos 310 and 616 Squadrons both attacked too late to be effective. The Germans were already alerted by the time that these squadrons became involved in the fray. A group of No 616 Squadron pilots charged a group of Bf 109s head-on in line abreast, but there was already total chaos. It was hard to distinguish friend from foe. Pilots were so preoccupied avoiding collisions that snap-shooting was all that could be managed. It was luck: a few pilots entered tentative 'damaged' claims but the stalwart Yorkshireman, Flight Lieutenant Ken Holden of No 616 Squadron, did make a 'destroyed' claim for a Bf 109 on which he had fired – it had promptly exploded. It was luck: one of No 616 Squadron's most experienced pilots, Flying Officer D. S. Smith, died. No 310 Squadron, despite all their experience, entered a solitary 'destroyed' claim.

Nos 242, 19, 310 and 616 Squadrons claimed four, seven, one and one Bf 109s 'destroyed' respectively, a total of thirteen, plus a total of 'five' probables' and three 'damaged'. The British losses were small in comparison. Five fighters were damaged or lost. Three pilots were missing: D. S. Smith, a Regular who had served with No 616 Squadron since the outbreak of war; the No 19 Squadron veteran Flight Lieutenant E. Burgoyne; and one of No 242 Squadron's new men, Pilot Officer M. G. Homer, who had only been posted in from No 1 Squadron, RAF Northolt, on the 21st.

The squadrons were well pleased with the statistics. They had not been on the ground long before they received a message from Park of No 11 Group to say that they had been poaching on No 11 Group's preserves. The pilots laughed at the humour, but later they found that the man was serious, and had made an official complaint. Leigh-Mallory was too satisfied with the result to use Park's complaint as anything other than further fuel to add ardour to their mutual hostility.

From the German point of view, the statistics were exaggerations. Four British squadrons – nearly fifty fighters – had engaged twice their number of German fighters from a superior position. Having no reason to stay to fight, the Bf 109s had dived and headed for home. This was one of their established reactions when they did not have the advantage of height. A few had fallen in the pursuit; a few British fighters had been picked off in the brief dogfight. The Bf 109 'upper guard' had cut off the attack of the second squadron – a tactical success, which the British 'upper guard' failed to prevent. The third and fourth British squadrons had arrived too late to be decisive, although they had not been the main British force.

When they had the opportunity to fight as cohesive units, like the Germans, the British fighters had split their forces and had fought individual battles. That Bader's fighter pilots were working independently is clearly evident in each and every combat in September. This is particularly relevant as the British knew, as a Fighter Command Memorandum to Squadrons noted, that:

> 'German fighters often work in pairs. If you get on the tail of one, the other immediately tries to get on your tail. . . . Formations quickly become broken up in a dogfight. Aircraft of Sections should try, as far as possible, to keep together for mutual support.'

The Duxford Wing pilots did not consciously protect each other's tails. Fighters in some squadrons in No 11 Group – Tuck's No 257 Squadron, for instance – were working in loose pairs, like the Germans. This was an aspect of fighter warfare upon which Bader later expended much thought.

A third Duxford Wing patrol was flown later that afternoon, but the enemy had retired. The sky was British. From now on, German raids by day became a dribble until they had all but ceased in early October. The Germans went over to night bombing, the final, traumatic phase of the Battle of Britain – the Blitz. The Duxford Wing flew several more times as a Wing, but the need for such concentrations of force had gone.

No 242 Squadron pilots had been awarded several decorations during the month. On 14 September, Bader was awarded the DSO for outstanding leadership and Flight Lieutenant Ball was awarded the DFC for gallantry. On 23 September, Sub-Lieutenant Dicky Cork was awarded the DFC, a rare award for a Naval officer, and the squadron was well pleased. On 27 September, two more DFCs were awarded to members of 242 Squadron, Acting Flight Lieutenant Turner and Pilot Officer Stansfield, and Pilot Officer McKnight was awarded a Bar to his. Two days later, Noel Stansfield was posted to No 229 Squadron as a Flight Commander.

☆   ☆   ☆

In order to avoid perceiving the Duxford Wing as unique in all respects as a result of scrutinizing it in isolation, No 11 Group experience provides perspectives. After 7 September, No 11 Group had reacted to the larger German formations, heavier escorts and more predictable targetting more cautiously than No 12 Group with two-squadron 'wings', which Park believed would give as good results as larger formations. One of the squadrons was to go for the bombers while the other distracted the escorts. The Debden Wing, Nos 17 and 73 Squadrons, began operations on 11 September with a successful engagement and fought on the 15th in the morning only – the squadrons fought separately in the afternoon. For the rest of September, the significant features of the Debden Wing were that Fighter Control failed to order it to sufficient height to intercept the enemy who had taken to flying very high, and that it became a three-squadron wing.

On 16 September, No 73 Squadron led a three-squadron patrol over Gravesend at 20,000 feet with Nos 257 and 504 (County of Nottingham) Squadrons. No contact was made with the enemy. No 257 Squadron joined the Wing, but No 504 Squadron did not fly with the Wing again. No 257 Squadron was commanded by Acting Squadron Leader 'Bob' Tuck, who had first led a wing during the Dunkirk fighting – in one of which Bader had flown! At mid-afternoon on 17 September, Nos 17 (leading), 73 and 257 Squadrons flew a wing patrol over RAF Hendon at 20,000 feet, but No 73 Squadron's ORB recorded: 'No contact made, the enemy fighters keeping above 30,000 ft, as seems usual when they are not escorting bombers.'

The next day, 18 September, Red Section of No 73 Squadron flew an early morning patrol at 10,000 feet over RAF Martlesham Heath, without seeing the enemy. At 09.20 hours, Nos 17 and 73 Squadron took off at 09.20 hours and patrolled Chelmsford at 20,000 feet, but again the Germans kept to over 30,000 feet. That afternoon, No 73 Squadron flew two squadron patrols. The first scrambled at 13.27 hours and patrolled over Rochford at 20,000 feet, but again the enemy fighters were too high. Another patrol took off at 16.00 hours, flying over Colchester at 15,000 feet, but, as No 73 Squadron's ORB recorded:

'The Squadron had an entirely wasted afternoon as e/a were seen but at 33,000 ft and as Sgt. Garton ['B' Flight leader] so aptly reported to the Controller over his R/T, "I can see bandits all right, but God knows how we can get to them". At no time was the Squadron ordered to sufficient height and after 1 hour 40 they were ordered to pancake. This made the 4th useless patrol of the day and all pilots were mightily tired and greatly uncomplimentary about the way the Controllers had dealt with them . . . '

The next four days brought no relief; bad weather cancelled flying on the 19th and 22nd; there was a three-squadron patrol over RAF Debden at 12,000 feet on the 20th in the late morning, when nothing was seen; and on the 21st, despite a fine day, there was no flying until the evening when a three-squadron patrol was flown on the RAF North Weald–RAF Hornchurch patrol line at 20,000 feet, seeing nothing.

Although the two-squadron wing had not been in major combat regularly, further large-scale German bomber attacks were expected. On the 21st, the three-squadron wing was put on a more permanent basis, as No 73 Squadron's ORB noted: '257 Squadron from Martlesham . . . are to operate with [Nos 17 and 73 Squadrons] from [Debden] until further notice returning each night to their base.' No 17 Squadron was to provide the top cover against escorts for Nos 73 and 257 Squadrons who were to break up bomber formations and shoot the bombers down, and between whom the lead would alternate.

The problems of controlling this formation became evident very soon. On 23 September at 09.20 hours, Nos 73 (leading), 257 and 17 Squadrons joined over Debden with orders to patrol Chelmsford at 20,000 feet. It went very badly, as No 73 Squadron's ORB recorded:

> '12 Hurricanes from 73 Squadron took off but only 8 returned. None of them fired . . . something had gone badly wrong. . . . Most of the returned pilots were almost speechless with anger and . . . each blamed the Operations Room for the setback. The Squadron was patrolling Chelmsford at 20,000 feet and were then reckoned over Rochford and Gravesend at the same height when they were told there were bandits at Angels 5 [5,000 feet] approaching from the East. When told to intercept at that height the leader of the Squadron was so astounded that he repeated the figure and obtained confirmation. The Squadron had got down to 12,000 ft when they were ordered up again to Angels 20 [20,000 feet] in the direction of Dover. It was while climbing back that the whole Squadron was pounced upon by 15 Me.109s and an odd He.113 [sic] diving at 360 m.p.h. compared with their climbing speed of perhaps 160 m.p.h. To make matters worse, the escorting Squadron (17) did not follow 73 Squadron down in the first place, thus leaving us entirely unprotected. The results were bad [four shot down] but might have been far worse.'

The rest of the Debden Wing's existence was characterized by frustrations – insufficient height, and problems with formation control and tactics. On 24 September, Nos 17, 73 and 257 Squadrons flew a Wing patrol over Gravesend at 20,000 ft and saw Junkers Ju 88s with Bf 109 escorts at about 09.00 hours, but again had insufficient height to intercept. Another Wing patrol took off at 11.25 hours, but produced zero. On the 25th and 26th, the Wing was at readiness but there was no flying. There was success on the 27th: Nos 17 and 73 Squadrons flew a morning patrol at 12,000 feet on the RAF Hornchurch–RAF North Weald line. They saw Bf 110s in a large circle at 19,000 feet, they climbed above them and dropped into the middle, shooting down several Germans. At midday, Nos 17, 73 and 257 were to patrol RAF Hornchurch, but No 257 Squadron had not finished refuelling and did not join the patrol. The next day, the three-squadron Wing patrolled at 09.30 hours but No 17 Squadron, which was the normal protection for the other two: 'once again failed to take up their proper position in the Wing formation and the opinion is expressed that it may be well that no interception of e/a was made.'

Another three-squadron patrol took off at 13.31 hours, but there was no interception. When they saw the Germans, the enemy was too high; usually, the Wing saw nothing; it was pointless flying three squadrons together in such circumstances.

The Debden Wing had now been operating for over a fortnight. They had much experience but had encountered several problems to which they clearly needed to find solutions. Moreover, the Germans were flying at 30,000 feet, and Fighter Command's intelligence system suggested that the daylight offensive was about to end. As No 73 Squadron's ORB recorded for 28 September, 'In the evening a conference between the C.O.s of 73, 257 and 17 Squadrons took place at Debden on tactics, which it is hoped will prove most useful'.

As a result, No 257 Squadron ceased to operate with Nos 17 and 73 Squadrons, and the Debden Wing again became a two-squadron wing, as flown elsewhere in No 11 Group, in recognition of German tactics.

The Wing continued to operate into October, seldom seeing the enemy, who flew too high. By mid-October, the German day offensive had died. German fighters could fly at altitude over the United Kingdom, but they posed no threat to the integrity of British airspace; Section or Flight patrols were again the appropriate response; and night defence became a priority. The Debden Wing last flew on 20 October; ironically, three days later, No 73 Squadron became a night fighter squadron.

CHAPTER 9
Evolving Tactics

No 242 Squadron's Adjutant, Flight Lieutenant Peter MacDonald, played an important if almost clandestine role in the evolution of Bader's tactics. MacDonald supported Leigh-Mallory and Bader in their views about larger formations and forward defence, but he felt that they were not being given a fair hearing. He wrestled with his conscience for some time. As a Member of Parliament, he had a right to see Ministers. Early in October 1940, he approached the Under-Secretary of State for Air, Mr Harold Balfour, who refused to discuss Service matters with a serving officer.

As a back-bencher, MacDonald had access by custom to the Prime Minister, Mr Winston Churchill. He balanced his Parliamentary rights with his duty as an officer. Soon afterwards, he spoke to Churchill, but kept the approach totally secret, from everyone, most of all from Bader and Leigh-Mallory. Churchill greeted him gruffly, but warmed to his presentation: Leigh-Mallory and Bader could influence the outcome of the battle positively if they were given the support that they needed. Churchill initiated a series of enquiries via his Ministers. Although they undoubtedly overlapped, these proceeded independently of the Air Staff's own analysis of the tactical situation.

☆   ☆   ☆

On Tuesday, 15th October, Bader went on four days' leave. Next day, Leigh-Mallory telephoned him and asked him to meet him the following morning at the Air Ministry in London. He might just be able to get him into the Air Staff Fighter Tactics Conference. At that meeting, the main characters in the 'Big Wing' controversy came together.

The meeting, held in the Air Council Room at the Air Ministry, was convened to discuss the 'major day tactics' in Fighter Command. In the chair was Air Vice-Marshal W. Sholto Douglas, Deputy Chief of the Air Staff. In the place of Air Chief Marshal Sir Cyril Newall, Chief of the Air Staff, who was ill, was Air Marshal Sir Charles Portal. It made little difference for the future of the fighter force: Portal was due to succeed Newall before the end of the month.

Portal sat at Sholto Douglas's right hand, and on his left sat Air Chief Marshal Sir Hugh Dowding, Air Officer Commanding-in-Chief of Fighter Command. Beside Dowding sat the three Group Air Officers Commanding, Air Vice-Marshals Keith Park (No 11), Trafford Leigh-Mallory (No 12) and Sir Quentin Brand (No 10).

The Assistant Chief of the Air Staff (Radar), Air Marshal Sir Philip Joubert, and the Director of Plans, Air Commodore John Slessor, the Director Home Office (DHO), Air Commodore D. Stevenson and the Permanent Deputy Director Signals, Air Commodore O. Lywood and the Assistant Director of the Air Tactics Branch, Group Captain H. G. Crowe were also present.

Acting Squadron Leader Douglas Bader sat next to the two men taking the minutes, Wing Commander Theodore McEvoy of the Fighter Command Headquarters Stanmore Staff and the permanent Air Council Official, Mr J. S. Orme. Bader was more than a little nervous about being in the company of such high-ranking officers. He had been aware of the cold scrutiny of some of the men, particularly Slessor.

The agenda stated that the meeting had been convened to discuss major day and night fighter tactics against bomber attacks because the enemy might make:

> ' . . . more determined, better organised and heavier attacks . . . in the spring of 1941 . . . It is necessary that the lessons we have learned should be applied generally to enable the fighter defence to operate at maximum efficiency.'

This is the key to understanding the meeting: it was called not to dissect the Battle of Britain so far, but to ensure that the night attacks were met effectively if possible and to ensure that Fighter Command was applying the most successful tactics to meet the renewed onslaught that was to be expected in the spring of 1941. It is only with hindsight that it can be seen that there would be no German offensive by day in 1941, but it was a very real threat in 1940. It was necessary, therefore, to prepare tactics, organization and command many months in advance. To say that the meeting was a post-mortem on the Battle of Britain is only a partial truth; to say that it was part of an elaborate plan to get rid of Park and Dowding is a gross simplification.

Sholto Douglas opened the meeting by setting forth the matters to be discussed. There were three propositions. First, he asked the meeting to consider the proposition that Fighter Command wanted to meet enemy formations with superior forces; secondly, that these forces should have a co-ordinated plan of action, whereby part of a covering force engaged the escorts and the main part of the force attacked the bombers; and thirdly, that the covering force should always be higher than the top of the enemy formation. Sholto Douglas said that he realized that this was an ideal solution. The time factor was critical: if it were necessary to engage the enemy before they bombed a crucial target, there might be inadequate time to gather the full force or to climb to superior altitude.

However, the meeting had not been convened to discuss the tactics used to fight the Battle of Britain in general, nor solely to examine the use of concentrations of force – Wings, specifically the No 12 Group Wing. It had been convened to discuss the tactics with which the RAF would meet what was seen as the very real threat of the Germans renewing their bombing attack on Britain in the spring of 1941 by day, and, rather more urgently, the tactics with which the RAF's inadequate night defence force was to tackle the menace of German night bombing now pounding the nation's cities.

Park, who was visibly exhausted, spoke first. He said that in No 11 Group, three factors – time, distance and cloud – meant that it should not be a general principle that a 'Wing' was the right formation to oppose all attacks – even mass attacks. He observed that the No 12 Group Wing was best used when conditions were ideal and the enemy bombers were already retreating and separated from their escorts. When No 11 Group was operating against large formations of bombers with fighter escort, Park said he worked on the principle of using squadrons in pairs at different altitudes separately to engage the enemy top and close escort and the bombers. The results from one- or two-squadron formations' operations compared well with those of the No 12 Group 'Wing' sorties.

Dowding brought in the overall perspective. He said that the main problem was determining early enough which was the major raid when several could be seen developing. While the Observer Corps had performed well, the altitude at which raids had been flown often defeated them. The answer in future lay in improved radar – the 'Gun-Laying' and 'Low-Cover' chains.

Park remarked that he had obtained useful early warning reports of German build-ups from high-flying reconnaissance Spitfires (No 421 Flight, RAF Gravesend) over the French coast. VHF radio would speed up results, by allowing direct contact with the pilot. The Spitfires observed the enemy formations, and then shadowed them. Park said that he believed that the only way to meet the fighter-bomber threat which had now developed was to use the system employed in No 11 Group. The reconnaissance Spitfires were supported by a full Spitfire squadron on standing patrol on the Maidstone patrol line at 15,000 feet. When radar warning of a raid was confirmed, the squadron climbed a further 15,000 feet, and then to 35,000 feet to cover other squadrons as they climbed to fighting altitude. Although the 'tip-and-run' raids demanded that No 11 Group be at a high degree of readiness, one squadron was always at instant readiness.

At this point, Leigh-Mallory brought up the issue he thought was the most important: 'I would welcome more opportunities of using the "Wing" formation, operating from Duxford and going down to help No 11 Group. All five squadrons of the Duxford Wing can be airborne in six minutes after being called and will be at 20,000 feet over RAF Hornchurch just twenty-five minutes later. I am sure that if a counter-attack of this magnitude were to intercept a large German formation on just ten per cent of occasions, it would repay the effort. On the 18th and the 27th September, the Wing obtained fine results in just such an operation – and one of those engagements was against fighters alone.'

Joubert pointed out that the warning that his radars had been able to give Groups had been very short on some recent occasions – too short for the squadrons to make effective use of it.

Dowding pointed out that the enemy's approach at great height posed great difficulties. He had instructed that an 'arrow' should go down on the

Operations Board when the first indications of a raid were put on the board, so that the direction could be seen.

Park said that as far as he was concerned No 11 Group could face the problem when a large raid was coming in. With some exasperation, Park stated the nub of his approach to meeting the bombers: 'Can it not be accepted that if No 11 Group had, say, twenty squadrons at readiness, that was generally sufficient to meet any enemy formation?'

In the debate which followed, the minutes recorded that 'it was generally agreed that additional fighter support would often be advantageous since the more we could outnumber the enemy, the more we should down'.

The rift between Nos 11 and 12 Groups became very obvious. It was deep. Sholto Douglas supported Leigh-Mallory. Dowding supported Park. The personal antagonism between Park and Leigh-Mallory was also very obvious as they faced each other. It was more than professional rivalry.

Park accused Leigh-Mallory of having failed to support his squadrons on several occasions, leaving No 11 Group's sector airfields exposed.

Leigh-Mallory said that No 11 Group requested No 12 Group assistance so late that it was useless and quite dangerous. It was of no value to send one squadron to guard an airfield from one hundred bombers – that was why he had sent several squadrons. Could Park not see that he was not using the assets wisely?

Park retorted by citing one occasion when it had taken the wing almost an hour to be in position over Sheerness. Leigh-Mallory, glancing at the disbelief on Bader's face, retorted: 'Nonsense! The Wing is airborne in six minutes and over Tilbury less than eighteen minutes after take-off. Our record proves it! If we were only given enough warning, we could have the Wing in position to meet a raid while your squadrons are still climbing.'

Dowding came under criticism for not having co-ordinated the two Groups, but now he asserted that: 'With my Group Commanders, I can resolve any difficulties of control involved in sending large formations from No 12 Group to support No 11 Group.'

However, he said that the other main difficulties to be met were those that involved the time factor. This was generally agreed. However, it was pointed out that whereas Bf 109 fighters might fly at 30,000 feet, which did not pose a threat, the bomb-carrying Bf 109s had never been found above 22,000 feet, so the climb was not a problem.

Sholto Douglas called on Bader to comment from his practical experience. Bader clambered to his feet, but Sholto Douglas bade him sit. Bader thanked him but said he would rather stand. Bader said that he thought that time was the essence of the problem. If enough warning could be given, then a large number of fighters could be brought into position, and he had no doubt that they would get most effective results against German formations.

Bader was faintly embarrassed and did not talk for long. He told Lucas that he recalled saying:

'You, gentlemen, learnt the lessons in the Great War. They are still the same today. Height, sun, position and strength in numbers, getting in really close – this is still what counts. It follows that to gain the tactical advantage, we must be got off the ground in time to win it. It also follows that it is more economical to put up one hundred fighters against one hundred bombers than it is to put twelve against one hundred. Practically, sixty against two hundred are acceptable odds. Once in the air, the fighter leader should decide where and when to meet the enemy – not the Controller on the ground. He can't see the enemy and doesn't know where the sun is because it isn't on his board.'

Portal asked Leigh-Mallory to what degree such a local concentration of forces, like a wing, affected the responsibility of a Group commander for the defence of the whole area of his Group. Leigh-Mallory responded: 'We have prepared satisfactory plans to meet the possibility of other attacks coming in. We always have other squadrons at readiness and availability. I am satisfied that concentrating a number of squadrons as a Wing when circumstances are right is not incompatible with my general responsibility as Group Commander.'

Brand seized on Leigh-Mallory's reference to having additional squadrons: 'Has No 12 Group a surfeit of squadrons? Need I remind the meeting that No 10 Group is currently rather weak were any concentrated attack to develop on the West of England. Ought these squadrons not be transferred to No 10 Group?'

Dowding answered him, showing fairness to Leigh-Mallory: 'I agree that No 10 Group could be considered somewhat weak should any major attacks develop in the West, but the protection of the Midlands and of the East Coast convoys is a big commitment for No 12 Group. It is a serious limitation, but, as Commanding Officer I have to keep in mind the necessity of meeting every threat with some force.'

Leigh-Mallory said that the forces could be used more effectively if a sufficiently long warning time could be got from radar – and this did not seem to be the case.

Joubert responded that the south-east coast radar stations had been badly damaged by the enemy, but that every effort was being made to get them back to full efficiency as soon as possible. He pointed out that it was not always the radar that was at fault in giving late warning – sometimes it was slow communications.

Sholto Douglas wrapped up the views of the meeting so far with a neatly balanced summary, as the minutes recorded:

'The employment of a large mass of fighters had great advantages, though it was not necessarily the complete solution to the problem of interception. In No. 11 Group, where the enemy was very close at hand, both the methods described by A.O.C. No. 11 Group and those of A.O.C. No. 12 Group could on occasions, be used with forces from the two Groups co-operating.'

Dowding's response directly addressed the essence of the wing question:

'I will ensure that No 12 Group "Wings" participate freely in suitable operations over the 11 Group area. I am sure that I will be able to resolve any complications of control.'

Dowding had managed to construct a highly sophisticated command and signals network before the war; now, with unlimited funds and operational experience, he saw no difficulty in controlling wings.

The Home Office representative asked if such co-operation could be employed generally throughout Fighter Command. 'They could not,' replied Dowding. 'Similar conditions seldom arise elsewhere.'

There was one significant conclusion. It was put forward that in conditions which enabled the enemy to operate in mass formations, the fighter leader could dispense with sector control. Once he had been given information about enemy movements, the fighter leader should be responsible for leading his formation to the combat.

It was generally agreed that where conditions were suitable, wings of three squadrons should be employed against large enemy formations. Where further forces could be made available without detriment to other commitments, even larger fighter formations should operate as tactical units. On occasion, two 'Wings' could be operated together as a unit – the meeting decided to call this a 'Balbo' (for want of a better name), after the Italian Air Marshal Balbo who had flaunted great armadas of flying-boats in the 1930s.

All the squadrons of a wing should operate from the same sector, but it would not always be possible to operate them from the same aerodrome. Wings would not be regarded as permanent units to be moved complete, but whenever possible the same squadrons should operate together as a wing. Where practicable, wings should be deployed at stations from which they could gain advantage in height over the enemy without having to turn. The wing or the 'Balbo' should be controlled by the Sector Commander, as at present, and it was undesirable for one of the squadron commanders to control it. The two wings of a 'Balbo' should be controlled by one of the Sector Commanders; they should work on a common HF radio frequency. No difficulty was anticipated in co-ordinating their operation. Theoretically, VHF radio would allow up to seven 'Balbos' to operate together.

The meeting then went on to discuss the fighter response to the night raids. Civilian morale was falling, so Sholto Douglas announced that single-seat fighters were to be used at night. Dowding argued that they would be largely ineffective. Brand, who had run many experiments with night fighting, agreed; unless supported by radar and searchlights, single-seaters were a waste of time. Dowding placed his faith in the development of the airborne interception radar and the two-seat, twin-engined Bristol Beaufighter. There were development problems but they were being overcome. This, he asserted, was the only way forward at night; others dissented; there was distrust of Dowding's technological approach to warfare. Dowding, bowing to the pressure, agreed to form a single-seat night fighter wing.

The meeting was dissolved after about an hour and a half.

When the minutes were produced, Dowding, Park and Brand all registered objections: they were slanted.

As to Bader's presence: it was abnormal, but perhaps there should have been more operational fighter leaders present, not one less. Balfour's pungent comment is worth repeating:

'I cannot find it so reprehensible that a breath of reality from someone who was doing the job was wafted into the Staff circles.'

Another gentleman in a position to comment with less than impartiality made a balanced statement that is worth recording here. Dowding's SASO, Strath Evill, had written on 25 September 1940 – before the meeting – though he was not talking about *big* wings, but wings:

'The strongest impression left in my mind is the absolute necessity for flexibility in our tactical methods. It is quite useless to argue whether wing formations are or are not desirable, both statements are equally true under different conditions . . . We must be careful not to be too rigid in our conclusions.'

☆   ☆   ☆

On 18 October, all No 11 Group's squadron and station commanders attended a conference at No 11 Group Headquarters on the subject of fighter tactics. Again, it was the time taken to intercept that was a prominent feature of the meeting. The Air Officer Commanding, Keith Park, said that he was particularly perturbed at the time taken by some Readiness Squadrons to become airborne – well over five minutes. He wanted far better reaction time than that. Leigh-Mallory's goad had clearly pricked Park.

☆   ☆   ☆

Leigh-Mallory believed that he saw the problem from the overall perspective of the threat facing Fighter Command. He held the view that No 11 Group was fighting the battle as a local affair and that it lacked co-ordination between Nos 11 and 12 Groups, whereas it should be controlled by the Commander-in-Chief Fighter Command himself. Dowding allowed Park to fight the battle. In the early stages, this worked, but once the target shifted to London, the front line also moved north. Dowding had made No 11 Group the strongest, but Park had the serious problem of being too near to the enemy to use his assets properly. No 11 Group's Operations Room only had a map of its territory, not No 12 Group's. At Fighter Command, a map of the whole of Fighter Command was used by the Operations Room, but they did not control, only plot: under each station was a list of each squadron and its availability. Had Dowding controlled the battle from there, he would have known his total assets, and would have seen the need to scramble the farthest squadrons first, not last, to hit the enemy coming in – in short, a defence in depth.

Bader saw the problem from the immediate tactical perspective of how best to reach and strike down each individual formation. He contended that he could get a wing into the air and into position to attack in force as the Germans were running in to their targets. All he needed then was the right information about the Germans' course and height. He would position his force.

In essence, he contended that fighters needed adequate warning of the raid and that the combat should be controlled by the most appropriate people – not the men in the Fighter Plot, not the Fighter Controllers, but by the leader in the air. He demanded one thing as a prerequisite: to be told as soon as a raid was seen assembling. However, he often found himself told only as it was coming in, and had to climb all-out to try to intercept at all, let alone get above it.

Bader believed that No 12 Group squadrons could have been used to spearhead the attack on enemy formations, with height and sun behind them. Meanwhile, the No 11 Group squadrons would have had time to climb to height and position to continue the onslaught. Bader thought that the senior officers in Fighter Command were failing to see the fundamental principles of fighter warfare. Charitably, Bader held the view that Dowding was under considerable stress during the Battle of Britain, preoccupied with daily contacts with the Air Staff, the War Cabinet, the other ministries. Bader believed that it was reasonable to assume that he was therefore unaware of the changing circumstances of the Battle of Britain, and therefore failed to change the tactical responses, and did not appreciate the need for overall control of the battle, rather than control at Group level.

Dowding was fighting the strategic battle. He saw rather more and rather farther than the acting squadron leader with seven months' experience of modern fighters and tactical control systems – and two weeks' combat experience. Dowding left Park to fight the Battle in the British tradition of the army commander deciding the battle plan, but leaving his corps commanders to fight the tactical battle. It was considered wrong to interfere, as this would be seen as criticism of the general.

In the heat of an intensive battle, a battle that decided history, a battle that made history as the first air-to-air confrontation ever, it was not the time to reassess tactics. How, in a matter of days could Fighter Command issue the directives to squadrons to change tactical ideas when it could barely train its replacement pilots to fly Spitfires? How, when no one really knew how modern fighters would perform, could they re-decide tactics? A modern fighter was designed to climb fast, to hit bombers, then return to base. It was not designed to engage fighters – as happened. Everyone was learning. As Bader himself said several times in later years, 'that was the point'.

It is all too easy to criticize with hindsight, but the important thing is to understand. Sometimes, in arguing a case, the need logically to explain everything clearly and to perform a chain-linked argument destroys the reality – the contradictions.

From the Battle emerged the new tactical ideas. That Bader and Leigh-Mallory experimented is both to their credit and their blame: they had excellent circumstances and, at the same time, inappropriate circumstances in which to test their theory.

Nevertheless, theirs were the tactical ideas that shaped 1941, but it was the Air Command structure – C_3I – that Dowding had employed which found its most succinct expression in the Allied Tactical Air Forces. Together, these tactical ideas and this structure dominated the future of British air power. The remainder of this book will unfold this theme.

☆   ☆   ☆

It is extraordinary to record that the matter of wings continued, and that ill-feeling between Nos 11 and 12 Groups continued to fester. This was perhaps largely the result of MacDonald's intervention with the Prime Minister. Late in October, the Secretary of State for Air, Sir Archibald Sinclair, visited RAF Duxford. He spoke to Bader and Woodhall. He heard enough from them to want his Under-Secretary of State, Balfour, to visit RAF Duxford and make a detailed report. Sinclair could see that the difference in tactical views held by the two Groups was severe. There was bitterness now not only between the two Air Officers Commanding, but between the Groups' squadrons themselves.

Balfour visited RAF Duxford on 2 November 1940. He too spoke with Bader and Woodhall. He then flew back to London, and wrote his 'Duxford Memorandum'. It stated Bader's and Woodhall's view succinctly. Sholto Douglas got the memorandum the next morning. Instantly, he sent Dowding a copy.

The ill-feeling had reached the level that control of operations was withdrawn from the Groups' Air Officers Commanding, and given to Fighter Command Headquarters.

Dowding laid the blame for the debacle firmly at Bader's door: he might be courageous, but he had an 'overdevelopment of the critical faculty'. The reader can judge the accuracy of this observation for himself. Dowding hinted strongly that Bader should be disciplined for talking so freely to Balfour and for criticizing his senior officers. It was a little too late for thoughts of discipline: Dowding should have acted before that.

The main fact is that the controversy should never have developed. Dowding should swiftly have crushed the disagreement between his two group commanders – the middle of a critical battle was no place for a tactical and personal clash. Dowding was a technocrat: he was no man-manager; and therein lay his weakness. A Montgomery would have had Leigh-Mallory straight on to the retired list, and Bader posted to a real front-line unit.

As to Leigh-Mallory, he remains an enigma. But it is not the last time that his inability to exercise his authority over his junior commanders was to do Bader a serious disservice.

CHAPTER 10
The Lion in Winter

W hile he went off on the four days' leave from 15 October 1940, during which he attended the Air Ministry fighter conference, Bader left No 242 squadron in the capable hands of Flight Lieutenant Ball. Bader returned on 19 October to mixed news. Not only was he told that Cork would have to wear the Distinguished Service Cross, not the Distinguished Flying Cross that he had been awarded, but he found a 'Most Immediate' order for the squadron to move from RAF Coltishall to Duxford, and, most upsetting, he had to read a report on the loss of one of the squadron's most popular pilots, Pilot Officer Neil Campbell.

During a patrol on 17 October, Campbell's Section had been vectored on to a 'bogey'. They caught a Do 17 some miles off Yarmouth. As Campbell went in for his attack, one of the Dornier's gunners must have got in a fortunate burst, for the Sector Controller was unable to raise him again on the radio. He was reported as missing. He was posted killed in action when his body was washed ashore a few days later. He was buried with full military honours on 31 October.

On 23 September, the standard telegram had arrived from the Air Ministry notifying No 242 Squadron that, on the recommendation of the Commander-in-Chief Fighter Command, His Majesty The King had been graciously pleased to award Sub-Lieutenant Richard Cork, RN, the Distinguished Flying Cross. He thus became the first Naval pilot to be awarded this, a Royal Air Force, decoration. The squadron considered this a fine award, and celebrated in style.

It did not please Their Lords of the Admiralty who by telegram amended the award to the Distinguished Service Cross, the Royal Navy's equivalent of the Air Force's Distinguished Flying Cross. Douglas Bader knew precisely how to handle this; he rested his case on the firm ground that HM The King had given Cork the Distinguished Flying Cross, and only His Majesty could change it.

Now, on Bader's return from the fighter conference, he learnt that the Sea Lords had outwitted him. In the *London Gazette* of 18 October 1940, the Admiralty gazetted the award to Sub-Lieutenant Cork of the Distinguished Service Cross for his service with the Royal Air Force. The award was effective from 20 October. Cork was ordered by the Admiralty to change the decoration (a subject of various apocryphal stories). Bader forbade him to wear anything other than the Air Force ribbon while with No 242 Squadron, but there was nothing further Bader could do.

On 20 October, the squadron moved from Coltishall to Duxford, as instructed, where they remained until the end of November.

On 27 October, Pilot Officer John Latta was awarded a well deserved DFC. He had consistently shown great courage.

The routine transfers and postings continued. On 17 October, Pilot Officers Wareham and Millard reported for duty from No 1 Squadron, Wittering, and the next day Pilot Officers Savory and Kemp were posted from No 85 Squadron, Church Fenton. On 3 November, Pilot Officer Smith was posted to No 615 Squadron, at Northolt, but the posting was changed to No 141 Squadron the following day.

On 5 November, operating from Duxford, Bader led No 242 Squadron and Lane's No 19 Squadron on a wing sweep over the Thames Estuary and out into the near reaches of the North Sea, looking for trouble. As they swung out over the Estuary, Willie McKnight called a warning. Two dozen pairs of eyes swung towards the sun and saw a stream of Bf 109s, hypnotic yellow flames stabbing from their cannon towards the Hurricanes and Spitfires.

Willie McKnight, the first to see the enemy and the first to react, turned hard into the attack and loosed off a quick deflection shot at the nearest Bf 109. Once past the British fighters, the Bf 109s pulled out of their dives and streaked away, but McKnight's target went into a steeper dive. Alongside it, a solitary Hurricane began to tumble towards the earth. The British and the German fighter impacted on the hard slate face of the sea within seconds of each other. Neither pilot got out. To set against Willie McKnight's quick victory was the loss of young Norris-Hart.

The round of postings continued. On 6 November, Pilot Officer Wareham, who had been with the squadron a few weeks, and the long-serving, reliable, Sergeant Brimble were posted to No 73 Squadron. They were soon bound for the Middle East, across North Africa, but sadly Brimble's Hurricane crash-landed in the desert and he was killed. Two new pilots were posted in from No 6 OTU, Flying Officer Lang on the 6th and Sergeant Truman on the 7th.

On 7 November, Squadron Leader W. E. G. Taylor was attached to No 242 Squadron from No 71 (Eagle) Squadron, for a fourteen-day course. No 71 Squadron was the first of the three RAF squadrons to be formed with American volunteer pilots. It had received its full complement of Hurricane Mk Is when it had moved to Kirton-in-Lindsey for operational work-up. Taylor was being trained for command of the squadron. It was a compliment to Douglas Bader that he had been selected to do part of the training.

Towards the end of the month, there was a change in leadership when, on 22 November, Flight Lieutenant Powell-Sheddon was posted to No 258 Squadron at Leconfield, and Stan Turner was made up to full flight lieutenant and took over his Flight. On 22 November, Pilot Officer Edmunds reported to No 242 Squadron from No 615 Squadron. On 28 November, Flying Officers Price and McKenna, RCAF, reported from No 56 OTU.

The Germans had turned to a night offensive, and the Blitz against British cities began. City after city was set aflame. Bader, like other contemporary day fighter squadron leaders, was deeply frustrated by the inadequacy of their equipment to fight at night.

On the night of 14/15 November, the Luftwaffe's bombers struck Coventry. Streams of bombers bore in on the city and added to the conflagration that engulfed several square miles of the city's ancient heart and outlying industrial and residential areas. Bader had been asked if any of No 242 Squadron's pilots were night-qualified; three were: himself, Turner and Ball.

They were instructed to patrol initially at 18,000 feet, and to be stepped up at intervals of 1,000 feet. They were to stay above the range of the heavy anti-aircraft guns, 12,000 feet. Bader remembered his training with No 23 Squadron, and felt confident that if anything could be done, they would do it, but the reality was different. The Hurricanes were no better than the Spitfire for night fighting – the long nose with the six exhaust stubs spurting out blue and yellow flames destroying night vision, the wings, the framed flat-sided canopy . . .

There was a full moon in a cloudless sky. While no doubt their silhouettes were clear to the bombers below, Bader, Ball and Turner could see nothing below. He led the formation over the city, looking for bombers for an hour. The frustration deepened. They knew the bombers were there but they could not be seen against shadows and the fires raging below.

There was little that the day fighter pilots could do to alleviate the plight of the cities in the German Night Blitz that winter, although the Hurricanes flew many patrols. Before, Bader's hatred of the Germans had been impersonal, thinking only of destroying machines. Now, he began to feel real, emotional hatred.

Douglas Bader turned to matters that he could influence, and continued to explore tactics boldly. Between 23 and 28 November, the No 242 Squadron ORB recorded: 'Squadron operating from Duxford. Wing and Sqdn Patrols carried out daily.'

However, on the 28th, the squadron received orders from No 12 Group Command, dated the previous day, ordering a 'D' move from Duxford to Coltishall. Owing to fog, the squadron was unable to begin the move until 30 November, and took until 2 December to complete it. The squadron was not operational on 3 December 'owing to VHF on station not being completed', but became operational the following day.

On 5 December, Dicky Cork and 'Jimmy' Gardner signed off No 242 Squadron. Gardner had three and a half victories flying with the unit. Squadron Leader D. R. S. Bader endorsed Cork's logbook: 'Ability as a fighter pilot on Hurricanes – Exceptional. One of the best pilots I have had in my squadron.'

On 7 December, Cork and Gardner made their last Hurricane Mk I flights with No 242 Squadron. The following day, they left No 242 Squadron and proceeded to No 252 Squadron, Coastal Command, at Chivenor, flying twin-engined Bristol aircraft – quite a change.

The Fleet Air Arm pilots had served with several famous units, including No 19 Squadron at Duxford with whom Sub-Lieutenant A. G. Blake, known in the RAF as 'The Admiral', flew; also No 213 Squadron at Tangmere and

No 46 Squadron at Stapleford Tawney. By the time the Navy recalled its pilots, eighteen had been killed. These included Sub-Lieutenant Dawson Paul, RNVR, a gifted pilot who had served with No 64 Squadron, RAF, and had shot down five German aircraft in July alone, Blake and Midshipman Ronnie Patterson of No 242 Squadron.

In November, there were changes in the leadership of Fighter Command and No 11 Group. Air Vice-Marshal Sholto Douglas took over as Commander-in-Chief of Fighter Command from Hugh Dowding. Bader's mentor, Air Vice-Marshal Trafford Leigh-Mallory, was transferred from command of No 12 Group to the premier No 11 Group. It did not take long for this to have its effects on No 242 Squadron.

For No 242 Squadron, 12 December was a day of surprises. Early in the day, the squadron received orders to move from Coltishall to Debden, a sector airfield in No 11 Group. Later in the day, this order was counter-manded. Instead, they were ordered to move to another No 11 Group airfield, Martlesham Heath in the North Weald sector. Within a space of a few hours, No 242 Squadron also received notification of the award of the DFC to Squadron Leader Bader and Flying Officer Tamblyn. Into the midst of this confusion and elation, a new pilot, Pilot Officer Arthur, arrived on posting from No 141 Squadron.

Nos 242 and 257 Squadrons were to swap bases. On 15 December, No 242 began to move to Martlesham, and the following day No 257 began to move to Coltishall in its place. No 242 Squadron completed its move to Martlesham on the 17th and became operational there the next day. In the process of the move, on the 17th, two of No 257 Squadron's pilots, both Polish, Pilot Officers Surma and Szczesny, were transferred to No 242 Squadron, thus remaining in the 'front line'.

Fighter Command were thinking out the tactics for 1941. Bader had led wings, and Fighter Command was interested in developing the concept. There were several meetings during November and December. They did not let up even for Christmas – No 242 Squadron's ORB recorded on 25 December 1940 that 'Squadron Leader Bader attended a conference of Squadron Commanders at Headquarters No 11 Group.'

On the last day of a momentous year, No 242 Squadron's ORB summarized:

> 'EXIT 1940. The Squadron has a proud record of achievement in this its first year as an operational Squadron. Having well over one hundred confirmed E/A to its credit. Having taken a notable part in the Battle of Dunkirk (from Biggin Hill and Manston). Afterwards in France as part of 67 Wing AASF. Covering the successful evacuation of the remainder of the BEF the whole of the BAF and AASF from there and after reforming at Coltishall under the Command of Squadron Leader DRS Bader, DSO, DFC leading the Duxford Wing in the Battle of Britain. This Wing has 158 confirmed E/A to its credit with 9 casualties and 15 aircraft lost, and of these 242 Squadron had 62 E/A confirmed. One DSO and ten DFCs have been awarded to Pilots of the Squadron to date.'

The process of postings went on, even as the year turned. On the penultimate day of the old year, Pilot Officers Dibnah, who had been with the squadron since September but had recently suffered ill-health, and Deschamps were posted to Central Flying School at Upavon. However, postings slowed down in the new year. On 4 January 1941, Sergeant Pilot Vaughan was posted in from No 5 RSS, Duxford, but he was 'not yet operational' [ORB].

On 7 January 1941, there was an important change. The Squadron Adjutant, Pilot Officer E. A. Summers, was 'posted to the Air Ministry Unit, Stafford House, for course at School of Oriental Languages' [ORB]; and Pilot Officer J. M. Williamson was posted in from Duxford to take over his duties. On 12 January, Flying Officer MacDonald left the squadron on posting to Headquarters Technical Training Command.

During January 1941, the routine continued of base patrols and patrols over coastal towns, like Felixstowe. However, the squadron also began to fly 'Mosquito' patrols over the French coast, and took part in the first sweep. Fighter Command was about to go over to the offensive.

A 'Mosquito' patrol, or raid, was the original code-name for low-level fighter intruder missions, which preceded 'Rhubarb'. The name itself says what the operation was intended to achieve. Trafford Leigh-Mallory conceived the idea: a pair of fighters sent across the Channel to shoot up targets of opportunity when low-level cloud over northern France gave good concealment. This was a method of using fighters offensively when there was little in the way of major attacks that Fighter Command could do. The first had been flown by a pair of No 66 Squadron Spitfires – although they had a specific objective, strafing Le Touquet aerodrome – on 20 December 1940. No 242 Squadron's first 'Mosquito' raid was flown on 9 January by Bader and Sergeant Richardson from Duxford. They did not engage the enemy. The same day, five fighter squadrons swept 30 miles into France, opening the offensive.

The next day, No 242 Squadron took part in No 11 Group's first offensive sweep. Leigh-Mallory especially asked Bader to lead his squadron on this mission, a wing escort for No 2 (Bomber) Group Blenheims on a bombing raid over France. Observation of German practice had shown that it was necessary for medium bombers to attack in small numbers and be escorted by large numbers of fighters. Therefore, Leigh-Mallory applied the concept of the wing to the escort. Three North Weald Sector Hurricane squadrons led by Wing Commander Victor Beamish were to escort a dozen Blenheims, formed up in two boxes of six. Another wing, of three squadrons of Spitfires, carried out a sweep.

Bader led No 242 Squadron off Martlesham Heath to join up with the other two squadrons over RAF North Weald. They picked up the bombers over RAF Hornchurch. One squadron of Hurricanes detached itself and surrounded the two bomber boxes as close escort. Bader positioned No 242 Squadron as top cover at 17,000 feet, the most difficult position; Leigh-Mallory was relying on Bader's experience. In between, the other Hurricane squadron rode as middle cover, led by Beamish, a seasoned tactician.

The formation left the English coast over Ramsgate and crossed the

French coast over Calais. Bader's pilots scanned the sky methodically, warily, watching for the Bf 109s. A few miles inland, they passed over Forêt de Guisne. The bombers bombed their target. Then the formation turned for home. There was still no response from the Luftwaffe. They crossed the French coast on the way home near Calais. No 242 Squadron returned to Martlesham Heath. The RAF fighter pilots saw nothing of the enemy, except accurate flak!

No 242 Squadron was active throughout 12 January 1941, but the day brought sadness and change for the unit. The squadron flew four 'Mosquito' patrols. It is interesting that they were flown in twos and fours, and that one of them was a lone effort. Bader (V6913) and Flight Lieutenant Turner (P3048) flew the first 'Mosquito' between 10.15 and 11.35 hours. As they swept in towards the coast of France between Dunkirk and Calais, they spotted the wake of a small vessel. It looked naval. In line astern, they strafed it, broke off into the cloud and wheeled around for another attack.

Next off at 12.15 hours were two pairs, Flying Officer McKnight (P2961) and Pilot Officer Brown (P3207), and Flying Officers Tamblyn (R4115) and Rogers (W9112). Both pairs headed for Gravelines. They fired on small vessels and machine-gunned troops on the beach. Then they were set upon by six Bf 109s, and a low-level dogfight developed, every man for himself. Tamblyn and Rogers landed back at 13.15 hours, and Brown touched down five minutes later, but Willie McKnight, DFC, failed to return. A Bf 109 had caught him at low level and gunned him down. He was killed.

At 13.25 hours, Pilot Officer John Latta (V7203) and Flying Officers Arthur (V6985), Edmunds (P3515) and Cryderman (P2982) took off on a 'Mosquito' raid. They found an interesting target, a schooner, and machine-gunned it. But again the Bf 109s had intervened. Latta failed to return. He too was dead. His death and that of McKnight were serious blows to the squadron.

At 15.00 hours, Ben Brown (P3207) flew the last 'Mosquito' of the day. It was a solo effort, an hour long and unproductive, as were so many. The loss of two experienced pilots, both very valuable to the squadron, was hard to justify in view of the results of the day's operations.

On 22 January, the squadron was engaged on convoy patrols. On one, Bader's section (Flying Officers Edmond and Cyderman) shared in the destruction of a Ju 88 east of Yarmouth. It was three against one, and Bader led the Section in for a series of passes, one fighter at a time, but then he held off to let Edmond and Cryderman have the main chance. Out of ammunition, they retired, frustrated. Bader issued the coup de grâce, a lethal burst into the cockpit area at close range; flames leapt from the bomber and it dived vertically. It was a valuable lesson for the two flying officers in conserving ammunition.

On 23 January, Squadron Leader Arthur Donaldson was posted to No 242 Squadron from No 56 OTU, 'supernumerary for Flying Duties' [ORB]. This was the youngest of Thelma Bader's three cousins. Tall, fair and good-looking, he was a fine pilot, with many flying hours. He had been an instructor on the staff of Central Flying School, and held the rank of squadron leader. As such, he was entitled to have his own squadron, but he had no operational experience. He argued long enough for someone to post him to No 242 Squadron. Although this was his cousin's husband's unit, coincidentally, it was no sinecure. Bader was recognized as a man who could teach a pilot the essentials of combat flying and survival, and who would be able to give a strict assessment of leadership qualities.

Arthur Donaldson would learn about leading in the air from Bader. It was mooted that he might take over from Bader when Bader left the squadron, but this would have been irregular for an officer from within to assume command. At the end of the learning period, Bader had to tell the AOC that Arthur Donaldson lacked the operational experience to take over command of such an aggressive, experienced squadron whose members needed firm handling. Bluntly, you had to be a bit rough to lead them. One day, for instance, Donaldson, Turner and Crowley-Milling had been flying a patrol. They intercepted a Ju 88. Arthur Donaldson was always honest. Turner and Crowley-Milling knew how to urge their aircraft for more performance, how to angle in for a shot, how to keep the hose of bullets on the target, all of which took time to learn. Donaldson just dropped farther behind. The aeroplane vanished in clouds, but Donaldson said he 'never even got a squirt at it' (Lucas).

On 28 January, the squadron was honoured by a visit to Debden by Their Majesties The King and Queen, who received Squadron Leader Bader and all the squadron's commissioned pilots.

On the evening of the 28th, both the officers and the sergeants messes had cause for a farewell celebration. Eric Ball, a cornerstone of the squadron, and Sergeant Pilots Pollard and Redfern, were leaving. The pilots let their hair down after a few tough weeks. Next day, Flight Lieutenant G. E. Ball, DFC, 'proceeded to Uxbridge on posting overseas' (ORB), while Sergeant Pilots Pollard and Redfern were posted to No 232 Squadron.

Early February brought several sweeps in wing strength. On 4 February, the ORB recorded a two-squadron sweep:

'Squadron took off in company with twelve Spitfires of No 266 Squadron to carry out offensive sweep of Boulogne area. English coast was crossed between Dover and Dungeness and landfall was made on French coast below Le Touquet where course was set for St Inglevest and out by Dunkirk. Absolutely no activity of any sort was experienced. Both Squadrons returned to Martlesham.'

On 5 February, the ORB recorded a failure of a three-squadron wing sweep:

'Squadron took off for North Weald to meet 256 and 249 Squadrons for operational flying, but did not operate with partner Squadrons. Four Hurricanes landed at North Weald, eight Hurricanes returned to base 1500 hours. Nothing to report.'

At 15.45 hours on 8 February, an experienced three-aircraft Section took off on an interception, Flight Lieutenant Stan Turner, Pilot Officer Crowley-Milling and Flying Officer Cryderman. They caught the enemy close to the coast, a Do 17. All three Hurricanes attacked and jointly shot it down in flames, but the return fire hit Laurie Cryderman's fighter and he 'reported on R/T that he was landing in the sea approximately two miles off coast.' [ORB].

Turner was back at 17.15 hours and Crowley-Milling at 16.40 hours. They had not seen Cryderman in the water. Air-Sea Rescue were on the scene swiftly, but without results. Reluctantly, Laurie Cryderman was posted missing. A few days later, Ian Smith was posted missing, too.

On 12 February, Bader went to London for a recorded interview with the British Broadcasting Corporation about the squadron's operations 'during last September's Blitz' (ORB). This was mandatory listening for the squadron, even if they did not exactly take it seriously, when it was broadcast the same evening at twenty-to-seven on the Home Service programme 'World Goes By'. Next day, it was broadcast again at half-past-twelve on the 'Forces Programme'.

On 15 February, three patrols were flown. Two of them were of three aircraft, but the last was flown by two, after one of their number had been damaged by enemy aircraft. As yet, the combat formations of the Battle of Britain endured – a 'Vic' of three, although 'Mosquito' patrols involved pairs of aeroplanes.

On 18 February, three new pilot officers reported for duty from No 56 OTU, Hicks, McKechnie and Oak-Rhind. There was no urgency for pilots to replace combat losses, and the training was unhurried. Now, pilots who had had sufficient time to master flying the Hurricane were being posted.

Also that day, there was a happy reunion for Bader when Dicky Cork reappeared, but there was sadness too for Cork to note the faces already missing. Cork brought with him Lieutenant-Commander Judd, No 880 Squadron's great bear of a Commanding Officer, to visit No 242 Squadron to introduce him to the Hurricane. They borrowed a couple of Hurricanes for some familiarization and aerobatic flying around the airfield.

Bader quickly spotted the absence of the DFC ribbon and the presence of a DSC ribbon. Cork told him an old sailor's tale, embellished with a touch of Irish. A few weeks after he had been posted back to the Royal Navy, he had visited that dangerous enclave of 'Very Senior Officers', the City of Bath. There he had been stopped by one such officer who had spotted the purple and white medal ribbon of the DFC. 'An unparalleled scene' followed. Since then, Cork had dressed 'properly'.

On 21 February, Flying Officer M. K. Brown was killed near the base. He pulled out of a dive at low altitude, but his aeroplane went into a high-speed stall and flicked into the ground. He was one of the original members of the squadron and his loss was keenly felt by the air and ground personnel.

The same day there was also cause for celebration. Squadron Leader Arthur Donaldson was posted to take command of No 263 Squadron, which was re-forming on Westland Whirlwind twin-engined single-seat fighters with four 20mm cannon. It was poetic justice. This was the unit that his brother, Squadron Leader 'Baldy' Donaldson, had died commanding during the Norwegian campaign.

February ended on two high notes for No 242 Squadron. The re-equipment of No 242 Squadron with Hurricane Mk IIs began on 21 February, when ten were received. A further eight followed on the 23rd to bring the squadron to a full establishment of eighteen machines. Then, on 24 February, Bader went to London, where, next day, he attended an investiture at Buckingham Palace when he was presented with his DFC. He returned quickly from London, keen to get his hands on the new Hurricanes.

Bader had wanted to have Hurricane Mk IIs for some months. There were detail improvements: they had the better VHF communications, a longer nose to improve stability and a larger rear-view mirror. Performance was better. Compared with the Mark I's Merlin II or III engine, the Mark II's Merlin XX produced 1,850hp at 21,000 feet and gave a marginal improvement in top speed, raised the ceiling to 36,000 feet and significantly increased the rate of climb. Moreover, the Mark IIB had a 50 per cent increase in firepower – it had a battery of twelve, not eight, .303-inch machine-guns.

March began unremarkably for No 242 Squadron, with unremarkable patrolling, but the squadron was about to be changed fundamentally. Sholto Douglas agreed to the establishment of wings at all the main Sector stations and to the creation of the post of wing commander flying at these stations. In early March 1941, Bader was summoned by Leigh-Mallory who offered him the choice of Tangmere or Biggin Hill. 'Sailor' Malan would have the one he refused.

Bader chose Tangmere. For him, Biggin Hill was too close to the distractions of London. He did not want his pilots tired out by living it up by night in the capital. He wanted them fit to fight the crack Luftwaffe fighters over the Channel. Malan accepted the command of the Biggin Hill Wing. They were the first two wing leaders. Within months, there were several more.

Bader returned to No 242 Squadron and broke the news to them. It was a week of change. In a matter of days, four pilots, including their Commanding Officer, left, and two pilots, including a new Commanding Officer, arrived at the squadron. On 11 March, Sergeants Jessop and Pollard 'proceeded to Northolt for posting', and on 13 March, Pilot Officer Surma 'proceeded to Baginton for flying duties'. Next day, the 14th, Squadron Leader W. P. F. Treacy – 'Treacle' Treacy – and Sergeant Etchells 'joined the unit for flying duties'. Then, on 16 March, the ORB baldly stated: 'S/Ldr D. R. S. Bader DSO DFC proceeded to Tangmere to take up Wing Commander's duties. Patrols carried out without incident.'

The entry in Bader's logbook was equally undemonstrative: 'Handed over command of 242 (Canadian) Squadron & posted to TANGMERE as wing commander.'

Bader wanted to take No 242 Squadron, but he knew that it was not realistic. Tangmere had three squadrons of Spitfires allocated to it. Bader and No 242 were both saddened and elated by the news. What Bader could do, however, was take his best men from No 242 Squadron. He began to make his arrangements.

☆   ☆   ☆

After Bader left and Treacy took over No 242 Squadron in mid-March, there was little other change until 28 March when Flying Officer Smith crashed at Bradfield St George during a patrol and was killed. There were now few of the Battle of Britain pilots left in the unit, and fewer of the November 1939 orignals. Pilots included: Squadron Leader Treacy; Flight Lieutenants Tamblyn and Turner; Flying Officers Arthur, Edmond, Grassick and Lang; Pilot Officers Crowley-Milling, Hicks, Kemp, McKechnie, Oak-Rhind and Richardson; and Sergeants David, Etchells, Kee, Redfern and Vaughan.

April 1941 was a very bad month for No 242 Squadron, although it had begun well. On the last day of the previous month, there had been good news for Pilot Officer Denis Crowley-Milling, the award of the DFC. On 1 April, Flight Lieutenant H. N. Tamblyn received his DFC from the King at Buckingham Palace, but only two days later his body was recovered from the sea after he had attacked a Do 17.

On 9 April, the squadron moved from Martlesham Heath to RAF Stapleford Tawney, still in the same No 11 Group Sector, North Weald. No 11 Group was about to enter an offensive phase, and No 242 Squadron was being included in the wing sweeps over France. Anticipation ran high in the squadron, but on 20 April the unit suffered a great misfortune, as the squadron's ORB recorded:

'Squadron took off for sweep. S/Ldr Treacy, F/O Edmond and F/O Lang believed to have collided in air. Three "baled out", two seen on sea, later picked up dead and found to be F/O Edmond and F/O Lang. S/Ldr Treacy missing.'

Fighter Command made good the loss of the leader rapidly, and on 23 April the charismatic Squadron Leader Whitney Straight, MC, became Commanding Officer; but within hours of his arrival, the squadron had lost Sergeant David on a night patrol. Three days later, A. J. Vaughan died when he forced-landed through lack of fuel.

The bad luck which had dogged the squadron lifted in May, and No 242 Squadron began regularly to fly sweeps with No 11 Group. On one of these, over the St Omer area on 21 May, Pilot Officer Oak-Rhind went missing. He had been with the squadron barely three months.

Stan Turner had already been 'poached' by Bader to lead a Flight of his Tangmere Wing, and on 12 June 1941 Denis Crowley-Milling was posted to Tangmere.

No 242 Squadron was no longer the unit that Bader had led. The pilots he had inspired were either dead, or posted to other fighter squadrons, or in the Tangmere Wing. However, some of the pilots who had joined other squadrons soon became outstandingly successful. Jimmy Gardner won renown flying Fairey Fulmars from HMS *Ark Royal* in the Mediterranean, but Dicky Cork had to wait for his turn to shine again. George Powell-Sheddon made a name in night-fighter operations from Malta during 1941. Two pilots who had been attached to No 242 Squadron to learn the art of fighter leadership from Bader came of age during 1941, Squadron Leaders Taylor and Donaldson.

In February, Squadron Leader W. E. G. Taylor took over the command of No 71 (Eagle) Squadron from Squadron Leader Walter Churchill, a relative of the Prime Minister. He had been groomed for this post. It was the first 'Eagle' squadron. It was Churchill's job to get the unit into shape, for all-American operations. Pronounced operational in early 1941, it was attached to No 11 Group airfields for offensive sweeps, undertaking its first on 5 February 1941, after which Taylor took over command.

Arthur Donaldson soon revealed the full potential he had been so keen to use. After his month with No 242 Squadron, Donaldson was appointed to command No 263 Squadron, which had begun re-equipment with Whirlwinds in late 1940. The squadron was very successful in its initial role of long-range and low-level bomber escort. On 12 August 1941, the medium bombers of No 2 Group, Bomber Command, made their deepest penetration so far. Fifty-four Blenheims attacked two power stations near Cologne in daylight. They were escorted by Whirlwinds of No 263 Squadron, the only fighter with the range to undertake such a mission. Later, the Whirlwind excelled in the role of intruder/fighter-bomber. It was dangerous, low-level work. Arthur Donaldson proved his qualities as a leader, and eighteen months later, in July 1942, he was posted to Malta as a wing leader – another satisfied customer of the Bader school.

PART IV

CHAPTER 11
Yorkshire Auxiliaries

T he RAF regarded the possibility of the Luftwaffe renewing its daylight offensive in the summer of 1941 on the scale of the previous year as high, but under its new commander, Air Marshal A. M. Sholto Douglas, who believed in aggressive fighter warfare, Fighter Command was now going over to the offensive. The Command was now much better prepared, tactically. No 11 Group still formed the spearhead, now commanded by Air Vice-Marshal Leigh-Mallory, a man who also believed in taking the offensive. Wings were ideally suited to offensive operations. The components already existed at sector station level; it was necessary to forge them into a coherent tactical fighting unit. Previously, squadrons in a sector had been treated as individual tactical entities under their squadron commander who was responsible to the station commander, who in turn was responsible to the sector commander; if squadrons flew together, one squadron leader was nominated as the formation leader, whch meant that tactics were never consistent and cohesion was inadequate. Now, each sector station was allocated three squadrons and a wing commander charged with co-ordinating their training and tactical employment and leading all three under his direct command as a wing in combat.

On 18 March 1941, Wing Commander Douglas Bader became Tangmere Wing Leader. The Wing flew the Spitfire Mk II, which had been introduced in the closing stages of the Battle of Britain. It was basically a Mark I re-engined with the 10 per cent more powerful 1,175hp Rolls-Royce Merlin XII, driving a de Havilland or Rotol constant-speed propeller which gave an appreciable improvement in climb and ceiling over the Mark I's two-pitch propeller. The Mark II was slightly faster than the Mark I in level flight, 370mph, and in the climb, 2,600 feet per minute, but had a one thousand foot greater ceiling, 32,800 feet. It had the same range, 395 miles, rather poor for an offensive fighter and a factor which limited RAF fighter sweeps to the Lille-Amiens area. The Mark IIA was armed with eight .303-inch machine-guns.

The Tangmere Wing comprised three squadrons, all combat tested. No 145 Squadron was a Regular Air Force unit with mainly Regular pilots. No 610 (County of Chester) Squadron was an Auxiliary Air Force unit, the majority of whose pilots were Auxiliaries. No 616 (South Yorkshire) Squadron was also an Auxiliary unit but had many Volunteer Reserve and some Regular pilots as it had been seriously depleted during the Battle of Britain. Bader had led Auxiliary units before, notably No 611 Squadron at Duxford, and had in fact led No 616 Squadron as part of the Duxford Wing the previous September.

Bader elected to lead the Tangmere Wing at the head of No 616 Squadron, with No 610 as top cover and No 145 on a flank between them. Thus it was the pilots of No 616 Squadron who were most directly exposed to Bader's thinking and leadership. This had a profound influence on several pilots in that squadron. The Squadron Commander was a Cranwell Sword of Honour Regular, Squadron Leader 'Billy' Burton. He and Bader had hit it off when they had first met at Duxford in 1940. Burton was a thorough professional. He had no qualms about Bader leading his squadron: he realized that he had much to gain from the relationship. Bader put his Spitfire in the care of No 616 Squadron's 'A' Flight, commanded by Ken Holden; the second in command was Flying Officer Hugh Dundas. From his arrival at Tangmere, Bader normally chose 'Cocky' Dundas and Pilot Officer 'Johnnie' Johnson for his Section and either Sergeant Jeff West or Allan Smith as his wingman, enabling them to learn rapidly from a superb tactician and leader.

☆   ☆   ☆

No 616 (South Yorkshire) Squadron was typical of the Auxiliary squadrons and was the last to be created. Formed at Doncaster airport, it began flying training on 5 December 1938, simultaneously launching a recruiting drive in its catchment area, South Yorkshire. Until Spitfires became available, it flew Gloster Gauntlet Mk IIs, the first of thirty arriving on 30 January 1939. Pilots and ground staff gave up considerable spare time, flying each weekend, to be ready for the onslaught that seemed not far away, but most of the young men joined because they wanted to fly. A perspective on the Services and life known as the 'Auxiliary attitude' set them apart from their Regular colleagues – a certain laissez-faire in regard to rank, an informality in dress, like red-silk-lined tunics . . .

Typical of No 616 Squadron's pilots was Hugh Spencer Lisle Dundas, who was born in Yorkshire on 22 July 1920. On leaving Stowe public school, he was indentured to a Yorkshire firm of solicitors. He wanted to fly. His elder brother, John, a promising foreign affairs journalist, had been commissioned as an Auxiliary pilot officer on 18 July 1938, flying with No 609 (West Riding) Squadron. So, attracted by No 616 Squadron's recruitment drive, Hugh Dundas applied. In early 1939, he was accepted for flying training. His application was well timed and he was attached to No 616 Squadron at Doncaster, in his catchment area.

Using six Hawker Hinds, two Avro Tutors and two Avro 504Ns, No 616 Squadron's first purely squadron-trained pilots to gain their wings were Ken Holden, Hugh Dundas and Buck Casson on 26 March, 17 June and 18 June 1939 respectively. Fairey Battles were used for pilot familiarization with enclosed-cockpit monoplane flying and the Merlin engine from May 1939. When the squadron had sufficient trained pilots, it relinquished its Hinds. It officially formed at Finningley as a fighter squadron attached to Fighter Command on 30 June 1939.

No 616 Squadron was at summer camp at Rochford (Southend), when the Auxiliary Air Force was mobilized along with Britain's other arms on 23

August. No 616 Squadron hastened back to Finningley. When war was declared on 3 September, it was not yet fully operational or embodied, although it had twenty Gauntlets, fourteen on first-line strength, but they were hardly a match for the Luftwaffe's Bf 109s or bombers.

All Auxiliary squadrons had to be brought up to Fighter Command's exacting standards: Regulars joined No 616; Squadron Leader Walter Beisiegel – 'Bike' – became Commanding Officer on 18 September and Flight Lieutenant Denys Gillam took over 'B' Flight. In late October, assigned to No 12 Group, Fighter Command, the squadron moved to its war station, Leconfield in the Church Fenton sector. On 31 October, its first Spitfires arrived from Duxford. Re-equipment was completed by December, No 616 being the last UK-based squadron to relinquish its Gauntlets.

Throughout the winter, No 616 trained intensively. It had flown a few monotonous but vital North Sea convoy patrols but flew them regularly from March. In May, Squadron Leader Marcus Robinson from No 602 (City of Glasgow) Squadron, AuxAF, became Commanding Officer and the squadron was declared fully operational. On 27 May, it moved to Rochford tasked with patrolling between Calais and Dunkirk to cover the Dunkirk evacuations, flying with Nos 19 and 65 Squadrons. It was blooded within minutes of first landing and refuelling at Rochford. The evacuation over, the unit returned to Leconfield on 6 June to resume convoy patrols, with a smattering of victories over bombers by day and night.

Thursday, 15 August 1940 was a turning point in the Battle of Britain. The Luftwaffe flew 1,786 sorties, attacking targets in the south-east of England throughout the day, but the two heavy raids it launched on the north-east were the last it launched in strength from Scandinavia. No 616 Squadron was fully involved in countering the raids. The enemy entered the area at 13.15 hours. Ten miles off Flamborough Head, No 616 Squadron encountered the enemy, who was flying in irregular formation at 15,000 feet, unescorted. The squadron turned east to bear on the enemy, and attacked. An hour later, the last bomber had gone from the north-east. No 616 Squadron claimed eight bombers destroyed.

On 19 August, No 616 Squadron was thrown into the Battle of Britain proper, posted to Kenley in No 11 Group. It had twenty-two pilots and eighteen Spitfires. Just three weeks and eight new pilots and twelve replacement Spitfires later, the squadron had only three pilots fully fit to fly. But in those three weeks, with only three days' rest, the squadron had faced the raids on the airfields, then on London, and had destroyed 23 enemy aircraft.

Dundas was among the casualties. On the evening of 22 August, the squadron was at readiness. At 18.45 hours, it was scrambled. Fourteen aircraft got into the air, an unusually high number. Dundas was one of Green Section's three pilots. At 12,000 feet, the unit arrived over Dover at about 19.30 hours, just as the second large free-chase of the evening was leaving the Kent coast. Still climbing – the most vulnerable situation – the squadron was immediately bounced by a dozen Bf 109s.

Dundas's aircraft was hit many times by a Bf 109. Shells and bullets tore into his engine, glycol tank and cockpit. His controls were smashed and his hood was jammed. He spun down out of control from 12,000 feet to below 400 feet before he managed to free the hood and bale out from the burning aircraft. His parachute jolted open and he landed only four seconds later. He was slightly wounded in leg and arm and his shoulder was dislocated, but he was traumatized by the experience of escaping death so narrowly.

The Battle's third and critical phase began on 24 August with widespread attacks on fighter stations inland. Next day, No 616 Squadron lost seven Spitfires to Bf 109s over Essex, with two pilots killed and four wounded; only Gillam scored. The free-chasing fighter battle climaxed between 30 August and 6 September, with the RAF losing the equivalent of a squadron a day.

Kenley had been bombed to a shambles. On 3 September, the severely depleted No 616 Squadron was withdrawn to Fowlmere, which it shared with No 19 Squadron. There, Squadron Leader Burton took over command but No 616 could not sustain operations, so undertook various training flights. It needed many replacement pilots. On 5 September, three young pilots joined it, fresh from OTU via No 19 Squadron who had no time to train them: Flying Officer Forshaw, Pilot Officer Johnson and Sergeant Ward, one of whom would bring fame to the unit in the months to come.

James Edgar Johnson had not found it as smooth as Hugh Dundas to gain his wings. Born on 9 March 1915, the son of a Melton Mowbray police inspector, and educated at Loughborough School, he had graduated in civil engineering from Nottingham University in 1938. He too was keen to fly and saved hard from his salary from his job near Loughton to take flying lessons. He attempted to join the somewhat socially elite Auxiliary Air Force, but the interviewing officer was most unimpressed that he spent his cash and spare time on flying and not on chasing foxes. When the Munich Crisis accelerated RAF expansion, Johnson reapplied, again unsuccessfully. He then tried the RAF Volunteer Reserve, but they had a surplus of trainee pilots. However, being a horseman, he joined the mounted Leicestershire Yeomanry, but when the RAFVR began to expand in January 1939 his application was reactivated. He began training in airmanship on weekday evenings in London and flying training over weekends on Tiger Moths at Stapleford.

European events were meanwhile gaining implacable momentum. On 23 August 1939, the RAF, Auxiliary Air Force and RAFVR were mobilized, together with Britain's other armed services. Johnson's flying course was suspended and he was called up and billeted in a Cambridge college, an instant sergeant. In December, he began his RAF ab initio flying training, a ten-week course on Tiger Moths at Marshall's of Cambridge, a civil flying training school, providing 25 hours dual and 25 hours solo. He completed the course with 84 hours' flying time logged.

On completion, pupil pilots went to RAF Uxbridge for two weeks' disciplinary training, before going to a Flying Training School (FTS). The FTS course was divided into two terms, Intermediate Training Squadron for basic flying training and an Advanced Training Squadron which encompassed navigation, instrument flying and night flying. Pupils spent thirteen weeks and flew about 50 hours in each term. In the ITS, pupils did five hours in the Link

Trainer and on average 50 hours of flying; and in the ATS, 6½ hours on the Link and an average of 45 hours' flying. In the ITS the pupil went solo after four or five hours' dual, and then made his advanced solo after seventeen or so hours. In the ITS, about half the time was solo, but in the ATS, over 80 per cent of the time was solo. Courses were run for about forty trainees, of whom three-quarters made it. The ATS course lasted six weeks. Under this arrangement much was done to relieve the service squadrons of the individual training tasks that had been theirs – applied training such as night flying, navigation and armament.

After enduring his fortnight at Uxbridge, Johnson passed to No 5 Service Flying Training School at RAF Sealand, Cheshire. He flew Miles Masters for enclosed cockpit and instrument training. Johnson soloed after two dual flights. When the course ended in July, he had accumulated 180 hours of flying time. No 48 Course of forty-one pupils completed ITS training and transferred to ATS on 1 July; thirty-four completed training on 10 August. That day, Johnson was commissioned as a pilot officer (probationary) – the probationary period was twelve months – and posted to No 57 OTU, at RAF Hawarden, Chesire, to fly the Spitfire.

At OTU, trainees flew some twenty hours in operational types under experienced instructors before being passed to squadrons who would give further training prior to the pilot's release for combat duty. Preparation is a key to survival in air combat, let alone success. Johnson had high hopes of learning how to fight in the air at Hawarden, especially as the instructors had recently fought in France. But there were too few instructors and too few hours to do more than familiarize the fledglings with the Spitfire – not to know how to fight in it. Moreover, the squadrons had no time to give new pilots combat training, as it was the height of the Battle of Britain. In spite of crashing after a bad landing, Johnson completed the course with just 23 hours on Spitfires.

Johnson was luckier than many inexperienced pilots that summer who were thrown into the intense air fighting without real training in the arts of fighting and surviving. On 2 September 1940, Johnson and two other pilots, Forshaw and Ward, were posted to No 19 Squadron at Fowlmere, a Duxford satellite. As narrated in Chapter 7, No 19 Squadron, equipped with cannon-armed Spitfire Mk IBs, was a frustrated unit: there was too little action, and when there was, their cannon jammed. The day Johnson arrived, there were four squadron patrols, all unrewarding, and the squadron's spirits fell further when told that they were probably to be withdrawn to Digby as a result of their armament problems. The squadron was too busy even to get their new pilots' names right – Johnson was recorded in the ORB as 'Johnstone'.

The following day brought greater satisfaction with two victories and the news that they would swap their Spitfires for eight-gun machines the very next day. But the new pilots still did not get to be initiated properly for, on 5 September, No 19 Squadron's Commanding Officer, Pinkham, was killed in combat. The unit was too preoccupied to deal with unblooded pilots. Therefore, on the 5th 'F/O Forshaw, P/O Johnston and Sergt. Ward posted to No 611 Squadron at Digby' [ORB].

The posting was reversed as soon as it was made. No 611 had no time to train pilots with less than 30 hours on Spitfires in the art of fighting and staying alive. Ironically for Johnson, the three new pilots were posted to an Auxiliary squadron – No 616. It needed replacements but was about to be rotated north for rest. Its ORB sums up its position on 5 September: 'No operational flying. Various training flights took place. F/O Forshaw. P/O Johnson and Sgt Ward posted from 19 Squadron.'

It was at Coltishall that No 616 Squadron first encountered Douglas Bader, commanding No 242 Squadron. His magnetic personality galvanized the unit, and inspired Johnson. No 616 Squadron continued operations for a few days nominally with the Duxford Sector 'Big Wing', but on 9 September moved to RAF Kirton-in-Lindsey, Lincolnshire, its home base, to rest and train replacement pilots, displacing No 74 Squadron. The base had recently been transferred from No 12 to No 13 Group. Several of No 616 Squadron's pilots were transferred to other squadrons. Denys Gillam left to take command of No 312 Squadron, the second Czech fighter unit to be formed, and Flight Lieutenant Colin Macfie took over his 'B' Flight. No 616 Squadron was one of six Auxiliary Air Force squadrons to take part in the Battle of Britain, but, apart from a few uneventful operations as part of the Duxford 'Big Wing' in late September, its role was now over. Dundas had rejoined the squadron. He flew on these 'Big Wings'. Dundas found that Bader's cool, humorous leadership in the air helped him greatly to get his nerves in shape after his bad experience. Dundas knew that he could rely totally on Bader as a leader.

Johnson was placed in 'A' Flight, commanded by Flight Lieutenant Ken Holden, who had served with the unit since its formation in 1938. Dundas was in the same Flight. Throughout the autumn of 1940, against the sombre background of the escalating German night Blitz against Britain, the squadron engaged in air exercises and training flights, enabling Johnson to familiarize himself with the Spitfire and combat flying, for which he was grateful. He did not forget this experience when he later dealt with new pilots under his command.

No 616 Squadron undertook East Coast convoy patrols again, destroying two bombers during these missions. Convoy patrols permitted new pilots – many straight from OTUs – to gain experience before joining No 12 Group operations with the Duxford Wing under Bader. No 616 Squadron was in action with the Wing on 27 September, when Ken Holden and Sergeant Copeland fought with Bf 109s, but Pilot Officer D. S. Smith was mortally wounded.

To enable No 616 Squadron to rebuild, one Flight left for Ringway, Manchester, while the other Flight busily trained seven new NCO pilots. However, 'Johnnie' Johnson went into hospital in November to have his collar bone reset – an old rugby fracture which had been causing pain since his crash at OTU. It came close to ending his combat flying career but he rejoined the squadron just into the new year.

On 28 November 1940, Dundas's elder brother, John, was killed. He was a Flight Commander with No 609 Squadron. Engaging Bf 109s off the Isle of Wight, with other No 609 Squadron Spitfires, he shot down Major Helmut

Wieck, the Luftwaffe's leading ace, but was immediately shot down by Wieck's wingman. He had amassed 13½ victories. His loss profoundly affected Hugh Dundas.

Dundas was now in Holden's 'A' Flight. From around New Year, Pilot Officer J. E. Johnson began to fly as his wingman. Shortly afterwards, Johnson had his first combat. On 15 January 1941, Dundas and Johnson were at readiness section. Twice the dispersal operational telephone rang, but the third sent them climbing hard out over the North Sea after a raider.

Vectored by the Sector Controller, they found the two target convoys, and then spotted the Do 17. They were just in time. They dived on the raider from up-sun, but it spotted them and turned south-east for home. The fighters each attacked twice in rotation. Dundas, as senior pilot, attacked first. Dundas hit the port engine which began to smoke, and the undercarriage fell down. Johnson followed, but opened fire too soon – a lesson he remembered. Dundas bored in again, silencing the rear gunner. On his second attack, Johnson pressed in close and scored hard hits. The bomber's rear gun had stopped firing, its undercarriage had dropped and its port engine smoked, but before Dundas could go in again the bomber escaped into cloud and they lost it. A kill could not be confirmed and the pilots were credited with a 'shared damaged'.

The offensive phase in No 616 Squadron's existence began on Wednesday, 26 January 1941 when it was posted back to No 11 Group, to join Nos 145 and 610 Squadrons at Tangmere. It relieved No 65 Squadron, and exchanged its Spitfire Mk Is for No 65 Squadron's Mark IIAs, after which No 65 flew back to Kirton to begin their rest.

The Tangmere squadrons began training to fly as a wing, and also took part in fighter sweeps over France. The three squadron leaders took it in turn to lead the squadrons. By March 1941, the squadrons were slowly gaining proficiency. When they were not busy with operations, they did a considerable amount of exercises of various types, including local reconnaissance flights, ciné-gun practice, formation flying, fighter attacks and gun tests, and, more occasionally, battle climbs and 'squadron Balbos'. In the late afternoon of 4 March, Nos 145, 610 and 616 Squadrons undertook practice wing operations, including a sector reconnaissance and a battle climb. However, the following day, an operation revealed shortcomings. The Tangmere squadrons were detailed to act as high wing cover for bombers on a raid into France. Taking off separately, the three squadrons rendezvoused over Hastings at approximately 13.00 hours. It was an unsatisfactory operation, as No 616 Squadron saw neither the bombers nor the other two squadrons after leaving the English coast. They were all back at Tangmere by 15.00 hours. There was much to learn.

They were also exploring modes of operation, especially at high altitude. On 9 March, a section of No 616 Squadron made a battle climb to 30,000 feet where the Spitfires' guns were test-fired, because the outer port and starboard guns sometimes failed to fire above that altitude due to cold. This was a necessary prelude to the operation the following day, 10 March, when three sections of No 616 Squadron (nine aircraft) took part, flying a high-altitude sweep with Nos 145 and 610 Squadrons. They crossed the English coast over Hastings. No 616 Squadron flew at 31,000 feet, very near the Spitfire Mk II's fighting ceiling. They flew over Calais and Boulogne, returning over Dover. They did not meet any enemy aircraft and experienced no flak at that altitude. This, like many of the activities in this period, was an experiment.

That night, 10/11 March 1941, No 616 Squadron mounted two 'Layer Patrols' over Portsmouth, each of four aircraft. Known as 'Fighter Night' in No 12 Group, flown at high moon, the objective was to pick out enemy bombers silhouetted by searchlights. In order to cover the sky, fighters flew up and down a designated patrol line, above the heavy anti-aircraft fire zones, stacked up at thousand-foot intervals from 13,000 to 23,000 feet. It was a frustrating task in a Spitfire for the wings obscured downward vision, the nose obscured forward vision and the exhausts gouting away feet from the eyes destroyed peripheral vision. When there was bomber activity, the intensity of fires and bomb flashes masked the bombers. The re-equipment of Tangmere's fourth squadron, No 219, with twin-engined Bristol Beaufighters with airborne interception radar changed the success rate of interceptions at night in the sector; both equipment and aircrew training were appropriate. Single-seat day pilots were trained to fight as part of a cohesive, nervous formations reliant upon long sight, not as a calm, cunning, solitary stalker.

On 13 March, the Wing flew another high-level sweep. No 145 Squadron flew top cover at 39,000 feet, No 616 ten thousand feet below and No 610 a thousand feet lower. The squadrons each flew in four sections of three, in 'Vics', in line astern or boxes, as they had done during 1940. The Wing crossed the French coast at Cap Gris Nez. Nos 145 and 616 Squadrons saw no enemy aircraft, but No 610 became engaged in a small action and destroyed a Bf 109, but also lost a Spitfire.

On 18 March, Wing Commander Douglas Bader arrived. The immediate effect was that sweeps ceased, although section patrolling continued, and the amount of exercises and their intensity was stepped up considerably. Bader was reshaping the Tangmere Wing.

☆　　　　　☆　　　　　☆

The Tangmere squadrons had not flown together operationally as a wing. For the next eight weeks, the Tangmere Wing was engaged in flying a routine of base patrols, convoy patrols over Selsey Bill, St Catherine's Point and other nearby points over which the enemy might enter the Wing's sector. More importantly, the Wing was also involved in a constant training programme overseen by Bader to prepare them for offensive wing operations. Bader swiftly won the Wing's confidence. He had his initials 'D-B' painted on his Spitfire in place of codes, a wing commander's privilege, the better to identify him in a fast fight. It also led the Station Commander to give him the call-sign 'Dogsbody'. As Bader led at the head on No 616 Squadron, the activities of that squadron are those principally followed in this narrative.

At midday on 19 March, the new Wing Leader got his command moving with a wing patrol at 30,000 feet over Hastings by Nos 610 and 616

Squadrons. The latter thought they saw a pair of Bf 110s, which disappeared. Wings were not yet permitted to cross the French coast, so the majority of operations were along the British coast and out into the Channel. There were two scrambles in the morning by No 616 Squadron's Blue and Green Sections. Exercises that day included air drill, aerobatics, ciné-gun, dog-fighting and local flying.

On 20 March, bad visibility and low cloud prevented flying. Next day, there were exercises and five scrambles when all sections went up on various patrols, chiefly of the Isle of Wight and a convoy. On 22 March, bad weather returned, so pilots used the Link Trainer and attended lectures instead of flying. The weather improved the next day and considerable flying was done. The exercises included a squadron 'Balbo' of twelve aircraft – a most useful exercise for wing operations. There were three scrambles when Red, Yellow and Blue Sections were ordered to patrol St Catherine's Point and Selsey Bill. Flying Officer Casson flew a dusk patrol, taking off at 19.29 hours. On 24 March, No 616 Squadron undertook two flying practice sessions, and mounted five scrambles, all sections taking off and patrolling St Catherine's Point and Selsey Bill. The next morning, a battle climb and dogfighting were practised, together with three scrambles, in two of which a patrol was made over a convoy. The weather deteriorated in the late afternoon and stayed bad the next day, with low clouds and rain preventing flying.

On 27 March, the local, formation and aerobatic practices were overshadowed by a combat success. 'B' Flight's Blue Section, Flight Lieutenant Colin Macfie and Sergeant Sellars, was scrambled at 14.36 hours to patrol base at 15,000 feet. After nearly three-quarters of an hour in the air, during which the pilots had climbed to 30,000 feet, they were vectored on to two smoke trails 10 miles south-east of Selsey Bill, but these soon petered out. Shortly before 15.30 hours, the Fighter Controller gave Macfie another vector. When the section was nearly over Arundel at 28,000 feet, the Controller told Macfie that there should be a 'bogey' ahead. Colin Macfie recorded:

'Almost immediately I sighted 1 Me 110, which passed 500' above us flying in opposite direction. When we had turned, the E.A. was about a mile in front. It went into a vertical dive and crossed the coast E. of Littlehampton, flying S. I got within range 10 to 15 miles out to sea and closed from 250 to 150 yds firing several short bursts, amounting to about 6 secs. (200 rds per gun). The rear gunner opened up when I was well out of range (600 yds). I concentrated on port engine, and saw two flashes from it, and a cloud of oil came out, which I found on my machine when I landed. I broke away in order to deliver an attack from the beam, but my windscreen iced up completely inside and while trying to clear this, I lost E/A.'

The enemy had descended to 1,000 feet, where the attack was delivered. Macfie landed at Tangmere at 15.50 hours, and claimed a 'damaged'. Sellars had lost both Macfie and the enemy when icing obscured his vision. He had no luck: he forced-landed near Durrington because of a faulty petrol gauge, the R/T breaking down and the frosting over of his perspex hood. Later, there was an unproductive scramble by Green Section and a solo dusk patrol by Sergeant McDevette.

Poor weather intervened on the 28th and 29th, with no operations other than a scramble at 17.38 hours on the 29th when Yellow Section was ordered to patrol St Catherine's Point. However, on the 29th, six aircraft flew to RAF Sutton Bridge for air firing, then flew back. This was a most useful exercise, when the fighter pilots could assess their own abilities at shooting – too few were any good without training.

On 30 March, one battle climb and three scrambles were carried out. Blue Section, patrolling St Catherine's Point, sighted a Ju 88 but lost it in clouds before they got near enough to engage. One dusk patrol was flown. There was air drill and local flying after lunch on the 31st, but otherwise the squadron was busy with standing patrols – eight, mainly over base and Portsmouth.

Although the first day of April was very cloudy and there was no flying, the weather improved on Monday, the 2nd. A detailed description of the next week shows the kind of routine of operations and training that No 616 Squadron pilots had during the period March to June 1941. Thus, at 06.20 hours on the 2nd, Blue Section was scrambled to patrol over Tangmere, landing an hour later. Meanwhile, Green Section came to readiness and was scrambled at 06.34 to patrol Selsey Bill. From morning until early afternoon, a number of pilots undertook local flying practice, but the weather closed in again during the afternoon. At 14.58, a lone Spitfire was scrambled to patrol base for twelve minutes.

On 3 April, a Tuesday, considerable flying was done. In the morning and early afternoon there was air-to-sea firing, ciné-gun practice and formation flying to enliven the routine. The squadron came to readiness in the late afternoon, and there were four scrambles to 'patrol base'. At 16.59 hours, Red Section was scrambled to patrol base, followed by Yellow Section six minutes later. Yellow was down at 17.30 hours, and Red seven minutes later. At 18.37 hours, Blue Section, then Green at 18.46 scrambled to 'patrol base'. Blue landed at 19.05 hours, Green at 19.25. A solitary aircraft undertook a dusk patrol over Selsey Bill, taking off at 19.17, landing 35 minutes later.

On 4 April, there was formation flying, sector reconnaissance, dog-fighting and ciné-gun practice. The only operational flying was two consecutive patrols over the base in the late afternoon by Red Section (18.08–19.12 hours) and Yellow Section (19.10–20.03), and a dusk patrol over Selsey Bill (19.50–20.35).

On 5 April, training continued with a squadron battle climb and sector reconnaissances. There were two section scrambles at 11.54 hours: Green to patrol Shoreham, returning at 12.35, and Blue to patrol St Catherine's Point, returning at 11.57. On 6 April, poor weather prevented operational flying, although there was a sector reconnaissance and local formation flying. The next day, two scrambles occupied the whole squadron. At 10.49 hours, 'A' Flight (Red and Yellow Sections) was ordered to patrol Shoreham; they were back an hour later. At 11.45 hours, 'B' Flight (Blue and Green Sections) scrambled to patrol St Catherine's Point for an hour, landing at 13.00 hours.

In addition, a battle climb, ciné-gun practice and local flying were carried out.

On 8 April, there were three scrambles: Red Section patrolled base between 07.39 and 08.34 hours; Blue patrolled base between 16.53 and 17.25; Green patrolled Selsey Bill between 19.16 and 19.40. The squadron also flew ciné-gun practice and a 'GL Carpet Run', a practice bomber interception in co-operation with the Army's Gun-Laying 'Radio Direction Finding' (Radar) sets in the area.

The 9th was a busy day. There were five section scrambles in which the squadron was occupied in covering convoys and a battleship: Blue (Shoreham, 13.20–13.51 hours); Green (St Catherine's Point, 13.34–15.00); Red (Convoy, 13.50–15.22); Yellow (St Catherine's Point, 13.55–14.58); and Blue (Convoy, 15.10–16.50 hours). To show that the Luftwaffe had not forgotten about Fighter Command, a Ju 88 dive-bombed Tangmere and 'caused quite a lot of damage' [ORB]. With two long pre-war runways that lay partly uncamouflaged (the civil contractors were being tardy in camouflaging the base) and its proximity to easily identified coastline and waterways, Tangmere was easy to find from the air, for friend and foe. There were several attacks on Tangmere during these weeks – one nearly demolished the mess and a score or more of pilots during 'happy hour'.

That night, 9/10 April, No 616 Squadron flew two Layer Patrols. Five pilots took part in each, patrolling a line between Tangmere and Bembridge. The enemy objective was Portsmouth.

On the 10th, local flying, ciné-gun practice and cloud flying were undertaken. There were scrambles at 11.50 and 11.55 hours when Red and Yellow Sections patrolled St Catherine's Point and base. The return of good weather the next day allowed much aerobatic and local flying to be done. There were two dawn patrols carried out by single aircraft and six scrambles later, mainly to patrol Selsey Bill and Shoreham. On 12 April, ciné-gun, local flying and flight air drill were carried out, and there were two section scrambles, both after lunch when Blue patrolled Littlehampton and Green patrolled Bembridge. On the 13th, in addition to three patrols over convoys, there was 'concentrated formation practice under the supervision of Wing Commander Bader' [ORB].

On 14 April, apart from night flying training in the early hours of the morning, the squadron was busy with seven various patrols, including one at dawn and one at dusk. The squadron was at readiness most of the next day, so only local flying and individual aerobatics were carried out, but there was a continuous patrol over Selsey Bill for convoy protection. A more adventurous assignment perked up weary spirits when thirteen Spitfires were ordered to escort bombers returning from a raid on Brest. It was a start.

There was one base patrol and two dusk patrols on 16 April, but it was 'a good day for training flying' [ORB] and much was done with sector reconnaissance, fighter attacks and dogfighting at 25,000 feet, and ciné-gun practice, local flying, searchlight co-operation and aerobatics. 'Aerobatics' in the ORB frequently meant the Wing Leader, either solo or with Burton, performing at low level over the station in defiance of regulations. It buoyed up the pilots' spirits to see their Wing Leader misbehaving and gave them confidence in his ability when they saw the beauty he could extract from an aeroplane in flight. His favourite stunt was to try to pull off the very difficult three slow upwards rolls – nearly always falling out of the third in an untidy recovery.

This was one of Bader's ways of raising the stakes and keeping his wing interested. However, a few days earlier Leigh-Mallory had called Bader, Malan, Peel, Broadhurst, Kellett and other wing leaders to his HQ at RAF Uxbridge. He told them that although the results from the 'Circus' operations were mixed so far, the wings would soon start to work up for full-scale offensive operations over northern France.

The Tangmere Wing flew its first 'Circus' operation on the afternoon of 17 April. Local flying and flight practice occupied the morning in preparation. In the afternoon, the squadron came to readiness but, as the ORB recorded, there was an anti-climax. The squadron was scrambled 'to act as bomber escort over Le Havre and Cherbourg. Bombers failed to find their target'.

On 18 April, the squadron flew patrols in the morning over Beachy Head and Shoreham. One section acted as a Lysander escort in the early afternoon. There was local flying in the afternoon. The next day, there was dogfighting, air drill, aerobatics and local flying, two patrols over a convoy, one over Selsey Bill and a fourth over base. On the 20th, the squadron's principal occupation was constant patrols over the base when at readiness because of enemy activity over the French coast and the uncertainty of the identity of aircraft coming over the English Coast. In the early afternoon, there was dogfighting, aerobatics and local flying practice.

No 616 Squadron had its first taste of hostile attentions over France on 21 April, but sadly also sustained its first combat loss from Tangmere during a sweep. The ORB recorded:

> 'The Squadron of twelve aircraft took off at 07.47 to escort Blenheims on a bombing operation over Le Havre. Unfortunately the bombers did not find their target and flew west of it. As our fighters were running short of petrol they had to leave the bombers and on the return journey Sergeant R. L. Sellars was shot at by a Me 109 and baled out over the sea. One aircraft remained over him and transmitted in order to obtain a "fix". Eight aircraft took off later on, in order to escort a Lysander and make a further search, but no trace was found.'

The 22nd April was a 'busy operational day'. Eight scrambles, mainly patrols over base and Selsey Bill, were made. Local reconnaissances and an interception exercise were the only training carried out. The squadron carried out local formation and local flying, gun firing and battle climb on the 23rd, plus six scrambles, chiefly over convoys entering the Solent. Convoy patrols might be boring and rarely eventful, but convoys were the lifeblood of Great Britain, and the very presence of fighters over a convoy had become a strong deterrent to German anti-shipping operations.

On 24 April, two offensive patrols, 'Rhubarbs', were carried out by two pairs of aircraft. First, Dundas and Sergeant Mabbett (Red Section) took off at 14.25 hours and crossed the French coast between Dieppe and Le Tréport and turned north-east towards Abbeville. They saw no enemy aircraft and landed at 15.48 hours. Next, Macfie and Sergeant McDevette (Blue Section) took off at 14.35 hours and flew to the Cherbourg area. Blue 1 dived on Maupertus aerodrome and machine-gunned at least seven Bf 109s on the ground, two of which were taking off. Macfie returned at 15.41 hours but he had not seen Blue 2 again after they regained the French coast and 'was probably shot down by A.A. or another fighter, but every hope is entertained that he is alive' [ORB].

On 25 April, despite being rather cloudy, there was a great deal of flying practice, notably air-to-sea firing, fighter attacks and ciné-gun practice. There were two scrambles, one over base at 18.55 hours and one over Selsey Bill at 19.56 hours.

On 26 April, there was a high-altitude offensive patrol over the French coast: Macfie and Dundas took off at 17.10 hours, but saw no enemy aircraft and nothing of interest. Training included local formation practice and cloud flying. There were six scrambles, most of them over base and Shoreham. Even when there was good weather, German single-seat fighters were seldom seen over England.

On 27 April, the squadron flew eight patrols, mainly over the sea to protect convoys and minesweepers. Another five pilots flew over to Sutton Bridge for air-to-ground firing practice; they also did cloud flying. During the morning of 28 April, cloud and local formation practices were carried out, followed later by a patrol over Bembridge, but the 'main activity took place after tea when almost continual convoy patrol was made, altogether nine in number' [ORB].

There were four scrambles early in the morning of 29 April to patrol over their own base and nearby RAF Ford. The new pilots and non-operational pilots spent the rest of the day in local and formation flying and practice dogfighting. Once the new pilots had honed their skills in such sessions, they still had much to learn, as attested by the eleven operational No 616 Squadron pilots who took off behind Bader at 13.53 hours that afternoon and headed for France with No 610 Squadron as a two-squadron wing. They formed part of an escort for No 2 (Bomber) Group Blenheims which were returning from operations over the French coast. Johnson was the instrument that taught the new relatively inexperienced squadron an essential lesson.

Returning from France, No 616 Squadron was flying in three sections of four in line astern – a formation they were testing – when Johnson spotted three Bf 109s above, and yelled over the R/T: 'Look out! Huns!' The Spitfire formation disintegrated while a lone Bf 109 plunged harmlessly through the chaos, loosing off cannon shells. The Spitfires landed back at Westhampnett in one and twos. When Johnson got back to base, Bader gave him a public lecture which left an indelible memory as to the absolute importance of reporting *calmly* to the leader the height, bearing and strength of enemy formations, and of taking appropriate and cohesive action.

It was very cloudy on 30 April, and there was little activity, except for a patrol over Beachy Head at 10 o'clock. However, advantage was taken of the weather to give new pilots cloud flying experience. Operational pilots had to be content with local formation practice.

There was a regular flow of new pilots from the OTUs to the Tangmere Wing squadrons. No 616 took on a distinctly Empire flavour and lost its Auxiliary predominance. During April, it received five from Grangemouth OTU. Three arrived on the 1st, Pilot Officer R. M. Lintoot and two New Zealand sergeants, R. C. Brewer and, a man to note, Jeffrey C. West. On the 17th and 19th respectively, Pilot Officer E. P. S. Brown and Sergeant E. Sherwood, a Rhodesian, arrived. On the 21st, Pilot Officer R. G. Sutherland, RCAF, followed from Heston OTU.

There were several ways to be taken off operations without wanting to be taken off. On 23 April, there was great disappointment for one No 616 Squadron pilot, Sergeant Walters. He fainted in the air but managed to recover himself and the aircraft and land at base. The Medical Officer was quick to examine him. The ORB recorded the result: '. . . ear trouble and it is very doubtful whether he will resume fighter pilot duties'. A week later, on 27 April, there was an accident that could have been avoided. It drew serious disapproval, and could have resulted in punishment. Sergeant Mabbett of No 616 Squadron had, as the ORB stated: ' . . . landed at dusk with his undercarriage up. . . . This accident was entirely due to negligence on the pilot's part'. The Spitfire was a write-off. As a routine transfer, a week later on 4 May, Mabbett was posted within the Wing to No 610 Squadron, but was later posted back to No 616 Squadron's 'A' Flight.

The month of May began with dismal weather and the continuance of the ban on flying over the French coast. On May Day, low clouds meant little activity and prevented training flights, but three convoy patrols were carried out by the experienced pilots of No 616 Squadron. The next day, the squadron's readiness section flew four patrols, three over the base and one over a convoy. The low cumulus cloud was put to good use. The squadron was introduced to 'ZZ' procedures: let-down through cloud under radio control. The base had a radio caravan with direction-finding equipment. On hearing a radio transmission from an aircraft, the DF operator in the caravan would establish the aircraft's relative direction and then give the pilot a QDM, a magnetic course to steer to reach base, followed by further QDMs for accuracy. Once the aircraft had passed overhead – judged by a null signal on the operator's equipment – it was sent out along a safe path (clear of mountains or other obstacles) along a series of QDRs (magnetic course to steer away from base) for a specified distance. The pilot was then instructed to do a 180-degree turn and was brought back by QDMs. All the while the pilot was losing height as directed. The process was repeated until the pilot was in visual contact with the airfield. This was a very useful technique for a pilot who had become disorientated during combat over enemy territory, especially as pilots had to make landfall on the English coast only along certain corridors – the other zones were covered by trigger-happy anti-aircraft gunners! This was one of the techniques which made the highly controlled yet flexible offensive fighter operations of 1941 possible.

On 3 May, the operational pilots of the squadron flew a twelve-aircraft 'Balbo' and then practised fighter attacks – not the Fighting Area doctrines but attacks under the direction of Douglas Bader. The routine of patrols also continued with two section patrols and a dusk patrol by one aircraft.

Although 4 May was a 'lovely day but not very much activity', there was a foretaste of action. Camera-gun practice, dogfighting and aerobatics were carried out. There were two patrols. The foretaste came when Macfie's 'A' Flight was scrambled to provide withdrawal escort for bombers returning from operations over France.

On 5 May, there were two section patrols – and action! On the first patrol, two of No 616 Squadron's veteran fighters, Pilot Officer Roy Marples and Flying Officer 'Buck' Casson, attacked a Ju 88, but Casson's aircraft was badly damaged by cannon fire. He was forced to bale out, landing east of Littlehampton, uninjured but 'peeved'. There were no fewer than four patrols flown at dusk by single aircraft. The 6th was a lovely flying day, but the squadron's operational members were occupied mainly with patrolling convoys; there was one dusk patrol.

As Wing Leader, Bader was responsible for inducting the new pilots, and the tactical framework of the Wing was his decision. He delegated to squadron leaders the training tasks, but he took a direct personal interest in his pilots. At first, after a rigorous period of local, formation and aerobatic flying, then practice attacks and dogfighting, the new pilots were put on convoy patrols, then point patrols and scrambles, before flying a first sweep in the middle of the formation.

Sunday, 7 May was overcast, ideal for cloud flying practice, but Bader also introduced fighter attacks to the practice flying. There was one patrol over Selsey Bill and one dusk patrol, after which one of those parties developed in the mess. Bader was the centre of attention as always, ebullient, charismatic, and the talk as always was of tactics, fighting and bringing down Germans. In common with other wings, the Tangmere Wing had begun rewriting fighter tactics and re-applying old lessons. The lessons of the Battle of Britain had not been forgotten in this offensive mood. The 'Vic' and 'line-astern' battle formations of the peacetime and 1939–40 RAF were suitable for attacking large, unescorted bomber formations. The events of 1940 had shown them to be seriously lacking against determined fighter escorts. They were also difficult to lead as more than one squadron. Bader had his own theories about tactics.

The fighter attacks practised that day had raised controversy. The squadron had been experimenting with flying in three sections of four in line astern, as Malan advocated. The fourth man was the weaver and was as vulnerable to being picked off as he was in a 'Vic' or a 'Five'. Bader invited comments from the pilots gathered round with their half-pint and pint pots that Sunday evening. Dundas suggested the idea of flying four abreast, rather than in 'Vics' of three. A long discussion ensued, with many pilots giving their views. Based on observing the successful German Rotte, the 'finger-four' consisted of two sections of two aircraft. Each section would be composed of a leader and a wingman flying 50 yards apart. The wingman's duty would be to guard his leader at all times, but not to engage the enemy themselves. One section leader would be the unit's leader. The four aircraft would be disposed in relation to each other as the fingers of an outstretched hand, and staggered in height. The wingmen would look inwards and behind; the leaders looked forwards and outwards – thus everyone would cover everyone else. It would permit total visual cover of the sky, and would be defensive and offensive. It was what the Germans flew.

Perfecting the tactic would take time, but for Bader it was a matter of urgency: the fighting season was upon them! Early next morning, a bleary-eyed Dundas and Squadron Leader 'Paddy' Woodhouse, Commanding Officer of No 610 Squadron, and one of his pilots, Sergeant Mains, were dragged into the air by a breezy, teetotal Bader keen to try the idea out. Dundas flew Number 2, wingman to Bader. Woodhouse and his wingman, Mains, made up the second section, Numbers 3 and 4. They took off at 11.00 hours on a 'high-altitude offensive sweep over the Channel'. Just what Bader wanted to happen, happened. Over the Straits of Dover, they ran into six Bf 109s from Jagdgeschwader 51.

Bader took the four fighters at 25,000 feet towards Dunkirk. A thin vapour trail appeared behind the fighters. He dropped the section to eliminate that tell-tale sign. Then he swung a full 180 degrees to starboard as they approached the French coast on a westerly heading. They would be within range of the German radars. Bader was teasing the Germans. They just cleared Calais. Woodhall called up to say that he had detected 'trade' in the area. Bader was not surprised. All four pilots scanned the sky. Dundas saw them first – up high and behind – as one of the enemy slipped too high and made a condensation trail. He told Bader: six Bf 109s at five o'clock high, three miles behind them. Bader located them assessed their intentions and said: 'OK. I've got them. Now wait for it everyone! Wait for it!' The four pilots flew on with their stomachs churning, as if they had not seen the enemy fighters. They could see the Bf 109s scything down, thinking they had got a beautiful set-piece . . . Then Bader called 'BREAK!'

Bader broke left. Dundas followed closely in the tightest turn he could remember, to come round on the Bf 109s' tails. But they lost sight of the other pair which had broken right. And Dundas lost sight of the Bf 109s. Suddenly, cannon shells struck Dundas's wing roots and glycol tank. Gushing white smoke, Dundas lost height. With Woodhouse screening him, he just made RAF Hawkinge.

Dundas had to come in too high and too fast. His engine died. He bellied in at 150mph, and bounced to a scrapyard halt just short of a line of factory-fresh Spitfires for No 91 Squadron. The unit's Commanding Officer was an Auxiliary too, but he blistered any camaraderie to ashes with his choice reprimand. Hawkinge was losing too many aircraft to too frequent strafings, while only a month before, Czech pilots had cascaded on to the airfield in a wet panic to land all at the same time. The Commanding Officer was very upset. Dundas was badly shaken. His Spitfire Mk IIA (P7827 QJ–A 'Cock of the North') was badly bent. Mains had a damaged tail and landed at another airfield.

Bader only made rude comments to Dundas on his return to Tangmere and then announced that he had found the errors and the solutions. He was satisfied that the basic formation had been proved, but they seemed to have mistimed the break, so that one or more of the enemy fighters was behind them when they broke, and so could fire on a wide target. The two wingmen had turned inside the last two Bf 109s, which opened fire on them as they turned, hitting both. The moment for calling the break was critical and it was essential to retain a cohesive defensive and offensive formation and to keep sight of the other aircraft and observe their tails. The two pairs ought not to have broken outwards, but either the same way, or crossed below and above one another. The wingman would fly further from the leader to prevent collision. The essence was to cover the leader, who did the killing.

In this encounter on 7 May, six Bf 109s and four Spitfires were involved. Back at Tangmere, Bader claimed one 'destroyed' and a 'probable' and Woodhouse a 'probable', for the loss of one Spitfire. Back at Wissant, Oberst Werner Mölders, Jagdgeschwader 51's Commanding Officer, submitted his Combat Mission Report Number 292, claiming his sixty-eighth combat victory, a Spitfire off Dover. It is a matter of historical irony that the leader of the German section who attacked the first Schwarme flown by RAF fighters should have been the man who had introduced it to the German fighter arm during the fighting over Spain!

The 'finger-four' gave considerably more flexibility and safety to aggressors in enemy air space than the defender-orientated 'Vic' or the 'five'. The line-abreast formation gave pilots more room, more manoeuvring space, less need to keep attention on formation. It provided a greater margin of security. In turns, each pair would cross over, to maintain cohesion, so that neither ended up on the wide outside arc. If the wingman was on the inside of a turn, he went low so that the other pair would swing to the top; if he were on the outside, his would be the highest aeroplane in the turn, and the other pair would slide inside the leader. Thus, no one would lose sight of each other, and they could keep the cross-over manoeuvre fluid even in the tightest of turns.

One pair flew 100 to 150 yards apart. Each pilot looked inwards. The pilot on the left led and navigated and kept watching the sky to his right. His Number 2 on his right concentrated on his leader to his left. Thus, two pairs together would survey the whole sky – pilots would dip their noses to see down in front and raise their nose to see behind to clear their lower six o'clock, and would waggle their wingtips to see below their wings. The sections were always twitching, the pilots' heads constantly turning.

Oswald Boelcke, the great German fighter pilot of World War One, had originated the pair in 1915. The RAF turned to theoretical tactics in the late 1920s, based on scientific principles not on experience; so did the Luftwaffe. The Germans had the chance to unlearn such unempirical tactics and 'rediscover' the value of pairs – termed Rotte – and the pair of pairs – Schwarm – spread across a thousand yards. The leader led from the second port position, out in front, with the other three stepped up or down and on either side as the situation demanded.

There were criticisms of the 'finger-four'. One was that the wingmen had no time to look forwards but at the moment of attack they simultaneously had to ensure that their flank and tail were clear, avoid collisions and perhaps fire, an onerous task. However nerve-racking, the results of combat suggest this was successful, not dangerous. The most serious was that in a turn the wingmen would always be on the outside of the turn and would have the furthest to go, and would therefore be vulnerable. There is some truth in this, judging by the ratio of wingmen to leaders who were brought down, but in practice the wingman would not stay on his leader's wing during a turn but would slip in behind him in line astern. In fact, one of the values of the formation was that one pair could slide under the other when making a sharp turn, or when breaking to meet a sudden attack.

Bader immediately began to have all three squadrons fly together in 'pairs of pairs'. Although other senior fighter commanders used a line-abreast formation, the Tangmere Wing exploited the 'finger-four' to perfection. The formation was not universally adopted by British fighter squadrons, squadron tactics being an individual matter for the squadron commander, but wherever a Bader protégé went in command, so did the 'finger-four'.

Once the basics had been established, Bader selected Sergeant Allan Smith as his wingman, and Dundas and his wingman Johnson to be the second section in his 'finger-four'. Bader had his eye on Johnson, a vividly alive young man, a born fighter. He had a keenness and an intuitive grasp of fighter tactics that Bader wanted to foster. To be placed in Bader's section was, as Johnson later put it, 'like getting the nod from J. C.'.

RAF fighter tactical thinking had been defensive until 1941, but during the summer of 1941, in common with the other No 11 Group wings, Bader and the Tangmere Wing were formulating the tactics that became standard for the next three years. This was part of the wing's function. Wings were the vanguard of the air offensive over German-occupied Europe, becoming important elements of the tactical air forces formed in 1943. Increasing use was made of them in North Africa and Italy.

On 9 May, No 616 Squadron's major activity of the day centred around moving, as the ORB recorded, 'from Tangmere to its satellite at Westhampnett. Although the accommodation is not quite so good for all concerned the change is for the better'. There were several reasons for the move. First of all, Tangmere was a pre-war two-squadron station and was overcrowded with three Spitfire squadrons and a Beaufighter night fighter squadron. No 610 Squadron was already based at Westhampnett, a grass airfield below the Goodwood racecourse at the foot of the East Sussex Downs. No 145 Squadron was already dispersed to another satellite, Merston on the other side of Chichester. The Sector Operations Control Room was relocated in a requisitioned college in the Chichester suburbs. Secondly, there had been numerous German fighter-bomber attacks on RAF stations, and Tangmere had been struck several times. The Germans soon realized that the Tangmere Wing had been dispersed and, noting that the grass airfields would be less easy to find, the raids ceased. Thirdly, a squadron is like an Army regiment and needs its unique sense of identity and corporate spirit, and having its own mess is a vital part of fostering that camaraderie that builds a fine fighting unit. No 616 Squadron's office was moved to Shopwyche, a large country house between Chichester and Tangmere, and its officers were billeted in

Rushmans in the village of Oving.

The members of the squadron relied on each other for social companion-ship, and Bader usually had a small coterie around him in the messes or in pubs in the evening. He went a stage further. Bader actively encouraged the members of the Wing to socialize, and the house which his wife had taken, 'The Bay House', which she shared with her sister Jill, was frequently visited by his pilots, helping to forge not just a squadron spirit, but a unique wing spirit.

The day after their move, the 10th, the grass airfield effect was completed when No 616 Squadron reverted to a 1940-style of operations. During the early hours, there were Layer Patrols over Beachy Head by four aircraft. Then a large enemy raid was reported in the early morning, and No 616 Squadron scrambled patrols over base and Portland Bill but could not find the raid.

On 11 May, the squadron was busy in the morning with convoy patrols over the Solent, plus training. On the 12th, the only activity was in the evening when three sections patrolled base and there was one dusk patrol over Selsey Bill. The next day, there was cloud and local flying, but during early morning patrols over Selsey Bill and base the weather closed in, causing aircraft to return after a quarter of an hour's flight. There were two convoy patrols in the evening. On 14 May, there was local formation and 'ZZ' practice, together with a squadron 'Balbo' and a patrol over Selsey Bill.

On 15 May, Burton and Johnson flew an offensive sweep over the French coast using cloud cover at 4,000 feet – an uneventful 'Rhubarb'. For the majority of No 616 Squadron, there were three patrols, a dusk patrol and 'ZZ', local formation, cloud flying, aerobatics and ciné-gun practices.

The next day, 16 May, there was much operational flying, mostly convoy patrols. Ciné-gun practices and dogfighting were carried out. Bader took great care to ensure that his pilots had total confidence in their machines. No longer did he restrict his training programme to formations and fighter attacks and aerobatics, but added stern close-in fighting disciplines, 'one-on-one' training that taught pilots how to exploit weaknesses in opponents. Bader stressed that pilots had to know how to wring the best out of their mounts. He had metal ailerons fitted to his Spitfire Mk IIA as soon as he heard that they were available. They worked – rate of roll almost doubled and rate of turn was greatly increased. Bader knew the value of turning hard and lost no time in pulling strings and having all No 616 Squadron's aeroplanes fitted with them, unofficially. They simply flew the Spitfires over to Hamble airfield where Vickers-Supermarine were manufacturing the new ailerons and had them changed on the spot. It confused officialdom but endeared Bader to his pilots.

On 17 May, Dundas brought down a Bf 109, the first enemy aircraft to be shot down by the squadron while at Tangmere. Three Bf 109s were flying over the sea off Worthing, and came in to attack the two No 616 Squadron Spitfires. Dundas's New Zealand wingman, Sergeant Brewer, was not in a position to engage the enemy. Green Section, while up practice dogfighting, met two Bf 109s over Brighton. Only Sergeant Morton (Green 1) could catch the Bf 109s who, seeing the Spitfire, dived towards France. Morton put in several bursts which seemed to have no effect.

On 18 May, No 616 Squadron flew several patrols over its base and Newhaven in the morning. The next day, the squadron flew patrols over its base, and spent the rest in training, including a squadron 'Balbo', until after tea when patrols were flown over a convoy.

The 20th brought a period of bad weather which restricted flying. The Tangmere Wing squadrons made a few scrambles and patrols over base, Selsey Bill and St Catherine's Point, plus a few convoys. A reduced scale of exercises was run, mainly local flying and dusk landings, with a few sessions of fighter attacks, sea-firing and ciné-gun practice and a battle climb. With the introduction of the 'pair of pairs' formation, the battle climb had become a much better tactic. It consisted of a squadron climbing in fours in a tight spiral so that each section crossed and recrossed every 360 degrees. It was a refinement of the old tactic of two-seat Bristol Fighters, with fore and aft guns. At all points across a wide span of sky and through a fair depth, guns could be brought to bear instantly on any assault on the squadron, which simply had to keep spiralling, and no Bf 109 would be able to get into the loop.

The weather picked up again on 28 May. No 616 Squadron alone flew seven patrols in the early morning and afternoon, and put in several hours of local flying, ciné-gun and fighter attack training. The next day, the weather worsened, staying bad until 2 June when there were three patrols off Selsey Bill, and camera-gun practice, local flying and aerobatics. Flying Officer Sutherland had the misfortune to hit a tree when coming in to land at Westhampnett, writing off his Spitfire and slightly injuring his spine; he went off to hospital.

Although bad weather returned on 3 June, it was not poor enough to prevent No 616 Squadron making two scrambles over base, and carrying out one 'local flying' – though the latter term sometimes masked an unofficial 'Rhubarb' by Bader. The following day brought an offensive sweep by twelve No 616 Squadron Spitfire Mk IIAs over the Dover-Dunkirk-Boulogne area at 22,000 feet. They met no enemy aircraft, but at least now were more visibly, in Sholto Douglas's phrase, 'leaning towards France'. The next day, apart from the usual local flying practice, an unusual 'S/L [searchlight] co-operation and weather test', there were two scrambles.

There followed four days without operations, when weather was poor, but 11 June was a very busy day with twelve scrambles, most of them for the protection of convoys. Dogfights, aerobatics and spinning exercises were carried out.

A week of excellent days for flying practice for non-operational and operational pilots alike began on 12 June, with local day, dusk, night and dawn flying for non-operational pilots, and air fighting, 'ZZ' practice and a GL Run for others, and dogfighting, ciné-gun, aerobatics and stalking. Significantly, on the 12th, a section went to RAF Redhill to rearm and refuel as a rehearsal for forward staging during the operations that were about to commence. The next day, No 616 Squadron flew a squadron 'Balbo' up to 30,000 feet, also an important rehearsal for the Wing operations. The routine of patrols and scrambles continued, for the Tangmere Wing remained at all times a part of the air defence of Great Britain: on the 12th, there were four scrambles, three in the early morning and one at dusk, and four scrambles on the 13th, two over base and two over Shoreham. On 17 June, No 616 Squadron flew seven scrambles. However, during the week, offensive operations began to take precedence over training and patrolling.

As the squadrons began to blend as operational entities, the flow of pilots to and from No 616 Squadron slowed during May and June, and was mainly sergeants. Two pilots were posted to other units and one on detached duty. On 19 May, Pilot Officer Walter was detached from No 616 Squadron to No 1 Delivery Flight, Hendon, to give him further non-operational flying experience before he rejoined the squadron. On 31 May, the Rhodesian Sergeant Sherwood was posted to No 266 Squadron (by now designated a Rhodesian unit) at Wittering. On 12 June, Sergeant S. C. Walters was posted to No 11 Group Flight, Croydon. On 5 May, Sergeant Bowen, RCAF, arrived, followed by Sergeant Scott on the 11th and on the 12th by Sergeant Crabtree from No 57 OTU, Hawarden. On 16 June, Pilot Officer T. F. Leckie was posted from No 53 OTU, followed on 20 June by Pilot Officer Trench from No 65 OTU, both at RAF Hawarden. No further officer pilot was posted to No 616 Squadron until Pilot Officer W. M. Murray, RCAF, arrived from No 403 Squadron, RCAF, based at RAF Ternhill, on 12 July.

Underlining the reason for the considerable amount of training and practice that the Tangmere squadrons undertook, Leckie, only two days after arriving, crashed his Spitfire: 'overshooting the airfield and turning over. He is injured in the spine and will not be able to fly for several months. This crash was due to inexperience.' The pilots had been trained at the OTUs more solidly than their 1940 counterparts, but by no means had they a full or practical understanding of air-to-air gunnery, hence the ciné-gun and dogfighting practice; nor did they know the new flexible formations, for they would have been given hours of 'Vics' at the OTU to teach them 'formating' but not observation. It was the role of the squadrons to induct them into the ways of combat. With the fighting season upon the Wing, there was an urgency.

While the routine process of acceptance and posting of squadron pilots was going on, Douglas Bader was refining his 'team' of leaders. On 5 June, another of No 616 Squadron's originals, Acting Flight Lieutenant Ken Holden, was promoted to the rank of squadron leader and given command of No 610 Squadron, based on the other side of Westhampnett. No 616 Squadron's ORB recorded: 'We wished him the best of luck in his new command – in the usual way.'

Flight Lieutenant E. P. P. Gibbs, from No 56 Squadron, North Weald, took over his duties as 'A' Flight Commander. 'Gibbo' was Bader's age. He was a Regular, a true professional with instructor's credentials, whose aerobatic mastery turned even Bader's blood cold with jealousy when it was unostentatiously displayed – especially when he performed the elusive third upward roll without effort. He had no operational experience and was fixed in the habits of flying 'by the book'. No one expected him to last very long in combat. Later in the month, on the 29th, this officer was promoted to the rank of squadron leader, but he remained with the squadron as 'A' Flight Commander. Under him were 'Cocky' Dundas and his wingman, 'Johnnie' Johnson. For operations, No 616 Squadron would comprise the Wing Commander's section (four aircraft) and two composite sections from both Flights led by Burton and a Flight Commander.

Bader had two of his No 242 Squadron pilots posted to his Wing, Crowley-Milling came as a Flight Commander to No 610 Squadron, and Flight Lieutenant Ian Arthur as a Flight Commander to No 145 Squadron. Fearless Stan Turner became No 145 Squadron's Commanding Officer.

If it were a coincidence, then it was a happy one that 'Woody' Woodhall was promoted to group captain and appointed as Tangmere Station Commander and Sector Fighter Controller. At Duxford, Bader and Woodhall had developed firm confidence in each other's judgments. At Tangmere, the partnership continued to grow. From controlling a short-range interception of hostile invaders over friendly territory, they now developed the techniques of controlling a large-scale fighter penetration of hostile airspace at 150 miles range. Unlike some controllers, Woodhall appreciated that air war takes place in three dimensions. He would read the radar picture and the data on his Operations Room control board and give the fighter leader directions that allowed him to understand the larger implications of what the leader might be seeing from his cockpit. Bader could therefore position his fighters most appropriately and take the most effective action when and where it was needed.

Woodhall had the rare ability among controllers of being able to visualize and then, as 'Johnnie' Johnson wrote of him, 'paint a broad picture of the air situation' for the airborne fighter leader. He would follow the Tangmere Wing on radar and give the Wing Leader information on the developing threats, telling him where other wings were. He was always aware of the position of the sun, the headwind that might slow the Wing's return, the cloud moving into the Channel, the time flown and the fuel states of the fighters. He spoke to them in his measured, mellow, deep voice, always reassuringly, always encouraging, advising, rarely ordering, giving them a course for home when they were alone deep over France. The fighter pilots felt that they had a friend in the cockpit with them over hostile land. This was not always so with controllers, many of whom were brusque or unaware of the real needs.

Woodhall was no backroom controller, isolated from the fighter pilots. He was a First World War fighter pilot. A grey-haired, stocky figure, with a lined, weather-worn face, he affected a monocle and wore an air of avuncular confidence. He had the right temperament to win the confidence of the fighter pilots. He took part in their social life in the mess with gusto. He talked reassuringly with the new boys. He was a familiar figure at dispersal when the Wing returned from a sweep, always there to greet Bader, to hear Bader's graphic summary of the fight, and then to discuss the fight with him and his pilots – and to join in the celebrations if appropriate later on.

☆   ☆   ☆

On 6 June 1941, Hitler launched his armed forces against the Soviet Union in Operation BARBAROSSA, in what he hoped would be a lightning victory against the Bolshevik menace to his Reich. Immediately, Winston Churchill welcomed the Soviet Union as an ally, and pledged tangible support, including the mounting of operations to occupy German forces elsewhere than on the Russian front. This gave the proposed offensive by Fighter Command over northern France an additional impetus. It was a small contribution, but it laid the foundations for future success.

On 10 June, No 616 Squadron's ORB had made a significant comment:

> 'A period of glorious weather and intense activity over Northern France commences. In all the Tangmere wing patrols, W/Cmdr Bader flies with us and leads the wing. We are the bottom Squadron, 610 Squadron next and No 145 Squadron on top. All these wing patrols are to cover our bombers over Northern France.'

This was the beginning of Sholto Douglas's and Leigh-Mallory's offensive. A number of types of offensive operation were introduced in 1941, appropriately code-named; each operation was numbered. A 'Circus' was a fighter sweep accompanying a small bomber force, with the primary objective of drawing enemy fighters into action. Bomber crews became demoralized by this sort of thing. A 'Ranger' was a freelance fighter sweep by a wing operating independently from the main penetration force. A 'Rodeo' was a pure fighter sweep. A 'Roadstead' was a low-level attack on shipping and coastal defences or ports – in 1941 undertaken by Hurricanes, such as the four-cannon Mark IICs of No 615 Squadron led by Squadron Leader Denys Gillam. Spitfires provided cover for such fraught operations. The Tangmere Wing's duties were bomber escort operations, offensive fighter sweeps and 'Rhubarbs'. It had flown its first 'Circus' on 17 April, escorting Blenheims to Cherbourg, and flew them regularly from June. From 17 May, it had begun to fly 'Rhubarbs'.

When they had been conceived six months before, the objectives of the offensive operations were twofold: first, to destroy railways, communications and facilities, and factories working for the Germans in France; and secondly, to destroy the German fighters forced into the air to counter the raid. The Joint Air Staffs Directive summarized it neatly, if optimistically:

> 'The object of these attacks is to force the enemy to give battle under conditions tactically favourable to our fighters. In order to compel him to do so, the bombers must cause sufficient damage to make it impossible for him to ignore them and refuse to fight on our terms.'

From early June, with the forced alliance of Britain and the Soviet Union and the Soviet demands for a 'Second Front Now', a third objective was added: to compel the Luftwaffe to keep fighters in France rather than deploy them to other fronts, such as the Mediterranean or North African, but principally the Russian front. One positive advantage of the German assault on Russia was that it was now highly unlikely that the Battle of Britain would be reopened in 1941.

The new offensive operations produced mixed results. The Luftwaffe did not react strongly to the high-flying fighter sweeps introduced in early 1941, but reacted viciously to 'Circuses'. Several wings of fighters escorted a few light bombers, undertaking diversionary attacks, support and cover. Intended to force the Luftwaffe to deploy fighters wastefully and to sting them into the air, 'Circuses' produced many tough battles. 'Ramrod' operations, a fighter sweep accompanying a small bomber force with the primary objective of destroying ground targets by the bomber force, got a stronger reaction from the Germans.

Compelling the Germans to fight on British terms was a problem. The British now faced the problems the Germans had faced in 1940 – fighting at the limits of range, over enemy territory, tied to escorting slow bombers, and against a co-ordinated radar network and fighter control system. The furthest that they could reach was Lille, limited because of the Spitfire's 200-mile radius. Lille was an important communications and transport centre – it had been a major objective during the First World War – with notable heavy industries. However, the route to the target was long, and passed over two concentrations of German fighters. The German fighter controllers had long warning of the raid, and time to assess the range, predict the development and organize an efficient defence. Now, the British faced the problem of the sun, and the problem that when they were shot down, it was over enemy territory.

All these were wing operations. Small-scale operations were also continued. After the de Havilland Mosquito fast bomber appeared, 'Mosquito' raids were renamed 'Rhubarbs' – because they were flown 'down among the rhubarb'. If flown at night, it was termed an 'Intruder' operation. 'Rhubarbs' were carried out by pairs of fighters slipping into France under cover of poor weather to attack targets of opportunity, but results were dubious and losses heavy. The Spitfire's glycol tank was under its nose and unarmoured; one bullet there could bring down a Spitfire. Most pilots loathed them for they resulted in high losses of both pilots and aeroplanes combined with little real damage to the enemy. They were ordered by Group Headquarters. However, in No 616 Squadron's ORB the phrase 'local flying was carried out' sometimes disguised an unofficial 'Rhubarb' when Bader took Burton and two wingmen hunting, for Bader enjoyed hunting.

For the major operations, the bombers flew down from their bases in Lincolnshire and Yorkshire. They rendezvoused with the close support wing, three squadrons of thirty-six Spitfires or Hurricanes, over the fighter base. The bombers flew at 12,000 feet, the extreme height for flak, usually in two boxes of six if they were twin-engined bombers or in a single box of four if heavy bombers. The fighters enveloped the bombers from 12,000 feet upwards. The close escort wing, thirty-six Spitfires, built the formation up to 20,000 feet: the 'Beehive'.

As the 'Beehive' flew over the Channel, other target support wings, perhaps six, took off and flew to the target at 20,000–30,000 feet to arrive over the target at the same time as the bombers. These would have more petrol to 'mix it' than the close escort wings, which had to fly uneconomically at the bombers' pace. The target support wings were to tackle the Bf 109s which attacked the 'Beehive' close to the target, when the escorts were vulnerable. Soon, a target withdrawal wing was introduced to arrive over the target area withdrawal corridor as the 'Beehive' and its fighters turned for home. With experience, it was found profitable to have a wing waiting over the enemy coast to bounce any German fighters loitering in anticipation of attacking the bombers on the way out.

Such an operation, involving over a hundred fighters and twelve Blenheims or six Stirlings, had to be planned meticulously: a wing leader's task was to get his wing assembled and flown into position on time at the right height and speed, and to continue to chart progress and react swiftly to correct changes of tempo. A wing had to arrive over the French coast at the right point at the right time; after that, its height and speed were at the discretion of target support wing leaders. For a wing leader, it was not just the enormous strain that day-to-day combat imposed that produced fatigue, it was the weight of responsibility for his wing and for each operation, the task of overseeing training and equipment, of organizing operations and liaising with Squadron and Flight Commanders, with Group and other wing leaders.

Bader was well fitted for this very exacting task, having had the thorough Cranwell training and having worked for a management-orientated company like Shell. He also had a healthy ability to cut through the 'bumph', the masses of paperwork that any organization generates, and to get things done off paper, making snap decisions with complete Cranwellian confidence. Bader was decisive, a man people trusted, and therefore followed to the death; he was in an atmosphere where he had complete sway, served by a staff to whom he delegated the routine, surrounded by acolytes, disciples by the end, who had supreme confidence in him, and with Squadron and Flight Commanders whom he had selected and whom he trusted implicitly. He welded his three squadrons together in the air and on the ground so that their individual identities were forgotten and they became the Tangmere Wing.

No 11 Group, Fighter Command, was the RAF's spearhead in the offensive and fighter wings were the chief offensive formation. Each wing commander led three squadrons as a combat wing, each treated as flexible parts of a tactical unit. It became apparent that a wing had to be composed of several smaller units, operating cohesively. Bader revelled in developing and applying tactics. He was a man at the right time and the right place. It was part of a wing's function in 1941 to experiment. The whole offensive was an experiment.

Bader was a fortunate man. The Tangmere Wing was his instrument: he had the complete faith of Leigh-Mallory and Sholto Douglas. They were still learning, forging a weapon, the flexible employment of fighter forces, and revising tactics: for this was where ultimately Bader won – he had criticized No 11 Group in 1940 for inflexible and defensive use of the inherently flexible and offensive fighter resources, and for using tactics that were fine in theory but were lacking in practice. Now, he could show how it should be done. However, Bader was not leading 'Big Wings' – not even full three-squadron wings. Sometimes he led into France what would have been termed in 1940 three flights – three squadrons of eight aeroplanes!

CHAPTER 12
Tangmere Wing Leader

Fighter Command's wing leaders had been specially selected for their leadership, proven ability, experience and understanding of air war. The first three, Bader at Tangmere, Malan at Biggin Hill and John Peel at Kenley, had been joined by others. Wing leaders supervised training and unified the squadrons in the wing structure. They determined tactics. They led their wings on operations. They brought a continuity that had been absent in 1940. They were vital to the success of the offensive. Fully trained, Bader and the Tangmere Wing were hungry for combat.

Despite the almost daily sweeps being flown, there was little action for some days. There were high-altitude offensive sweeps over northern France on the morning of 14 and on 15 June, but nothing interesting was seen. On 16 June, one high-altitude offensive sweep was carried out by eight aircraft of No 616 Squadron, but they saw nothing. The Luftwaffe paid scant attention to these operations because they threatened nothing. On 17 June, there was a wing patrol over northern France. Only Derek Beedham of No 616 Squadron fired his guns, although he made no claim. On 18 June, there was early morning activity when five scrambles had been made by No 616 Squadron by quarter past six, but the offensive wing patrol flown in the afternoon did not live up to the promise of the day, for nothing was seen. The next day, one offensive wing patrol was flown. Colin Macfie claimed to have damaged one of just two Bf 109s they met. On 20 June, the Wing was released in the afternoon, ending the intensive training which had continued concurrently with these sweeps. The next day, the Wing settled down to a schedule of patrols and sweeps over France.

The usual practice for the Tangmere Wing was for each squadron to take off independently from Tangmere, Merston and Westhampnett and to form up over Chichester, before rendezvousing over Beachy Head (code-named 'Diamond'), along with a hundred other aeroplanes. This could be a nerve-racking time, for the risks of collision with so many fast fighters in a restricted piece of airspace, all in formation in orbits from zero feet up to 20,000 feet, was great. Once assembled and the bombers set off, the Tangmere Wing headed out over Pevensey Bay and turned to starboard, flying in tight formation across the Channel, sometimes at low altitude, sometimes in a climb. Radio silence was strictly imposed. Near the French coast, Bader waggled his wings, and the Wing drew into line-abreast 'finger-fours'. As they crossed the coast, the pilots flicked their guns to 'Fire' and their reflector sights to 'On' – just in case.

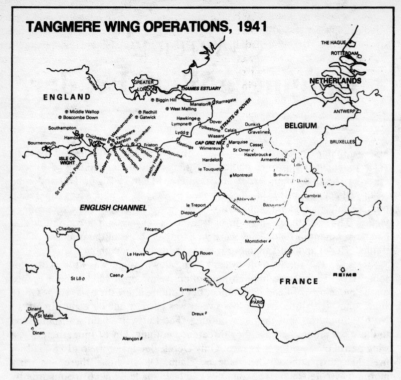

TANGMERE WING OPERATIONS, 1941

The positions of the sections, squadrons and heights varied according to conditions. As an example, No 616 Squadron as low cover would fly at 20,000 feet, with No 610 Squadron behind and to the left at 22,000 feet, and No 145 Squadron at high cover in a stretched crescent at from 24,000 to 30,000 feet flying either to the left of both of them in the sun in the morning, or to the right in the afternoon. The position of the sun was critical, just as for the Germans in attacking England during the Battle of Britain, for it affected the direction of the attacks. In the morning, the Tangmere Wing would try to enter and exit France further to the north-east near Gravelines and in the afternoon near Boulogne or Le Touquet to the south-west. From eleven in the morning until two in the afternoon, they fought with the sun high above them, favouring the Luftwaffe.

On the way back from a sweep, formation was maintained if possible; if they had had a fight, the rule was to form up with another Spitfire and get out low; there was no chance of reforming the Wing then. To release the tension, Bader had a habit of shoving back his canopy as he approached the English coast at Eastbourne and stuffing a ready-charged pipe into his mouth, and puffing away like Popeye. His wingmen would sheer off in ostentatious terror. But the lethal results of such flagrant regulation-breaking never caught up with Bader. It just added fire to the myth.

As soon as the sweep had landed, Group Captain Woodhall would meet Bader and they would discuss the operation, roping in any pilot whose part was material. Bader had the ability not only to observe the fight but to reconstruct it into a flow of events and to give it meaning. He would discuss No 616 Squadron's fight with the squadron's pilots, and then collate it with the accounts telephoned in by Holden and Turner of their squadrons' roles. A full picture would emerge of the whole operation. It was a valuable form of debriefing, making the pilots clearly conscious of what was happening around them; and that kind of awareness contributed greatly to survival and the development of fine leaders.

On 21 June, there were two wing patrols over northern France. On the first, Squadron Leader Burton destroyed a Bf 109, sharing it with a pilot from No 145 Squadron. The second wing operation of the day was a withdrawal cover for an escort of a raid to St Omer. The Germans had learnt to attack the 'Beehive' as it withdrew when the British fighters were low on fuel and the pilots were tiring. Therefore, Fighter Command sent a fresh wing out to meet the 'Beehive' as it came back. Today, the Tangmere Wing flew along the coast as 'withdrawal cover'. Bader brought down a Bf 109 over the sea, his first victory on a sweep. He wrote:

'I was leading Tangmere Wing which was milling around in and off the coast around Desvres. Saw the bombers and escort go out near Boulogne, followed by AA bursts. We stayed around above and behind the bombers and escort when I noticed two Me.109s in line astern about to turn in behind my section of four. I told them to break left and twisted round quickly (metal ailerons) and fired a very close deflection burst at the first Me.109E at about 50 yards' range, about ½ to 1 second. My bullets appeared to hit him as his glass hood dispersed in pieces and the aeroplane pulled up vertically, stalled and spun right-handed. I foolishly followed him down with my eyes and nearly collided with a cannon Spitfire.'

Sadly, Pilot Officer Brown was seen diving down out of control. He was the first officer casualty for No 616 Squadron that year. The ORB recorded that he was 'a great loss to us, as he was liked by both officers and men'.

On 22 June, there was an offensive wing patrol in the afternoon, to Hazebrouck, when Flying Officer Roy Marples destroyed a Bf 109 and Flying Officer Casson and Sergeant Beedham shared a 'destroyed' Bf 109 between them. It was a very successful offensive operation. The Tangmere Wing destroyed six enemy aircraft with no loss to themselves. The Wing celebrated in style.

On 23 June, the Wing flew two offensive sweeps to Béthune, one in the morning and one in the afternoon. There were no contacts with enemy aircraft. Sergeant Beedham ran out of petrol and baled out over the sea off Brighton. He was picked up by a lifeboat and received as a hero by the civilian population. The squadron less charitably thought that 'he could have easily made a forced landing on the Downs' (ORB).

On 24 June, one wing offensive sweep was flown to Béthune again, but the weather was bad and only two Bf 109s were seen.

Hugh Dundas had another successful encounter with a Bf 109, this time over France, on 25 June. It was a 'busy day for the pilots in which two wing sweeps were made' (ORB). A 'sweep' was technically a fighter offensive patrol, without bombers, but all wing operations became known as 'sweeps'. In the first sweep, actually a withdrawal cover operation, Bader claimed one Bf 109 destroyed and shared another destroyed with Sergeant West. Flight Lieutenant Gibbs and Sergeant Brewer claimed a 'probable' each and Flying Officers Hugh Dundas and Roy Marples claimed a 'damaged' each.

Bader recorded the combat from his position as Tangmere Wing Leader. No 616 Squadron had taken off from Westhampnett at 11.58 hours, and had joined Nos 145 and 610 Squadrons, flying out over Dungeness at 20,500 feet. Crossing the Channel in a steady climb, the Wing approached France at Gravelines, but turned south to the French coast at about 25,000 feet. Pilots saw a number of Bf 109s occasionally, but combat was not joined. Bader's combat report gives an interesting insight into the operation of a pair of fighters in a combat:

'When 145 Squadron informed me that they had found bombers and were escorting bombers back over Gravelines, I gave the order for the Wing to withdraw. As we crossed coast at Gravelines at about 18,000 feet my section ran into 4–6 Me.109Fs milling around over Gravelines-Dunkirk area about 500 feet below. We flew into them and I gave one a short deflection shot and my No 2 (Sgt West) followed in with another burst of two seconds. Sgt West broke to port and lost sight of enemy aircraft but I broke to starboard and saw it half roll and dive down and followed it down – giving it ½ second burst – seeing pilot baling out about 5 miles off Gravelines in sea. Then vectored 280 degress from this point, crossed over South Foreland and returned to Westhampnett at 13.35. This Me.109 was not visibly damaged although bullets were seen to strike i.e. no smoke etc.'

In the second sweep of 25 June, in the afternoon to St Omer, Bader destroyed one Bf 109. The Tangmere Wing Leader had led No 616 Squadron off Westhampnett at 15.49 hours. The squadron joined up with Nos 145 and 610 Squadrons at about 16.00 hours, and began a climb to 21,000 feet over the Channel. As it was the afternoon, the Wing crossed into France at Hardelot. Then, just over the French coast, the Wing picked up the bombers – the 'honey'. With the bombers below the fighters, the 'Beehive' flew eastwards. After a few minutes, a large number of enemy fighters appeared behind, below and to the north of the Wing. 'Eventually', Bader recorded, he:

'was compelled to engage them and disregard the bombers, since they were all round us and we were flying down sun. With the leading section I engaged eight to nine Me.109Fs which were climbing east to west i.e. towards Boulogne. We were then at 20,000 feet and the enemy aircraft between 16,000 and 17,000 feet. We dived on to them and F/O Dundas and his Number 2 attacked two who turned north and climbed. I attacked four Me.109Fs, with my Number 2, who were climbing in a slightly left-hand turn. I gave a short burst at one at close range from the inside of the turn and saw white, black and orange-coloured smoke envelop the aircraft, which went down in an increasingly steep dive which finished up past the vertical; I did not follow the aircraft down and claim it as destroyed. I straightened up from turn just as some more Me.109s (which were milling about some Spitfires) turned towards me. I gave a short head-on burst on one of them, who I don't think had seen me, but saw no apparent result of my fire. I then joined with Squadron Leader Holden of No 610 Squadron with my No 2 and gave a burst at another aircraft but saw no result.'

No 616 Squadron returned to Westhampnett at 17.22 hours, after an operation of an hour and a half, but they were missing three members. Sergeants Jenks and Brewer had possibly been 'pounced on' by Bf 109s after they became detached from the formation. Brewer had been with No 616 Squadron since 1 April, Jenks somewhat longer. There was relief when it was learnt that Sergeant Morton, who had been shot at by a Bf 109, had managed to land at RAF Hawkinge and was returning to the squadron.

Back at base, Bader learnt that his section's attack had been successful. Apart from his own claim, 'Cocky' Dundas had succeeded in damaging one of the two Bf 109s which he and his Number 2, Pilot Officer 'Johnnie' Johnson, had attacked, before the Bf 109s escaped.

On 26 June, there was an offensive sweep by Nos 145, 610 and 616 Squadrons, in which 'Johnnie' Johnson opened his score with a Bf 109 'destroyed' and Flying Officer Casson added a Bf 109 'damaged' to his mounting score. Johnson, although he had occasionally led a pair in Bader's or Burton's section, was frustrated as wingman to Dundas because, as on the day before, he had to protect his Number 1, not fire his own guns. The Wing took off from Tangmere and landed at RAF Redhill, where it refuelled and took off again at 10.54 hours. They flew south over South Foreland.

On its way inland from the French coast, at about 12.00 hours, the Wing was bounced by a fifteen-strong fighter force of Bf 109s over Gravelines, near Dunkirk. Johnson (Dogsbody 4) soon found himself completely alone – a dangerous position. As he wrote, he:

'became detached from W/C Bader's section at 15,000 feet through watching 3 Me 109's immediately above me. I saw them dive away to port and almost immediately afterwards saw an Me 109E coming in from my starboard side which flew across me about 150 yds away, turning slightly to port. I immediately turned inside the E/A and opened fire, closing to 100 yards. After two one-second bursts, the E/A jettisoned hood, rolled over and pilot baled out, his parachute opening almost immediately. I then broke away as there were other E/A about.'

He had needed only slight deflection and had expended only 278 .303-inch rounds. After the combat, Johnson obeyed a basic rule and joined up as a pair with Flying Officer Scott of No 145 Squadron. Together, they flew back and landed at Hawkinge for refuelling, flying on to Westhampnett and landing at 13.25 hours. His claim was confirmed by several No 145 Squadron pilots. One No 616 Squadron pilot who had been unable to reform as a pair, Sergeant Morton, mistook the north of the Thames Estuary for the south coast near the Isle of Wight, and crash-landed near RAF Coltishall. After this combat success, Johnson's score quickly mounted.

On 27 June, two wing sweeps were made, and an offensive sweep the next afternoon. All three sweeps were uneventful. There was no wing operational activity on 29 June, but the day was not wasted – there was much to do, and local flying, dogfights, sector reconnaissances and co-operation with Ground Control Interception were undertaken.

In late June, No 616 Squadron was called on to provide experience of a different kind from the round of 'bringing on' to operational status the pilots straight out of training units. On 28 June, Lieutenant Montgomery of the US Army Air Forces joined the squadron for a week's training. On 30 June, he did some air-to-sea firing but, before he could be settled into an operational role, he was 'suddenly recalled home' on 4 July.

On 29 June, Flight Lieutenant E. Gibbs was promoted to squadron leader. Although he remained attached to the squadron, the next day Flying Officer Casson was promoted to acting flight lieutenant as second-in-command of 'A' Flight to maintain the balance in the squadron.

On 30 June, Dicky Cork and his No 880 Squadron's Commanding Officer, Lieutenant-Commander Judd, stationed briefly nearby, dropped in on Tangmere to see Bader. The brooding, bearded, massively built 'Butch' Judd terrified the RAF pilots and amazed them when he managed to squeeze his 6ft 2in frame into a Spitfire Mk IIA. Bader expounded the new tactical formations to Cork and Judd, and then demonstrated them. No 616 Squadron was due over France in two hours' time on an offensive patrol: Bader put Cork (R9501) and Judd into Spitfires and took them with him as his wingmen. They flew an offensive patrol down the French coast, going in over Dunkirk and inland to St Omer, then out over Le Touquet and on to Boulogne; but the Luftwaffe did not react. Judd and Cork flew back to HMS *Daedalus* after lunch. For Cork and Bader, it was their last parting.

The Wing also flew a sweep. The only incident was when Sergeant McCairns was shot at, explosive shells entering his cockpit. He retained control of his aeroplane and landed safely and uninjured at base.

By now the Wing was working very effectively. The leader team, Bader and his three Squadron Commanders Burton, Holden and Turner, were indivisible and powerful. The Flight Commanders were experienced men. The squadron pilots had been taught well and were learning swiftly. Observing, assessing, deciding, then acting – these things in that order were what pilots who wanted to survive and be successful had to learn. Slowing down a situation, assessing the threats accurately, knowing where the enemy fighters were and which enemy aircraft were a danger, which in danger, that was the way to impose authority on combat.

Bader insisted that pilots should act as cohesive teams – the essence of any warfare, air, land or sea. Pilots should not play a lone hand. During one early wing sweep, a solitary Bf 109 appeared in front of No 616 Squadron's Spitfires. Bader was wary, thinking it was a decoy, but no one could see other Bf 109s. Bader led Dundas down. The 109 half-rolled and dived . . . and other 109s streamed down. No 610 Squadron, flying centre, turned into the attack and caught some. The other Bf 109s went for No 616 Squadron which, as usual, was flying at low position. Stan Turner led his No 145 Squadron into the fray from up-sun in his position as top cover. In the ensuing mêlée, Dundas got separated from Bader, and pitched against four Bf 109s. For five minutes he was unable to escape – then he flicked into a spin at 17,000 feet. He levelled off above the ground and headed for base, squirting at a 109 landing at an airfield en route, and finally shook off other 109s in mid-Channel. Bader was not sympathetic to pilots who got isolated, but Dundas was learning.

Despite the good weather, little training flying was being done. Operations were laying claim to time. On 1 July, there was no training at all; another offensive wing patrol in the afternoon was flown, without claims, and the squadrons were active on other work – sections of No 616, for instance, flew four protective patrols.

Bader had a good day on 2 July. First of all, he was informed that he had been awarded a Bar to his DSO, and then he led an offensive wing patrol that morning which met 'plenty of action' [ORB], after which the Wing was released. During the morning offensive patrol, Bader led No 616 Squadron's first section and he claimed a 'destroyed' and a 'damaged', as did his Number 2, Sergeant Allan Smith, who also machine-gunned some workshops and German soldiers on a beach. Pilot Officer Heppell, also in Dogsbody Section, destroyed a Bf 109, the pilot baling out. Bader recorded his own combat:

> 'Sighted approximately 15 Me.109Fs a few miles south-west of Lille so turned south and attacked them. They were in a sort of four formation climbing eastwards. They made no attempt to do anything but climb in formation so I turned the Squadron behind them and about 200 feet above and attacked from behind. I attacked a Me.109F from quarter astern to astern and saw his hood come off – probably he jettisoned it – and the pilot started to climb out. Did not see him actually bale out as I nearly collided with another Me.109 that was passing on my right in the middle of a half-roll. Half-rolled with him and dived down on his tail firing at him with the result that glycol and oil came out of his machine. I left him at 12,000 feet, as he appeared determined to continue diving, and pulled up again to 18,000 feet. My ASI showed rather more than 400mph when I pulled out. Found the fight had taken me west a bit so picked up two (610 Squadron) Spitfires and flew out at Boulogne round Gris Nez and up to Gravelines where we crossed the coast again and found a Me.109 at 8,000 feet at which I fired from about 300 yards.'

Bader's phrasing of his claim makes interesting points. He left the Intelligence Staff in no doubt about the results he saw, qualifying and supporting as necessary. When assessing his first and second claims, he obviously pummelled information out of his pilots: he took the business of claims and evidence very seriously, for the Air Force needed to make accurate assessments of the results of the sweeps. Bader expected his pilots to be equally scrupulous. His report continued:

> 'The first Me.109 is claimed as destroyed since, although I did not actually see the pilot leave the aircraft, I saw him preparing to do so, and several pilots in 616 saw two parachutes going down, one of which was shot down by P/O Heppell. The second Messerschmitt was seen by P/O Heppell and is claimed as damaged.'

The third Bf 109F he attacked he was careful to state was not damaged, but was claimed as 'Frightened'!

On 3 July, there were two offensive wing patrols. In the first, the German fighters were 'loath to engage', but Sergeant Bowen, RCAF, found an unfortunate Henschel Hs 126. After a No 610 Squadron pilot had fired at it, Bowen attacked the Henschel and fired. His judgment thrown by the unaccustomed slowness of this parasol monoplane target, he broke away just a fraction of a second too late. His port wingtip sliced into the Henschel's port wing strut and port tailplane, and it spiralled away. Bowen shared this Hs 126 as probably destroyed with the No 610 Squadron pilot. Sergeant Crabtree did not return from this operation. He had been with the unit since 12 May 1941. He escaped to Madrid and wrote to the squadron a month later from the British Embassy there to say that he was on his way home.

In the second wing patrol on 3 July, the activity was not so great. However, Sergeant Derek Beedham probably destroyed a Bf 109, one of his several successful encounters that summer.

On 4 July, there was an offensive wing patrol in the early afternoon. A number of small boats, thought to be E-boats, were seen off Boulogne, but were not attacked. Pilot Officer Johnson and Sergeant Morton each 'damaged' a Bf 109 'Emil'. Johnson as Yellow 1 was leading Yellow Section, behind Bader. He recorded the fight as follows, which took place at 14,000 feet five miles inland from Gravelines at 15.20 hours:

> 'I heard W/Cdr Bader instruct his section to break. As I was immediately behind, I broke away steeply to the left and after two tight turns saw a Me 109E firing at me, but no fire hit me owing to the tightness of the turn. There was also another Spitfire flying in the same turn. The e/a broke away to port in a fairly medium dive. I followed him down and gave him a short burst ["15°–20° deflection from 200 yards to 150 yards"] and observed glycol fumes coming out of it. I then broke away as there were other 109's in the vicinity, finally returning to base at 16.00.'

Later that afternoon, No 616 Squadron's ORB recorded that: 'Four aircraft did some local flying practice'. In reality, this was the Wing Commander and the Squadron Commander with their wingmen over France on an offensive sweep. The combat illustrates a number of facets of Bader's skill – just how close he meant by close; how it was more important to him to reassemble the section than to watch his victim fall; and how Burton could see the whole combat clearly. All this shows how Bader had digested the experiences of 1940. Bader recorded the combat thus:

> 'Intercepted one Me.109E some miles south of Gravelines at 14,000 feet, while with a section of four. Turned into its tail and opened fire with a short 1-second burst at about 150 yards. I found it very easy to keep inside him on the turn and I closed up quite quickly. I gave him three more short bursts, the final one at about 20 yards' range and as he slowed down very suddenly I nearly collided with him. I did not see the result except one puff of white smoke halfway through. Sqn Ldr Burton in my section watched the complete combat and saw the Me.109's airscrew slow right down to ticking-over speed and as I broke away the Messerschmitt did not half-roll and dive – but just sort of fell away in a sloppy fashion, quite slowly, as though the pilot had been hit. Having broken away I did not again see the Me. I attacked, since I was engaged in trying to collect my section. I am satisfied that I was hitting him and so is Sqn Ldr Burton . . .'

On 5 July, after a routine morning, an offensive wing patrol was flown at lunch time which brought several fights. Flight Lieutenant Colin Macfie, 'B' Flight Commander, was forced down in France during one of the fights:

'We were all very sad at his loss for he had been with the squadron since the beginning of September, 1940, and had endeared himself to everyone despite his taciturnity. We heard later that he had sprained his ankle when landing by parachute, and in a prisoner of war camp.'

Macfie had been recommended for the DFC, and he was gazetted in absentia on 27 July.

As a result of Gibbs' promotion and Macfie's loss, there was further change. On 7 July, 'Buck' Casson was confirmed in the rank of flight lieutenant and took over Macfie's 'B' Flight, and Flying Officer H. S. L. Dundas was promoted to flight lieutenant and took command of 'A' Flight. Dundas retained his wingman, Johnson, so both remained under Bader's direct tuition, but the position gave Dundas greater control. With freedom to initiate combats, Dundas destroyed a Bf 109 on 10 July, shared in destroying another on 19 July, claimed a probable on 21 July, and shared in the destruction of another on 23 July. Bader's teaching method was clearly sound. In addition to being able to control tactical situations, it meant that Dundas would now shoulder administrative responsibilities for ten pilots and fifty airmen, teaching him the necessary skills for further promotion – the next step was squadron leader.

On 6 July, there were two wing patrols. The first was a wing cover operation for bombers returning from a raid, but the wing saw no enemy aircraft. The second brought 'plenty of action' with Bf 109s. One of the Bf 109F pilots' most successful tactics was to dive from their superior altitude into a formation, shoot and break off, without staying to mix it, for the Spitfire Mk V could out-turn the Bf 109F and only had to keep turning to escape or close on a German. Sometimes the Bf 109Fs would break off and then pull up for a snap shot, and sometimes they would half-roll and dive away at a steep angle. On the second sweep of the day, the Bf 109s adopted their favourite tactics. Bader was flying with Johnson and Smith in his section and they stuck together throughout the fight, after which Bader and Johnson claimed a 'destroyed' each, and Smith a 'probable'. In another section, Sergeant Beedham claimed a 'damaged'. Bader described the second sweep:

'During the withdrawal from Lille to Gravelines we were pestered by Me.109s starting to attack and then half-rolling and diving away when we made to engage. Of an initial three bursts I fired at three Me.109Es I claim three frightened (P/O Johnson subsequently destroyed No 3). Finally, two Me.109Rs (I think) positioned themselves to attack from starboard quarter behind when my section was flying above and behind the bombers south of Dunkirk. These two were flying in line astern and I broke my section round on to them when they were quite close (250 yards away). They both did a steeply banked turn, still in line astern, and exposed their complete underside (plan view) to us. I gave one a short burst (no deflection) full in the stomach from 100–150 yards and it fell out of the sky in a shallow dive, steepening up with white and black smoke pouring from it, and finally flames as well. The pilot did not bale out while I was watching.'

Another long-serving and experienced member of No 616 Squadron failed to return from this operation, Sergeant McCairns. A couple of days later, a Spitfire pilot from another squadron saw a Spitfire that had crash-landed on the beach at Dunkirk and noted the squadron and aircraft code letters; it was McCairns' aircraft. Later the ORB recorded that 'he was a prisoner of war, slightly wounded. He had been with us since 14th October [1940] and had shown himself a very capable and keen pilot. He had just applied for a commission.'

On 7 July, a single-section patrol over St Catherine's Point and two wing offensive patrols were flown. In the first wing patrol, the aircraft took off from RAF Friston which, stated the ORB, was 'a new airfield just lately completed near Beachy Head. This airfield had proved unsatisfactory for landing owing to the small size and uneven surface of the ground, and one of our pilots crashed his aircraft there.'

The Wing picked up the bombers off the English coast, escorted them to the target area and back again. 'Odd Bf 109s' were seen but no attacks were made. In the second wing patrol, the Wing, after a quick lunch, flew to Redhill and took off from there. No casualties were inflicted on the German fighters, or the British fighters or bombers. The bombers managed to get bombs in and around the target at Chocques. Sergeant Bowen was shot at by a Bf 109 and had to crash-land, unhurt, at RAF Hawkinge.

On 8 July, the Tangmere Wing flew two wing offensive patrols. The first was an early morning escort for six Stirling four-engined bombers. Enemy fighters had attacked over the target, then, with the new day's sun low behind them, they loitered during the withdrawal but did not engage. However, sporadic flak opened up on the 'Beehive'. It was accurate and blew up one of the Stirlings, only two of whose crew baled out. 'It was not', No 616's ORB recorded, 'a very pleasant sight to watch.'

On the second wing patrol, a few Bf 109s were attacked but no claims resulted. No 616 Squadron had no casualties, but Nos 145 and 610 Squadrons suffered three pilots lost and one wounded. Flying Officer Marples came down too low over the sea while returning from the patrol and damaged his propeller and his starboard wingtip, but he managed to land at Hawkinge. There was no further flying activity that day.

On 9 July, there was a wing offensive patrol near Mazingarbe to escort a bombing raid. The bombing was accurate. However, as No 616 Squadron's ORB recorded, it was a frustrating operation for: 'enemy fighters were seen but were loath to engage but W/C Bader and Sgt Smith engaged and claim one probably destroyed and one "damaged".

Bader described his victory:

'Just after crossing the French coast (with bombers) at 18,000 feet I saw a Me.109 behind and above me diving very steeply, obviously intending to get down below and behind bombers and attack from underneath and then zoom away. I instructed my section I was diving down, and dived straight through and under the escort wing converging on this Me.109 who had not seen me. He saw me as he was starting his zoom and turned right-handed, i.e. into me, and dived away. I was very close by then and aileroned behind him and gave him a 1–2 second burst from 100–150 yards straight behind him. Glycol and heavy black smoke streamed out of his aeroplane and he continued diving. I pulled out at approximately 10,000 feet . . . When he was about 2,000 feet I lost him . . . I am claiming a probable . . . Just after leaving the target area my section was attacked from above and behind and we turned into the attackers, Me.109Fs, who started half-rolling. I got a good short squirt at one and the glycol stream started. Did not follow him down and claim a damaged. Several others were frightened and I claim one badly frightened who did the quickest half-roll and dive I've ever seen when I fired at him.'

Despite the reluctance of the Luftwaffe, No 616 Squadron lost two pilots, Squadron Leader E. P. P. Gibbs and Sergeant Morton. Although he was no longer leading 'A' Flight, Gibbs had been a steadying influence and his loss meant that No 616 Squadron had lost two experienced Flight Commmanders inside a week. This had a disruptive effect on the squadron on the ground, as well as in the air. As predicted, Gibbs, the 'aerobatic king', had not survived long in combat. He was too refined a pilot for the coarse hurly-burly of air fighting, but it was his ability that extricated him from certain death. Picked off by a Bf 109, he was descending without power to the ground but still in control, intending to level off and glide in for a wheels-up landing – no problem! Then he noticed he had company. His victor was following him down. Gibbs realized that as soon as he levelled off at 200 feet, the German would open fire, to make sure of the victory. So, without engine power, Gibbs levelled off and flipped over on to his back, 'out of control'. The Bf 109 backed off. Barely a score of feet above the ground, Gibbs yanked the Spitfire right way up and dropped on to the earth before the startled German could react. Gibbs took to his feet and escaped into unoccupied France and moved on to Spain. He was back in England before the fighting season was out with some story for the Line Book!

On 10 July, the Wing flew a patrol led by Bader, with seven No 616 Squadron Spitfire Mk IIAs and VBs. The Wing took off from Westhampnett at 11.38 hours, detailed for a patrol over France as high cover to the bomber escort of a 'Circus' and 'plenty of enemy fighters were encountered' (No 616 Squadron ORB). Dogsbody Section ('A' Flight) comprised Bader and West as Dogsbody 1 and 2, and Dundas was Dogsbody 3, leading Bader's second pair with Heppell as Dogsbody 4. Bader described their first fight of this sweep:

'Was operating in a four over the Béthune area at 24,000 feet when we saw five Me.109s below us in a wide loose vic. We attacked diving from above and I opened fire at one at 200 yards closing to 100, knocking pieces off it round the cockpit and pulling up over the top. I saw flashes as some of my bullets struck (. . . de Wilde). Was unable after pulling up to see it again, but saw and attacked without result three of the same five (so it is to be supposed that two were hit), immediately after pulling up and turning. My own aeroplane shielded my view immediately after the attack and I claim this one as a probable only, because of the incendiary strikes and the pieces coming off the cockpit.'

Of this same fight, Flight Lieutenant 'Cocky' Dundas, in Dogsbody Section, flying a Mark IIA, recorded:

'The two sections of two in line abreast were flying N from Béthune area, when several Me 109's were seen flying in the same direction. I followed W/Cdr Bader in to attack, but the a/c I picked out dived away and I opened fire at extreme range ["150 yards"], observing no results. . . . '

Just after the Wing had left the French coast over Calais at approximately 12.50, against the dense cloud Bader spotted three Bf 109s flying at 7,000 feet and diving south over Calais. Bader recorded his second fight of this sweep:

'Was flying with section of four northwards over 10/10ths between Calais-Dover. Sighted three Me.109Es below flying south-west over the cloud. Turned and dived to catch them up which we did just over Calais. The three Me.109s were in line abreast and so were my section with one lagging behind. I closed in to 150 yards behind and under the left-hand one and fired a 2-second burst into its belly under the cockpit. Pieces flew off the Me.109 exactly under the cockpit and there was a flash and flame and black smoke, and then the whole aeroplane went up in flames.'

Dundas recorded the second flight:

'After crossing the coast above 10/10 white cloud we sighted 3 Me 109's several thousand ft below flying in wide vic and in a gentle dive towards France. We rolled and dived, W/Cmdr Bader on the left, myself in the middle and P/O Heppell to stbd. Going in line abreast with the others I opened fire from below and behind at about 150 yds range. Fired short bursts amounting to approx. 5 secs, and last burst, when e/a was turning slightly to port, produced vivid flash and e/a commenced to burn. Then broke sharply to starboard, as W/Cmdr Bader had already broken over me, and 3rd e/a on my right had turned and was firing at me.'

Heppell recorded the fight:

'I was Dogsbody 4 flying in W/Cmdr Bader's section and being number two to F/Lt Dundas. . . . The Wing was patrolling in Calais area just prior to returning to Tangmere, when we sighted a section of 3 Me 109's several thousand feet below travelling in the opposite direction in a wide vic. We did a half roll and dived after them and below attaining a speed of about 400. We were diving almost line abreast, Wing Commander Bader on the left, Flight Lieutenant Dundas in the centre and myself on the right. I was slightly farther back than the other two. The e.a on the right which I was attacking saw the other two delivering their attack and turned to the left just as I was about to fire. I fired at him on the turn for a few seconds [at 200 yards] and then broke under him, by this time he was going down in a gentle dive with glycol streaming from him.'

After this attack, Dundas recorded that: 'Section rejoined and flew home just above cloud in wide line abreast at 1000'. Landfall at Dover balloons.'

Following the combat, Bader claimed a 'destroyed' and a 'probable', and Dundas a 'destroyed', West a 'probable' and Heppell a 'damaged'. Both West and Heppell had seen Bader's victim going down in flames in a vertical dive. Nos 145 and 616 Squadrons suffered no losses, but No 610 Squadron lost three pilots, including Sergeants Blackman and J. S. Anderson, who had been posted from No 616 Squadron only a week earlier.

The Tangmere squadrons were still part of the air defence of Great Britain. To give an idea of the flexibility already required of a fighter wing, during the same day, 10 July, two sections of No 616 Squadron also carried out patrols off St Catherine's Point, first Red Section (16.29–17.40 hours) and then Yellow Section (17.32–18.15 hours). Squadrons required a surplus of pilots. The establishment of No 616 Squadron exceeded a score. Of these, at any one time, a number would be non-operational – hence the amount of practice. Given that only seven or nine pilots flew on sweeps, and that Burton, Casson and Marples, and Dundas, Johnson, Heppell, West and Smith were regulars, the other squadron pilots did not fly frequent sweeps, and undertook the convoy and point patrol routines, which still went on even as the sweeps were flown. During the four weeks from 27 June, there was considerable change in No 616 Squadron's sergeants mess, leaving aside casualties.[1] There was always much movement of sergeant pilots between squadrons, and several non-commissioned pilots were posted to No 616 Squadron. Regrettably, an accident on 21 July, when Sergeant F. A. Nelson spun into the ground during local flying practice a week after arriving, reinforced the need for careful assessment and training of new unit pilots, even while the squadrons were mounting intensive operations. By now, the squadron was also suffering combat losses and could ill afford non-operational deaths and injuries.

On 11 July, in the morning (11.11–12.25 hours), eight Spitfire Mk IIAs and VBs of No 616 Squadron with eight Spitfire Mk VBs of No 610 Squadron carried out a Channel sweep led by Squadron Leader Burton: 'The object was to cover the return of bombers from an operation. They were sighted and escorted back.' No 610 Squadron engaged and 'damaged' two Bf 109s, but No 616 Squadron did not engage.

The Wing was now flying a mixture of Mark IIA and VB Spitfires. During July, the Wing exchanged its Mark IIAs for Mark VBs, a higher flying mark with two 20mm cannon and four machine-guns. (A number of the pilots thought they were flying Mark IIs with cannon.) The Spitfire Mk Is and IIs were fast-climbing, short-range point-defence fighters. In the early period between the wars, British fighters had been designed to climb very rapidly to intercept (French) bombers flying from France to bomb England. This was the kind of operation flown in the Battle of Britain, except that the Germans

---

[1] On 27 June, B. W. Kepton was posted from No 66 Squadron, Perranporth. On 28 June, I. Meltin was posted from No 234 Squadron, Warmwell. On 29 June, W. M. Menzies was posted to No 41 Squadron, Catterick. On 30 June, J. S. Anderson and P. F. Brooker were posted from No 152 Squadron, Portreath, and H. C. D. Blackman and J. E. Anderson from No 64 Squadron, Drem. On 3 July, J. S. Anderson was posted back to No 152. On 4 and 5 July respectively, Blackman and J. E. Anderson were posted to No 610 Squadron; they were lost in action on 10 July. On 9 July, L. M. McKee and B. R. Terry, an Australian, were posted in from No 66 Squadron. On 11 July, F. A. Nelson arrived from No 65 Squadron, Kirton-in-Lindsey; he died on 21 July. On 12 July, R. Large arrived from No 66 Squadron.

provided their bombers with a fighter escort. From 1941, British fighters were called upon for bomber escort duties and to engage in fighter-versus-fighter combat, which was not what they had been designed to do. They needed greater engine power, swifter responses, greater firepower and longer range. The Spitfire Mk V was the answer – a fast-climbing, hard-hitting, quick-manoeuvring, truly offensive fighter.

The Spitfire Mk II and V were identical in appearance, which gave the British a tactical advantage of surprise against the Germans. The Mark V used the new 1,475hp Merlin 45 and its derivatives, which were 25 per cent more powerful than the Merlin XII of the Spitfire Mk II. The top speed was no better but the rate of climb rose to 3,250 feet per minute at 15,000 feet, a considerable increase, and the ceiling rose by three thousand feet to some 36,000 feet. Now, the Mark V could climb to fighting height – 20,000 feet plus – in about six minutes. Standard range was not improved – if anything, it decreased because the more powerful engine was thirstier. However, a 24-gallon rear fuselage tank could be fitted, but Squadron Commanders asking their 'erks' to fit this would not be well loved! The radius of action remained only adequate, just under 200 miles – hence the area of operations in the summer of 1941 was restricted to the range of the Spitfire.

British pre-war fighters were designed for guns using the .303-inch British infantry cartridge. Unless fired at close range in large numbers, they lacked the power to penetrate the skin of a modern bomber, let alone its armour. The larger-calibre Hispano cannon fired ninety rounds a minute, and used a heavy solid steel or explosive 20mm shell which could penetrate any aircraft's skin and deal with armour.

No 145 Squadron was the first squadron in the Wing to get the Mark VB because they flew top cover and needed the extra performance the most. No 610 Squadron, the medium cover squadron, got them next, followed by No 616 Squadron. Bader kept his Mark II until everyone else was re-mounted – so that he flew the slowest aeroplane. This was a sign of an understanding leader, for it allowed those behind to keep pace without wasting fuel and attention on high power settings.

The new Spitfires arrived in ones and twos on the squadrons during early July. Most of No 616 Squadron's arrived on 22 July – twelve. The squadron 'experienced a lot of trouble with the cannons' [ORB] – shades of No 19 Squadron in 1940. Many cannon test and aircraft shake-down flights were carried out throughout July into August by the squadrons of the Tangmere Wing. No 616 Squadron's ORB did not pull its punches:

> 'Unfortunately the Armament and Maintenance Sections experiencd considerable difficulty with the cannons and engines, due to poor workmanship and faulty installation. The people responsible for seeing that the new aircraft sent out to operational units are fit to fly and fight in little realise the difficulties which the maintenance staffs have to contend with. In some cases it took a week before the aircraft was finally passed out for operational use. All this extra work had to be done during a period of intense activity, and no praise is too high for all the men engaged in a task which is usually taken for granted and receives very little recognition.'

The original Hispano cannon had a rather bulky drum ammunition box which required blisters on the Spitfire's upper wing surface to accommodate it. Problems were experienced with the feed. Ammunition was stowed with one layer over another, and the belt and cartridge above lay like stacked logs in the troughs of the lower belt. Normal feed was insufficient to pull the next round across the troughs and into the breech. This resistance was aggravated by high G in turns. On later marks, there was an assisted ammunition feed, a sprocket which pulled the belt out of its box. There were also problems caused by oversized rounds, jamming cannon during combat. At altitudes, cannon could jam if the heating were inadequate.

Bader wrote that 'we were entirely happy against the latest Me 190F' when they got the Spitfire Mk V. However, he asserted that cannon tempted pilots to open fire too soon, negating any advantage of cannon firepower. He stuck to a Mark IIA, then flew a machine-gun-armed Mark VA (W3185 from late July), of which a hundred were produced. He may have been so insistent because the cannon showed such reluctance to operate properly. As always, he had his initials 'D-B' painted on his aeroplane instead of squadron and aeroplane codes, to make his aeroplane more readily identifiable in the air.

In the afternoon of 11 July, there was a rather long wing offensive patrol (14.56–17.25 hours). Nos 145, 610 and 616 Squadrons joined up over their base, with Bader leading at the head of No 616 Squadron (seven Spitfires, plus Bader's). They crossed the English coast at Hastings and the French coast at Hardelot with No 616 Squadron leading in the lowest position at 24,000 feet. The Spitfire pilots spotted the bombers, then lost them in the haze over the ground, but continued on to the target area, which the Wing reached at 15.58 hours. Seven minutes later, the Wing began to withdraw. No enemy fighters were engaged, but Sergeant Smith of No 616 Squadron's 'B' Flight found action – which showed how effective the cannon could be as a weapon.

He had oxygen trouble and had to break away from the wing formation and dive down to a lower altitude. He flew home at low level. At 16.15 hours in the St Omer-Longuenesse area, he spotted an aerodrome on which were parked about twenty Ju 87 Stukas. He was flying a Spitfire Mk VB and put the cannon to good use. He made a diving attack on the aerodrome. He:

> 'swooped down low so that his line of sight was in line with the cockpits and engines of the e/a. He opened fire and could see his cannon fire going into the aircraft and observed two emitting flames. . . . He also observed some more e/a on the farther side of the aerodrome, but could not positively say if these were Ju 87s. He did not attack these e/a as by now he was being fired at by several gun positions, and did not think it advisable to go back and attack them, and continued on previous course and crossed the French coast.'

As he sped at high speed and zero feet, making his escape on his previous course, he was heartened to see women in the fields waving at him. As he crossed the coast, he:

> 'observed a soldier in a hut on the ground and fired a short burst at him. Just off the coast he observed a fishing smack but did not attack this. He also observed what appeared to be an E-boat but, unfortunately, was not in a position to attack. This E-boat opened fire on Sgt Smith . . . '

It missed and Smith made landfall slightly west of Dungeness. He put down at Friston to refuel, and returned to base at 17.30 hours.

Firing from close range with no deflection, Allan Smith had 'destroyed' two aircraft and 'damaged' several others for a total expenditure of ammunition of 113 20mm cannon shells and 370 rounds of .303-inch ammunition; his armourers were relieved that he had experienced no stoppages. The sighting of the 'Ju 87s' was important enough for No 616 Squadron's Intelligence Officer, Flight Lieutenant C. R. Gibbs, to submit a full Headquarters Fighter Command Combat Report on 19 July, quoted above.

On 12 July, there was one wing offensive sweep (led by Bader plus seven No 616 Squadron machines, 09.27–11.15 hours). Bader had a very successful engagement, which he described in his combat report:

'When orbitting the wood at Bois de Dieppe about to proceed to St Omer at 26,000 feet, we saw approximately 12–15 Me.109Fs climbing in line astern from Dunkirk turning west and south. I told my section we would attack and told the two top squadrons to stay up as I thought I had seen more Me.109s above. We turned so that the enemy – who were very close and climbing across our bows – were down-sun, and I fired a very close deflection shot at the second last one at 100–50 yards' range. I saw De Wilde flashes in front of his cockpit but no immediate result as I passed him and turned across him and fired a head-on burst at the last Me.109 who had lagged a bit. A panel or some piece of his machine fell away and he put his nose down; as I passed over him I lost him. I then turned round 180 degrees to the same direction as the 109s had been going but could not see them. I called my section together and, after a little, made contact with them. I then saw the "Beehive" and bombers flying over the St Omer wood travelling south-east just below with a squadron of Spitfires above. I saw two Me.109Fs above the Spitfires and dived down to attack. These two flew away south more or less level and I closed up quickly on one which I shot from 100 yards dead astern and produced black smoke and glycol. The second one was banking to the left when I attacked the first and he dived a little after the first. I got in behind him with a good burst, followed him through 10/10ths cloud (about 100 feet thick) and gave him one more burst which set him on fire with a short quick flame under the cockpit, then black smoke, then the whole machine caught fire round the fuselage. The pilot did not bale out. I pulled away at 9,000 feet and I reckon this aeroplane crashed between St Omer and Béthune. I went up to 14,000 feet and called my section together, they were both above the cloud in the same area, and we had no more combat.'

Bader claimed one 'destroyed' and no fewer than three 'damaged'. Sergeant Smith claimed a 'probable' and Pilot Officer Heppell claimed a 'damaged'. The Wing had no losses.

Between 13 and 17 July, there was a break in the intense operations. The weather was too poor to fight on the 13th, and the other four days were occupied with flying practice and the odd convoy patrol, and just one offensive wing patrol, on the 14th, led by Bader with nine No 616 Squadron Spitfires (09.39–12.10 hours). A section of three Bf 109s engaged. One was destroyed by Pilot Officer Johnson, and another was 'damaged' by Sergeant

Smith. Bader cited Dundas and Johnson as witnesses to support his claim of one enemy fighter pilot 'frightened'. Bader had spotted a lone Bf 109, and dived on it himself, but before he opened fire, the pilot baled out. Strictly speaking, a fighter's guns had to be fired for a claim to be made. On 18 July, local flying continued, although three No 616 Squadron sections flew convoy patrols.

On 19 July, the Wing flew an offensive patrol (13.10–15.30 hours), led by Bader plus seven No 616 Squadron Spitfires. Many Bf 109s were encountered. Bader claimed one 'destroyed', and shared another Bf 109F 'destroyed' with Flight Lieutenant Dundas. Bader also claimed a 'probable' and Flight Lieutenant Casson a 'probable'. The Wing had no losses. As Officer Commanding 'A' Flight, but flying in Dogsbody Section, Dundas recorded the 'shared' as a Bf 109F, that the attack took place at 13.55 hours over the Lille area, and that the enemy were at 20,000 to 25,000 feet:

> 'I was Dogsbody 3, leading W/C Bader's second pair, when the wing took off 13.10 hours. Over Lille area section became engaged with Me 109s. I attacked one at long range without result, except a frightened ½ roll, and then pulled up to see another 109 ahead and slightly above. W/C Bader was going in to attack from dead astern, and I came in for a slight deflection shot. Two or 3 short burst with cannons, fired simultaneously with the W/C, destroyed the e/a. The enemy pilot catapulted from his a/c in a very surprising jack-in-the-box style, opening his parachute immediately. Patrol was then resumed.'

To add further to the day, Dundas received the DFC, the first member of No 616 Squadron to do so.

On 20 July, the Wing (Bader led, plus nine No 616 Squadron Spitfires) flew an uneventful offensive patrol, taking off in the late morning at 11.50 hours. Only a few enemy fighters were seen, and the Wing landed at 13.05 hours. A Channel patrol was made by 'A' Flight, No 616 Squadron, led by Dundas to cover destroyers (18.35–19.34 hours).

On 21 July, the Wing took off on the first of two offensive sweeps at 07.42 hours. Bader led, with nine No 616 Squadron Spitfires. Although the enemy refused to fight, Heppell claimed a 'probable' and Beedham a 'damaged' Bf 109. Sergeant Mardon fired at a flak ship with his 20mm cannon, and hit it, which caused the ship to make for shore 'hurriedly'. Heppell (Red 1) and his Number 2 attacked four Bf 109Fs at 09.00 hours at 10,000 feet over the Dunkirk area. He recorded the combat thus:

> 'We crossed the French coast at approximately Le Touquet at about 24,000', my section being stepped up to the right of the W/C. When we reached Lille we went into a left-hand orbit and I led my number 2 into line astern of the leading section. A 109 dived underneath the section in front and I gave chase with my number two. The e.a. turned diving towards the East and so I broke away after giving him a burst at about 400 yds.
> 'I then found that I had lost my number two and so turned around and joined the bomber escort. Just before we reached Gravelines two e/a dived to the right-hand side of the escort, with a Hurricane I gave chase and they dived inland. I again broke off as we were getting low and the

Hurricane had left. I climbed up and was some distance behind the Bombers when I saw two e/a coming up astern. I did a climbing turn to the right and stall turned meeting them head on. They both fired at me and I could see from the tracer coming from the wings that they were 109E's. Another two then arrived which were 109F's. I did violent evasive action of every type I knew, firing occasionally. I then fired at one who came straight through my sights and was a 109F. I very nearly collided with him. I did a steep turn to the left to avoid another who was firing at me and saw that the one I had just fired at was going down in a gentle dive with black smoke coming from him, one of the other 109's went after him. I then went into a steep dive doing turns over the coast and the last I saw of the one who had followed the smoking e/a, he was weaving about him. The other couple dived away to the South West. I then returned at sea level. About four miles from Dover I saw an e/a flying at sea level. I found it was a 109E and squirted it all around one turn without result. My ammunition ran out and I saw another 109 preparing to attack me from above. I did some very steep half turns and went hell for leather for Dover. I saw the 109's climb up to about 4,000' five miles off Ramsgate. I landed at Hawkinge to refuel. I claim the 109F with smoke as probable.'

This engagement illustrates how powerful even a few cannon shells could be when fired accurately. Heppell had opened fire on this Bf 109F from virtually point-blank range, as the notes to his Combat Report record: 'About 75 or 50 yds till it was necessary to break to avoid collision'. Although he had used all his ammunition in several bursts ('112 20mm cannon shells; 1075 0.303'), he suffered no stoppages. The problems with the cannon were being overcome. The Wing was back by 10.05 hours.

Before the late afternoon sweep, No 616 Squadron flew two convoy patrols, one by Red Section (16.45–18.00 hours) and one by Yellow Section (17.35–19.00 hours). The second sweep (led by Bader with nine No 616 Squadron aircraft, 19.50–22.00 hours) produced much fighting. Bader and Dundas each claimed a 'damaged' and Heppell a 'probable'. Sergeant Mabbett did not return from this fight. In the afternoon, Heppell was back as Dogsbody 4, and claimed a Bf 109 'probable' shared with 'Johnnie' Johnson (Red 1) at 20.45 hours in the Merville area:

'While on patrol over the target area our section was flying in an Easterly direction when about 6 Me 109's were sighted travelling to the south and about a thousand feet below us. Our section did a steep turn diving slightly. I took the e/a on the extreme right, diving slightly below him until I was within range. I then pulled up getting my sights on to him and giving him a burst with cannons and M.G.'s from dead astern ("250 to 150 yards . . . 4½-second burst"). Then someone called over the R/T telling us to break as there were more e/a behind us. Just before I broke I saw glycol start to stream from the 109 and his nose dropped slowly and went into a steep dive. I then lost sight of the e.a. in my turn and Red 1 (P/O Johnson) gave him a squirt. When I had turned around and seen there was nothing close behind me, I looked down and saw the e.a. was about five to ten thousand feet below still in the same attitude, pouring out glycol and black smoke. I then joined up with some other Spitfires, who were shooting at other 109's, who were diving for the ground.'

Johnson recorded this fight:

Above: The Royal Air Force College, Cranwell, flight-line at the start of the 1930s. (Courtesy of the Commandant, RAF College, Cranwell)

Below: The sight from the hangar mouth greeting Second Year Cranwellians on the fighter course each morning: the Flight's Siskins being warmed up. (Courtesy of the Commandant, RAF College, Cranwell)

Above: An Armstrong Whitworth Siskin operated by the RAF College, Cranwell. Douglas Bader graduated from the Avro 504N to the Siskin as his operational type. (Courtesy of the Commandant, RAF College, Cranwell)

Below: During Operation DYNAMO, RAF Spitfire and Hurricane Squadrons operated away from their home airfields closer to the action. This is RAF Gravesend. (Private)

Above: Firepower 1940! A No 611 Squadron Spitfire Mk I's eight machine-guns being tested in the butts at its home base, RAF Digby. No 611 Squadron joined the Duxford Wing. (Private)

Below: 'Dicky' Cork (left) beside Eric Ball with two other pilots of No 242 (Canadian) Squadron, RAF, at RAF Duxford in 1940. (FAA Museum)

Above: 'Dicky' Cork with another great Naval fighter pilot, A. G. Blake – 'The Admiral' – of No 19 Squadron, at RAF Fowlmere in 1940. (FAA Museum)

Below: Acting Flight Lieutenant P. S. Turner leaning on the tail of his Hurricane, No 242 Squadron, 1940 (IWM)

Above: Denis Crowley-Milling (right) and Pilot Officer M. G. Homer (centre) with an unidentified pilot, No 242 Squadron, 1940. (IWM)

Below: Flight Commander 'Johnnie' Johnson (with pipe), Bader's No 4 during the summer of 1941, photographed later with his No 616 Squadron Flight and a model signpost pointing to their combat areas. (IWM)

Left: Hawker Sea Hurricane pilot of No 880 Squadron, FAA. (P. C. Smith)

Bottom left: HMS *Eagle* with Hawker Sea Hurricane on approach, shortly before the carrier was torpedoed. (P. C. Smith)

Below: In 1942, Malta's tactical situation demanded Spitfires but it was hard to get them to the island. Mark Vs were quickly modified not only for the climate with tropical filters but with long-range tanks to allow them to be flown off carriers, like this one seen in unfamiliar British snow. (V–S)

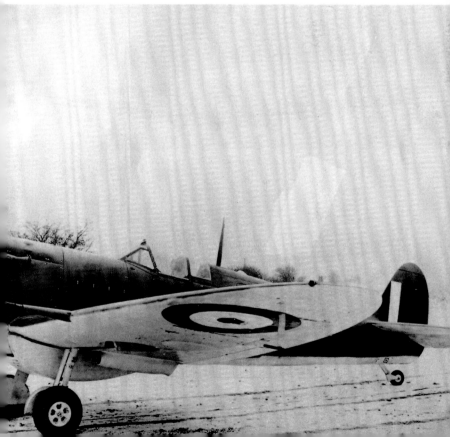

Below: Eight-gun fighter bullet patterns, superimposed on Heinkel He 111 at 100 yards' range.

25% of hits zone ~ 75% of hits zone

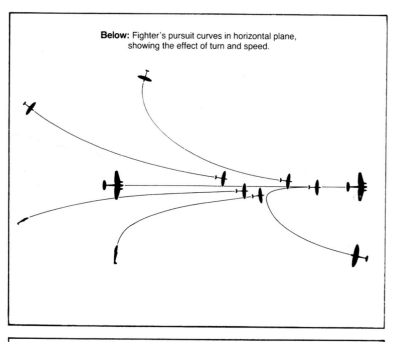

Below: Fighter's pursuit curves in horizontal plane, showing the effect of turn and speed.

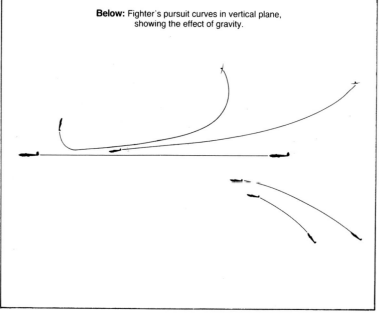

Below: Fighter's pursuit curves in vertical plane, showing the effect of gravity.

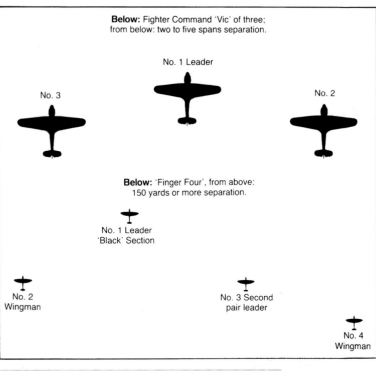

Below: Fighter Command 'Vic' of three; from below: two to five spans separation.

No. 1 Leader

No. 3

No. 2

Below: 'Finger Four', from above: 150 yards or more separation.

No. 1 Leader
'Black' Section

No. 2
Wingman

No. 3 Second
pair leader

No. 4
Wingman

Left: A Spitfire Mk VC of Malta's Takali Wing, showing its Mediterranean camouflage. (Private)

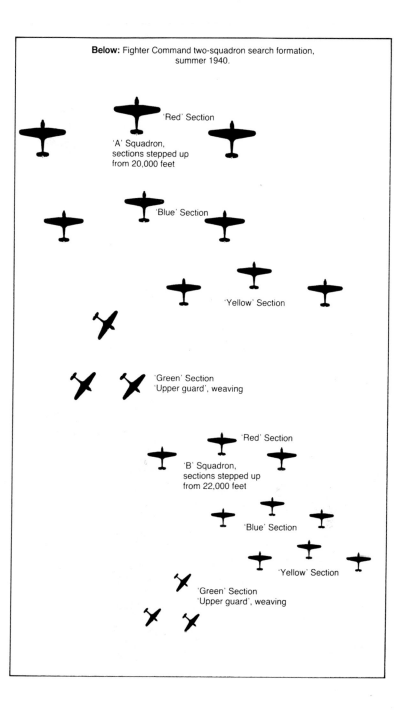

Below: Fighter Command two-squadron search formation, summer 1940.

'Red' Section

'A' Squadron, sections stepped up from 20,000 feet

'Blue' Section

'Yellow' Section

'Green' Section 'Upper guard', weaving

'Red' Section

'B' Squadron, sections stepped up from 22,000 feet

'Blue' Section

'Yellow' Section

'Green' Section 'Upper guard', weaving

Left: Hawker Typhoon Mk I instrument panel, 1942. (M.G. Burns)

Below: Hawker Typhoon Mk IA of No 486 (NZ) Squadron. (IWM)

Right: Wing Commander 'Johnnie' Johnson in his Kenley Wing Spitfire Mk IX, 1943. (IWM)

Bottom right: Hugh Dundas about to be presented to HM The King when His Majesty visited Desert Air Force squadrons in Italy. (IWM)

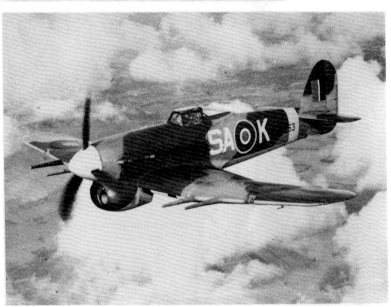

Left: Vickers-Supermarine Spitfire Mk VIII (AN–O) of No 417 (City of Windsor) Squadron, RCAF, No 244 Wing, commanded by Hugh Dundas, taking off on 10 January 1944. It has the extended span wing for high-altitude operations. (Canadian Archives)

Below: Group Captain J. E. Johnson, Station Commander of RAF Wildenrath, Germany, and his North American Sabre F.4, XB686, in the mid-1950s. (J. D. R. Rawlings)

Right: Douglas Bader on the course at the Royal and Ancient at St Andrews, drives his ball down the fairway with characteristic aggression. (*Dundee Courier*)

Above: Douglas Bader at St Andrews. Golfing was a game he could play on equal terms with anyone. Usually he set a cracking pace and was on the heels of those in front. (*Dundee Courier*)

'I was Red 1 on patrol with my squadron near the target area flying at 26,000'. I positioned by section (comprising Sgt Mabbett and myself) to starboard and slightly above and behind the Dogsbody section when 6 109s were sighted flying eastwards, and D.B. swung round to position his section for an attack from astern. I then brought my section slightly below and almost abreast of the D.B. section and at this stage my No 2 was with me. When about 250 yards from the enemy formation I saw D.B.4 (P/O Heppell) open fire at the right-hand 109 which emitted glycol fumes but continued to fly straight carrying out gentle swings to port and starboard. Unfortunately I did not hear the order to break and pressed home my attack on the right-hand e/a from 150 to 200 yards. After 2 short bursts [8 machine-guns] the nose of the e/a dropped slowly and it eventually went into a vertical dive, the white glycol fumes giving way to thick black smoke. I then broke away and did not see e/a again. My No 2 (Sgt Mabbett) was not seen again after this engagement.'

Johnson and Heppell joined up and made their way back to the French coast, over Boulogne. Both pilots commented on the very accurate flak they experienced when crossing the French coast. They crossed into England over Dungeness – one of the 'anti-aircraft gun safe' zones for returning fighters – and landed at Tangmere. The loss of his Number 2 moved Johnson deeply, for it was the first wingman he had lost. The Germans buried Mabbett at St Omer with full military honours.

On 22 July, the squadron had another busy day. In the first offensive sweep of the day, led by Bader with seven No 616 Squadron aircraft (12.10–13.47 hours), the Wing escorted Blenheims over Le Frait, where they bombed some E-boats, but though their bombs fell in the target area, hits were not observed. The sweep was without incident. No enemy aircraft were seen. During the late afternoon, No 616 Squadron also flew patrols: a six-aircraft patrol over Selsey Bill (15.10-15.47 hours), Blue Section taking over (16.10-16.49 hours). Concurrently, 'A' Flight flew a base patrol between 16.27 and 16.48 hours. After four hours' break, the Wing flew another offensive sweep in the evening (21.07–22.48, Bader leading eleven No 616 Squadron machines) as escort to Beauforts to Le Havre and Cherbourg to attack shipping in harbour. No results of the bombing were seen and no enemy aircraft were met.

On 23 July, a brief early morning patrol by No 616 Squadron's Blue Section confirmed that the weather was not good enough for a wing sweep, so Bader and Squadron Leader Burton made a Channel sweep off Dunkirk, Gravelines and Calais; they followed the Hurricanes of No 242 Squadron which were to bomb a ship off Dunkirk, in the hope of catching some of the fighters which rose to intercept the Hurricanes. They took off from Manston at 13.40 hours, just after No 242 Squadron, and landed back there at 14.25 hours, just after the Hurricane squadron. In a combat out to sea just around Dunkirk, Bader claimed a 'damaged', possibly 'destroyed' Bf 109. He recorded the sortie thus:

'The weather was very hazy from about 1,000 feet upwards but clearer below. We flew from North Foreland and near Gravelines were attacked by a Me.109 out of the sun. We countered and Sqn Ldr Burton had a shot at it. It flew low over the water to the French coast.

'We carried on up to Dunkirk and slightly past where we saw some flak and then a Spitfire . . . flying straight for home in a dive being attacked by a Me.109. We immediately turned on the Me.109 which saw us and did a left-hand climbing turn back to France, but I got a very close short burst (½ second) at him from underneath and behind him. It definitely hit him and produced a puff of white smoke under his cockpit. I turned away immediately as I had no idea how many were about and did not want to lose Sqn Ldr Burton.'

In the evening of 23 July, the Wing (led by Bader plus nine No 616 Squadron aircraft) made a sweep (19.40–21.24 hours) over northern France and met many enemy fighters. At about 20.30 hours, Casson's Blue Section became involved with thirty Bf 109Fs and two Bf 109Es at 18,000 feet over Hazebrouck. The manner in which Casson described the combat illustrates the way to handle pairs in combat:

'I was Blue 1 leading a section of four aircraft to port of and above the squadron. As we approached the French coast over Le Touquet at 22,000 feet the leading section broke up after somebody had informed the leader that he was about to be attacked from the rear.

'The squadron to port of the wing crossed over and we were ordered to continue our course inland, with the result that my section was flying about a mile ahead of the wing.

'Several enemy aircraft passed over us when we were about fifteen miles inland but did not attack and upon reaching Hazebrouck Wood about thirty Me 109F's were seen climbing up directly behind us in a very ragged formation. We split into two pairs and I turned to port with my No 2 and dived on the last two E/A which were in line astern and lagging slightly, giving two bursts of approximately two seconds each, one from about 350 yds and the other from 200 yds as the deflection decreased from 60° to 40°. The last aircraft turned over and dived away emitting black smoke and I lost sight of it in the haze as it dived down directly over Hazebrouck Wood. My No 2 who engaged these aircraft with me saw pieces fall from it as it dived away.

'Breaking right I climbed again and looked out for my No 2 (P/O Trench) but couldn't see him. He saw me however and was climbing up to rejoin when four Me 109's crossed his path, he followed them. After weaving about for a short time, I decided to make for the coast again and saw two Me 109's climbing up about 2,000 ft below me. I went into a half roll and tried to engage them but was travelling too fast and couldn't get my sights to bear on either of them. They didn't see my first effort and it was not until I had crossed behind them and was diving again from the port quarter that they saw me. They broke upwards in opposite directions and I opened up at the nearer aircraft from 300 yds and closing to about 100 yds, with one long burst. White smoke suddenly poured from his engine and turning very steeply he dived away almost vertically leaving a trail of white and black smoke. I followed him down to about 7,000 ft and saw him crash close to a small wood on the south side of Abbeville and burst into flames. I then turned north for home and hit the coast at Dungeness.'

Casson destroyed one Bf 109E and damaged two Bf 109s – his claim brought No 616 Squadron's 'bag' to fifty. Bader and Dundas shared a 'destroyed' claim, and Johnson claimed a 'damaged'. It is interesting to note that Casson, who recorded that he was flying a 'Spit IIB', fired fifty-six cannon shells in several combats and suffered no stoppages.

On 24 July, in the early afternoon, the Wing led by Bader (plus ten No 616 Squadron aircraft) took off to escort Blenheims to bomb Cherbourg docks, which was successfully carried out (13.10–14.34 hours). No enemy fighters were seen. Unlike the flak experienced a few days earlier over Boulogne by Johnson and Heppell, the flak over the Cherbourg area was, according to No 616 Squadron's ORB, 'very inaccurate and sparse, showing that the enemy have moved most of their guns and fighters to the northern France area'. This was a sensible move by the Germans, for the RAF was operating most intensively over northern France. This demonstrates the effect that the offensive was having. Nevertheless, the operation had taken its toll: at 15.54 hours, ten No 616 Squadron aircraft were scrambled to search for a Blenheim crew reported to be down in the sea, but although they searched for an hour and a half, they did not find them.

However, this was the last offensive sweep that the Tangmere Wing flew for a fortnight. The weather had held throughout the month, but now became unreliable with frequent low cloud and rain, and 'Rhubarbs' seemed to be on the menu. On 25 July, a day with no operational flying, No 616 Squadron's ORB pinpointed a change: 'From now on intense activity decreased owing to weather deteriorating.' There were two other reasons for a falling-off in operations. First, the Tangmere Wing was changing over to the Spitfire Mk VB but there were many problems with the engines and armament. Second, on 28 July, No 145 Squadron was rotated for rest to Catterick, Yorkshire. Predictably, Stan Turner raised hell and refused to leave Bader, but the order was enforced. No 41 Squadron, commanded by the Canadian Squadron Leader Elmer Gaunce, took their place: it needed to be inducted to the Wing's ways, and that would take some time. Many in the Tangmere Wing were concerned about making such a fundamental change to the Wing during the 'season'. It seemed dangerous to break up such a closely interdependent team as Nos 145, 610 and 616 – and so it proved.

On 26 July, the Wing took off in the early morning but the operation was cancelled by Bader before they were over the sea, because the visibility was so poor. Westhampnett was unserviceable owing to the excessive wetness. 'No further flying was done' (ORB). On 27 July, no operational flying was done, only cannon tests, local flying and formation practices. On 28 July, there was one patrol made over Shoreham and cannon tests. The next day, four sections of No 616 Squadron patrolled a convoy. There were cannon tests and local flying practice. On 30 July, there was no operational flying, but cannon tests, local flying practice and flight air drill; and on the 31st, 'only some local flying and cannon tests made' (ORB). On 1 August, several cannon tests were carried out, then the Wing was released for the afternoon. It looked as if a return to the existence of April and May was imminent.

There was another reason for 'resting' the Tangmere Wing. Bader had now flown more sweeps than any other pilot in Fighter Command, and he still insisted on leading his Wing on every sortie. In one seven-day period he had flown ten sweeps. He was approaching exhaustion. Many of his pilots were also fatigued, but Bader's responsibilities did not start and end with flying the sweep. They were all-embracing. He had to ensure that the orders were precise and correctly disseminated; he had to ensure that the squadrons took off on time and assembled over the rendezvous at the correct heights at the precise time; he had to ensure that the heights were appropriate and that the speeds, headings and timings were right at all points of an operation. He had to control the three squadrons; he had to be aware of all threats to the Wing, and had to be the focus of the control, until the point that combat was engaged – then it was every pair for itself. Even then, it was the principles which Bader had striven to inculcate in them which brought them victory.

Bader had also the routine of organization on the ground. At the end of a day, Bader would often have to fly over to No 11 Group's Headquarters where the wing leaders foregathered with the senior staff officers and Leigh-Mallory to discuss progress, exchange views and hear policy. Leigh-Mallory had instituted these meetings – a continuation of the process he had begun during Christmas 1940, of consulting with his fighter commanders. He called conferences of his station and wing commanders at Headquarters Uxbridge after important operations.

Bader put a great deal of effort into these meetings, always ensuring that his Wing was duly prominent, that its efforts were recognized, and his comments were often forceful and could be quite caustic, especially after the senior officers had withdrawn. Douglas Bader was putting out a great deal of physical, mental and emotional energy. He was thriving on the ultimate competitive game of fighter sweeps, but the strain was taking its toll on his nervous system, whether he recognized it or not. Bader was not chasing victories: he had a score, to Malan's and Tuck's thirty-plus; he was more content that the Wing should score high and that the Luftwaffe units should be defeated in their encounters with his Wing. Claims mislead; victory was hard to assess, but if the air were clear of enemy fighters, if they were unopposed, then that would be victory.

Wing Commander Adolf ('Sailor') Malan was the top-scoring RAF pilot at that point. He had been leading fighters on operations since Dunkirk in May 1940. He had led No 74 Squadron throughout the toughest battles of 1940. He had been leading the Biggin Hill Wing for as long as Bader had been leading the Tangmere Wing. Malan had self-awareness. He recognized in himself the tardy reactions, the dulled senses of danger and self-preservation and other signs of combat fatigue. He had seen it in others: they ended up dead and put at risk the lives of their fellow pilots. Malan had humility. He knew that he was no longer fit to take the responsibility for his men that his position demanded. With great moral courage, at the end of July 1941, he asked Trafford Leigh-Mallory to remove him from command. Leigh-Mallory did so immediately. Within days, a new wing leader had been found. Malan was sent off on an extremely useful lecture tour of the United States, to raise the consciousness of the American people to the plight of Great Britain. He was a fine ambassador.

The implications of Malan's request concerned Leigh-Mallory. He got hold of Bader as soon as he could and told him what had happened. Leigh-Mallory emphasized that no opprobrium attached to Malan's request – indeed, quite the reverse – and then invited Bader to step down. Bader was deeply touched by Leigh-Mallory's understanding of the pressures that he was under. He believed that the fighting season was nearly over, and he wanted to see it through, rather as if it were a rugby season. Bader had been leading constantly since late May 1940, fifteen months, and had been operational for eighteen months, but he did not feel that he was in any great danger of making mistakes, far less of crumbling. He declined Leigh-Mallory's invitation.

Exhaustion is its own drug, and Bader was at that dangerous stage when a dulled sense of his own feelings urged him not to let go. A harder commander than Leigh-Mallory would have ordered him to stand down, but, calmly, sadly, he acquiesced. Leigh-Mallory had commanded aircrew in the harsh 1918 campaigns and he knew the virtually inevitable consequences of Bader's continuing as Tangmere Wing Leader.

Peter MacDonald, who had served with No 242 Squadron under Bader, arrived on posting to Tangmere as Station Adjutant. It was more than a fortuitous posting. Peter MacDonald saw just how tired Bader was. There were great blue weals under his eyes, a quick tetchiness with anyone not associated with the Wing, a remoteness. MacDonald advised him to rest. He and Leigh-Mallory got as far as getting Bader's agreement that he would step down as Tangmere Wing Leader at the end of September, but that was the end of the fighting season, and there might be another forty or fifty sweeps flown by then. With an older man's paternalism and Thelma Bader's knowledge, Peter MacDonald organized a golfing holiday in St Andrews for himself with Douglas and Thelma Bader in the second week of August, a week when the cool wind of Fife would take the heat off the sweltering summer, and Bader could knock his nerves back into shape. Bader agreed to go.

There was still a requirement for offensive operations, but the weather was becoming uncertain. Instead of euphoria, there was often frustration. On 2 August, a Channel guard to cover bombers withdrawing from Cherbourg was cancelled after take-off owing to poor visibility. Two convoy patrols were made. On 3 August, there was no operational flying. On 4 August, there was an offensive sweep by six aircraft from No 616 Squadron led by Bader, as high escort, 'but it was unsuccessful owing to the poor visibility' [ORB]. On 5 August, one section patrolled over Beachy Head and one Lysander escort was carried out, despite a gale warning in the morning, but the weather improved in the afternoon. The next day, there were six convoy patrols, while an exercise with GCI made a change to the routine of cannon tests, local flying and aerobatics that had occupied the other four days.

Bader was concerned by the inactivity. So were his pilots. He telephoned the Air Officer Commanding late at night to point out that the Tangmere Wing had not flown a sweep since 24 July. The Wing wanted action! Leigh-Mallory agreed to include the Wing on the offensive operations being flown. The next morning, 7 August, No 616 Squadron carried out air tests and a squadron

'Balbo'; then it flew its first offensive wing sweep for a fortnight in the late afternoon. The Wing got the action it wanted. The sweep produced several fights in which Sergeants Derek Beedham and Jeff West claimed a 'damaged' each. Beedham flew at Yellow 2 with 'B' Flight. No 616 Squadron took off from Westhampnett at 17.15 hours, and joined up with the Wing. The Wing crossed the French coast just before 18.00 hours at Hardelot. Soon afterwards, at 20,000 feet just west of Béthune, the first enemy fighters were sighted. Derek Beedham recalled seeing:

> '20 plus Me 109F climbed past and starboard of us, behind us and into the sun. The whole wing orbited to starboard. Just about now 4 E.A. came round behind. Yellow Section turned inside them. I was just on the point of spinning when I saw an E.A. start diving away so I put my nose down and closing in to 200 yds gave him a short burst with 1 cannon, the other having never fired owing to faulty ammunition. No results. Turning and climbing back I could not see any other aircraft in the sky, so I started weaving back towards the coast, turning steeply . . . at about 300mph. Almost immediately I saw an aircraft coming in on the inside of the turn, it had a duck-egg blue spinner but was slightly "Bluer" than ours, at first I thought it was Yellow 1, on tightening up the turn it opened fire. I had no difficulty in out-turning the E.A. which was a Me 109F, 3 guns firing from the nose, altitude 20,000 ft (approximately). I completed the circle and saw the E.A. approaching from the port beam, so I turned head-on to him and opened fire with cannon and machine-gun. He also fired. We broke to starboard and started a dogfight, in which I had no difficulty in out-manoeuvring the E.A. Most of my attacks were from the beam either ahead or astern; E.A. opened fire wildly every time I tried to get in a head-on attack and I made him put his nose straight down. I was able to draw the fight across to the coast. At about 6,000 feet, while I was turning inside his steep turn, he reversed his bank and I got in a good 2-second burst of cannon and machine-gun, the E.A. put his nose down and dived away underneath towards France.
>
> 'I continued weaving towards England when the E.A. again appeared on the inside of the turn. I gradually tightened up the turn increasing the speed to over 300mph and then whipped over into a turn in the opposite direction and almost blacking out on the turn, I opened fire on E.A. from the port beam and continued firing until we were head-on, the E.A. opened fire just after me and stopped as we were head-on. I saw a cannon shell explode in his port wing and some engine cowlings coming off. The E.A. passed underneath me and as I turned it was spiralling to the left down to the sea, but did not appear to be completely out of control. Landed Westhampnett 18.37 hours.'

On 8 August, the weather was too bad for flying. Only one local flying practice was made. On 9 August, there was a wing sweep in the late morning. During the operation No 616 Squadron claimed four 'destroyed' and one 'probable', which was, as the ORB said, 'a very good effort'. But any sense of victory was taken away by the two losses. No 616 Squadron's ORB recorded:

> 'This was a very sad day because we lost our much admired wing leader, Wing Commander Bader, and F/Lt L. H. Casson, 'B' Flight Commander and one of the "Originals" of the Squadron. Both these leaders were very popular with everyone and their absence will be sadly felt.'

CHAPTER 13
Pas de Calais

On the morning of 9 August, the Tangmere Wing was detailed as high cover escort for a bombing raid on Béthune. Bader's usual Number 2, Allan Smith, had a heavy cold in his head. Regulations forbade a pilot to fly with blocked sinuses, so he was grounded and went off to London to buy a new uniform for he was about to be commissioned. The experienced New Zealander Jeff West flew instead as Dogsbody 2. Dundas and Johnson made the second pair, as Dogsbody 3 and 4. Bader, flying his Spitfire Mk VA (W3185), led his section of four off Westhampnett airfield at 10.40 hours, followed by No 616 Squadron's second and third sections, Yellow and Blue, led by Squadron Leader 'Billy' Burton and Flight Lieutenant 'Buck' Casson. It was a perfectly routine target support operation of the kind they had flown several dozen times, a high-altitude penetration of 30 miles inland.

As he settled into the climb a few minutes after take-off, Bader noticed that his airspeed indicator was not working. It registered a steady zero. This was a legitimate reason to return to base, especially for a leader. It was necessary to know how fast they were travelling in order to get the timings and speeds of the wing penetration right.

On time a few minutes later, No 616 Squadron's twelve Spitfires flew into position below No 610 Squadron's twelve Spitfires over Chichester and headed for the rendezvous at Beachy Head, but there was no sign of No 41 Squadron. The two squadrons waited, but the medium cover squadron failed to make the rendezvous on time. Strict radio silence was enforced, so Bader could not call up Squadron Leader Elmer Gaunce to ask where the hell he was. Nos 610 and 616 set out without the third unit.

However, without an airspeed indicator, Bader could no longer lead the Wing. Moreover, Bader's radio was not functioning properly or clearly. The Wing had to arrive over the French coast at a specific time; he had to know their speed. Bader signalled to Dundas to take over the lead. Dundas moved ahead. He had the time over the French coast and the required speed written in indelible pencil on the back of his left hand. Bader slipped into subordinate position, but he would have expected any other pilot to have turned back under such circumstances: but he did not.

It was imperative that the Tangmere Wing, already depleted, should arrive on time in the correct position and at the right speed and height. The difficulty did not lie in loss of numerical strength, but in the coverage of the sky that three squadrons permitted. It was a deficiency that could be made good by positioning. Although Bader's experienced touch was lacking, Dundas knew what Bader would do under the circumstances, and did it.

The Wing encountered heavy broken cumulus cloud up to 12,000 feet, which made conditions difficult. There was a brilliant sun high in the summer blue sky, with hazy cirrus clouds like a shift round it. An aeroplane would be silhouetted against the cumulus by such a sun. Dundas reasoned that Bader would want to go in high in such conditions and climbed the Wing to 28,000 feet; the force carried on its way, above the cloud. The Wing crossed the French coast south of Le Touquet on time. Bader called up Dundas on the radio to say he was resuming the lead: he did not need his airspeed indicator now. Dundas had done his job. It was very rarely that Bader delegated the lead. He was driven by his sense of duty and responsibility. He had no 'second-in-command'. He shouldered the whole burden on each and every sweep, made all critical judgments, and the strain was beginning to show.

The Spitfire pilots kept a wary watch for the Bf 109s from Abbeville and Wissant, the nearest bases to the coast, on the 30-mile run-in to Béthune. No 616 Squadron led at 26,000 feet, with No 610 Squadron 2,000 feet above to their starboard, between them and the sun. Later, as they approached the target, they would meet the Merville and St Omer Bf 109 Staffeln. On the return, they would face fresh fighters, with St Omer straddling their way like an aerial fortress.

As the 'Beehive' approached Béthune, Bader took the Wing in a slow orbit to port. Ken Holden, leading No 610 Squadron, spotted three loose sections of Bf 109s, twelve fighters, coming in quickly like sharks in a fast turn round the port forward quarter of Bader's section. Bader and Dundas could not see them for a second or two, as they were hidden from view. They rocked their Spitfires to see below their wing. Bader complained irritably to Holden: 'I can't see the bastards. Where the hell are they?' His usual calm humour had deserted him. Holden told him to look below his port wing. Simultaneously, both Dogsbody leaders saw the three Bf 109 'finger-fours', in line abreast two or three thousand feet below, and a mile or so in front. It was the perfect position for a classic 'bounce', but it was too good to be true. The Dogsbody pilots knew the ways of the Germans and sensed that something was not right.

Bader watched for a second or two, calculating. Then he told Ken Holden to keep his No 610 Squadron in position as top cover. Behind Dogsbody Section, Burton and Casson held position to give immediate protection against stern attack. There were three sections of four Bf 109s, each in line abreast – one section for each of No 616 Squadron's sections. Where was the catch? Then Bader signalled 'Attacking' to Dogsbody Section. He curved to port in a coarse turn and led his section down on the rear of the middle section of Bf 109s. Behind, Blue and Yellow Sections fanned out to attack the outer Bf 109 sections.

Dogsbody Section drew into line abreast, in a well-rehearsed manner, but there was a lack of smoothness. There was a target for each of them but they lost precious seconds setting up the attack. Bader selected the Bf 109 second from starboard. West was to Bader's port and Dundas to his starboard

with Johnson out to Dundas's starboard. Dundas chose the extreme starboard
Bf 109 as his target. That meant that Johnson had to slide beneath the
formation from the right to the extreme left, beyond West, to engage the
extreme port fighter. The pilots set their sights on their selected victims. The
Bf 109s flew straight and level.

Bader misjudged the attack. 'I was tense,' he wrote, 'and my judgment
had gone for some reason which I did not recognize at the time. One never
did.' He dived too fast and too steeply. He tried to get his fire on his selected
target, but he had no chance to steady his aircraft behind it. He nearly
collided with it as he went straight through the formation. The others
managed to open fire at the same time as he did – sound tactics – but only by
using their controls coarsely.

To starboard, Yellow Section hit the starboard section of Bf 109s and to
port Blue Section hit the port section. The seconds of delay cost them
surprise, and the Bf 109s turned on them. Philip Heppell (Yellow 3) and Roy
Marples (Blue 3) each knocked down a Bf 109 in the shock of the first clash.

Then everyone was split up into individual dogfights. Someone had
called loudly over the radio: 'BREAK!! For Christ's sake break!'

Bader was not conscious of hearing the command – he was already diving
away from his first false pass. Blue and Yellow Sections were already in a
tussle. Dogsbody Numbers 2, 3 and 4 were hammering their victims. No one
knew who had called the break or for whom it was intended, but they could
not take chances. Johnson, West and Dundas snapped out of their attacks and
reefed themselves round to confront the Bf 109s that had cut in from above, to
spring the trap.

Holden had kept his No 610 Squadron's twelve Spitfires orbiting. Now
he brought his own section down to even up the odds.

In the initial attack, Johnson got in a half-second burst and managed to
shoot pieces off a Bf 109 but in that instant that word 'BREAK' came through
his radio headphones, instantly given real meaning when cannon shells came
past his starboard wing – other Bf 109s had worked round from above or
underneath. He whipped round, his harness like strips of metal against his
shoulders. He was set upon by three Bf 109s. He kept turning. He spiralled
down into the cloud. The Bf 109s tried to cut in on his turns. Johnson was
heading for the ground. He lost the Bf 109s in the cloud.

Dundas and West had been firing when they too had heard the break
called and had glanced up and seen the nasty flickering of the cannon in their
rear-view mirrors. They turned to face their attackers, getting in short bursts,
but kept turning, jinking, instinctively trying to avoid getting tricked by one
Bf 109 into a move that forced them across the guns of another Bf 109. Then,
apart, they made for the clouds, and set the power high and their dive steeply
for the Channel coast 20 miles away.

Bader may have heard the order to break and reacted instinctively. He
was going too fast to turn. Diving away from his target, he levelled off at
24,000 feet – alone. The sky was entirely empty. West and Dundas and
Johnson had all become involved in individual fights and were isolated. The
'finger-four' had broken. Bader was at a dangerous height, silhouetted above

the cloud. He had no cover: in such circumstances, he had repeatedly told his pilots that they had to dive for the deck and head for home, preferably with another Spitfire as a pair. He debated whether to head home, or go on to the target. He decided to go on.

Then he saw six Bf 109s a couple of miles in front of him, six tempting targets, three line astern pairs, widely placed, too well placed to miss. They were heading for Béthune, too. He decided to stalk them; if they spotted him, then he would dive and go home. He slipped in behind and below the rear aircraft of the centre pair, gently, and fired steadily, a three-second burst from close range. A sudden flame spurted from behind the cockpit as the petrol tank was hit. Then the rear fuselage burst into fire. Bader watched it fall away on fire.

Bader moved forward to pick off his victim's leader. There were a pair of Bf 109s flying off each of his wingtips, but there was no danger from them unless they spotted him and turned at him. While they were going in the same direction as him, their guns did not threaten him. If they saw him and turned to attack, he would dive and break for home at low level. Alone, Bader thought he could get away with his attack. The Bf 109s did not seem to be on proper guard.

The Bf 109 filled Bader's gyroscopic sight graticule and his thumb was just pressing on the trigger. His guns chattered. He prudently looked right and then left and spotted the two Bf 109s on his left turning sharply towards him. They had seen him. They were going to attack him. Bader's gunfire was knocking chunks off the Bf 109 but he abandoned his attack: he had once before tried to finish off an attack when he himself had been under attack, and he knew it could be fatal. He broke off in a turn.

But he broke off in a turn away from his attackers, not towards them, the rule as old as fighter air war, as old as naval warfare. His attackers saw his tail through their gunsights. Bader could not see his attackers. If he had flown at them, they would have been unlikely to have hit him with gunfire. But he turned towards the pair of Bf 109s on his right because they represented no threat to him. They were still flying straight and level. They had not seen him. Bader intended to pass either over them or under them, and then dive for the deck and home – a Bf 109F could not hold a Spitfire Mk V in a dive.

It was only a short distance, but the Bf 109s behind were closing in. As he passed under the aftermost of the pair of Bf 109s on the right, Bader banked over hard right towards home and began his dive.

He saw the tail of the Bf 109 out of the corner of his eye, heard a rending noise behind him, saw pieces fly off his Spitfire, and then his Spitfire lunged forward. He tried to haul the control column back. Nothing. No resistance. No force. The Spitfire was diving vertically, spinning. Bader looked behind him. The tail had gone. He glanced forward at his instruments – habit – and saw the altimeter unwinding like a racing wheel – 20,000 feet already! Get out!

He reached up and grasped the hood release and pulled. The canopy flew off. The cockpit filled with noise and rushing air. He released his harness. As it fell off, he was sucked out of the cockpit by the rush of air. But he did not leave his aircraft. He was held against it, battered, his mind buffeted into confusion by the wind. Then, he was free. His artificial right leg had caught in the cockpit, then suddenly snapped off free. He pulled his parachute and drifted down. He was no more than four or five thousand feet up. He fell through a cloud, and heard an aeroplane coming fast towards him. A Bf 109 flew round him, then vanished. Seconds later, Bader landed. His remaining artificial leg crumpled hard into his ribs. He had no hope of evading capture.

Widely separated, the Wing's pilots were heading for the ground and making their way back in ones and twos at low level across the Channel. The fight was not entirely over, however. As Johnson hurtled through the cloud making his escape, he had heard Squadron Leader Burton order the Wing home. Recovering at low altitude, he made for base. A Bf 109 appeared below him. He warily checked the sky for others, then dropped beneath the careless German, stalking him, and closed to killing range. His cannon shells ripped the 109's belly open. It went straight down.

As they were heading out across northern France, West, Dundas and Johnson heard Woodhall repeatedly calling for Bader to answer. There was no response from Bader. West and Dundas were too low to respond. Johnson was higher and answered: 'We've had a stiff fight, sir. I last saw the wing commander on the tail of a 109.'

The Spitfires landed back at Westhampnett and Tangmere and their pilots told their stories. West, Dundas and Johnson already realized the implications of Bader's failure to answer. All the pilots had been accounted for by lunchtime, except Flight Lieutenant 'Buck' Casson and Wing Commander Douglas Bader. The pilots reconstructed the sequence of the fight with their Intelligence Officer, Flight Lieutenant C. R. Gibbs, and the Station Commander, Group Captain Woodhall. Burton had ordered the Wing out when a force of twenty more Bf 109s had entered the arena. However, No 616 Squadron pilots claimed four destroyed and one probable and were quite satisfied overall; but no one could remember seeing Bader after the initial engagement.

It became obvious that Bader and Casson had been brought down. On the afternoon of Bader's loss, No 616 Squadron's 'A' Flight flew what the ORB euphemistically described as a 'convoy patrol', to search for Bader and Casson. It was led by Dundas with Heppell, Johnson and West, Bader's closest associates on the squadron, who immediately volunteered. But they quartered the French Channel coast in vain. There was no word from the Germans and none from the Red Cross. Encouragingly, No 616 Squadron received a letter from Sergeant Crabtree who had been shot down on 3 July, written from the British Embassy in Madrid and telling the squadron that he was on his way home.

The Tangmere Wing assumed the worst. The loss affected different people in their different ways. It was particularly difficult for Dundas to accept, for Bader had stood for a great deal in the young man's life; and the loss of Casson at the same time left him with a sick feeling, for now he was the only one of the originals left on the squadron, and he knew the statistics of attrition. The young pilots also felt a great responsibility towards Mrs Thelma Bader who lived nearby. She had held 'open house' to her husband's pilots throughout the long, hot summer and there was a bond of affection between her and No 616 Squadron, wrought by the intensity of the lives that they were leading. The young pilots tried their best to support her, but it was she who helped them to come to terms with their loss. Some idea of the remarkable support that Douglas Bader and his pilots enjoyed from his wife may be discerned from the words spoken by Sir Dermot Boyle in 1971 of Mrs Thelma Bader at this time:

> 'When Douglas went missing for five long anxious days she devoted herself so whole-heartedly to comforting the pilots who lost their Wing Leader that it was hard to realise that it was she who had lost a husband to whom she was utterly devoted.'

Wing Commander Douglas Bader, DSO★, DFC, had led the Tangmere Wing for only five months, but his spirit, example and teaching were indelible, not only on the Wing but throughout Fighter Command. There were many messes throughout Britain where toasts were drunk to a man who had inspired hundreds by his courage and leadership when the nation was in gravest danger.

Air Vice-Marshal J. E. Johnson calls him the 'greatest tactician of all'. Being in Bader's section at the front of the wing, often as his wingman, taught Johnson invaluable skills. Within two years, Stan Turner, Denis Crowley-Milling, Dundas and Johnson were successful wing leaders, and Roy Marples, 'Nip' Heppell and several others had their own squadrons. By the end of the year, his two sergeant wingmen, Smith and West, were both officers, and went on to command flights, Smith in North Africa and West on Malta.

It was five days before they heard that Bader and Casson were alive and were prisoners of war. Woodhall broadcast the news of their safety over the station Tannoy system, and then drove to the Bay House to tell Thelma Bader and her sister, Jill.

A year and a week after his capture, Bader was incarcerated in Colditz Castle, the prison reserved by the Germans for incurably troublesome prisoners of war. It was recognition of a kind.

The Germans believed that they had shot down Bader, but Bader was certainly not going to give the Germans the satisfaction of crowing about having shot him down. It was somewhere between 11.20 and 11.40 hours when Bader baled out of his Spitfire over St Omer. The Tangmere Wing was fighting Bf 109s of Adolf Galland's Jagdgeschwader 26. 'Buck' Casson was also shot down, shortly after Bader. Two Jagdgeschwader 26 pilots, Oberfeldwebel (Sergeant) Max Meyer of 6 Staffel and Leutnant Kosse of 5 Staffel, each claimed one Spitfire destroyed 'in the region of St Omer', Meyer at between 11.15 and 11.30 hours, and Kosse at 11.45 hours. It was Meyer's eleventh victory; the timing tallies with Bader's descent to earth. It was Kosse's eighth victory; its timing tallies with Casson's shooting down.

Bader thought that he had collided with the second Bf 109 on his right as he banked and turned towards it. He had nearly collided with Bf 109s and Spitfires before. He had seen it happen. It had felt like a collision. He had heard the impact. He had seen the tail of a Bf 109 right above him when it had happened. Such catastrophic damage as Bader's Spitfire suffered – the ripping off of the entire tail unit – had to result from very serious force. Therefore, Bader reasoned that it had to be a collision. Were this the case, there would be a damaged, possibly destroyed German fighter; there is no positive record of this.

Bader had heard a terrific noise coming from the rear of his Spitfire. Pilots whose aircraft had been hit by cannon shells in the tail had often thought that they had collided with another aeroplane; Dundas had thought the same when he was shot down in 1940, the noise was so great. Moreover, cannon shell exploding in the joint between the tail section and rear fuselage of a Spitfire which was under heavy G force could easily induce sufficient stress to cause a massive fracture – the right damage at the right point.

Galland was sure that Bader had been shot down. He even introduced Bader to a young Jagdgeschwader 26 pilot as the victor when Bader visited St Omer after his capture. Galland wrote that Bader was most insistent to know that his victor was an officer. The pilots of the Tangmere Wing did not think anything else other than that Bader had been shot down until several years later they heard that Bader had collided with a Bf 109. In 1981, Max Meyer, now living in Australia, claimed in a Sydney newspaper that it was he who had shot down Bader. Meyer said that he had followed his victim down until his parachute opened; Bader recalled that as he hung on his parachute, a Bf 109 had swung past him. It is possible that Meyer was able to claim the destruction of a Spitfire because he had opened fire at the point that a collision had taken place and thought he saw a result to his fire. Recently, the Australian 'fighter mafia' attempted unsuccessfully to trace Meyer. There is no proof either way.

After his repatriation in 1945, four years after that fateful day over St Omer, Bader completed his combat report (Form 'F'), claiming one 'destroyed' and one 'probable':

> 'Attacked a climbing formation of about twenty Me.109F's. I told 610 Squadron to stay put, and dived with my section on to the leading four Me.'s. I nearly collided with the first one at whom I was firing, and had to go behind and under his tail. Continued downwards where I saw some more Me 109's. I arrived among these who were evidently not on the look-out, as I expect they imagined the first formation we attacked were covering them. I got a very easy shot at one of these who flew quite straight until he went on fire from behind the cockpit – a burst of about three seconds. In turning away right-handed from this, I collided with an Me.109 which took my tail off, it appeared as far up as the radio mast but was actually probably only the empennage. This was at about 24,000 feet, and I do not think it did the Me.109 much good. The collision was my fault. I baled out and landed alright, and became a prisoner of war. *Note*, the Germans told me later that they had shot down 26 Spitfires, and lost none that day.'

☆   ☆   ☆

The Tangmere Wing still had to fight through the rest of the 'season'. It had a sound grounding in tactics. It needed a new wing leader, but one fault to be found in Bader's leadership was that he had insisted on leading all sweeps and had not trained one of the squadron leaders as a natural successor. Until a wing leader was appointed, temporary leaders were found.

On 12 August, after two days without operations, Wing Commander Donald Finlay, the Olympic hurdler, led the Tangmere Wing on a sweep over northern France. Enemy aircraft were seen but there were no engagements. The operation was unsuccessful. In the early evening, Squadron Leader 'Billy' Burton led the Wing on a Channel Guard. No 41 Squadron engaged enemy fighters, and shot down one Bf 109 for no loss. The next day brought bad weather again and no operations.

On 14 August 1941, the new Tangmere Wing Leader took command, Wing Commander Woodhouse, AFC. He was formerly the Commanding Officer of No 71 'Eagle' Squadron, and before that of No 610 Squadron when it had flown with the Tangmere Wing under Bader. He was an appropriate choice, for he had led the second pair on Bader's first 'finger-four' combat. Woodhouse led the Wing in an offensive sweep over France the day he took command. No 616 Squadron, although not engaged by enemy aircraft, lost Sergeant McKee who had only been with the squadron since 9 July.

No 616 Squadron had received another jolt when Flying Officer Roy Marples, one of its original wartime members, was posted as a Flight Commander to No 41 Squadron, within the Wing on 10 August. To fill the vacancy as 'B' Flight Commander left by 'Buck' Casson, Acting Flight Lieutenant 'Mitzi' Darling was posted in on promotion from No 602 Squadron, part of Wing Commander Alan Deere's Kenley Wing. There were other changes. Sergeant Allan Smith, Bader's wingman, received a well-deserved commission as a pilot officer on 14 August. This was real justification of Bader's methods. It was not easy for an NCO to win a commission. Within twenty-four months, this young man from South Shields was a Flight Commander in North Africa. There was a temporary change in the squadron's line-up too: with the tension off after Bader was known to be alive, 'Cocky' Dundas was packed off for seven days' leave in the country. He was back on 21 August.

The same day as Allan Smith was commissioned, another pilot who had been commissioned in the field was posted to No 616 Squadron, Pilot Officer Lionel Pilkington, DFM. He came from No 145 Squadron, Catterick, in the exchange for Pilot Officer Maltin. He had already proved his mettle with the Tangmere Wing, flying for a short period the previous month with No 145 Squadron before it left for Catterick.

Pilkington, a native of Hull, had learnt to fly at weekends on Blackburn B.2 trainers at Brough airfield. When war broke out, he had volunteered for aircrew duty in the Air Force and underwent service flying training. In January 1940, a sergeant pilot of barely twenty years, 'Pilk' was posted to No 73 Squadron at Rouvres, France, with the Advanced Air Striking Force. He saw the 'Phoney War' out, and fought through the gruelling five-week Battle of France, retreating west with his squadron. On 18 June, he flew out from Nantes with the remnants of his unit. On 17 July, he was awarded the DFM.

Pilkington was posted as an instructor to No 7 Operational Training Unit, at Hawarden, flying Spitfires, because of his experience in France. However, on 7 September 1940, he qualified as one of 'The Few'. Airborne with a pupil, he was told over the radio of an approaching raider. He told his pupil to go home, then set off. He was flying R6924, one of the ex-No 19 Squadron cannon-armed Spitfire Mk IBs. He caught the raider, a Ju 88 reconnaissance machine, and shot it down. His combat report records the kind of experience that No 19 Squadron had faced: 'I fired approximately 3 rounds from my port cannon when it jammed, but fired 57 rounds from my starboard cannon.'

In November 1940, Pilkington was commissioned as a pilot officer, but had a long wait for an operational posting. On 16 July 1941, only two days after arriving on No 145 Squadron at Tangmere, he was appointed a section leader. Sergeant pilots had never flown as section leaders in France, although several were experienced enough. However, on 28 July, No 145 Squadron was rotated out of the Tangmere Wing, for rest. Two days later, on 30 July, 'Pilk' was made up to Acting Flight Commander. On 14 August 1941, he was transferred to No 616 Squadron, in order to stay with a front-line unit.

On the afternoon of 16 August, Nos 41, 610 and 616 Squadrons flew a frustrating offensive sweep. Enemy fighters were seen but they were loath to engage. A pair of No 616 Squadron pilots machine-gunned gun posts south of Boulogne. Early the following morning, there was another bomber escort for No 616 Squadron, but the bombing did not take place as the weather was too poor. Later, a section of four No 616 Squadron Spitfires flew a surprise sweep over northern France at 20,000 feet; they saw nothing of interest. On 18 August, an offensive sweep was carried out in the early afternoon, but No 616 Squadron did not engage the enemy.

On the morning of 19 August, as No 616 Squadron's diarist recorded, 'the so-called "leg operation" took place, in which Wing Commander Bader's artificial leg was dropped over the St. Omer area. The bombers went on to target area but had to turn back owing to storm clouds.' The Luftwaffe had offered a 'safe conduct' to an aeroplane carrying a replacement for the artificial leg Bader had damaged baling out. 'Woody' Woodhall had offered to fly the sortie. The Air Ministry coldly declined: the Night Blitz had left no room for chivalry; Bader would probably have agreed. His leg was dropped during a routine 'Circus' by No 82 Squadron's Blenheims. The Tangmere Wing flew close escort; Crowley-Milling was so close that he could see the bomb doors open and the stout, oblong wooden box fall out of the bomber into a peppering of flak. Wing Commander Woodhouse announced the delivery, in English, to the Germans over the radio. The Germans collected the leg and presented it to Bader. He made good use of it; now he could walk again, he could escape . . . The Germans had a lot to learn about their prisoner.

The mission on the morning of 19 August might not have been successful militarily, but, true to Bader's spirit, the Tangmere Wing took part in another offensive sweep over northern France that afternoon. Pilot Officer Allan Smith began to show his mettle as a leader when No 616 Squadron met Bf 109s and he damaged one.

After a day without operations, 21 August was a very busy day, and an unlucky one for No 610 Squadron. Sweeps were scheduled for morning and afternoon, and convoy patrols for the late afternoon. The early morning offensive sweep was frustrating. No 616 Squadron saw just three Bf 109s, but no one engaged. The early afternoon sweep, providing cover for a Blenheim bomber mission to Lille, was tough. No 610 Squadron lost a section of four Spitfires. One of them was Denis Crowley-Milling.

The Tangmere Wing fought at a serious disadvantage. Solid cloud at 19,000 feet squeezed the four escorting wings into the few thousand feet above the Blenheims below the cloud base. It was a hazy autumn day, with good visibility downward but very poor visibility horizontally. Such conditions were ideal for attackers. The Tangmere Wing was at the most serious disadvantage, and No 610 Squadron flying top cover was in the worst position, protecting the other two squadrons: No 41 middle and No 616 low cover.

The Luftwaffe used the weather superbly. In pairs and fours, they nibbled at the invaders on the way in. They picked off Spitfires, but never ventured enough to make a full retaliation worthwhile, forcing the Spitfires into tight defensive manoeuvres, denying them the initiative. After leaving enough manoeuvring room, they broke away, and flew back into the cloud or in a dive. They caused constant vigilance, constant tension. They isolated sections of Spitfires.

No 610 Squadron, as usual as top cover, took the brunt of these tactics. The other two squadrons had twelve or twenty-four men to guard above them. Under these circumstances, No 616 Squadron was lucky to escape without loss, and only the most aggressive could score, 'Johnnie' Johnson claiming one Bf 109 probably destroyed.

The Germans harried them home. Denis Crowley-Milling and his wingman, and Ken Holden and his Australian wingman, Tony Gaze, were isolated from the Wing. They strove to shake off their attackers, but when they lost one Bf 109, another latched on to their tails. They lost cohesion.

Cannon shells slammed through Crowley-Milling's cockpit. White smoke from leaking glycol belched out. The Merlin began to shake violently, coolant temperature soaring, and within seconds the engine thudded to a halt. Crowley-Milling spun the powerless Spitfire on to its back and went into a near vertical dive to get out of the combat zone, down through the other two squadrons. He was over St Omer and headed for open country. Still in full control, he pulled the Spitfire out of the dive and glided down.

He saw a cornfield coming up. He pushed back the hood, tightened his straps, and went in for a textbook wheels-up landing. He unstrapped and clambered out. Methodically, he destroyed the secret contents of his fighter. He became aware of running figures in Field Grey half a mile away so abandoned his attempts to set the fighter alight. He ducked down and headed off fast through the tall corn, away from the Germans.

He threw away his flying clothing, and begrimed himself with good workaday dirt. He was aware that patrols would be sent out to track him down. He set off at a fast pace to get as far away from the scene of his crash-landing as possible . . . there was every chance that he could make it back to Britain to continue the fight.

Crowley-Milling was luckier than Bader had been. He covered many miles that day, and avoided being picked up by the Germans. The French Resistance network in the Pas de Calais was extensive and cunning. His presence soon came to the attention of one of the most successful Resistance groups, the Fillerin family. They took Crowley-Milling under their care and hid him on their farm.

Meanwhile, plans were put in operation for the next stage of his journey. Monsieur Didery was a shoe and horseshoe maker and so had legitimate reasons to move around the Pas de Calais farming communities. The young fighter pilot was entrusted to Didery who smuggled him into his flat in St Omer and hid him there.

There, Crowley-Milling learnt of a scheme to rescue Bader from a hospital nearby in St Omer. A van was to be mocked-up as an ambulance. Two resistance workers were to don Luftwaffe uniforms. They were to drive up to the hospital in their ambulance. Using a forged authority to gain admission, they would take a stretcher upstairs and locate Bader. They would carry him back down to the ambulance and drive off with him to a safe house. Then, they would either pass Bader down the 'Line' to Spain, or radio London to have a Lysander come to pick him up from a secret field at night. It was all laid on, except the Lysander. The plan was being prepared by Dr Albert Guerisse, a Belgian, alias Lieutenant-Commander Patrick O'Leary. Would Crowley-Milling prefer to go straight to Spain, or stay and help to rescue his commander, and go with him to Spain? Crowley-Milling loyally agreed to stay.

The plan had to be abandoned when it was discovered that Bader had already been moved. He had already made an escape, but had been recaptured. He was being taken to Dulag Luft, the reception and interrogation centre for all RAF prisoners, in Germany.

Alone, Crowley-Milling was funnelled through Resistance channels south across France. Two weeks later he crossed the Pyrenees to Spain. The Spanish police quickly picked him up and threw him into the Miranda concentration camp. There he starved, caught typhoid and went blind.

Only slowly did his health improve and his sight return. Later he was evacuated to England. After his sufferings, this brave man did not intend to take a job anywhere else except in the front-line while there was fighting to be done.

For Crowley-Milling's comrades at Tangmere, the pace of operations was slowing. There were no sweeps for four days. On 22 August, No 616 Squadron flew three section patrols over Selsey Bill, then the entire squadron was scrambled on a base patrol at midday when enemy aircraft were detected coming in from Cherbourg. The enemy aircraft turned back. For the next three days the weather was bad and there was no operational flying. On the afternoon of 26 August, Air Vice-Marshal Leigh-Mallory visited Tangmere and presented No 616 Squadron with their Crest, approved by HM The King. It depicted the White Rose of Yorkshire with an arrow through it to denote speed and death. The motto was *Nulla rosa sine spina* ('No rose without a thorn').

During the morning of the 26th, the Tangmere Wing had acted as bomber escort for a mission over St Omer aerodrome. Only a few enemy aircraft were seen. The next day was different. In the early morning, the Wing flew a sweep over the Béthune area. Enemy fighters, already in good positions of height advantage, were encountered by the top cover squadrons, although No 616 Squadron met no enemy aircraft. The result was not satisfactory: the Wing lost three pilots but claimed only one 'destroyed' and two 'damaged'. Two days without major operations followed.

On 29 August, No 616 Squadron was detailed to provide escort for an anti-shipping bomber operation in the Straits of Dover. They flew to Manston, suitably located on the tip of Kent, and refuelled. They waited for the operational order, with the weather closing down, until the operation was cancelled when the weather became too poor. Nevertheless, hunter turned gamewarden, they flew convoy patrols for the rest of the day. The next day No 616 Squadron flew two patrols over Selsey Bill, plus the routine flying practice and cannon tests. The Wing was back to the routine of February to May. The 'season' was nearly finished.

During the 'season', No 616 Squadron had lost seventeen pilots on operations, of whom some had been killed and some were prisoners of war but two, Gibbs and Crabtree, were known to be coming back via Spain. No 616 Squadron had changed during August, with a total of five pilots leaving the unit or being lost and eleven new ones retained on the establishment. The loss of 'Buck' Casson over France and the posting of Roy Marples on promotion the very next day had great impact on No 616 Squadron, particularly as it coincided with Bader's loss. These two officers were long-serving members of the squadron, pillars of the social, disciplinary and tactical structures that are so essential to the smooth-running of a unit and the wellbeing of its members. On the 14th, another pilot who had served with the squadron many months, Pilot Officer Malton, was transferred to No 145 Squadron, in exchange for Pilot Officer Lionel Pilkington. In addition to Pilkington and 'Mitzi' Darling who had taken over 'B' Flight, three new officers were posted to No 616 Squadron, and Pilot Officer Sutherland made a welcome return from sick leave with his spine fully mended after his landing accident.

However, in early September, a Flight Commander's post became available with No 111 Squadron at North Weald and Lionel Pilkington, promoted to flight lieutenant, was transferred to 'Treble One' to fill it; sadly, this promising leader was killed near Hazebrouck on 'Circus' 100, on 20 September 1941. There were several changes in No 616 Squadron's sergeants mess, too, with Allan Smith leaving and six NCO pilots being posted in. As the offensive slackened, the high casualty rate among No 616 Squadron's NCO pilots did not continue. Only one was lost operationally, McKee, and another in an accident. Squadron Leader 'Billy' Burton held his men together with a firm paternal hand. The intense loyalty of the pilots and airmen to their squadron was manifest to the newcomers, who needed only a few weeks to identify completely. It was an intimate and close fraternity, like an army regiment, with its own traditions and its own battle honours.

The 30th August was a significant day: No 610 Squadron left the

Tangmere Wing. It had flown with Douglas Bader as part of the Duxford Wing and had flown throughout his tenure of the Tangmere Wing Leader post. It was due for rest. Now it followed the second member of the original Tangmere Wing trio, No 145 Squadron. It had performed well with the Wing. Its departure was much regretted, particularly by No 616 Squadron for Squadron Leader Ken Holden was a former member of the squadron. He was awarded the DFC for his leadership. No 610 Squadron was replaced by No 129 (Mysore) Squadron, which had formed at RAF Leconfield on Spitfire Mk IIBs in June 1941 but had re-equipped with Mark VBs in August before joining the Tangmere Wing. It was no longer the wing that Bader had created.

The Tangmere Wing was busy on the last day of August. At dawn, No 616 Squadron acted as a destroyer escort and then No 129 Squadron was broken in with an offensive sweep. The Luftwaffe put up scant resistance and the only pilot to have a fight was Sergeant Bowen, a Canadian, who shot down one Bf 109 and damaged another. In the second offensive sweep, in the afternoon, the Wing escorted bombers to and from the target area without meeting any opposition.

No 616 Squadron's ORB summarized the month of August as:

> 'a disappointing one from the operational point of view owing to the poor weather conditions. Although sixteen offensive sweeps were carried out over France, their effectiveness was in several cases hampered by too much cloud, making it difficult for the Squadrons in the wings to keep together. Wing Commander Bader, DSO (and Bar), DFC, and F/Lt. Casson were shot down on the 9th August and are now Prisoners of War. This was a serious loss to the RAF, the Wing and the Squadron.'

On 4 September, the Tangmere Wing took part in 'Circus' 93, taking off from Tangmere and Westhampnett at 15.50 hours. 'Johnnie' Johnson and Jeff West put their long-established teamwork together. Johnson led 'A' Flight's Yellow Section (Yellow 1), with West leading the second pair (Yellow 3). The Wing intended to cross the French coast near Le Touquet at about 16.30 hours. As they approached the enemy-held coast, No 616 Squadron was at about 27,000 feet, with Blue Section out in front and Yellow Section to the right, behind and slightly above.

They were still about five miles from the coast when Johnson and West saw eight or more Bf 109Es some two or three thousand feet above them, but down-sun from their section's position. One of the Bf 109Es peeled off in a diving attack on Blue Section. Someone shouted a warning. Blue Section took prompt evasive action, then reformed, though the enemy aircraft simply dived away. Johnson kept Yellow Section orbiting up-sun of the other enemy fighters, climbing, until he was in a good position. Johnson selected a Bf 109E, then led his four aircraft in a simultaneous attack on it from just 200 yards, all four gently turning to starboard to close the curve, taking the Bf 109E slightly from the rear starboard quarter. West fired two short bursts with slight deflection from a range of 150 yards, closing to 100 yards before having to break early in order not to distract Johnson who was gradually converging on West's line of fire. Johnson fired another burst.

West turned to cover the section's rear, to have a good look for other enemy fighters, and to wait for Yellow 4, to ensure safety. Yellow 1, 2 and 3 all saw the fire have effect, but could not say for certain whether the enemy aircraft had been destroyed; Yellow 4 was on the outside of the curve and so had to tuck in behind in line astern and was too preoccupied with formating and guarding to see the effects. (This was one of the criticisms of the 'finger-four', that wingmen could become vulnerable in turns, but in practice they simply went into line astern.) West and Johnson claimed a highly likely 'shared probable'.

☆   ☆   ☆

This was virtually the end of the offensive over northern France in 1941. The results were now being assessed by the Air Ministry. When Air Marshal Sholto Douglas had taken over as Commander-in-Chief of Fighter Command from Dowding on 25 November 1940, he had been told by the Chief of the Air Staff, Portal, to undertake a fighter offensive over France the following year as a way of hitting back, to change the focus of the war. Sholto Douglas was dubious. He felt that results would be low and casualties too high. However, the new Air Officer Commanding No 11 Group, Leigh-Mallory, also strongly and persuasively favoured offensive action. Sholto Douglas slowly but surely changed his mind.

The first low-level intruder missions – 'Mosquito' raids – had produced low results and double the casualties of interception work. The first 'Circus' operations also produced marginal results: the Germans did not respond to pinprick provocation forcefully. (Bader, as an advocate of offensive use of fighters, flew on these operations from their inception, analysed them and strove to devise better methods and tactics.) Bomber Command supplied bombers for the operations over northern France but was restive at this inappropriate use of the bombing potential. By the end of May the offensive was flagging.

Some historians argue that it might have been cancelled altogether were it not for the invasion of the Soviet Union by Germany and the subsequent requests for Britain to open a second front to relieve pressure on its new ally, the Soviet Union. Certainly, the focus of the offensive shifted, but the argument misses two fundamental points: the Fighter Command wings had not worked up by the end of May; and the offensive was only an opening round in the employment of tactical air forces. Conversely, the argument misses another point: that the RAF still anticipated that the Germans would reopen their day bombing campaign on Britain in the early summer of 1941. As suggested earlier in discussing the October 1940 'Big Wing Meeting', the fighter wings had been formed and deployed to fight 'the Battle of Britain 1941' with an aggressive defence. With the German invasion of the Soviet Union, the day-bombing threat to Britain became minimal; the wings' roles now became 'aggressively offensive'.

In June 1941, it had been manifestly impossible for Britain to meet the Soviet Union's request for a second front – Britain was sorely stretched in North-West Europe, the Mediterranean and Egypt, and in the Atlantic; in the Far East, she had a thin-spread defence against Japanese aggression. The only weapon available to open a 'second front' was Bomber Command, which was thus committed to opening a campaign against Germany's transport system and civilian morale from July 1941. One of the objectives of the offensive over northern France was to force the Germans to base more aircraft there to defend it, so diverting them from the Eastern Front.

The Air Ministry played the numbers game to make sense of the offensive. During the main period of the offensive, 14 June to 3 September, Bomber Command losses over northern France rose from 4 to over 7 per cent per sortie. In the same period, No 11 Group claimed 437 enemy aircraft 'destroyed' and 182 'probably destroyed', but it was realized by the Fighter Command analysts that these figures were inflated; if they had been accurate, the Germans would have had to keep more than 200 serviceable fighters in the region to cope with attrition. In fact, post-war analysis of German records reveals that they lost 128 destroyed (plus 76 damaged) in the same period. Ironically, No 11 Group in the same period lost over France 194 aircraft and pilots – when a British pilot baled out, he was captured; if a German baled out, he was recovered. No 616 Squadron alone lost twelve pilots between mid-June and mid-August.

If the British were not winning the attrition battle, neither were they forcing the Germans to concentrate their forces in France and depriving the Eastern Front. First, the Germans withdrew 100 aircraft and their units from France, leaving 200 in France. Secondly, German production of fighters and trained fighter pilots was high. Thirdly, 60 per cent of Germany's day fighter strength was concentrated on the Eastern Front – and the remaining 40 per cent was not all in France either! The irony is that it was Britain who was forced to concentrate its forces: retaining nearly 70 per cent of its day fighter squadrons in the United Kingdom – seventy-five squadrons.

Over France, the British fought at a disadvantage. They were attacking a stable fighter defence system with modern radars, efficient fighter control systems and excellent fighters and leaders. The Germans had warning of attacks from well out and could assess and prepare a defence in depth from Wissant on the coast to St Omer 35 miles inland. At intervals, small groups of fighters attacked the great herds of British fighters and attempted to pierce through to the bombers – the tactics used by Park in 1940. The British at first made the same mistake as the Germans had in 1940, allocating too many fighters to the immediate defence of the bombers, but later the British learnt and supplied freelance wings to sweep ahead, around and behind the main force. They were going to the maximum range of their fighters. There was little margin for error in fuel: fighter wings needed other fighter wings to support them on the withdrawal. Thus, during 1941, the number of aircraft in the air on a sweep became very cumbersome; it was some time before it was discovered that better placing of fewer aircraft would achieve a better result. 'Johnnie' Johnson felt that the number of aircraft on sweeps in 1941 was excessive; later, in 1943, he led three- and five-squadron wings, but came down to preferring to lead two-squadron wings. It is of note that Bader frequently led wings composed of an equivalent number of aircraft as a two-squadron wing.

It was decided that the offensive would be continued in 1942, but the four-engined heavy bombers would not be used; they would be reserved for bombing Germany – a more rational use for their long range, heavy bombload and great defensive armament, for Germany was much farther away than France, the targets were larger and the heavy bombers went unescorted. The twin-engined 'light' bombers, the Blenheims, would be used against targets in northern France – as bait perhaps – but they were more appropriate to the shorter ranges and smaller pinpoint targets and they could not be used over Germany. This was not a compromise: it was a logical application of resources.

The essence of the 1941 offensive was that the RAF could fly over France at will even if not unopposed – daily, twice daily, in great numbers. Air superiority had constantly to be contested: it can be won and lost in a day; those whose primary concern is terrain's supremacy neglect the fact that contesting air superiority over occupied France was an essential prelude to prosecuting the war successfully.

In strategic terms, the results of the 1941 fighter offensive were poor, but the offensive was not strategic: it was tactical. It won a measure of air superiority over northern France. It sought to prove principles. It was an exploration. It trained fighter leaders, controllers and planners. The offensive laid the foundations for future success. From the pilots who flew on the sweeps emerged the leaders of the next four years, who fought in North Africa, Malta, Italy, Normandy, the Falaise 'Gap', Belgium and through into the heart of Germany. From the operations emerged the techniques of controlling large numbers of aircraft in a confined airspace, the tactics of applying air power, of using a wing, squadron, section and pair in combat, the methods of fighting in the air and winning. Above all, there emerged new tactical formations and a sense of the flexibility of fighters. At the forefront of these developments were Bader's men.

☆   ☆   ☆

During September, No 616 Squadron underwent further change in both the officers and sergeants messes. In mid-September, when Al Deere reclaimed 'Mitzi' Darling to fill a vacancy for a Flight Commander in No 602 Squadron, he created a vacancy for a Flight Commander in No 616 Squadron. Darling was not on the list of available flight lieutenants, but Deere and Burton were old friends and arranged things, with Fighter Command's approval, and Burton had a man in mind to replace him. The choice was obvious. Flying Officer James Johnson, who had learnt rapidly under Bader's guidance, was promoted to flight lieutenant and placed in command of No 616 Squadron's 'B' Flight. During August and early September, Johnson had damaged a Bf 109 and claimed three probably destroyed, two of which he shared. Now, as a Flight Commander, he could not only control a combat and perform the killing himself, but would have the opportunity to control the tactical situation.

The day after his promotion, 'Johnnie' Johnson along with Philip Heppell was awarded the DFC, and the aggressive and experienced New Zealand

Sergeant Jeff West was awarded the DFM. Shortly afterwards, West was commissioned, remaining with his squadron. This was swift: he had only joined the squadron on 1 April, straight from OTU. Already, those who had flown with Bader were showing progress.

The last of the original No 616 Squadron members, Hugh Dundas, left the squadron on Sunday, 21 September, on a posting for 'rest' – instructing at No 59 OTU, a Hurricane unit based at Crosby-on-Eden, in No 81 Group. Not enamoured of the prospect, he was determined to be back on operations before Christmas: he made himself dispensable and was back on operations in four weeks – a record!

The same day as Dundas left (despite the previous night's mess party) Johnson had a very successful combat inland from Le Touquet. Flying as Yellow 1, he initiated the combat at 20,000 feet, descending to 18,000 feet. He destroyed two Bf 109s. Significantly, the other 'gun' in Johnson's Section, Pilot Officer W. W. 'Huck' Murray, a Canadian (Yellow 3), also registered success during this encounter. Johnson destroyed another Bf 109 later in the month, bringing his score to six.

In October, No 616 Squadron was rotated north to its 'home station', RAF Kirton-in-Lindsey, in its parent No 12 Group, to rest. No 65 Squadron took over its place in the Tangmere Wing, Indisputably, this was now no longer the wing that Bader had led. It was part of overall Fighter Command policy to rotate squadrons between the front line and the rear areas to ensure that front-line squadrons were fresh. Wings were not considered to be entities (unlike the German system) and squadrons were relieved as necessary.

At the same time, Squadron Leader 'Billy' Burton left the squadron. He was posted to No 11 Group Headquarters where his experience as a fighter leader, the right-hand man of Douglas Bader, would be invaluable; and he was exhausted. When Burton had taken No 616 Squadron over in September 1940, it was a shattered unit, quite literally decimated on the brunt of the Luftwaffe's assault on No 11 Group. He was a Cranwell Regular, with the deep understanding of flying, discipline, training and comradeship that the squadron needed. He oversaw the induction of the new pilots and put the squadron through a long and thorough training for which the pilots had every reason to be grateful. He had groomed them and pumped their morale high during the frustrations of convoy patrols, until finally he had led them in to the front line in January 1941, at Tangmere.

Burton had continued to train the unit rigorously, and to supervise its integration into the Tangmere Wing. Bader and Burton had struck up an instant understanding, and Burton had been content for Bader to lead the Tangmere Wing; he and his men could learn much from such a leader. It is of note that Johnson, who had joined No 616 Squadron at the same time as Burton as a raw Spitfire pilot straight from OTU, had accumulated nearly 400 hours in just over a year. Since June 1941, No 616 Squadron had seen intense fighting and had nearly a score of pilots. As a measure, Dundas, Johnson, West, Smith and Heppell, who had been at the very centre of it all, had flown over sixty sorties each during the summer. The squadron was well in need of a rest.

Squadron Leader Colin Gray, the New Zealander, took over command of No 616 Squadron, and flew with them back to Kirton-in-Lindsey. As it was re-equipping with Spitfire Mk VBs taken over from No 616 Squadron at Tangmere, No 65 Squadron had left at Kirton its cannon-armed Mark IIBs for No 616 Squadron, which operated them alongside its remaining Mark VBs. At Kirton No 616 Squadron spent the winter on North Sea convoy patrols, uneventfully.

The character of the squadron had changed by now. Philip Heppell and Jeff West were posted to Malta. Johnson alone remained of the 1940 pilots. He led 'B' Flight, comprising eleven pilots, the Canadian Pilot Officers Sanderson, Strouts and Bowen, who had been commissioned, the New Zealanders Crafts, Ware, Bolton and Davidson, an Australian, Smithson, a Rhodesian, Pilot Officer Winter, and just one Briton, apart from himself, the Englishman Welch. No 616 (South Yorkshire) Squadron, Auxiliary Air Force, was neither Yorkshire nor Auxiliary: it had become representative of the highly mixed units of the mid-war RAF.

The pattern of air fighting was about to change, too. In early 1942, No 616 Squadron was posted to RAF Kings Cliffe, a satellite of Wittering. They formed part of the Wittering Wing. The Wing had two famous leaders. The Wing Leader was the legendary Wing Commander Pat Jameson and the Station Commander was Group Captain Basil Embry. This produced more action. In March, the Wing escorted Whirlwind fighter-bombers against targets in Holland, operating from RAF Matlask.

The major change in 1942 was wrought by the appearance of the Focke-Wulf Fw 190. No 616 Squadron occasionally flew operations as part of a No 12 Group wing from a forward base, usually West Malling, Kent. On 15 April, No 616 Squadron was part of such a wing flying escort cover to a 'Hurribomber' squadron which was attacking Desvres. The Wing took off from West Malling at 13.45 hours and crossed the coast near Le Touquet. The Wing was about six miles inland when Johnson saw a number of German fighters against the hazy sky. Some had round wingtips – Bf 109Fs, a familiar opponent. The others – blunt tips, bulbous nose, thin fuselage – were lethal Fw 190s, which were the masters of the Spitfire Mk V. Some three or four thousand feet above the Spitfires, the Messerschmitts and the Focke-Wulfs confidently manoeuvred for position in the sun . . . In the coming months, this was to be an all too familiar situation.

When it returned to Kings Cliffe shortly after this, No 616 Squadron re-equipped, not with the answer to the Fw 190 but an answer to the perceived threat from German high-flying reconnaissance and bomber Junkers Ju 86Ps, the high-altitude Spitfire HF Mk VI. No 616 Squadron was the first squadron to receive the type, of which only a hundred were built. Johnson, however, did not have to bear the discomfort of the sealed, pressurized cockpits of these fighters for long, for he was given his own squadron.

CHAPTER 14

Operation TIGER

O n 8 December 1940, still attached to the FAA's parent unit, HMS *Daedalus*, RNAS Lee-on-Solent, Dicky Cork and Jimmy Gardner were posted to No 252 Squadron, Coastal Command, based at RAF Chivenor. The following day, Cork recorded that they experienced their first flights on Bristol Beauforts but on New Year's Day 1941 Cork first flew one of the unit's Bristol Blenheims. A week later, on 7 January, Cork and Gardner were posted away from No 252 Squadron. With that their attachment to the RAF ended.

On 8 January, Cork and Gardner were posted to No 759 (Fighter) Squadron, at HMS *Heron*, RNAS Yeovilton, for a week's course on the Fairey Fulmar, which included carrier deck landing. They first flew a Fulmar the day they arrived. Cork and Gardner signed out of No 759 Squadron on 15 January, and each took a week's leave. Their flying careers now took different courses. Cork was posted to No 880 Squadron, flying Grumman Martlet single-seat fighters. Gardner was posted to No 807 Squadron, flying Fulmar two-seat fighters.

No 807 Squadron had formed as the third Fulmar squadron on 15 September 1940. The squadron had embarked in HMS *Pegasus* during December 1940 and January 1941 to prove the CAM-ship idea. Gardner joined the squadron as it completed this task, and became one of its section leaders. The squadron was intended to embark in the new aircraft carrier HMS *Victorious*, but that ship's completion was so delayed that No 807 Squadron was diverted to HMS *Ark Royal*, whose last of two Skua squadrons it was to replace.

Commissioned in 1938, *Ark Royal* was the first truly modern aircraft-carrier built for the Royal Navy. She displaced 22,000 tons and carried 70 aircraft. Goebbels had made the first of his legendary claims that she had been sunk while she covered the Norwegian campaign. From Spring 1940, she operated in the Western Mediterranean and Atlantic as part of Admiral Somerville's Force H, whose operational port was Gibraltar. She was extensively used on the Malta convoy runs and in April 1941 she joined HMS *Argus* in the 'Jaguar' runs to Malta, flying off fighters within range of the island.

With such an excellent aircraft carrier and successful attack aircraft, it is surprising that the Fleet Air Arm had no truly effective carrier fighter; and the RAF did not have effective fighters with sufficient endurance to provide a substitute. The Navy had to 'make do and mend' with the Skua and the two-seat Fulmar. It had to withdraw from the North Sea, and operations in the Mediterranean were dangerous.

No 807 Squadron worked up for carrier embarkation, before flying on to HMS *Furious* at the end of March for ferrying. In April 1941, No 807 (Fulmar) Squadron arrived off Gibraltar in *Furious* and on 4 April replaced No 800 (Skua) Squadron in *Ark Royal*. Also aboard *Furious* were four ASV-radar-equipped Swordfish for *Ark Royal*. They increased *Ark Royal*'s search perimeter to 140 miles radius. With the new arrivals, *Ark Royal*'s Carrier Air Group comprised Nos 807 and 808 Squadrons, each with twelve Fulmars, and Nos 810, 818 and 820 Squadrons, each with twelve Fairey Swordfish TBRs.

No 807 Squadron had little time to spend working up with the carrier, and familiarization with the launch and recovery procedures aboard *Ark Royal*, and practising deck landings. The squadron also needed to work with the Fleet's air defence. The threat to a Fleet is 360 degrees, unlike that to a land target which may be more or less 180 degrees. The Fleet must protect its complete perimeter. To do this it has guns, fighters and manoeuvrability. It is important therefore that the guns are allocated an arc in which to function and the fighters are allocated another arc.

After the Hurricane, Gardner found the humble combat performance of the Fulmar a shock. The main bomber opponent was the Italian Savoia-Marchetti SM.79, whose performance was as good as the Fulmar's. The Fulmar's speed was so low that bomber interceptions frequently became a stern chase, a dangerous procedure, especially as the .303-inch machine-guns with which the aeroplane was armed needed to be fired at a range of 75 yards to ensure a kill. At that range, the Fulmar's large frontal area, with the radiator mounted vulnerably under the nose, provided the enemy gunners with an unreasonably good target. Fulmar pilots had only the engine to deflect bullets, as no armour was fitted.

Ark Royal carried air search radar and had an experienced Fighter Direction Officer. During his period with No 242 Squadron, Gardner had become fully accustomed to the ground controller directing fighter operations, using radar. He had learnt to rely on it, yet had observed how Bader had made allowances for the system's weaknesses by placing his fighters more appropriately. Now, in the Mediterranean, Gardner found that the Fulmar allowed very little flexibility. However, he found that he could rely on Fighter Direction Officers to interpret the radar picture, place Fulmars appropriately to meet incoming threats and make best use of the assets to prevent the Fleet defence from being saturated.

The performance of the fighters affected their tactics. The Fulmar tactic could only be to gain as much height as possible and dive against the enemy aircraft and try to inflict damaging hits in the first pass. They flew in pairs because they usually lacked the numbers to fly in larger formations, and two was the number that could safely be scrambled at the same time.

One factor striking a pilot who had flown single-seat RAF fighters as odd was the presence of a navigator in his fighter. Bader had insisted on each pilot developing his navigational skills: for the North Sea convoy patrols it was essential, and its relevance had become apparent during the battles in the high skies over Essex. Now, Gardner had someone, Petty Officer R. Carlyle, who did all the navigating, estimates of engine setting for precise endurance times, and who was another set of eyes to quarter the skies. A navigator might add weight to the aeroplane but made the pair of Fulmars a feasible defensive fighter formation with four pairs of Eyeballs Mk I checking the sky – and many navigators toted a Thompson with which to spray the enemy in combat!

On 24 April 1941, *Ark Royal* sailed from Gibraltar with twenty-three Hurricanes aboard. They were due to fly off for Malta on the 26th, 450 miles from the island, but the weather over Malta was very poor and the fly-off was delayed by 24 hours. This was a dangerous time for the carrier, and sixteen Fulmars were aloft for four hours. Normally, the Fulmars had to fly constant patrols of two aircraft, with two aircraft at readiness on deck, and four pilot warned for readiness. It was good training for No 807 Squadron. On 27 April, in three waves, each led by a Fulmar navigator aircraft, the Hurricanes took off and headed for Malta. All landed safely. *Ark Royal* turned back for Gibraltar.

Within a fortnight, *Ark Royal* made the run again but this time as part of Force H as escort to a convoy carrying tanks to the British North African forces: Operation TIGER, the passage of part of Convoy WS.8 through the Mediterranean. Tank losses had been very high in the Desert, and some three hundred cruiser and infantry tanks, plus some fifty crated Hurricanes, in five fast freighters were being sent urgently, under the eyes of the Axis air and sea forces. The tanks were vital for success in North Africa. It would take the convoy eight days to cross the Mediterranean; Force H would escort them almost to Malta.

Force H left Gibraltar on 5 May, and rendezvoused with the convoy. The weather was overcast and concealed the Fleet. The third day out from Gibraltar was always the most critical for a convoy, as it passed below Sardinia, within easy range of the Axis bombers and fighters. In the early morning of 8 May, the ASV Swordfish searched but found nothing, then at 11.15 hours a signal was intercepted from a shadower. A seaplane was spotted and attacked by *Ark Royal*'s Fulmars. It fled, unharmed, but the damage was done. Soon the bombers would arrive.

The defence of the Fleet depended on the anti-aircraft gunfire screen from the medium- and small-calibre weapons of the capital ships, cruisers, destroyers and carriers, and on the fighters of HMS *Ark Royal*'s Air Group – a nominal twenty-four Fulmars. *Ark Royal*'s company had been called to action stations at dawn on 8 May. Twelve of the Fulmars were serviceable, but the CAG maintained a permanent combat air patrol of at least a pair throughout the day by rapid repair and re-equipment. When a raid was anticipated, every serviceable fighter was launched as swiftly as possible – there were no reserves to hold back. Use was intensive. Jimmy Gardner, who was Blue Section leader, carried out four fighter patrols on the afternoon of 8 May, and was in combat on three of them.

At 13.45 hours, eight Italian SM.79 torpedo-bombers attacked *Ark Royal* and the battle-cruiser *Renown*. Escorted by Fiat CR.42 fighters, the SM.79s came in below radar height. Sighted close in, the terrific anti-aircraft barrage forced them to drop early. The ships easily evaded the torpedoes. Three bombers went down to the guns. The Fulmar patrol dived on the CR.42 escort. Lieutenant-Commander R. C. Tillard, RN, saw three CR.42s 200 feet below him and turned towards them and attacked head on. The Fulmar broke to port and dived vertically, flattened out at 500 feet but disappeared . . .

From 16.20 hours, attack followed attack. Gardner was on patrol almost constantly. During one of these attacks, Gardner and three other pilots latched on to an SM.79 at low level and hammered it. Gardner fired the final burst that sent it into the sea.

The main attack came in three waves just after 19.00 hours: twenty-eight Ju 87s escorted by six Bf 110s. They came in over the top of a large black cloud which rose from the waves to 9,000 feet to the north of the Fleet, in an otherwise clear sky.

By now, *Ark Royal* had only seven Fulmars fit to fly. Three were flying patrols and went straight for the enemy. Two sections of two were on deck on standby. There was far too little wind to get them airborne, and *Ark Royal* had too little forward speed. To get her aircraft airborne, an aircraft-carrier in convoy had to draw away from the protective screen of the convoy and escorts to get up speed – a dangerous evolution.

As *Ark Royal* increased speed, the first pair of Fulmars sat ready on the catapults. Barely was there enough wind over the deck when the first pilot opened his throttle, and hammered into the air, dropping over the round-down of the bow, sinking, skimming over the waves as his aircraft clawed for lift. The second machine followed, wallowing as it gained flying speed. The second pair took to the air with only a little less trauma.

The four Fulmars climbed for height . . . The two sections of two Fulmars went directly for the large bomber formation, joining the three already engaged. It was Jimmy Gardner's third combat of the day. Swiftly, on the first pass, while he had speed to manoeuvre, Gardner shot down one of the Ju 87s, which exploded in a fireball. He fired on others, inflicting damage but he was forced out of the combat when return fire badly damaged his machine and shattered his windscreen. Other pilots damaged other Ju 87s and a Bf 110, but the important point was that the Fulmars behaved as if they were many and scattered the enemy, who jettisoned their bombs miles from the convoy.

Gardner thumped his Fulmar down on to *Ark Royal*'s deck, almost blind with the crystallized windscreen, peering around the side of the canopy frame. He was very fatigued, but was insistent that he should have another aeroplane and be prepared to fly again. The other pilots were very tired as well, but the serviceability of the Fulmars was in serious doubt if further attacks came.

Weary eyes scanned the horizon. Just as the day was closing, three SM.79s sneaked in low on *Ark Royal*'s port quarter. The radar plot just caught them, but too late. Lieutenant R. C. Hay, RM, and Lieutenant Guthrie, RNVR, were flown off but could not stop the SM.79s. The gunners failed, too. The brave Italians pressed in very close, flying a tight, low attack pattern, but *Ark Royal*'s Captain turned the ship to avoid the well-aimed torpedoes, heeling her hard to port. Two torpedoes ran true, passing parallel 150 feet down her starboard side.

All the air attacks on 8 May were beaten off without bomb or torpedo hits. By the end of the day, seven enemy aircraft had been shot down, three by the Fulmars and four by the ships' guns. Several enemy aeroplanes were damaged. Gardner claimed one destroyed and shared another; later, another which he had claimed as 'probably destroyed' was confirmed by his gun film. Two Fulmars were lost in combat, one of whose crew was saved. Victories were not the important element. The overriding consideration was that the Fulmars had countered the attacks, letting the enemy know that they must expect heavy opposition. In that respect, Gardner led by example.

As darkness fell on 8 May, the convoy entered the Skerki Channel. The job of the Fulmars was over; Ark Royal and Force H turned about for Gibraltar. A Royal Navy escort from Alexandria met the convoy on the other side of Malta and took it to Egypt. TIGER was a brilliant success, due in no small measure to the Fulmar aircrews of Ark Royal. The tanks allowed the British to hold the balance in North Africa, if not achieve success.

Jimmy Gardner remained with Ark Royal, and only a fortnight later was in the midst of great events when Bismarck broke out into the Atlantic. Ark Royal left Gibraltar in company with Force H to intercept. She flew off Fulmar reconnaissance flights into the hazardous mid-Atlantic weather, but there was little chance of combat during this operation for the Fulmars. The carrier's Swordfish crippled the German battleship, allowing the Home Fleet to catch her.

Gardner took part in two further intensive convoys that year, providing essential air cover for convoys in the Western Mediterranean. He made three further victory claims, one on 23 August over a Ju 52, and shared claims on 27 September and 18 October. Ark Royal's fame continued to mount. Jimmy Gardner was still aboard Ark Royal with No 807 Squadron when a U-boat torpedoed her off Sardinia. Under tow to Gibraltar, she sank on 13/14 November 1941. The Fleet Air Arm was saddened by the loss of a fine carrier, a legend, but it was a severe blow to the Royal Navy, Malta and the British Army in Egypt. HMS Formidable had already been forced to leave the Eastern Mediterranean. Now there was no carrier operating in the Mediterranean at all.

Many pilots from Formidable were fighting in the Desert. Now, others from Ark Royal joined them. Now with a DFC and the rank of lieutenant-commander, Jimmy Gardner was posted as Commanding Officer of No 889 Squadron, RN, flying Hurricane fighters in the Western Desert. There he brought his score to eight and seven/twelfths victories. At the end of 1942, Gardner was posted as Commanding Officer of the School of Naval Air Warfare, a post in which he served with distinction until the end of the war.

CHAPTER 15
Furious **and** *Indomitable*

On 21 January 1941, Dicky Cork was posted to No 880 Squadron, based at HMS *Condor*, RNAS Arbroath. The Commanding Officer was a South African, Lieutenant-Commander J. E. U. Judd, who was known as 'Butch' – short for 'The Butcher'. His reputation was legendary throughout the Fleet Air Arm, and Cork was ribbed mercilessly about him in the mess when he learnt of his posting to 'The Butcher's Squadron'. Judd had won his sobriquet deservedly. Massively built and over 6ft 2in tall in his naval flying socks, he was a man of violent tempers and great ferocity who rode his pilots hard and ruled the squadron's airframe and engine fitters with rods of iron.

No 880 Squadron was scheduled to equip with Grumman Martlets, the US Navy's F4F Wildcat, but there were several problems with this fighter and the squadron was re-scheduled to pioneer the Sea Hurricane into service. So, on 18 February, Cork took Judd with him to visit No 242 Squadron. In Hurricane Mk IIs borrowed from the squadron, Cork (V3818) and Judd indulged in local flying and some aerobatics. Dicky Cork's success in the momentous Battle of Britain and his experience made him an ideal selection for the FAA's first Sea Hurricane squadron. He was placed in command of 'A' Flight, although as this was the only Flight formed as yet, Judd led it.

The Admiralty had persisted in its attempts to secure Hurricanes and Spitfires for carrier service. The FAA was now receiving navalized Hurricane Mk Is (Merlin III engine) fitted with catapult spools and arrester hooks and designated Sea Hurricane Mk IB. However, it was still slower than land-based fighters, although faster than the Fulmar and Martlet but it lacked their endurance. Of greater concern was the poor performance of the Sea Hurricane's Merlin at the low altitudes at which most naval interceptions took place, but the Sea Hurricane was better at medium and high altitudes than the Fulmar or Martlet. It was clearly an interim type but it was a start.

On 22 June 1941, Hitler attacked the Soviet Union. The Soviets asked Britain for immediate aid. A specific request was naval assistance against the two main ports beyond the North Cape which were used by the Germans to supply their effort in northern Russia. These ports, Kirkenes in Norway and Petsamo (now Petenga), 40 miles east in Finland, were 250 miles inside the Arctic circle and 1,300 miles from Scapa Flow. Churchill decided that it was politic to attack these ports very soon.

Despite recent experience in the *Bismarck* chase, HMS *Victorious* was a new ship and her Air Group were still working up. Nevertheless, as she and HMS *Furious* were all that were available, her Air Group was given a fortnight to work up as fast as it could, before embarking.

By now Cork had seen another side to Judd, and had come to respect him as a thorough professional. The respect was mutual, and Judd's respect for his Flight Leader was strong. Judd's was an inflexible regime, but his men were exceptionally well prepared. For Cork, the main difficulty was that Judd lacked Bader's humour and ease. After Bader's thorough training of Cork, he was not only able to realize Judd's expectations, but to benefit from the driving leadership.

On 30 June 1941, Cork and Judd again visited Bader, now at Tangmere. Bader shoved them into Spitfires and took them along on an offensive patrol to Dunkirk, St. Omer, Le Touquet and Boulogne. Cork (R9501) and Judd flew as Bader's wingmen. There was no action on this sortie, but it was illuminating for both Cork and Judd to fly in the new fighter formations that Bader's wing was developing. That evening, Cork and Judd signed on at HMS *Daedalus*, RNAS Lee-on-Solent. They had much to discuss concerning tactics. Judd was swift to learn and adapt, while Cork had hard-won experience.

On 20 July, they flew north and landed late in the evening at RNAS Twatt, a strip of tarmac laid into a moor on the Orkneys. There, Dicky Cork, 'Butch' Judd, Johnnie Forrest, Jack Smith and Dickie Howarth prepared to embark in *Furious*. The squadron was far from ready for combat. Indeed, it had less than half its establishment of pilots and Sea Hurricanes but the pilots were experienced. They formed a temporary 'A' Flight for a special operation. They had only a day to wait. At crack of dawn on 21 July, Judd led Cork and the other pilots off from Twatt and flew out over the Atlantic looking for *Furious*.

No 880 Squadron 'A' Flight and its pilots, led by Lieutenant-Commander Judd and Cork, embarked in *Furious* who was waiting in company with *Victorious*. No 880A Squadron was to provide the top cover for the Carrier Task Group. The Admiralty plan stated that, during the perpetual daylight of the Arctic, *Victorious*'s Albacores would bomb and torpedo shipping in Kirkenes; simultaneously, *Furious*'s Albacores and Swordfish would bomb and torpedo shipping in Petsamo. The Kirkenes strike's secondary target was to be the Kirkenes iron ore plant, and the Petsamo secondary target was to be the oil storage tanks located there.

German anti-aircraft gun defences were said to be minimal and little Luftwaffe fighter opposition was anticipated. The carriers' Fulmars would cover them, while the Sea Hurricanes flew cover over the Fleet. The Sea Hurricanes were being rushed into service on their first operation in order to give the best possible cover to the carriers themselves. They did not have the range to accompany the strike force, or to meet it, or to cover it with a withdrawal CAP. Besides, no opposition was expected, so the Fulmars were thought able to cope.

On 23 July, *Victorious* and *Furious* sailed from the United Kingdom with the 8-inch gun cruisers HMS *Devonshire* and HMS *Suffolk*, and six destroyers. Force P was commanded by Rear Admiral W. F. Wake-Walker in *Devonshire*. They went via a stop at Iceland, approaching the North Cape from an oblique angle. Judd lost no time in getting the Sea Hurricanes prepared for launching and inducting the pilots new to carrier decks – including Cork – into the practice.

On 30 July, Force P sailed into the attack zone, but, as it neared the launch point 80 miles north-east of Kirkenes, it was sighted by a German He 111 reconnaissance aircraft which radioed its sighting. Surprise was lost, but the attack had to go ahead.

Furious launched her four No 880A Squadron Sea Hurricanes to fly CAP over the carriers as they flew off their strike aircraft. Then she launched her eighteen strike aircraft and *Victorious* launched her twenty strike aircraft. Just over a quarter of an hour later, *Victorious* launched her twelve Fulmars to defend the strike and *Furious* her six.

Furious's strike on Petsamo was an anti-climax – there were no ships in port to sink – but the Kirkenes raid was a tragedy. *Victorious*'s Albacores braved flak only be set upon by Bf 110s and Bf 109s which outclassed the escorting Fulmars, which had a hard time defending themselves. Alerted by R/T, the Sea Hurricanes could do nothing to help.

Furious lost two Fulmars and one Albacore, but *Victorious*'s losses were a disaster for her new air group: eleven Albacores and two Fulmars failed to return and eight Albacores were damaged, and no fewer than thirty-six aircrew were lost. The operation failed for lack of preparedness and intelligence, but it succeeded in political terms.

The last survivor touched down on *Victorious* at 18.45 hours, and Force P shaped course for home. Some hours later, a Do 18 reconnaissance flying-boat sought them out. If they located the fleet, the Luftwaffe would attack. Judd and Howarth were scrambled and shot the Do 18 down – the first Sea Hurricane combat, the first victory. Judd was ebullient! No 880A Squadron disembarked from *Furious* on 30 September.

Cork took a week's leave. To add to his Hurricane experience, Cork now had the as yet unusual operational experience of flying from a carrier the new generation of naval fighter, the Sea Hurricane. He had learnt his fighter craft under a hard master, Bader. He had begun to learn the naval fighter craft under another hard master, Judd. In the months ahead, his position as one of Judd's trusted Flight Leaders developed his leadership abilities and gave him direct contact with a man who knew the business of naval fighter operations thoroughly. Cork was learning from great mentors.

On 5 October 1941, Cork attached himself to HMS *Raven*. Meanwhile, No 880 Squadron's Headquarters had moved to RNAS Machrihanish, at the back of Campbeltown on the Mull of Kintyre, to prepare for embarking in their new carrier. New pilots were arriving to form 'B' Flight and bring 'A' Flight up to establishment, under the care of the Senior Pilot, a laconic Canadian Lieutenant 'Moose' Martyn. Dicky Cork was 'A' Flight Leader and 'B' Flight Leader was Lieutenant Brian Fiddes, RN. Among the pilots were Lieutenants Lowe, Steven Harris and Richard ('Dickie') Howarth, and Petty Officer 'Bungy' Williams, RN, and Sub-Lieutenants John ('Johnnie') Forrest, John ('Jack') Smith, John ('Jack') Cruickshank, Hugh Popham and 'Paddy'

Brownlee. Most of them were Royal Naval Volunteer Reservists.

Judd flew in to Machrihanish on 6 October, and two days later led the squadron aboard their new home, HMS *Indomitable* (Captain T. H. Troubridge, RN), as she steamed off Ailsa Craig. *Indomitable* was the fourth of the six-ship 'Illustrious' class of carriers to be completed. Cork joined the ship on 9 October. The Admiralty had an important role for the carrier, but first the carrier and air group had to work up.

Indomitable's Carrier Air Group comprised two fighter squadrons, one with Fulmars and one, No 880, with Sea Hurricanes, and two Albacore strike and anti-submarine squadrons. The complexities of operating a carrier fighter squadron are far greater than operating a land-based fighter squadron. Patrols have to be dovetailed, landing-on timed to just ten seconds between aeroplanes; patrol areas around the fleet have to be determined. The Sea Hurricanes provided the top cover and close cover, while the Fulmars provided the medium-range and low-level cover. There was considerable rivalry between the two fighter squadrons, fuelled by 'Butch' Judd's perfectionism, aboard ship and in the air. Judd might have terrified his crews, but his obsessionalism was not unrealistic: a carrier needed to have high serviceability and swift recovery of its aeroplanes because of the nature of the air threat to it, especially when the ship had to steam into wind, for a possibly vulnerable period to launch and recover its aircraft. If Judd could land all his squadron on in two minutes, he would significantly reduce the risks to his carrier.

For Judd and his pilots, there followed a long period of frustration, with little sight of the enemy. While working up, *Indomitable* ran aground off Kingston, Jamaica, suffering serious damage to her bow. From 10 to 22 November, she was in Norfolk Navy Yard, Virginia, USA, undergoing repairs. It was during this period that the crew learnt that *Ark Royal* had been sunk. More serious news was to follow. It had been planned to include *Indomitable* in Force Z, a task group comprising *Prince of Wales* and *Repulse*, but they were sunk by Japanese air attack in the South China Sea on 10 December, three days after the attack on the US Navy at Pearl Harbor. Had *Indomitable* not been damaged, she would have been alongside the British capital ships and the story might have been very different.

Early in 1942 *Indomitable* was in the east ferrying Hurricanes to Java, Sumatra and Ceylon. Later, she joined Admiral Somerville's hastily as-sembled Eastern Fleet which spent several weeks evading the more powerful Japanese carrier force at large in the Indian Ocean – Somerville had to keep his force extant at all costs. After that, *Indomitable* was called to Bombay, where she arrived on 12 April and stood by to repulse the threat to India from the Japanese carrier fleet. That fleet was heading back to Japan. *Indomitable*'s squadrons spent a week at Bombay and were then re-embarked just before the carrier set sail for the Seychelles. En route, the Air Group learnt that they were about to get their first taste of real action: Operation IRONCLAD, the invasion of Madagascar, off the east coast of Africa. The operation was being mounted because it was feared that the Vichy French might permit German and Japanese submarines to operate from a base on the island to attack the Allies' vulnerable sea routes.

There was no possibility of land-based air power assisting the landings. The two sister carriers *Illustrious* and *Indomitable* co-operated under *Illustrious*'s former Captain, Rear Admiral D. W. Boyd. *Illustrious* embarked two fighter squadrons, Nos 881 and 882 with twelve Martlets each, and two Swordfish TBR squadrons, Nos 801 and 829. *Indomitable* embarked two Albacore squadrons, Nos 827 and 831, and the fighter squadrons – Nos 800 and 806 with twelve Fulmars each, and No 880, now reduced to nine Sea Hurricanes through attrition. The carriers came together and joined up with the huge convoy of troop landing vessels on the afternoon of 4 May. This was the first time that a Royal Navy strike force provided cover for troops until airfields were secured. It was an operation that would be repeated many times before the war was ended. A third carrier, *Formidable*, provided distant guard in case the Japanese fleet were to intervene. IRONCLAD coincided with the great Battle of the Coral Sea, in which the Japanese fleet was defeated: the Japanese did not interfere in IRONCLAD.

The fighting on the ground was some of the most vicious and unpleasant of the war. In the air, the French showed little resistance, but all members of the Royal Navy's Air Groups were blooded.

From dawn on 5 May, the Sea Hurricanes were to fly offensive patrols over the town and harbour of Diego Suarez and the Vichy French naval aerodrome to the south of the town at Antsirane. The Martlets were tasked with flying cover patrol over the invasion beaches. At this point early in the war, the Fleet Air Arm had little experience of carrier-borne Army support operations. Sea Hurricanes were the fastest aeroplanes available to the Navy and were therefore used as offensive fighters. They also had more firepower than the Martlets, so were used for strafing while the Martlets were tasked solely with air defence.

Judd and Cork were aware of the new RAF fighting formations as Bader had taken the opportunity of their operational flight with him the previous year to ram home the advantages! Cork was the only truly combat-experienced pilot in the squadron, but the extensive work-up undertaken by the Carrier Air Group had given the squadron commanders and their pilots and the Fighter Direction Officer sound experience of fighter handling. *Indomitable*'s Commander Flying adhered to Naval practice and denied Judd his head over No 880 Squadron – for the time being.

In the small hours of 5 May 1942, landing vessels put ashore 13,000 British Empire assault troops at two points on the west of the island's northern isthmus. It was the first major Allied amphibious landing. The troops' task was to capture the town and harbour of Diego Suarez on the other side of the northern isthmus. This was done without great difficulty.

Before dawn on the 5th, *Illustrious* and *Indomitable* launched air strikes in support of the landings. The Swordfish and Albacores attacked ships in Diego Suarez harbour, bombed harbour installations and strafed Diego Suarez aerodrome, destroying aeroplanes. By 04.30 hours, No 5 Commando's 600 men had seized the town of Diego Suarez. The troops consolidated.

At dawn, Cork took part in a strafe of Antsirane aerodrome. Three Morane-Saulnier MS.406 fighters and a Potez 63.11 reconnaissance-bomber were destroyed in a hangar they set alight. A later attack was less successful. Cork flew another Hurricane that day when the Sea Hurricanes strafed the airfield at Diego Suarez.

The next day, 6 May, Cork led a section of No 880 Squadron in an attack on a gun battery in the Antsirane naval base in preparation for the assault on the base, which continued to resist. Later, in line astern, six Sea Hurricanes led by Judd strafed a grounded armed sloop whose guns, covering the approaches to the town, were still giving trouble. They left her burning. Judd's reputation as a bloodthirsty sailor was well reinforced by his positive glee at the destruction he wrought. Cork, however, was jealous of the Martlet pilots of No 881 Squadron who had met a formation of MS.406s in the air over the landing ships, and shot down four of them. Cork thirsted for real action.

Antsirane lay on the southern side of the bay. The ground forces had failed to take it. During the night of 6/7 May, the destroyer HMS *Anthony* pressed right into the harbour under the gun batteries to land fifty Royal Marines on the dock. The marines swiftly seized the depot and the base fell to the British troops within hours.

On 7 May, No 880 Squadron flew combat air patrols over the town, the shipping and the landing beaches. With Diego Suarez and Antsirane secure, only routine patrolling was anticipated. It was hoped that the French troops throughout the island would surrender, but the Vichy Governor, Armand Annet, would not capitulate.

Following the operation, *Indomitable* anchored in Diego Suarez harbour on 8 May. Ten days later, she sailed for Kilindini, the naval base of Mombasa. The final, unforgettably bloody campaign began in September 1942, supported by *Illustrious*. Annet surrendered on 5 November. Madagascar was one of the Allied victories that marked a turning point in the war in late 1942.

Indomitable took no part in the final campaign: the Admiralty had other plans for her. At the end of the first week in July, she headed south again. She paused at Durban, and more briefly at Capetown, then ran up the west coast of Africa, where she put in to Freetown to replenish in a bare few hours. The squadrons disembarked at Durban, Capetown and Freetown, for further working up. This piecemeal training was not ideal.

Indomitable then began the run up from Freetown at high speed. There was clearly urgency. Rumours started about the next deployment. The two favourites were the hot option and the cold option: the Malta convoy run, the hotter in every sense, and the Murmansk convoy run. On 4 August 1942, the rumoured deployment was confirmed: The Malta gauntlet. The Carrier Air Group was to cover Operation PEDESTAL. It would be a good deal tougher than Operation IRONCLAD. In fact, this was one of the major British naval air battles of the war, and made Cork's name a second time.

CHAPTER 16
Typhoon Troubles

On 19 October 1941, 'Cocky' Dundas was posted to No 610 (County of Chester) Squadron as a Flight Commander. He arrived at Tangmere just before it was rotated north for rest to Leconfield. Dundas himself had been posted away from No 616 Squadron for 'rest' as a flying instructor on No 59 OTU, but had connived his way back to operations in four weeks. Until November, No 610 Squadron was busy escorting Stirling and Halifax heavy bombers and the last of the raids by the RAF's Fortress Mk Is before they were withdrawn from bombing.

However, on 18 November, Dundas broke a leg during a mess game. As a result, he missed the opportunity to command the first Spitfire squadron which was to be sent to Malta off an aircraft carrier's deck, No 601 – no job for an invalid. Instead, he was given command of No 56 Squadron at Duxford, the first to get the new Hawker Typhoon fighter, the latest, fastest, most powerful and most heavily armed single-seat fighter in the world!

On 20 December 1941, wearing new squadron leader's rings, Dundas took command of No 56 Squadron, relieving Squadron Leader Prosser Hanks. The squadron's first two Typhoon Mk IAs (R7582 and R7583) had arrived on 11 September, but delivery was slow. The squadron was converting to Typhoons from Hurricane Mk IIBs, and continued to fly them as well until March 1942. No 56 Squadron was joined by No 266 Squadron on 29–30 January 1942 and No 609 Squadron on 30 March to form the Duxford Wing, commanded by Hanks, now promoted to wing commander.

No 56 Squadron's main task was to work the Typhoon into operational service, and they worked closely with the Duxford-based Typhoon Air Fighting Development Unit. It was not an easy task. Severe problems with carbon monoxide seeping into the cockpit, forcing the pilots to breathe oxygen throughout flight at all altitudes, were cured when Gloster's Chief Test Pilot, Gerry Sayer, visited No 56 Squadron and recommended fitting 4-inch stub exhausts as standard.

Tail structure failure was a persistent danger, lessened initially by riveting fishplates around the tail/fuselage join. It was later found to be caused by vibrations in the fuselage induced by elevator and tailplane flutter. Once the cause had been identified, the cure was effected relatively easily, but fatalities had been considerable.

The Sabre engine took longer to tame. Prone to catching fire when starting and to failing inexplicably in flight, and with only 25 hours between overhauls, it also set up sympathetic resonance in the fuselage, which, according to pilots, had dire effects on their potency.

Pilot conversion was prolonged as the Typhoon was not an easy aircraft to master, with heavy torque, high speeds and poor vision from the cockpit, coupled with great weight. All these factors kept the Typhoon from operations.

In March 1942, No 56 Squadron received four-cannon-armed Typhoon Mk IBs, which it operated alongside its twelve-machine-gun-armed Mark IAs for some time. As both marks were from the same serial range and the squadron's records do not distinguish between the marks, it is uncertain when the Mark IAs were phased out, but they were still operational in August, for both marks were involved in the Dieppe operation (Operation JUBILEE).

The Duxford squadrons, Nos 56, 266 and 609, gradually moved out to operational bases while others formed at Duxford. On 30 March, No 56 Squadron moved to a new Duxford satellite, Snailwell, Cambridgeshire. It brought the station its first taste of real action, beginning to practise 'Rhubarbs' in April and was shortly declared combat ready. On 29 May, 'A' and 'B' Flights moved to Manston, Kent, and Westhampnett, Tangmere's satellite respectively, becoming operational there the next day.

The Flights were detached to these stations, both near the Channel coast, in a brief attempt to intercept the Fw 190 Jabo high-speed, low-level fighter-bombers which made tip-and-run raids on southern targets, sneaking in below radar, a German version of 'Rhubarbs'. On 31 May, Dundas and his wingman, Pilot Officer Dininger (in 'B' Flight Typhoon Mk IAs R7648: US-A and R7694: US-R respectively) flew the first Typhoon operation from Manston. They were scrambled on an anti-Jabo patrol, patrolling between Sankey Bill and St Catherine's Point, uneventfully.

On 1 June, No 56 Squadron took off from Manston and Westhampnett to join other parts of the Duxford Wing (led by Wing Commander Denys Gillam since April, after Hanks left for Malta) to take part in the first Typhoon wing sweep, from Mardyck to Boulogne. After the operation, No 56 Squadron landed at Snailwell before flying on to Manston and Westhampnett. Similar operations followed. From 7 June, the squadron was again operating from Snailwell.

Throughout the first half of 1942, the future of the Typhoon was intensely discussed at Fighter Command HQ and Duxford. Group Captain Harry Broadhurst, a proven tactical leader, was the Group Captain Operations at Fighter Command, and fighter policy was his to decide. He did not think that the Typhoon had much of a future as a fighter. The pilots at Duxford disagreed. The arguments reached a point where they had to be resolved. The Duxford leaders and the Fighter Command policy-makers met at Fighter Command HQ during June. The Typhoon had been rigorously evaluated, but there was little combat time on it.

Broadhurst asserted that there were some seventy squadrons of Spitfires, which were fulfilling all the fighter roles required of them satisfactorily, and were a known quantity. On the other hand, there were only three Typhoon units, and they had had a host of problems to solve. Production was less than swift, too. He argued that there was no fighter role for the Typhoon, as it could not be used as a close escort, cover or freelance fighter. The Typhoon was too much of a handful and lacked the necessary agility to be a close escort fighter, like the Spitfire Mk V. The performance of the Typhoon's Sabre engine fell off above 18,000 feet, and its manoeuvrability deteriorated at altitude, but most fighter-versus-fighter combat took place above 20,000 feet, so it could not provide cover or succeed in a freelance role. It was the Allison-engined Mustang Mk I all over again; and Broadhurst proposed the same solution – use them for special duties and ground attack.

In contrast, the fighter leaders flying the Typhoons – Grandy and Richey, and particularly Dundas who had the most experience on the type – argued for an offensive role for the Typhoon, not a secondary tactical role. Sholto Douglas asked Dundas to put forward the leaders' views. Dundas proposed how the Typhoon could be employed on fighter sweeps to use its strengths and avoid its weaknesses. As the main formations were withdrawing, the Typhoon wing would sweep round their rear at high speed to catch enemy aircraft leaving or entering the combat zone. Going in at 21,000 feet, they would gradually descend as they curved round so that they were at their best fighting altitude at the point where they were most likely to engage the enemy. The Typhoons would use their superior speed and dive to bounce anything that they spotted, but they would not engage in manoeuvring combats as they were inferior dogfighting machines to the Fw 190s and Bf 109s.

Sholto Douglas considered the proposals. He concluded that, as Broadhurst could not argue from experience of the Typhoons, it was worth trying the offensive role proposed by those who could. The Duxford Wing did take part in several sweeps, but did not engage enemy fighters on any of them. The Fighter Command Operations staff were careful to keep them away from the main battles being fought during the sweeps. The climax of the argument came with JUBILEE, in mid-August.

No 56 Squadron's first 'combat' had been on 1 June 1942. Pilot Officer Duego and Sergeant Pilot Stuart-Turner had been scrambled to intercept hostile aircraft located off Dover by radar. Two No 41 Squadron Spitfire Mk VBs were also scrambled from RAF Gravesend. The two sections were unaware of each other's presence. The Typhoons, however, saw the Spitfires above them. Identifying them correctly, they were not alarmed. But the Spitfires mistook the Typhoons for Fw 190s and shot them down. Only Duego baled out.

This mistake in recognition was not an isolated incident. Typhoons and Mustangs were too often mistaken for enemy aircraft by RAF fighters, and by British anti-aircraft gunners on the Channel coasts as the fighters returned home from sweeps. The Typhoon's and Mustang's wing resembled those of the Bf 109F and the Bf 109E or Fw 190A respectively, while the Typhoon's deep chin radiator could be confused with the Fw 190A's annular nose. Typhoons had sported all-white noses in November 1941, but this had only given enemy pilots a bull's-eye, so from December 1941, black and white stripes were painted below the wings. From late July 1942, nine-inch wide yellow chordwise bands, already carried by Army Co-Operation Command Mustangs, were added above each wing inboard of the guns – some had two bands – to identify them to friendly aircraft considering a quick bounce.

In the first nine months of operations, more Typhoons were lost through structural or engine failure than combat, estimated at one per sortie in July-September 1942. Of the first 142 Typhoons delivered to operational squadrons, 135 were involved in serious accidents or lost through engine or airframe failure. Accident and loss rates declined as the engine problems were solved, but problems remained into 1943. Moreover, the rate of climb and altitude performance were poorer than expected. Nevertheless, in countering Jabo raids and exploring fighter-bomber tactics, the Typhoon's early introduction to operations was judged to be worth the problems and the high cost. Dundas had been given a heavy responsibility when he was placed in command of No 56 Squadron but had successfully worked a very difficult aircraft into service, evaluated its strengths and weaknesses and had championed its tactical fighter merits at the risk of alienating Harry Broadhurst.

CHAPTER 17
'Rhubarbs'

On 14 January 1942, a month after 'Cocky' Dundas's departure, No 610 Squadron was moved from Leconfield to Hutton Cranswick. It was not long before one of its 1941 members reappeared. Straight from survivor's leave, Denis Crowley-Milling came to take over a Flight as an acting flight lieutenant on 6 February 1942. The next day, a new commanding officer was posted in, Squadron Leader G. S. K. Haywood, on promotion from No 616 Squadron.

On 4 April, No 610 Squadron was moved again, to Ludham, Norfolk, and began the staple diet of No 12 Group squadrons – work over the North Sea protecting convoys, flying fighter patrols and mounting 'Rhubarbs'. On 3 July, an attachment of part of the squadron to West Malling, Kent, as a temporary reinforcement for No 11 Group was greeted with keenness, but resulted in no action and much disappointment. It was curtailed after four days. In reality, it was a rehearsal for a future operation.

In further preparation for this operation, during July, the squadron was re-equipped with a full complement of eighteen Spitfire Mk VBs. Powered by Merlin 46 engines, these fighters were equipped to carry long-range jettisonable fuel tanks, and the squadron termed them 'LR Mark VBs'. The first seven arrived on 9 July, followed by nine on the 11th and two on the 14th.

There were changes in personnel too. On 9 July, Flying Officer 'Johnnie' Johnson was posted from No 616 Squadron as an acting flight lieutenant. On 13 July, Squadron Leader Haywood left the squadron and Johnson was appointed to the unpaid rank of acting squadron leader on appointment as his successor. Johnson carefully selected his wingman, choosing the solid New Zealander, S. C. Creagh, who had been promoted from sergeant to flight sergeant on 1 June.

No 610 Squadron was part of No 12 Group, but Johnson was determined to get the squadron into No 11 Group where the action lay, and set the highest standards. However, the squadron had to be content with shipping reconnaissance and convoy patrols, and 'Stooge' patrols, with the occasional interception and offensive patrol, the normal operations of Nos 12 and 13 Group squadrons. 'Stooge' patrols were mounted by a pair of Spitfires, often a pilot officer and a sergeant. Lasting about an hour and twenty minutes, they were intended as casual patrols to intercept any enemy aircraft that might be operating in the area. There were also some fighter sweeps and 'Rhubarbs' into Holland.

An offensive patrol flown by No 610 Squadron on the evening of 2

August off the Dutch coast clearly shows the nature of such operations. Red Flight of six Spitfire Mk VBs was scrambled from Ludham to intercept enemy bombers returning to Holland after a raid on England. They were airborne at 18.10 hours, led by Johnson (EP254:B), with his wingman Creagh (EP253:K), and Pilot Officers Wright, Pabiot, Collinge and Hokan. Johnson set course on 117 degrees and headed out over the North Sea at high speed, hoping to overhaul the bombers.

Visibility was excellent, up to 20 miles, but there was ten-tenths cloud at 4,500 feet with patches of mist and low haze. At 18.50 hours, 2 miles off the Dutch coast and 15 miles north of Ymuiden, Johnson turned the formation to starboard and set up a search pattern. The Spitfires were stepped up between zero feet and 3,000 feet. First, the formation swept south down the coast to try to head off the bombers. Some 4 miles north of Ymuiden, they spotted a convoy of eight ships in two columns 3 miles off shore. The convoy was not deploying balloons but there appeared to be two flak ships ahead of the convoy, so the formation skirted the convoy to seaward. The Spitfires continued on down the coast. Heavy flak batteries at Ymuiden opened up on them, but inflicted no damage.

The formation reached the limit of its patrol, 15 miles south of Ymuiden, turned, and flew back north up the coast. They flew up to the convoy, then headed back south to the same point, where they again turned. They flew all the way back up the coast to 15 miles north of Ymuiden, then back to the convoy again before heading home on a course of 290 degrees. They saw no enemy aircraft. They landed at Ludham at 19.55 hours.

'Rhubarbs' were limited daylight attacks by small sections of two or four fighters, under cloud or bad weather cover. The objectives were to destroy enemy aircraft and attack targets of opportunity on the ground. They were instituted on a large scale by Fighter Command in 1942, and were flown at the discretion of group commanders, usually in quiet periods between escorts to 'Circuses' or flying in 'Rodeo' fighter sweeps or smaller 'Ramrod' attacks. They were flown by Spitfires, Typhoons, Hurricanes, Mustangs and Whirlwinds. The operation's lack of planning meant that time over the target area was at a premium in order to find targets. The Spitfire's maximum radius was the same as the Typhoon's and Hurricane's at 150 miles, and similar to the Whirlwind's at 165 miles, but it was half that of the Mustang at 300 miles.

On 3 August, No 610 Squadron flew a 'Rhubarb' involving the entire squadron. The basic operation had been planned in advance and the instructions came from No 12 Group Headquarters, but the detailed execution of the orders was left to the squadron commander. Sections of two Spitfires were assigned to specific areas, and targets were sought within those areas. A section of four Spitfires acted as withdrawal cover in case the offensive sections ran into trouble, and also to take advantage of any fighter response the Luftwaffe might make.

On that day, three pairs of Spitfires were involved in three co-ordinated penetrations, Green, Blue and Red Sections. After they had taken off, Yellow Section (led by Squadron Leader Johnson with Flight Sergeant Creagh, Pilot Officer de Patoul and Sergeant Harris) took off at 12.20 hours to cover their withdrawal. Johnson climbed Yellow Section above cloud and continued to climb. He set the section up in an orbit pattern over the Dutch coast at 10,000 feet between Zandvoort and Ymuiden, hoping that any enemy aircraft taking off during the 'Rhubarb' would be silhouetted against the cloud.

Green Section (Warrant Officer Jackson and Pilot Officer Gaudard) took off at 12.10. They flew on a course of 117 degrees, climbed to 1,000 feet and crossed the Dutch coast just north of Katwijk. They saw one electric passenger train on the Leyden-Haarlem railway line but they did not attack it. They flew up the Sassenham-Haarlem canal and saw a hutted army camp 2 miles west of the canal, some 5 miles south of Zandvoort.

Sweeping in from the north at about 200 feet, Jackson (Green 1) strafed a group of accommodation huts, watching his cannon shells burst in the huts. About fifty men were seen, half of whom fell to the ground. Gaudard (Green 2) followed, strafing the same huts, and also saw several soldiers tumble down.

On breaking off the attack, the pilots found themselves separated. Jackson flew over Zandvoort. There was nothing on the roads or railway. He flew west. On the cliffs 3 miles north of Zandvoort, he spotted a machine-gun post. He set his gun switch to machine-guns only. He dived down and gave the post a long burst. He saw flashes inside the post and two soldiers ran out of it. His attack seemed to be productive. He decided to continue the attack, so he flew out to sea and curved in again but light and heavy flak along the coast opened up on him. He veered away and turned on to 300 degrees and returned to base. He landed at 13.40 hours.

Gaudard (Green 2), meanwhile, had orbitted near the camp at 500 feet for some minutes looking for Jackson and targets. He spotted a small barge by a bridge just west of Vijfhuizen and strafed it. Cannon shells exploded on the vessel. He was now short of ammunition and low on fuel. He turned for the coast and crossed it just south of Zandvoort, on 270 degrees. Gaudard and Jackson joined up near base and landed at 13.40 hours.

Blue Section (Pilot Officer Smith and 2nd Lieutenant Hvinden) took off at 12.15 hours. They flew on 104 degrees at 100 feet across the North Sea. At 12.55 hours, they were 8 miles off the Dutch coast. There was bright sunshine and little cloud cover over this stretch of coast, and visibility was 15 miles. They decided that conditions were too hazardous for a 'Rhubarb' and turned back to base, arriving at 13.40 hours.

Red Section (Pilot Officers Collinge and Wright) took off from Ludham at 12.20 hours. Collinge and Wright flew on a course of 097 degrees at 200 feet, climbing to 2,000 feet when they were 3 miles off the Dutch coast. The visibility over the Dutch coast was 10 miles. There was a ground haze and nine-tenths cloud at 2,000 feet. The conditions were good for a 'Rhubarb'. First, they flew up and down the coast for five minutes, looking for targets. They spotted a group of barges a little south of Zandvoort, and crossed the coast at 2,000 feet.

Doug Collinge (Red 1) attacked three 150-foot oil tanker barges from 700 feet, hitting them repeatedly with cannon and machine-gun fire. Wright (Red 2) followed him, hitting the deck of one barge with a long burst. Collinge flew on north a mile and attacked two 100-foot barges, seeing many strikes on their decks.

The section then turned and headed for home on 290 degrees. About 10 miles off the Dutch coast they saw two Ju 88s flying east directly towards them, but just above. The visibility over the sea was very poor and the two Spitfires were low on ammunition, so the section did not take this opportunity to engage.

Squadron Leader Johnson kept Yellow Section orbitting for ten minutes after the withdrawal of all Red, Blue and Green Section aircraft. No enemy fighters had come up to attack the intruders. He turned around and took the section back to base on 294 degrees. Yellow Section landed at Ludham at 13.50 hours. The last pilots of the squadron, Collinge and Wright, arrived back at 14.05 hours.

The Intelligence Officer debriefed the pilots, seeking reports of damage inflicted, of enemy reactions, of flak positions, of useful information about deployments and transports. Johnson led the debriefing. The squadron had been lucky this time: there had been no losses. One section had aborted because the weather was too good to give them adequate cover. Four aircraft had attacked targets. The gains were one army encampment damaged, with a number of soldiers killed, and several barges and a machine-gun post damaged.

Over a third of 'Rhubarb' operations were aborted due to unsuitable weather. On better days, locomotives, rolling stock, small vessels and transportation systems were attacked successfully. Very few enemy aircraft were destroyed. Losses approached 10 per cent, mostly to flak, the highest loss percentage of any type of air operation in 1942–43, which must weigh heavily in any assessment of the effectiveness of 'Rhubarbs'.

PART VI

CHAPTER 18
Takali

In late May and early June 1941, Royal Navy carriers had managed to fly off sufficient Hurricanes to Malta to bolster the day air defence of the island to three full squadrons. These were sufficient to maintain the island's air defences against the assaults by the Italian Air Force. Further carrier-transported Hurricanes were flown in during the year.

In November 1941, Hurricanes of Bader's old unit, No 242 Squadron, were flown off HMS *Ark Royal* – they were the last the carrier sent for she was torpedoed a few hours later. One of No 242 Squadron's former members had already made a name for himself on Malta, George Powell-Sheddon, who had flown as one of Bader's Flight Commanders during the Battle of Britain.

Although the main bombing raids on Malta came by day, there was bomber activity at night, which had to be countered. With Hurricanes to spare in July 1941, a special night fighter unit was formed with Hurricanes surplus to the establishment of the day fighter squadrons. The unit was termed the Malta Night Fighter Unit (MNFU), and was commanded by Squadron Leader George Powell-Sheddon. After a tour with No 258 Squadron, he had become one of the many battle-tested fighter pilots sent to the beleaguered island. Powell-Sheddon set the example for the Hurricane pilots with two victories at night during his period of duty on Malta. In December 1941, the MNFU was redesignated No 1435 Flight (later Squadron).

In December 1941, to stabilize the situation in North Africa, the Germans became involved in the air battle for Malta, whose chief importance lay in its capacity for air and sea offensive operations against the Axis air and sea supply routes to North Africa. The British had not prepared Malta's defences before the war and were suffering the consequences. On the other hand, Rommel warned his High Command of the dangers of leaving Malta unsubjugated. Malta posed severe problems both for defender and would-be subjugator. The German policy was to hit the fighter bases to deny Malta defences, hit bomber and torpedo-bomber bases to deny Malta offensive capacity and hit the docks and harbours to deny Malta an offensive naval role and the ability swiftly to unload supply vessels. Others argued that Malta had to be invaded.

The problems involved in the air defence of Malta were complex. The nerve centre was the Central Fighter Operations Building. The only adequate part of the air defence control system of Malta, it was run on similar principles to those in the Metropolitan Fighter Command Sectors. It was underground, hewn out of the island's solid rock. However, in equipment and mode of operation, it was amateur.

The problem for the air defence was similar to Park's during the Battle of Britain. Malta also faced a 360-degree threat. The German bombers would join up over Comiso in Sicily with their Bf 109 escorts. Generally, the force units comprised six Ju 88s and between twelve and twenty Bf 109s. The German formation then headed for Malta. The bombers crossed the Maltese coast at one point, such as Zonkor Point or Grand Harbour. Their principal targets were the aerodromes and Grand Harbour. Enemy bombers approached at high or medium altitudes. They released their bombs in either a shallow diving attack across the target, or a steep dive-bombing attack.

The bombers were heavily escorted by Bf 109Fs. A formation of Bf 109Fs swept ahead of the formation and another acted as top cover. The Bf 109F had an advantage in ceiling and rate of climb over the Hurricane. When flying as top cover, the Bf 109Fs would always have the advantage of height and position over the Hurricanes. As the bombers made their run, the Bf 109s orbitted overhead. After their attack, the Bf 109s closed on the bombers and the force headed back, usually over Filfla island or Kalafrana Bay.

The Hurricanes had been hard-pressed to defend Malta adequately after the Luftwaffe had first become involved over the island in December 1941. The Hurricanes were manoeuvrable, but had insufficient speed and climb to catch the fighters and the bombers, and the fire-power of their eight .303-inch machine-guns was inadequate against the skin of modern bombers.

Even if the Hurricane pilots sat in their cockpits at readiness, they could not be scrambled in time to reach the bombers, and then fell prey to the diving Bf 109Fs. The Hurricanes, in fact, had to climb away from the bombers in order to gain altitude, and even then could not gain enough height. The fighter controller had to tell the fighters when to turn back towards the enemy formation. This required very fine judgment. The timing was made rather more difficult because the fighter controller was underground and there was no Ground Controlled Interception radar on Malta. This all had the inevitable result that the interceptions took place far too close to the targets, and often the bombers were only intercepted after they had bombed.

In January 1942, there was no senior officer on Malta with current experience of fighter operations. The wing commander in charge of the Central Fighter Operations building was an experienced fighter pilot who had been promoted from command of a fighter squadron, but had no experience of controlling fighters from the ground.

One of the war's most successful operational leaders, Basil Embry, was asked by Tedder to visit Malta in mid-January 1942, and make recommendations. He analyzed the situation and made a forthright report. First, it was evident that only Spitfire Mk Vs had the necessary rate of climb, fighting ceiling and firepower to deal with the tactical situation. Secondly, he rejected the argument that ground radar would not operate on Malta, and recommended that it be installed. Thirdly, he recommended that the job of fighter controller be made that of a group captain to give authority and that a seasoned controller with current experience be appointed, preferably a

Fighter Command Sector Controller, because the task was so complex.

Embry's recommendations had immediate effects. The British Government, which was already considering sending Spitfires, now made it a matter of urgency. On 7 March 1942, HMS *Eagle* flew off the first batch to the island. Shortly before that, ground interception radar had been installed on the island. Raids could now be seen forming up over Sicily. Finally, within days of Embry's recommendations, Group Captain A. B. Woodhall, who had guided Bader from Duxford in 1940 and Tangmere in 1941, was on his way to become the Senior Fighter Controller. He instructed the pilots on Malta that he would scramble them in formations of four aircraft, in pairs. For their part, the pilots flew in pairs once airborne.

Once Woodhall was installed and had seen the poor tactical fighter control on Malta, it was almost inevitable that one of the Bader team should then be appointed to take command of the Takali Wing – Wing Commander P. S. Turner. 'Woody' Woodhall and Stan Turner between them transformed the fighter defence of Malta.

Turner's arrival was not low-key. A Sunderland flying-boat collected him and four other pilots – Flight Lieutenant P. B. 'Laddie' Lucas, Raoul 'Daddy Longlegs' Daddo-Langlois, Bob Sergeant and Tex Putnam – from Gibraltar in the small hours and flew them through the safety of the Mediterranean night to Malta. The flying-boat put down in Kalafrana Bay, and the new pilots, straight from the gloom of the English winter into a crystal blue island day, were pulled ashore in a dinghy.

As they collected their kit, and walked towards the mess for breakfast, the air raid sirens began to wail. A few minutes later, the pilots heard the note of Merlins under power and looked up. There, at barely 4,000 feet and struggling upwards, were four machine-gun-armed Hurricane Mk IIs.

Then the pilots caught a different note from higher in the sky. There, at 10,000 feet they could see a dozen Bf 109Fs, sweeping in ahead of the raid in three sections of four, in loose, open, line-abreast formation – 'finger-four'.

Stan Turner looked back at the Hurricanes struggling aloft in a catch-me-if-you-can line astern. He exploded: 'Jesus Christ! They're not going to fly that way with me!'

Turner arrived at Takali asking insensitive questions. He was told, equally bluntly, that they had had only four Hurricanes aloft that morning because they had only four Hurricanes able to fly out of the twelve that were nominally serviceable. The reason that they flew in line astern? There was no time to form up in a neat formation, and climb as hard as you can was the only instruction.

Turner was not impressed. When he met the Takali pilots, he told them bluntly: 'I don't know who taught you your formations, but no one is going to fly line astern or vics with me. I'm interested in living. From now on we fly line abreast, and I'm going to show you how, starting now!' – and he did.

It was another month before the first Spitfires arrived in Malta and during the intervening weeks, Turner, coming from the immaculately maintained squadrons in England, learnt the hard way what Malta's pilots had endured in their clapped-out Hurricanes. Only too often Woodhall could only send up four, five or six Hurricanes to meet the large German and Italian formations, and the Hurricane's guns could not bring the bombers down. But the new formations and tactical instructions began to have an effect. When the Hurricanes did engage successfully, the results were more conclusive. The rate of losses began to decrease.

Turner had been flying operationally since March 1940. He was exhausted, but his strong leadership and tactical skill were needed in this crisis – he could teach offence in defence. He led the Takali Wing for only a few brief weeks in the spring of 1942, but, as 'Laddie' Lucas who was one of his Flight Commanders has written, in that time he passed on the essence of Bader's teaching. And those who learnt it from him, and survived, passed it on to others.

When the first Spitfires arrived, on 7 March, they were turned around in minutes and sent against the Bf 109s while the Hurricanes tackled the bombers. It was a beginning.

With the arrival of Spitfire Mk Vs, with more powerful Merlins and two 20mm cannon, new tactical possibilities opened up. The ideal was for the Hurricanes to attack the bombers while the faster-climbing Spitfires covered them against the Bf 109s which flew top cover to the bombers. In practice, this was not possible. The German escorts were often very heavy.

However, it was much better than in 1941. Now, Woodhall could watch on radar the raid form up over Comiso, estimate the number of 'big jobs' (bombers) and follow the raid on its progress across the sea. It took fine reading of the radar picture and an intimate knowledge of German and Italian tactics to know where the fighters were placed and how to direct his own thin forces on to the raid in order to get at the real prize – the bombers.

Stan Turner was not the only Douglas Bader pilot who flew in Malta in 1942 and brought his teachings. Pilot Officer Geoff West and Flight Lieutenant W. E. 'Nip' Heppell, DFC, arrived in early March 1942 to fly the new Spitfires. Heppell and Flight Lieutenant P. B. Lucas each commanded a Flight of No 249 Squadron at Takali. Heppell, known to all in Fighter Command as 'Nipple' for some reason (or 'Nip' or 'Hep' for polite consumption), was, according to Paul Brennan, 'a tall, languid, apparently indifferent Englishman who had proved himself in air battles over France'. Heppell was now fighting a different kind of war from the one he had fought under Bader in the Tangmere Wing, a defensive not an offensive war. The principles of flying in pairs remained the same, but there was now the overriding necessity to scramble fast and climb rapidly. He had the best aeroplane for the job. This was the kind of warfare for which the Spitfire had been designed – a fast-climbing, short-range interceptor.

On 17 March, Heppell had a fight against high odds, for he was leading a raw section against a strongly escorted force of bombers and he himself was new to defensive warfare. He led Red Section of four aircraft, for dawn readiness. The pilots were Flight Sergeant Ian Cormack (Red 2) who flew as Heppell's wingman, and Pilot Officer Paul Brennan, RAAF, (Red 3) with Sergeant Junior Tayleur (Red 4) as wingman. Brennan and Tayleur had flown in on 7 March; Cormack had scarcely more experience.

Just before 06.30 hours, the Fighter Controller telephoned Heppell to order the section to strap themselves into their aircraft at readiness. The pilots ran up their machines and then 'buckled them on'. They flicked their gun switches from 'Safe' to 'Fire'.

They waited for what seemed to be an interminable time, the cool Heppell and the tense new boys. Then the duty airman rushed from the dispersal hut and fired a Very pistol in the air, yelling: 'Scramble'. The four Merlins, already primed, popped and crackled into life.

The four Spitfires taxied out, lined up and Heppell waved them off. They sped across the soil, tails bobbing up swiftly . . . swinging, correcting . . . undercarriage retracting it seemed before the wheels had left the earth, a dust cloud spiralling behind them . . . the Spitfires floating, then climbing hard.

Forming up on Heppell in the centre in the position of the long finger, Red Section climbed south-east. The sun had been up only a short while. It was a very clear day, with a red sun hanging in a blue sky. There was slight haze low over the sea to the north which was beginning to disperse.

Heppell called up Woodhall for instruction. Woodhall instructed him to climb quickly to meet a raid coming in from the north. The enemy formation was about 40 miles off. The Spitfires passed through 10,000 feet, spaced out in the classic 'Malta formation' – line abreast – Heppell scanning over and beyond Cormack to his left, while Cormack swept the skies over and around Heppell's Spitfire.

Woodhall called up again on the radio: 'Hullo, boys. The party is now 20 miles north of St Paul's Bay, moving south. There are some big jobs, with fighter escort.'

Heppell continued to climb the section, hoping that he could gain enough height, hoping he was in the right position. They passed through 17,000 feet 6 miles east of Zonkor Point, still heading north.

Woodhall had the bombers now, he said. They were heading for Grand Harbour. For Heppell, accustomed to being the aggressor with height and sun to play with, taking on such odds from such a weak position was still a new and dangerous way to fight.

Heppell scanned the sky to his left and above, dipping his wings to clear the blind spots. Seconds later, through the top left of his canopy just beside the frame, he spotted them. Eight Ju 88s, twenty Bf 109s . . . at least . . . there would be other Bf 109s somewhere too. His heart began to race, but he was calm as he called to his section:

'OK, boys. They're at ten o'clock, slightly above us. Break into them.'

Heppell pulled his Spitfire into a climbing turn towards the Germans. His wingman followed him closely. Heppell kept his head swivelling, checking his wingman's far side, up and behind . . . experience told him that's where he would be if he were them . . . he spotted the Bf 109s behind him . . . he'd known they had to be there. He said over the radio:

'More above us at five o'clock. Keep turning, boys.'

Heppell lost sight of Cormack, Brennan and Tayleur. Paul Brennan, new to this game, broke left and lost contact, but fortunately Junior Tayleur swiftly reorientated himself and swung back into position on Brennan's wing.

Cormack, after the first break into the Germans, and following Heppell's warning of more behind, kept turning and had simply found himself in a sky without aircraft – a not unusual but still mystifying experience for a fighter pilot.

Heppell plunged into the bombers, but the Bf 109s latched on to him, and forced him to take swift evasive action. He was heavily outnumbered. The Bf 109s were queueing up on the Spitfires' tails. Heppell called up the other Spitfires for help, but two of them were too busy or too inexperienced to respond, and Cormack, having got separated, knew better than to fly around trying to re-engage from a weak position and alone.

Heppell kept turning, juggling out of the way of the bursts of cannon fire. There were five on Heppell's tail. He caught a Bf 109 in his sights and fired, a pot shot. He broke off when a Bf 109 boresighted him, and swung out of the way. He caught another Bf 109, and gave it a burst before breaking off to guard his own tail. It was no time to gain victories. Once in a while, Woodhall fed him brief information on the progress of the raid.

Then Brennan called up Heppell to say that he was clear and how was he doing and could he help? Heppell thanked him and declined, paused breathlessly and added: 'These Huns think they can shoot me down. Not bloody likely!' But he was sweating and afraid.

However, the Bf 109s were only interested in protecting the bombers. They had no brief to stay and fight. They succeeded in guarding their bombers from the Spitfires. Then, as the bombers began to return, the Bf 109s simply broke off and headed north.

The fight had lasted fifteen minutes and the whole sortie less than forty minutes. When they got back, Heppell learnt that Cormack had not engaged, and that Brennan had knocked down his first German aircraft, a Bf 109. Tayleur's seat had broken under the pressure of turning, and he had done the only sensible thing – dived out of the combat and headed home.

An hour later, the section was scrambled again, but the call came too late for them to get into a good tactical position. The German formation was already over them as they began their long climb. Woodhall kept warning the section that there were strong forces of Bf 109s orbiting Malta.

After passing through 8,000 feet over Filfla island, Cormack drew Heppell's attention to Bf 109s above them. Heppell looked around, and saw a pair flying along in front of them, too casually, he thought. He looked behind and saw the second pair. The pair in front were the usual decoys. Heppell broke the section left in a steep cross-over turn to shake off the real danger from the pair behind.

As they turned, Heppell saw a dozen Bf 109s plummetting down from out of the sun. The Spitfires were very badly placed. There was nothing that they could do. Heppell quickly ordered: 'On your backs and dive. Get out!'

The four Spitfire pilots rammed their throttle levers hard forward, half-rolled, skidding to make themselves slippery targets and dived. The Spitfires accelerated to 550 mph, the pilots struggling to control them with trim alone, as the controls jammed at that speed. At under 4,000 feet, three of the Spitfires pulled out, but Cormack's controls had locked solid. He went straight into the sea.

Heppell led the other three back to Takali and landed. The loss of a pilot went deep. They still had another two hours or so on duty in which to relieve the strain with talk.

The Huns did catch 'Nip' Heppell later over Malta, with a cannon shell, and he was retired from the action to recover. He later became a squadron leader, running his own squadron of fighters.

Squadron Leader E. J. Gracie arrived with new Spitfire pilots on Malta towards the end of March 1942. He was a stocky, balding Englishman, a Battle of Britain veteran, with eight victories over Malta, who had joined the RAF as the only service with which he could do his fighting sitting down. He was promoted to wing commander in mid-April 1942, and took over the Takali Wing, becoming Station Commander.

CHAPTER 19
Operation PEDESTAL

Lieutenant Richard Cork did not need the briefing to tell him how critical Malta was to the Allied cause, and the size of the escort made him aware of the importance of the convoy. Any convoy being sent through would confront very heavy air and naval opposition from the Germans and Italians who would seek to annihilate it, starting with the aircraft carriers.

By the middle of July 1942 Malta's position was again desperate. The island was short of food, ammunition, fuel and aircraft. Axis successes in North Africa had turned the tide. Convoys had failed to get through. HMS *Eagle* had made two sorties to fly off a total of fifty-nine Spitfires to Malta, but by the end of June there were only eight serviceable fighters on Malta. On average, the RAF was losing seventeen a week. Kesselring had told Hitler that the 'aerial attack on Malta has, I feel, eliminated Malta as a naval base'. Thus, it would no longer threaten the supplies to Rommel's Afrika Korps. Victory in North Africa was within the Axis reach.

The British decided upon a massive operation to save Malta, code-named PEDESTAL. The convoy was composed of fifteen fast merchantmen and the American fast oil tanker *Ohio*, and was escorted by Force Z, under the command of Vice-Admiral Sir Neville Syfret, comprising the 16-inch gun battleships HMS *Nelson* and HMS *Rodney*, the carriers *Eagle*, *Indomitable* and *Victorious*, plus three anti-aircraft cruisers and fourteen destroyers. Between them, the carriers embarked sixty-eight fighters. They would be outnumbered ten to one by Axis fighters and bombers operating from Sardinia and Sicily.

New fighter control techniques had been developed by the Fleet Air Arm. To iron out problems, during 6–7 August, the three carriers ran an exercise, BERSERK, with the old carrier HMS *Argus* acting as a fighter direction ship. Fighter direction relied on effective radar and efficient radio communication between fighter and ship. It would be upon the success of the radar detection, shipborne fighter direction and the skills of the fighter pilots that the success of the convoy would depend.

Naval fighter direction faced a 360-degree threat, from all altitudes. Fighters had to be vectored on to the targets on time and at the right height. To do this, *Victorious*'s Type 79B radar was to concentrate on height finding, while the Type 281 sets mounted on *Indomitable* and the cruiser *Sirius* were to concentrate on the all-round, low-altitude threat. All aircraft carried VHF radio and IFF, and the ships had VHF. The cruisers *Nigeria* and *Cairo* were fully equipped for fighter direction, a generous provision for a single convoy.

On 7 August, the convoy was joined by HMS *Furious* and her escort, which was to carry out Operation BELLOWS in company with the PEDESTAL convoy. *Furious* was carrying forty-two Spitfire Mk VBs which she was to fly off to Malta on 11 August, and then turn back. She also embarked six Sea Hurricanes of her own No 804 Squadron to bolster the PEDESTAL fighter strength to seventy-four.

The next day, Saturday, 8 August, the main carrier force joined the convoy. The three carriers *Victorious*, *Indomitable*, *Eagle*, were to operate independently within the destroyer screen to the rear of the convoy. Each carrier had an anti-aircraft cruiser and anti-submarine screen, and had to run its own defensive fighter patrols. For greatest efficiency, each carrier's fighter group was allocated a role best suited to its equipment. *Victorious* had most Fulmars so drew low cover below 5,000 feet, above which *Indomitable* and *Victorious* mounted medium cover with Martlets and top cover at 20,000 feet with Sea Hurricanes. A Malta convoy was one of the most intense combat experiences yet devised.

The convoy passed through the Straits of Gibraltar on the night of 9/10 August. While in the Straits it was joined by replenishment ships and further escorts. By now, the Italians already had sufficient information from which to deduce what was happening.

Monday, 10 August dawned fine and clear, a beautiful Mediterranean day. From dawn, four fighters were kept at immediate readiness on *Indomitable*'s flight deck, their engines warmed up and their pilots strapped in. Albacores flew anti-submarine patrols. The look-outs scanned the horizons and the high skies and the air warning radar and the sonar swept for the enemy above and below the sea.

At 05.25 hours, four Sea Hurricanes were scrambled after a suspected shadower, but failed to catch it. There were further alarms. In the middle of the afternoon, two Martlets were scrambled after a suspected shadower. It turned out to be a Vichy French flying-boat on a regular Toulon to Morocco flight. It was a security risk. Admiral Syfret's instructions were clear. The airliner was shot down. To be undiscovered for a few more hours might make a big difference to the convoy.

At this point, the British fighter strength had already fallen. *Indomitable* had embarked three fighter squadrons: No 806 with ten Martlets, nine of them serviceable; Nos 800 and 880, each with twelve Sea Hurricanes, of which twenty-two were serviceable. However, Nos 800 and 806 Squadrons had only recently re-equipped and had worked up in haste; they did not have the deep training that Judd had given No 880 Squadron. *Indomitable* also carried twenty-four Albacores. *Victorious* embarked three fighter squadrons also but two had the less effective Fulmar, and two were at half strength. No 809 Squadron had twelve Fulmars and No 884 Squadron had six, but four were unserviceable. In order to embark six Sea Hurricanes of No 885 Squadron, *Victorious* had landed six of her twenty-one Albacores, but one of the Sea Hurricanes was unserviceable. Ten of her fighter pilots were new, with no combat experience. Aboard *Eagle* were No 801 Squadron with twelve Sea

Hurricanes plus four crated, and No 813 Squadron with four Sea Hurricanes. None of the British fighters was a match for the land-based fighters they would meet, and they lacked the performance and the teeth against the bombers. A few of the Sea Hurricanes had four 20mm cannon, but the rest of the fighters had machine-guns.

The night of 10/11 August passed peacefully but in the early hours of the 11th an Italian submarine, on station 50 miles south of Ibiza, reported to the Axis command accurate information about the convoy and its formidable escort. The Axis response was uncompromising. The Italian Fleet was deployed for action. The Germans deployed twenty-three E-boats. Nineteen Italian and two German submarines were deployed in waves across the convoy's path. Two minefields had been prepared. From the air, 784 Axis bombers and fighters were prepared on the airfields of Sardinia and Sicily. However, the Germans asserted that they would deal with the convoy with air power alone, without help from the Italian Navy. The Italian Navy was checked, by Mussolini.

From dawn on 11 August, the carriers had standing patrols aloft of six aircraft at a time, at each level in pairs from different carriers. They circled the Fleet, watching, waiting for a call from the Fighter Direction Officers. They were forbidden to break radio silence unless something happened. Each patrol lasted an hour and thirty minutes. *Indomitable*'s first patrol of the day was flown by Hugh Popham and Brian Fiddes.

The first shadower was caught on radar at 08.15 hours, and fighters were vectored on to it, unsuccessfully. Cork (in Sea Hurricane Z4642) and three wingmen flew the mid-morning patrol. Ten minutes into the patrol, *Indomitable*'s radar detected 'bogeys' at 22,000 feet, shadowing the convoy. Just as one of them was passing the vital message giving the Fleet's composition, bearing and speed, Cork was vectored on to it, at 10.10 hours. He and his wingmen climbed fast to gain the advantage, although there was no chance of getting into the sun. He spotted it ahead, a Ju 88. He swiftly dived on it, from the beam. He had only time to fire once before it dived away. He hit its port engine, which immediately began to smoke. The Ju 88 began to lose altitude – too swiftly, but was travelling too fast for the two Sea Hurricanes to follow it. Cork claimed it was probably destroyed. Other shadowers appeared throughout the morning and afternoon.

Readiness was stepped up. In addition to the eighteen fighters in the air, six at each level, six pilots were strapped in their cockpits on the deck of each carrier, engines warm, ready to fly off the deck. Four pilots waited on stand-by in each carrier's Ready Room. Throughout the day, pilots were on duty three times in rotation, once in the morning, once in the afternoon and once in the evening. Cork (Z4642) flew twice more that day.

Shortly after noon, *Furious* began to fly off the Spitfires. Forty-one were ready. The first group of eight left from 12.29 hours. The second eight began to fly off at 13.09 hours.

By this time, the submarine pack had closed in. Kapitän-Leutnant Helmut Rosenbaum of *U-73* had been stalking the carrier group for several hours. He had specific instructions: sink carriers, not merchantmen. At 13.15

hours, *U-73* got through the destroyer screen and put four torpedoes into the old hull of *Eagle*. She sank in seven minutes, taking with her 131 of her crew. With *Eagle* went her vital aircraft; almost a quarter of the convoy's air cover had gone.

A raid had hit the Fleet before *Eagle* went down and was being driven off by fighters from all the carriers. Four of *Eagle*'s No 801 Squadron Sea Hurricanes were airborne. Acting Sub-Lieutenant Douglas MacDonald, RN, and the squadron's Commanding Officer, Lieutenant-Commander Rupert Brabner, RNVR, landed on *Indomitable* and were incorporated in No 880 Squadron. Sub-Lieutenants (A) Michael Hankey, RNVR, and Peter Hutton, RNVR, landed on *Victorious*. Hankey was incorporated in No 885 Squadron. Hutton refuelled and took off on patrol again, and landed on *Indomitable*, and joined No 880 Squadron.

Ten minutes after *Eagle* had sunk, a submarine launched a fan of torpedoes at *Victorious*. One of them was seen to pass across her bows. It was the first of several torpedo and periscope sightings that afternoon – all threatening the carriers. It kept the Albacores busy. The destroyer screen darting around them, the carriers defensively zigzagged and jinked. It became fully clear now to the pilots of No 880 Squadron why 'Butch' Judd had driven them so hard to reduce the deck-landing interval between aeroplanes. A pair of Sea Hurricane pilots had less than thirty seconds to make a return to the deck between the carrier's defensive course changes.

At 13.47 hours, after a break while the submarines were hunted, the next group of Spitfires began to fly off *Furious*. The last Spitfire left her deck at 15.12 hours, 555 miles from Malta. *Furious* and her escort immediately turned back to Gibraltar. Malta's air defence was secured for a further month.

Later that afternoon there was a lull. However, on his second patrol of the day, Cork recorded that he: 'intercepted a Vichy French airliner. Let it go.' The element of surprise had gone. There was no point in shooting down this aeroplane, even though it was known that Vichy airliners were radioing information of value to the enemy.

Like patient vultures, shadowers circled in the sun, beyond the altitude and range of the ships' anti-aircraft guns, watching, diving away if fighters tried to set upon them, sending back their reports. By early evening, the attacks would begin as the convoy came within range of the Sicilian air bases.

Indomitable had a squadron patrol up in the mid-evening, led by Judd. Cork's third patrol, it was flown very late in the day – very late, considering how late it gets dark off Africa in mid-August. As a number of *Eagle*'s former fighters were aboard, they were incorporated into No 880 Squadron.

At 20.40 hours, *Indomitable*'s readiness Sea Hurricanes were scrambled to reinforce the standing patrol. The carrier's Fighter Controller, Stewart Morris, gave them a northerly vector, and told them to climb to 20,000 feet. Then they were told to descend to 12,000 feet, then up again to 20,000 feet. Yellow Flight's two pairs – the Flight Leader Brian Fiddes and Hugh Popham; and Steve Harris and Paddy Brownlee – spotted the 'trade', a large group of Ju 88s, perhaps three dozen, coming in from the east.

In line astern, the pilots went in to attack the bombers. The enemy formation broke. Brian Fiddes and his wingman Hugh Popham managed to hold on to one of the jinking bombers, but only just. They fired at extreme range. Pieces came off it. Smoke issued from one engine. The Sea Hurricanes could not get closer. The bomber disappeared in the gloom, leaving the Sea Hurricane pilots frustrated at the slowness of their mounts. Nevertheless, the raid had been driven off.

When the fighters returned to their ships after intercepting the raiders and patrolling, all the Fleet's anti-aircraft guns were firing. The fighters flew around the perimeter, and the gunfire followed them. They waggled their wings and the fire intensified.

Ten of *Indomitable*'s Sea Hurricanes were aloft and, by the time the gunners had been persuaded to stop, the fighters were running very short of fuel. *Indomitable* was keeping dark in order not to be an illuminated target for a U-boat, but Captain Troubridge decided that she had to get her aircraft down, dark or not dark. He turned the carrier into wind. He accelerated and put the deck lights on.

The whole Fleet had been blazing away at the returning fighters and although the ships were quiet now, Judd was taking no chances. Wheels down, he led the Sea Hurricanes along the starboard side of *Indomitable* before finally landing on to ensure that the gunners knew they were friendly. The starboard aft pom-poms gave them a burst. The temperature in Judd's cockpit soared.

Judd landed on first. Hardly had his Sea Hurricane come to a halt beyond the barrier, than he had leapt out the cockpit, hurled a deck crewman out of his way, and sprinted back up the length of the deck. He sprang down into the pom-pom gun-pit and grabbed the gunnery lieutenant by the throat, picked him up bodily and shook him, his bristling face thrust into the young man's unbearded mouth: 'You bloody useless bastard! You brainless oaf! Don't you know a Sea Hurricane when you see one!' Satisfied, he dropped the startled lieutenant and stormed off into the night to make an official report.

Cork took the matter less seriously, recording: 'Whole squadron shot at by Fleet landing at night.' The patrol, as a result of the delay in landing on, was two and a quarter hours in duration, of which the last half an hour was by night.

Indomitable managed to land on eight of her own fighters, and five of *Victorious*'s. Hugh Popham, low on fuel, mistook carriers and landed on *Victorious*. The carrier was slewing under rudder, trying to put him off, and his engine cut out through lack of fuel as he came over the round-down and he crashed. He broke his and another Sea Hurricane. He was stranded until the next day, at least.

Troubridge had steamed *Indomitable* dead ahead for over an hour at 26 knots, way out beyond the destroyer screen, an easy target, until he was sure that all the fighters that were still aloft must be down on a deck or in the sea. Troubridge's decision was critical: without her fighters, *Indomitable* was useless to the Fleet. The Axis bombers were going for the carriers in order to establish their own air superiority over the Fleet, before picking off the

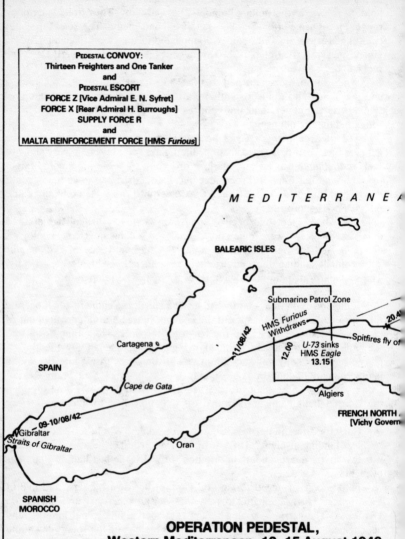

PEDESTAL CONVOY:
Thirteen Freighters and One Tanker
and
PEDESTAL ESCORT
FORCE Z [Vice Admiral E. N. Syfret]
FORCE X [Rear Admiral H. Burroughs]
SUPPLY FORCE R
and
MALTA REINFORCEMENT FORCE [HMS Furious]

MEDITERRANEA

BALEARIC ISLES

Submarine Patrol Zone

HMS Furious
Withdraws

20.4

Spitfires fly of

12.00

U-73 sinks
HMS Eagle
13.15

Cartagena

SPAIN

11/08/42

Cape de Gata

Algiers

FRENCH NORTH
[Vichy Govern

09-10/08/42

Gibraltar
Straits of Gibraltar

Oran

SPANISH
MOROCCO

OPERATION PEDESTAL,
Western Mediterranean, 10–15 August 1942

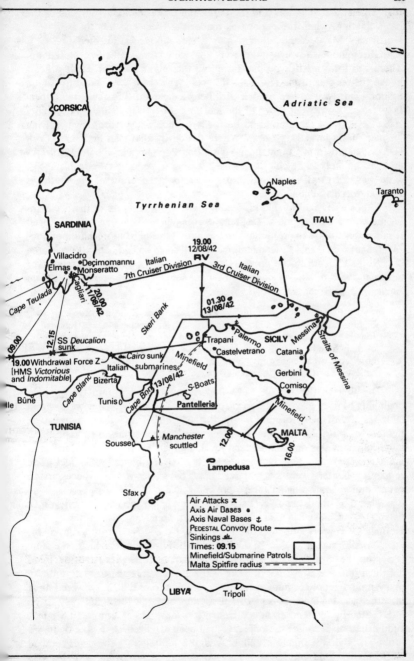

real targets, the freighters and the plum, the tanker *Ohio*. At the end of the day's fighting, when the count was made, the Fleet had less than fifty Sea Hurricanes, Martlets and Fulmars fit to fly. Troubridge was justified.

Throughout the night, the warships' gun crews remained closed up. There was little rest for the hangar crews that night, and the senior officers of the fighter squadrons found rest difficult. The crew were called to Action Stations shortly after five o'clock. Just before dawn on 12 August, the critical Day Three, Cork went down to the hangar deck to inspect the serviceability states. He found that Judd had been there since well before dawn, driving his men. Judd turned on Cork: 'Where the devil's that man Popham?' Cork had just heard from Commander Flying that Popham was aboard *Victorious* and was unlikely to be able to get back, owing to operational circumstances. Judd was not at all impressed, but Fiddes took the brunt of his wrath, as Popham was his wingman.

Judd's gruff exterior hid his feelings. He was well aware of the pressures on the young fighter pilots. Lieutenant-Commander Brabner, late of *Eagle*, recalled that Judd sought him out to tell him of 'his high appreciation of Sub-Lieutenant MacDonald's leadership and skill' since he had been incorporated into No 880 Squadron the previous afternoon. Judd knew the importance of personal bonds in a naval single-seat fighter squadron. The young pilots from *Eagle* were, as Brabner wrote:

> '. . . cut-off from that . . . support which is so necessary in a Single-Seat Fighter Squadron and which comes from flying among close personal friends . . . cut off from their base, disturbed by uncertainty as to the fate of their friends . . . cut off from their Squadron, and, while receiving a hospitable welcome, were flying in strange Squadrons among new colleagues in the heat of an extensive battle.'

The first fighter patrols were flown off the carriers into the sunlight beginning to filter above the horizon in front of the convoy. They were within 50 miles of North Africa, and a little further from Sicily – they could expect fighters to escort the bombers. Eighteen naval fighters were to be kept in the air throughout this day, six at each level, Fulmars at low cover, Martlets at medium cover and Sea Hurricanes as top cover above 18,000 feet. The remaining fighters were kept at readiness, to be flown off as necessary to counter raids. Many fine balances were being held.

That day, almost two years since his first combat success, Cork flew four patrols. He achieved in that day a score that would make men heroes over Germany two years later. On the first patrol, No 880 Squadron, led by Judd, attacked a formation of a score of Ju 88s at 09.15 hours. It was the first enemy attack on the 12th. The fighters had no advantage of height or sun, but Judd led them into the attack. Cork destroyed a Ju 88 before the formation broke up. Within a couple of minutes of interception, two of the Ju 88s were falling into the sea, ten had jettisoned their bombs and run for home only to be intercepted by fighters scrambled from *Victorious*, and two more Ju 88s fell. Judd called off a chase: the objective had been achieved. A couple of Ju 88s broke through the fighters and braved the anti-aircraft fire and bombed ineffectually. One pilot was lost, Hankey of *Eagle*, flying with No 885

Squadron. Twelve enemy aircraft were claimed as 'destroyed' or 'damaged' – a good opening.

Indomitable's Fighter Controller told 'Butch' of a faint blip he was getting to the south, and Judd turned his formation and headed for Tunisia. There they found another similar formation, just off the coast. Ignoring the escorts, they homed in on the few bombers. They had to make their first pass count.

Cork was lucky. He (Blue 1) and his wingman, 'Crooky' Cruickshank (Blue 2), destroyed another Ju 88 before the bombers pulled out of range. They stuck together and chased the bombers, but had to avoid the fighters.

Judd turned on to a skidding, diving Ju 88 and tried to hold it in his sight, but the bomber was opening the range. Judd had no alternative but to make a stern attack – an attack that he had so often told his young pilots would probably be fatal for the attacker. Judd also knew that his duty was to attack at all costs, to bring down bombers and to demoralize the enemy. He bored in on the bomber. The rear gunner opened fire. Judd pressed in. He saw the tracer whipping past his Sea Hurricane's nose. He knew the bomber's fire was accurate, but he had a V-12 engine in front of him and armoured glass. He concentrated, then began to fire. Bullets struck his engine and cockpit. His aeroplane spun out of the sky, streaming smoke and plunged into the Mediterranean.

Brian Fiddes was unlucky. He had disappeared from the patrol, shot down by the Fleet's anti-aircraft fire, but he managed to bale out. He bobbed around in his Mae West from some time, as the convoy and escort passed him by; then the last destroyer in the screen spotted him among the waves and picked him up.

On return to *Indomitable*, Cork was appointed to command No 880 Squadron, in place of Judd. The squadron had lost two Sea Hurricanes – Judd's and Fiddes's – and most of the others were damaged. Cork's own aeroplane (Z4642) was damaged and needed attention from the overworked mechanics.

Behind Cork and his squadron there was a great support structure all working to get them into the air to counter the enemy aeroplanes. Activity was ceaseless on *Indomitable*'s flight deck and in her hangar. The men, mostly Able Seamen, were too busy even to be cheerful. Most men were so tired that they felt cold even in the sweltering hangar. The anti-submarine patrols had to be prepared and flown off, and recovered. The fighters for each standing patrol had to be ranged and tested, lashed and chocked. Then they had to wait while the carrier came round into wind, briefly, only seconds, and then the fighters were unleashed like whippets and flown off in just eighteen seconds before the ship would turn hard to confuse submarines. Then, a couple of turns later, returning fighters would be flown on and unhooked, all within twenty seconds.

When the fighters were aboard, they had to be rearmed and refuelled, checked and repaired and maintained. To the list of the usual ailments of fighter aircraft – leaking oil, low pressures, etc. – was added combat damage. The fitters and riggers strove to change windscreens, engines, propellers, rudders as the hangar deck became cluttered with components and tools and slippery with oil.

Cork and his men could not fight if they did not eat and drink. In the galleys, food was prepared and doled out to the aircrews and deckcrews when they could snatch time to eat it. Biscuits and cocoa were popular.

Upon the teamwork of the deck crew and the skill of the pilots a great deal depended. The hard regime of Judd began to make sense to the pilots of No 880 Squadron. With Judd gone, Cork had an immense burden to shoulder, but he did so with admirable confidence.

On *Indomitable*'s bridge, the Captain kept watch, ready to react to threats, controlling the overall timing of the operations on his vessel. In the Fighter Direction Room, the operators watched their air direction radar screens, with the Fighter Direction Officer nervously fingering his microphone. The radar plot showed a boiling picture of enemy air activity. The Fighter Direction Officer and his operators picked out the relevant echoes, the clusters forming and moving more clearly than the others. Attacks went on throughout the day. They increased in weight as the convoy drew nearer to the Sicilian airfields. The FAA fighter pilots' task was made many times more difficult and dangerous now, for enemy single-seat fighters could now escort the bombers.

Cork and Cruickshank sat in the cockpits of the leading two readiness Sea Hurricanes ranged on the deck one behind the other, engines warmed, deck crews ready. The pilots were fully kitted, parachutes hard under their buttocks, Sutton harnesses tightly secured. They sweated constant warm trickles. Almost unconscious of doing it, they searched the sky to the north-east, waiting for the call. As the carrier changed course, the wind carried the smell of sea salt mixed with aviation fuel and rubber and oil and metal in the heat, but the pilots were used to the swell of the sea. They only noticed the carrier heeling into a vicious zig or zag by the way the horizon tilted and their gaze was swung around over the men on the carrier, away from the threat in the air which, after all, the ship's radar would see long before they would.

Constantly, as they sat on the flight deck, they contemplated the hundred and one things that they needed to remember, the take-off drill, the landing drill, the drill for ditching – 'canopy back . . . tighten harness . . . release parachute but not harness . . .' remembering the hints and the tips from colleagues, the little things and the big things that might save their lives today, within five minutes. Thinking of these things and the pain that tickled them in the gut, the sweat that broke out on them was not caused by the heat.

They could see the flight deck officers standing by, looking too tense to be bored, too keyed up to think about anything clearly. Around their Sea Hurricanes were the men who tended these fighting machines, the Able Seamen holding the lanyards securing the wingtips, the hunched backs of the men who lay on the scuffed armour of the deck ready to pull the chocks away from their wheels, the men sitting ready with the starter motor. The pilots' eyes kept coming back to see Commander Flying pace his walkway on the island superstructure to their right.

At last, the cry from the Bosun's Mate: 'Fighters stand to!' and they were on their way, too engaged to feel anything but the metallic taste of adrenalin. The ship was on a straight course into wind, just for them. Their Merlins fired. Cork poured on power to drag his fighter off the deck. He felt the sink and lift in the same fraction of a moment as he went off the end of the deck. Behind, Cruickshank was rising off the deck, undercarriage coming up. Twenty seconds after the Bosun's Mate's cry, and already behind them the carrier was veering away to port to keep the submarines guessing.

At 12.15 hours, the Axis had launched a major air attack, seventy aircraft combining all categories of attack to saturate the defences of the Fleet – Ju 87 and Ju 88 dive-bombers, He 111 torpedo-bombers, SM.84 and SM.79 torpedo-bombers and level bombers, and SM.84s carrying Motobomba FFs ('circling mines') and fighter-bombers. They had a heavy Italian fighter escort.

During this, his second, patrol of this momentous day, Cork flew another Sea Hurricane (N2435). The squadron hit a large formation of SM.79 bombers. Cork shot down one of them, but the Sea Hurricanes were then jumped by Bf 110s. Sub-Lieutenant A. J. Cruickshank, Cork's wingman, was shot down by a Bf 110, but Cork then shot down that Bf 110. The crew was picked up by a destroyer, so confirming the victory. Cruickshank was not picked up; he had been killed. Cork's aeroplane was also badly shot up in this action. When he arrived back on *Indomitable*, his Sea Hurricane was removed for repair work.

Indomitable's No 806 Squadron also lost its Commanding Officer, Lieutenant-Commander R. L. Johnson. He was chasing a bomber when he was bounced by fighters. He was badly wounded, but he managed to put his Martlet down on *Indomitable*'s deck and catch a wire, but he was too fast and the Martlet had been damaged. His fighter's hook pulled out. He went over the side.

The Fleet's defences survived. The fighters and massive anti-aircraft barrages had beaten off this attack by 13.45 hours, although one of the merchantmen, SS *Deucalion*, was disabled and forced out of the convoy. Two Italian Reggiane Re.2001 fighter-bombers stayed behind and joined the circuit to land on *Victorious* and then swept over her deck, taking everyone unawares, and dropped a bomb each. Amazingly, they did no damage, but hurt many vanities.

The fighter assets were being rapidly depleted, but there was now a lull in attacks in the afternoon. There were frequent submarine alerts and contacts. One Italian submarine, *Cobalto*, was depth-charged, forced to the surface and rammed by the destroyer HMS *Ithuriel*.

Shortly after 17.00 hours, the carrier air direction radars began to show active plots again. All available fighters were scrambled and began a continuous series of operations, countering the shadowers which relayed intelligence information, breaking up groups of raiders and nibbling at the incoming formations until the fighters could muster for a head-on attack to send them scattering.

At 17.45 hours, the largest formation of the day began to appear. It was the climax of the battle. Every available fighter was flown off *Indomitable* and *Victorious*. Heavily escorted formations of Ju 87s, Ju 88s, Cant Z.1007s and SM.79s were coming in with heavy fighter escort, over one hundred enemy aircraft. It was Cork's third patrol and he had to take yet another Sea Hurricane (Z7093). No 880 Squadron ran into a large formation of fighters. Cork found an SM.79 which he shot down – it was confirmed destroyed – but they were jumped by Bf 109Gs and Reggiane Re.2002s. The anti-aircraft fire opened up as the bombers came in range, and hits began to be scored.

The attack was well planned and competently executed. The enemy saturated the Fleet's defences and went for *Indomitable*. Four Ju 87 and eight Ju 88 dive-bombers pinpointed her, and peeled off in line astern from 12,000 feet into an intense barrage of flak. Three of them were hit and burnt out, but the carrier was badly hit forward, aft and on the beam. The water towers fell back into the sea and the spray dispersed. *Indomitable* appeared, beginning a slow circle, listing badly, smoking heavily and losing way.

The bombers had done a thorough job. One bomb penetrated her deck armour aft of the after lift, and had buckled the lift. This made it impossible to fly on aeroplanes. A second bomb exploded forward in the hangar mouth. Most of the maintenance crews at work in the hangar were killed or badly burned or injured. The explosion hefted the 7-ton lift, which was at full elevation, up on its chains and jammed it two feet above the deck. The carrier could not fly off any more aircraft.

A third bomb sliced through the side of the vessel and exploded in the wardroom anteroom. It killed many of the carrier's Albacore crews, and one of No 880 Squadron's Sea Hurricane pilots. There was damage below the waterline from bombs exploding close to the hull. Fires raged through the hangar and after areas. There was flooding below the waterline. *Indomitable* lost way, listing, circling for twenty minutes before the pumps began to work; then, slowly, the smoke began to disperse. Her Captain signalled that the situation was under control. By 19.30 hours, the carrier had begun to move forwards with the Fleet, but she was no longer an asset. She was the third British carrier to be disabled by the Luftwaffe.

Half of *Indomitable*'s fighters were aloft, including No 880 Squadron. The pilots were being diverted to *Victorious*, the only surviving carrier. The arrival of twelve of *Indomitable*'s aeroplanes on *Victorious* between 18.50 and 19.30 hours caused confusion on her deck.

Cork's Sea Hurricane had been seriously damaged in the nose area, and as he approached to land on *Victorious* the engine began to lose power. He held the power up. Just as he hit the deck, the engine died. The arrester hook caught a wire, held and the hydraulic mechanism hauled the fighter to a jarring halt. Men rushed from the deck edge and manhandled the fighter forward, into the jam of aeroplanes in the park.

Despite the pandemonium on *Victorious*'s deck, Cork's place was in the air. His Sea Hurricane was unflyable. He seized another from *Victorious* (Z4056). Though demonstrably exhausted, he insisted on taking off on his fourth patrol of the day. Attack waves were still coming in, others circling. Cork intercepted enemy aircraft and managed to damage another Re.2002.

He landed back on *Victorious*.

Another of Cork's pilots, Sub-Lieutenant Peter Hutton (one of the *Eagle* No 801 Squadron survivors), was in the air when *Indomitable* was crippled. He landed on *Victorious*, out of fuel. He also insisted on being refuelled and launched immediately for another sortie. He shot down an attacker and gave chase to another, but was killed by fighters.

It had been intended to fly off two four-fighter cover patrols, one for the Fleet from *Indomitable* and another from *Victorious* for Force Z at the point they parted, but this was now impossible. At 18.20 hours, *Victorious* put up four Fulmars to cover the convoy, but they became entangled with the attackers, shooting one down and losing one. It was 19.30 hours before the last enemy had disengaged – thirty-five minutes after Syfret had had to turn Force Z about to return to Gibraltar. *Indomitable* went with Force Z, remarkably now working up to 28 knots.

By 19.30 hours, *Victorious*'s deck was crowded with aeroplanes. The Fulmars could be struck down below in the hangar, but it was soon over capacity. The Sea Hurricanes could not be struck down below because their wings did not fold and the carrier's lifts were not large enough to take them. *Victorious* had only been able to embark six of her own Sea Hurricanes at Gibraltar (No 885A Squadron) and these had been parked on outriggers on the aft flight deck. Of *Indomitable*'s Sea Hurricanes, Martlets and Fulmars, those that were clearly irreparable were manhandled overboard.

Indomitable's flight deck was blocked by broken lifts at either end. *Victorious*'s deck was blocked by aeroplanes at either end. It was clear that *Indomitable* was incapable of operating aircraft, and it was equally clear that were another raid to fall on them now, *Victorious* could not fly off any fighters to counter it. Despite *Indomitable*'s damage, the last attack had failed – the convoy was still intact, but now the omens were good for a decisive Axis naval victory.

Cork reported to the Commander Flying, *Victorious*, to assess the state of his squadron, and told him that, as Judd had been killed and Fiddes was presumed missing, he was Acting Commanding Officer of No 880 Squadron. There was one entirely fresh No 880 Squadron pilot on *Victorious*, Hugh Popham, who had unkindly been marooned aboard the vessel since his crash-landing the previous evening. He was fretful away from his own squadron and anxious to take part in the great day. Cork, wisely, had a Sea Hurricane made available and gave Popham a patrol to fly as soon as the deck had been cleared.

Every available man aboard *Victorious* laboured to clear her flight deck in order to fly off the last patrol of the day. Within the hour, six Sea Hurricanes of assorted units were ranged aft, in line astern, engines primed and warmed, pilots ready, the deck clear for them to fly off. Upon *Victorious* fell the task of putting up the Fleet's fighter defence, two fighters at each level. As soon as the deck was ready, Popham was flown off, followed by two others, at 20.07 hours, landing on again at 20.45 hours as night fell.

Only one merchantman had been sunk so far, although several had been hit. They were 130 miles from Malta. At 19.30 hours, the heavy warships of Force Z had had to turn back west because they were low on fuel. As the wake of the battleships and carriers disappeared, the convoy prepared for the worst phase of the battle. No capital vessels remained to counter the Italian Fleet and there were fewer heavy anti-aircraft guns and no fighters to counter the enemy bombers, but the convoy was within range of Malta's Beaufighter fighters – and the next day would have the effective cover of Malta's Spitfires.

Within hours, the bombers, the E-boats and the submarines struck. At 19.55 hours, the Italian submarine *Axum* (Tenente di Vacello Renato Ferrini), fired a fan of torpedoes that caught three vital ships: the two with fighter direction, the cruisers *Nigeria* and *Cairo*, and the oil tanker *Ohio*. Although none sank, it was a brilliant attack, and disrupted the Fleet, its control of the escorts and its control of the air assets from Malta. Later, the cruiser HMS *Manchester* was crippled by torpedo-boats, and scuttled. By the next day, eight merchantmen had been sunk, and *Ohio* had been struck repeatedly.

From dawn next day, the RAF from Malta mounted a massive cover operation, but it was hindered by the lack of fighter direction facilities due to *Axum*'s attack.

Late in the afternoon of 13 August, the Feast of Santa Maria, three merchantmen entered Valletta's Grand Harbour. The next morning, a fourth made harbour. They were scarred and battle-weary, but their 30,000 tons of essential supplies represented salvation for the island. The tanker *Ohio* was not with them. She was fighting a battle against the seawater that was flooding into her. Lashed between the destroyers HMS *Penn* and HMS *Ledbury*, and towed by the minesweeper HMS *Rye*, the tanker finally reached Grand Harbour with her 11,500 tons of kerosene, petrol and aviation fuel on 15 August. Malta now had sufficient food, supplies and fuel to continue the struggle against the Axis siege.

From *Victorious*, Cork flew one patrol (Z7093, re-engined) on 13 May. He flew daily (Z7093) until the 16th, when they disembarked at Gibraltar. All the patrols were uneventful.

Victorious accompanied *Indomitable* into Gibraltar. There, the damaged carrier was put in drydock for inspection. No 880 Squadron left its aircraft aboard *Victorious*. Most of the squadron's maintenance crews were dead or injured. Cork let his aircrews rest and enjoy 'The Rock'. The squadron felt Judd's loss, in Hugh Popham's words, as the 'sudden, nagging absence of a familiar pain'. Yet, the pilots had reason to be grateful to 'Butch' Judd. His pressurized reign had given them the professionalism that had enabled them to fight with great distinction one of the toughest air battles of the war with remarkably few losses.

In the two days of intensive fighting over PEDESTAL, Cork himself was credited with five enemy aircraft confirmed destroyed, one probably destroyed and one damaged. More important, No 880 Squadron had kept fighting throughout the period of greatest danger, repeatedly breaking up enemy atacks, even after their carrier had been knocked out and their Commanding Officer had been killed. Cork had acted as Commanding Officer with admirable calmness and authority under very trying conditions, continuing to lead effectively. The success of the Fleet air defence had depended upon men such as Cork.

The FAA claimed to have destroyed between thirty and forty enemy aircraft during the PEDESTAL air battles. Their own losses amounted to thirteen aircraft in air combat, plus those lost on *Eagle* and *Indomitable*, but the damage to the latter by air attack must also be weighed in the balance. Vice-Admiral Syfret commented:

> 'The speed and height of the Ju 88s made the fleet fighters' task a hopeless one. It will be a happy day when the Fleet is equipped with modern fighter aircraft.'

For the five score naval fighter pilots who had defended PEDESTAL he gave unstinted praise:

> 'Flying at great heights, constantly chasing the faster Ju 88, warning the Fleet of approaching formations, breaking up the latter, and in the later stages doing their work in the face of superior enemy forces – they were grand.'

In the last week of August, *Indomitable* sailed for the United Kingdom. On 8 September, Cork signed off the ship at Liverpool. No 880 Squadron was given a week's leave, before reassembling at RNAS Stretton. 'Moose' Martyn became Commanding Officer and Brian Fiddes the new Senior Pilot. The squadron was scheduled to re-equip with Seafires. Cork, however, had left the squadron, and spent the next fourteen months as an instructor at Yeovilton and Henstridge.

PEDESTAL was an important, though not critical, strategic success for the Allies, one wave in the turn of the tide in the middle months of 1942. On 10 November 1942, Cork was gazetted the DSO for PEDESTAL. Cork had now been involved in two of the most momentous air battles of the early war years, the Battle of Britain and the PEDESTAL air operation – as well as seeing the nadir of British Imperial fortunes in the East.

CHAPTER 20
Operation JUBILEE

Operation JUBILEE, the combined services amphibious raid by Allied troops on Dieppe on 19 August 1942, was intended to prove the theories of amphibious warfare. There was to be a continuous air umbrella over Dieppe, and Fighter Command was mustering every available squadron. The RAF's objectives at Dieppe were threefold: close air support for the landing forces; keeping the Luftwaffe's bombers away by achieving air superiority; and destroying the enemy in the air, the bait being 252 ships close off shore. The pilots were enthused with purpose. Victories were anticipated. Heavy losses were expected.

On 16 August 1942, most of 'Johnni' Johnson's No 610 Squadron's personnel and all its aeroplanes – thirteen officers and sixty-four airmen with eighteen Spitfire LR Mk VBs (Merlin 46) – moved to West Malling, for temporary reinforcement of No 11 Group for JUBILEE. The squadron was to fly top cover for a wing led by Wing Commander Pat Jameson formed from three No 12 Group squadrons, Nos 411 (RCAF), 485 (RNZAF) and 610.

The first Allied forces landed just before 04.00 hours on 19 August, but were pinned down on the beaches. No 610 Squadron's ORB recorded:

> '"Dieppe Day". Egg and chips breakfast for sleepy eyed pilots in the wee sma' hours – readiness by 03.00 hours – tension of waiting for orders . . . Pilots were very early astir, but ground crews were before them – busy as bees through the night fitting long range jettisonable tanks to the Spitfires – tanks that specially proved their worth on this occasion, with the Squadron airborne the longer because of providing top cover.'

No 610 Squadron took off from West Malling at 07.40 hours and formed up over the base with Nos 411, 485 and another squadron. Ten minutes later, the Wing, led by Wing Commander Pat Jameson, set course for Dieppe. No 610 Squadron were detailed as top cover, to be over Dieppe at 10,000 feet, the most difficult position, while Nos 485 and 411 Squadrons prevented enemy aircraft from attacking ground forces.

The British fighters approached the French coast in good wing formation. About ten miles off the French coast, Squadron Leader Johnson began to climb No 610 Squadron to its allocated position. The previous wing was retreating, badly mauled, and they flew into a massive battle. About three miles off the coast, as they were passing through 7,000 feet, Johnson saw a gaggle of thirty, forty, perhaps fifty Fw 190s and Bf 109s jockeying for position about 2,000 to 3,000 feet above No 610 Squadron.

The Spitfires were vulnerable, but they had to engage, as they were protecting the squadrons below them. Johnson forced the squadron to climb faster. Urging their Merlins, Johnson and his eleven men watched the Germans. The Germans were flying singly, in pairs and in fours.

Suddenly, the German attack broke. In classic fashion, Johnson immediately turned his squadron to meet the onrush. The British and German forces closed fast on each other.

Johnson, his squadron closed up tight on him, climbed hard after an Fw 190 which was at 11,000 feet. He got on its tail. At 200 yards, he opened fire and closed to 150 yards. The Fw 190 turned to port away from the fire, but Johnson skidded after it, cutting the turn and closed in again from the beam, hitting it repeatedly with shells and bullets. Smoke belched from the stricken enemy. Its wheels dropped as it lost hydraulic systems pressure and it dived steeply towards the sea – other pilots saw it crash.

No 610 Squadron still retained cohesion, a tribute to the control and discipline exacted by Squadron Leader Johnson and Flight Lieutenants Crowley-Milling and Pool. The squadron was attacked three or four times by the German fighters which wheeled overhead, and the Spitfires had to make violent countering manoeuvres. Attacks developed from both flanks and astern, simultaneously. Operating singly, in pairs and fours, the Germans fought with great persistence.

The whole of Jameson's wing was being subjected to attacks from all quarters. Under the repeated pressure of attacks and the breaks to counter them, the British squadrons became split up. Combat developed which broke up sections and Spitfire pilots found themselves fighting independently. Their critical fuel position gave them very little room for error if they became cornered.

Johnson's long experience enabled him to retain control over his section. With his Number 2 (Flight Sergeant S. C. Creagh), Number 3 (Pilot Officer L. A. Smith), and Number 4 (Pilot Officer Wright), he chased a Bf 109F. They got on to its tail, and Johnson opened fire at 250 yards, closing to 200 yards, before Creagh and Smith took over, knocking pieces off it. It began to smoke and Johnson moved in for the coup de grâce. It half-rolled and dived vertically into the sea.

But the squadron leader's success had been noted by the Germans. As his section killed the Bf 109F, enemy fighters closed in on them. Within minutes, an Fw 190 picked off Creagh from Johnson's wing. Creagh's Spitfire was badly damaged, so he dived out to sea and baled out. He floated down to land in the sea at 08.20 hours.

Meanwhile, Flight Lieutenant Crowley-Milling had also gained a victory in the first rounds of the attack. He got on to the tail of a Bf 109F and gave it a burst of shell and bullet. The Bf 109F rolled over, and glycol poured from it – it was hit in the engine cooling system and could not last long. But other Germans pounced on Crowley-Milling and he had to counter them. Recovering, he searched briefly below him and was rewarded by seeing a pilot bale out of a Bf 109F – his, he deduced.

As Johnson reorientated himself after losing Creagh, he spotted a member of his squadron – whom, he could not tell – trailing white glycol, but under control and heading for the emergency landing ground to the east of Dieppe.

Johnson and Smith turned inland at 20,000 feet and saw heavy enemy reinforcements approaching Dieppe from the south-east. Johnson warned Wing Commander Jameson of this force.

Almost immediately, he spotted an Fw 190 flying on his port beam at the same height. Johnson turned to outflank him, tightly followed by Smith. He closed in on the Fw 190's starboard beam. He opened fire – machine-gun only, his cannon shells exhausted – and saw bullets strike around the cockpit, and pieces flying off the aeroplane. The Fw 190 began to emit a thin stream of glycol. Johnson broke off at 50 yards. Smith dived in on the Fw 190's tail, engaging it successfully (they claimed it as a shared damaged).

Then Johnson found himself separated from Smith, and alone in a very dangerous sky. Making for home, he spotted a solitary Fw 190 over Dieppe, bearing the markings of an Italian – one of a number encountered that day. The Italian saw him approach, and charged. Johnson reefed his fighter into the tightest of turns to get on to the 190's tail, but he was alarmed to find that the 190 was gaining on his tail – in theory, the Spitfire Mk V could at least out-turn the Fw 190.

Johnson dived for the ground at full power and near vertically, pulling out at ground level and streaked across Dieppe's roof tops. The 190 followed every evasive move. Johnson rammed the throttle to emergency and headed straight at a British destroyer off shore through the barrage of flak it was putting up, and hurtled over it, the Merlin 46 running at +16 pounds boost! The 190 did not follow. The chase lasted twenty minutes. In Johnson's estimation, it was his toughest combat.

In the mêlée above Johnson's solitary duel, Pilot Officer 'Hokey' Hokan closed on an Fw 190's port quarter, fired, and saw strikes on its tail. But this Fw 190's partner got on Hokan's six o'clock and evened the score by severely damaging the Spitfire's tail with cannon shells. Hokan broke off the attack, and immediately made for home.

Soon, all the other No 610 Squadron pilots still airborne began to turn for home, flying back low and independently. Johnson was the first to arrive back at West Malling, setting EP254:B down on the grass at 09.10 hours. Ground personnel swarmed around his fighter, whose burning hot engine cowling told its own story. Johnson reported that it was a 'terrific party'.

Within seconds, 'Hokey' Hokan eased his stricken Spitfire (EP238:D) into West Malling, with the remains of his lacerated tail only just staying on. He won 'hearty congratulations' for this fine piece of airmanship. Pilot Officer Wright arrived back five minutes later, followed by a victorious Crowley-Milling (EP361:X), and Pilot Officers R. W. Pearson and R. M. Gaudard and Warrant Officer W. M. Jackson at 09.20 hours. Pilot Officers L. A. Smith and P. R. Pabiot landed at 09.30 hours.

Three pilots were missing: Creagh (EP198:H), Flight Lieutenant P. D. Pool (EP235:F) and Sergeant J. C. Leech (EP342:S). During the combats several Spitfires were seen to go down. None of the pilots was able to give any hard information as to what had happened to Pool or Leech, or confirm who it was Johnson had seen going down. The total claims amounted to one Fw 190 and two Bf 109Fs destroyed and two Fw 190s damaged.

These were No 610 Squadron's first combats with the formidable Fw 190 – Der Würger (The 'Butcher Bird'). Superior in most respects to the Spitfire Mk V, it was wresting from Fighter Command the air superiority which had been won so expensively during 1941. During Summer 1942, No 610 Squadron suffered heavy losses to the 'Butcher Bird'.

When JUBILEE had been planned, Typhoons were not involved, but the Duxford Wing Leader, Wing Commander Denis Gillam, pressed their case: they should be used to sweep behind the main operational area, as outlined at the discussion at Fighter Command in June. A converse view was that the most profitable role for the Typhoons was low-level day cover of the beaches. A negative view was that the Typhoons were simply not yet reliable enough for such a major operation. In fact, only the Duxford Wing's three Typhoon squadrons were operational, owing to continuing problems: Nos 56, 266 (Rhodesian) and 609, commanded by Squadron Leaders Dundas, G. L. Green and Paul Richey respectively. Persuaded by Gillam, Leigh-Mallory overruled Broadhurst and agreed to let them fly, provided the pilots were sure that their squadrons were ready.

At 09.00 hours on the day before the operation, 18 August, Group Captain John Grandy, DSO, Duxford's station commander, and Wing Commander Denis Gillam briefed the Typhoon Wing. The pilots were given the choice: if they did not think that their aircraft were sufficiently problem-free for a major operation, they could still opt out. The raid was a very emotive thing: it was taking British Empire forces back to France. Without dissent or hesitation, the pilots opted to fly. After the long, frustrating development of the fighter, it would be a boost to get on an operation.

By 09.00 hours on 19 August, the vital beachhead withdrawal operations were under way. From 10.00 hours, the RAF Blenheims, Bostons and Hurricanes gave intense close-support to ground forces, while Spitfires broke up the bomber formations. The Typhoons were kept well away from the main battle, although ironically the Typhoon was first mentioned in the Press during reports of the JUBILEE operation! Typhoons flew diversionary feints to draw off enemy bombers flying south from Holland and Beauvais.

At 11.00 hours, the Duxford Typhoon Wing took off from West Malling on its first sortie, a diversion mission. It made rendezvous with nine Defiant 'calibration' (electronic deception) aircraft off Clacton at 11.15 hours. With the Typhoons flying escort at 18,000 feet, the formation flew to within ten miles of Ostend. The Defiants were equipped for electronic warfare, acting to deceive German radars. The intention was to appear on radar like a bomber raid, and so distract the Luftwaffe from Dieppe, and give the Typhoons an opportunity to fight. Dundas (R7825) led No 56 Squadron.

Near the enemy coast, the fighters left the Defiants and swept on to Mardyck/Calais, but did not encounter enemy aircraft. The Wing returned over the Channel and landed at West Malling, which was hot and dusty in the warm midday sun and crowded with Spitfires, 'Hurribombers' and

Beaufighters. The Typhoons were immediately refuelled and rearmed, while the pilots grabbed some lunch.

It was not long after the impressive take-off by the Duxford Wing's Typhoon squadrons, that Johnson led No 610 Squadron off to battle again. No 610 Squadron's losses on its first sortie meant that the squadron's reserves were called out. Sergeant K. A. Edwards (EP443:Q) replaced Creagh as Johnson's Number 2, his all-important wingman. Two pilot officers, de Patoul (EP398:E) and F. Musgrove (EP252:T), made up the dozen. Hokan strapped on a reserve Spitfire (EP346:J).

No 610 Squadron took off again at 11.20 hours on a fighter escort mission to cover the withdrawal of the naval forces from Dieppe. There was by now very little fighter opposition. The Luftwaffe was not staying to fight. Four Fw 190s were chased inland behind Dieppe. Although they were too far away, Johnson gave them a burst from about half a mile.

Crowley-Milling attacked another Fw 190. His cannon shells struck home, signified by a brief cloud of black smoke. He chased it, firing another burst, but it escaped into clouds below.

The squadron saw four Do 17s approaching the naval forces off Dieppe and were swinging in to attack, but all four bombers were despatched by other Spitfires before No 610 Squadron was near them.

The Luftwaffe had been taken completely by surprise by the Dieppe landings, and was slow to react, their bomber units only beginning to respond in strength by 10.00 hours. During crucial phases of evacuation, no bombers succeeded in attacking landing craft, and by 13.00 hours the RAF had air superiority. Nevertheless, the German fighter units had reacted more quickly, and the Fw 190s that did appear had an edge over the Spitfire Mk V.

No 610 Squadron landed back at base without loss at 12.56 hours, in time for lunch, but, as the No 610 Squadron ORB recorded: '. . . if it was eggs and chips for breakfast it was only "nearly Spam" for lunch, the pilots being called for another spell of readiness almost before they could take the food off the plates at the midday meal break.'

Jameson's Spitfire pilots and the Duxford Typhoon pilots sat strapped in, sweltering, at readiness. Then the green Very light arced up slowly, and activity broke out around the fighters as the groundcrews laboured to start the Spitfires and Typhoons. It was an unpleasant task starting up thirty-six temperamental Sabres and taxi-ing out in the dusty, hot air, but thirty-five Typhoons took off again at 14.00 hours. Seconds later, the thirty-six Spitfire Mk Vs of Jameson's wing followed them into the air. The No 610 Squadron ORB recorded the scene: 'Not the least memorable activity of the day was the take-off in rapid succession in the early afternoon of six fighter Squadrons – three of Spitfires and three of Typhoons.'

The Typhoons' second mission of the day was a diversionary sweep from Le Touquet to Le Tréport, to the north and east of the main operational area. The objective of the sweep was to catch any enemy aircraft heading in to the beachhead from the Pas de Calais airfields.

The Typhoons formed up in search formation over Beachy Head. Nos 56, 266 and 609 Squadrons flew as top, middle and low cover. Broken cumulus lay at 2,000 to 4,000 feet, and they flew stacked up from 10,000 feet, ignoring enemy radar, making a 300mph fast target penetration and turning west from the Somme estuary to Dieppe.

The Typhoon Wing searched for targets. Gillam, at the head of No 609 Squadron, led the Wing at 400mph round behind Dieppe, down through broken cloud, looking for action. Near Dieppe, a section of No 266 Squadron chased three Do 17s with an escort of twenty Fw 190s. The Typhoons claimed one Do 17 destroyed and one probable and one Fw 190 probable for the loss of one Typhoon pilot. Gillam took Nos 266 and 609 Squadrons down to engage some Fw 190s, but there were no real gains or losses, though they claimed three damaged.

Gillam ordered Dundas (R7714) to keep No 56 Squadron above at 17,000 feet to give top cover throughout this evolution. There were more enemy aircraft at a higher altitude which kept zooming down and making nibbling attacks on No 56 Squadron but, sure that the Typhoons could not hold them in a dogfight, they did not engage them. Dundas could only respond defensively, as he had to act as the 'umbrella' for the other two squadrons, fighting below. The Germans kept up the nibbling attacks, but when Dundas took the squadron in a steep countering turn, the Germans broke off.

Meanwhile, No 610 Squadron was proceeding with a cover patrol over the withdrawal of the ships from Dieppe, as part of Jameson's Wing. The Luftwaffe was not so aggressive now as it had been in the early morning. Johnson fired on two Fw 190s at a range of 800 yards. They half-rolled and flew clear.

Shortly, four other Fw 190s were seen approaching No 610 Squadron. The Duxford Typhoon squadrons were in the vicinity and took care of them.

Pilot Officer R. W. Pearson had a problem and turned for home, followed by Warrant Officer W. M. Jackson; mutual support was important. Pearson landed at West Malling at 15.05 hours, followed by Jackson. Johnson's section (Sergeant Edwards, Pilot Officers Smith and Musgrove) touched down at 15.20 hours. Flight Lieutenant Crowley-Milling's section (Pilot Officers P. B. Wright, P. R. Pabiot and L. E. Hokan) touched down at 15.25 hours, and the remaining pair, Pilot Officers G. de Patoul and R. M. Gaudard, were back by 15.25 hours.

With JUBILEE reaching its final stages, requiring further fighter cover, Jameson's Spitfires and Gillam's Typhoons were called on for one further patrol each. The Duxford Typhoons took off for their final patrol at 17.00 hours, tasked with sweeping the area from the Somme estuary to Cap Gris Nez. Again, this was away from the main action. Both Gillam and Richey had to abort, and flew back to base, accompanied by eight No 609 Squadron pilots who misinterpreted their actions as a general withdrawal. Green of No 266 Squadron took over the lead of the Wing. Dundas (R7825) led No 56 Squadron. The Typhoons crossed the coast of France north of the Somme at 12,000 feet, but were faced with total cloud cover so flew back to Duxford instead of to St Omer. It was the end of a disappointing day for the Wing.

Squadron Leader Johnson's last mission of the day, an escort, began with wheels-up at 17.35 hours. No 610 Squadron, on its own, was again detailed to protect shipping. This time they orbitted in mid-Channel. Four Fw 190s approached and were intercepted, but they dived and headed back to Dieppe followed closely by a section of No 610 Squadron. The Spitfires could only close to firing range as they crossed the French coast at zero altitude. Johnson tried a burst from 400 yards, but then called off the pursuit.

The squadron resumed its orbital patrol pattern. About 5 miles off Dieppe, they picked up a British rescue vessel which was patrolling parallel to the coast. They gave it close escort until their low fuel forced them to return to base, where they touched down at 19.05 hours. The pilots were stood down, but the ground crews still had a lot of work ahead of them, for the Spitfires had been hard used that day – No 610 Squadron had flown a total of nearly 69 hours. The senior officers also had forms to fill in and letters to write.

There was good news though for No 610 Squadron. Creagh was safe. He had parachuted into the sea some 6 miles north-east of Dieppe. *MGB 317* had picked him up and brought him back to England.

Over France and the Channel, other RAF fighters continued to fight until 21.00 hours, but already a picture was beginning to emerge of the day's fighting. There was much information to be collected, collated and assessed by the squadron 'spies'. It was clear that the Fw 190 had an edge over the Spitfire Mk V and the Typhoon. The Spitfire Mk V pilots readily admitted that they had had a very tough time. JUBILEE was the first major operation in which the Typhoon and Fw 190 were involved, but Typhoons were only committed to the air superiority battle when the forces were actually returning. The pilots of the Duxford Wing felt that they could have met the Fw 190 on equal terms, saving the Spitfires a mauling, had they been committed earlier.

However, although several Fw 190s were destroyed by Typhoons during JUBILEE, it was shown that Typhoons were inferior to Fw 190s in some important respects and superior in others. The Typhoon could out-pace, out-dive and out-gun but not out-manoeuvre the Fw 190 – the reverse of the Spitfire Mk VB – nor could it out-fight it at altitude, which was distressing because the Typhoon was intended as a high-altitude fighter; its wing was just too thick.

Moreover, the problems with the Typhoon continued. In one combat, three Typhoons of one squadron were lost when their tails broke off when pulling out of a diving attack. The writing was on the wall. Group Captain Broadhurst now had the evidence he needed. The Typhoon was no longer a fighter: it simply did not fit the tactical requirements of the fighter war that was developing. This was a considerable personal blow to Dundas and the pilots of his unit who had worked so hard and at such cost to free the aeroplane of bugs and get it operational.

For Fighter Command, the following day, 20 August, was quiet in comparison. Wing Commander Pat Jameson's No 12 Group Wing was still operating from West Malling, but there was 'more waiting for action than flying', as No 610's ORB put it. The Wing flew only one patrol, late in the afternoon, a cover patrol for the withdrawal of Fortresses which were returning from bombing targets at Amiens. The operation reveals interesting aspects of the fighter game.

The squadrons began to assemble on the airfield by 17.00 hours. Led by Squadron Leader Johnson, with Flight Lieutenant Crowley-Milling leading the second Flight, No 610 Squadron's twelve Spitfires took off at 17.12 hours. They were again top cover and took up position over Cayeux at 28,000 feet.

The Fortresses began their withdrawal across the Channel without intervention from German fighters. To protect the withdrawal, the Wing patrolled east and west parallel to the French coast. The early evening sun was bright in the west. At about 18.20 hours, just after the bombers had crossed the coast, about a dozen Fw 190s appeared inland at about 30,000 feet. Johnson decided to hold No 610 Squadron in position as top cover, which would prevent the Fw 190s flying west and attacking the bombers out of the sun.

The German squadron leader, seeing the British fighters' lack of reaction, sent down two of his Fw 190s to fly across the front of No 610 Squadron. They were a decoy. They quickly turned and flew back inland, hoping to lead the Spitfires below the German squadron. No 610 Squadron held its position.

The German leader sent down another decoy pair across No 610 Squadron's front. The Spitfire squadron was up-sun of them. Johnson spotted that the Fw 190 Number 2 did not appear to see his Spitfires in the sun from where he was, and dived on the Fw 190's port beam. He opened fire at 150 yards, giving the 190 a 1½-second burst of cannon and machine-gun fire, closing to 120 yards. He did not seem to have hit it – there were no strikes on the fighter – but the enemy aircraft suddenly pulled vertically upwards, tumbled over and went into a lazy vertical spin. Johnson broke away and did not see the enemy aircraft after that.

Wing Commander Louden, who was flying with the squadron, saw that the Fw 190 spun for several thousand feet and was 'of the opinion that either the pilot was killed or the controls were shot away'. Pending the ciné film being developed, the Fw 190 was claimed as probably destroyed.

After Dieppe, No 610 Squadron went back to No 12 Group and was faced with the prospect of resuming 'Stooge' patrols, convoy patrols, 'Rhubarbs' and sweeps. However, compared with the first half of the year, August under Johnson's and Crowley-Milling's exacting leadership had been very successful. Combat victories carried the unit's total 'bag' to 123 'destroyed', forty-one and a half 'probables' and forty-one 'damaged'. Indicative of the intensity of the squadron's operations during August, the total flying time amounted to 873 hours 20 minutes, of which 461 hours 35 minutes were operational – and the intensive operations over JUBILEE accounted for less than 70 hours of that total. The squadron had had their Spitfire LR Mk VBs barely a month, but attrition and hard flying had taken their tolls. Besides, they had little call for their long-range capability. On 21 August, No 610 Squadron received its first three Spitfire Mk VCs, and the fourth the next day.

In the first week of September, Denis Crowley-Milling was posted away from the squadron on promotion to squadron leader to take command of a new Typhoon squadron, No 181. 'Crow' had great experience as a fighter leader and was among the strongest candidates for a squadron command. Johnson himself was hoping that No 610 Squadron would be posted to No 11 Group, but within days the squadron was posted to RAF Castletown, in northern Scotland. After their hard but successful summer, Johnson was highly indignant, but it was policy, and that was that.

CHAPTER 21
'Bombphoons'

There was a great deal of hard thinking to do after Operation JUBILEE by all three British Services. For the RAF, it was clear that the Typhoon was not a success in a pure fighter role. From now on, Typhoons would be used in specialist roles. They were to be used in the defensive role. Plans were made to distribute the squadrons to southern airfields in order to exploit their ability to intercept the Germans' fast, low fighter-bombers (Jabos). These carried out the Germans' more limited version of 'Rhubarbs'. In the second half of 1942, there were five operational Typhoon squadrons. Apart from opposition to Jabos, their main tasks were bomber escorts and offensive sweeps. In the latter operations, they began to display the promise in the low-level role in which they found success as fighter-bombers during 1943.

No 56 Squadron went to RAF Matlask, Norfolk, from where it could cover the North Sea coast, No 257 Squadron to RAF Exeter, Devon, and No 266 Squadron went to RAF Warmwell, Dorset, to defend the south-west. No 609 Squadron went to RAF Biggin Hill, Kent, and No 486 Squadron, RNZAF, to RAF North Weald, Essex, to cover the south-east. New Typhoon squadrons would be formed as fighter-bomber units. On 18 September 1942, the Duxford Typhoon Wing was formally disbanded.

On 24 August 1942, 'Cocky' Dundas's No 56 Squadron moved to RAF Matlask which it made home for eleven months. The officers were billeted in a picturesque mill-house on a mill stream. 'Johnnie' Johnson and Denis Crowley-Milling were also based in the sector and visited Hugh Dundas. Wing-sweeps had become a regular duty for No 56 Squadron at Snailwell, and from Matlask the squadron undertook offensive sweeps with other No 11 Group fighter squadrons, and defensive patrols against Fw 190s and Ju 88 bombers until the end of the year.

From June 1942, German Jabo sorties had become more frequent, increasing towards autumn as their long-range bomber offensive failed. Fighter watches and standing patrols near frequent targets were instituted. The Typhoon could defeat the Fw 190 but had first to find it, and results were limited until November. Typhoons of No 266 Squadron claimed victories over Ju 88s on 9 and 13 August and those of No 1 Squadron over Me 210s on 6 September, but, although involved in several combats, No 56 Squadron's Typhoons did not score until 14 September when Flight Lieutenant Mike Ingle-Finch and Pilot Officer Coombes destroyed a Ju 88 (the former later got his own Typhoon squadron command).

Denis Crowley-Milling's great experience as a fighter leader placed him among the strongest candidates for a squadron command. In September 1942, shortly before it was posted north to RAF Castletown for rest, Crowley-Milling left No 610 Squadron, was promoted to squadron leader and appointed Commanding Officer of No 181, the first Typhoon fighter-bomber squadron. A new wing was to be formed. Two squadrons were being formed with Typhoon fighter-bombers as initial equipment, Nos 181 and 182 Squadrons.

No 181 Squadron formed at Duxford on 7 September 1942, followed by No 182 formed at Martlesham Heath on 12 September 1942 under Squadron Leader T. P. Pugh, DFC. A third fighter-bomber squadron, No 183, formed shortly afterwards. Crowley-Milling formed No 181 Squadron in the model taught to him by Douglas Bader.

On 1 November 1942, No 183 Squadron formed at RAF Church Fenton, followed by No 195 Squadron at RAF Hutton Cranswick on 27 November, by No 197 Squadron at RAF Drem the next day and by No 198 Squadron at RAF Digby on 8 December. At the end of 1942, the No 12 Group Order of Battle boasted three operational Typhoon squadrons, Nos 56, 181 and 182, and three non-operational squadrons, Nos 183, 195 and 198. On 30 December, No 245 Squadron re-equipped with Typhoons at RAF Charmy Down.

Dundas and No 56 Squadron had pioneered many fighter-bomber techniques. Towards the end of 1942, No 56 Squadron turned to shipping attacks, 'Rhubarbs' and some bomber escorts and began to specialize in ground-attack, eventually dropping 250-pound bombs. These were eventful weeks for No 56 Squadron, which began flying daily 'Rhubarbs' to Belgium and Holland from November. For example, on 17 November 1942, it flew one to Flushing airfield, strafing German fighters. Also from mid-November, No 56 Squadron began flying the first Typhoon 'Intruders' – night 'Rhubarbs'. From this point on, the Typhoon was increasingly used as a fighter-bomber.

However, on 23 November 1942, Dundas handed over command of No 56 Squadron to Squadron Leader A. C. Johnston, DFC. His task of working the squadron into service had been completed successfully. Dundas went to a staff job, overdue for rest. On 1 December 1942, he was granted a regular commission with the rank of squadron leader, a well-deserved reward.

A normal feature of combat aircraft today, equipping high-performance aircraft, particularly fighters, as standard with the means to carry a range of external bombs and munitions ('stores'), was still a novelty in 1941–42. The Germans had pioneered the carriage of bombs on the Messerschmitt Bf 109, but specialized modifications had had to be applied, which reduced performance and limited the aircraft's performance in its original role. A solution was required which could be fitted as standard during production, to give an operational squadron the flexibility to fly with or without stores, and which did not affect either the capability in the primary fighter role or reduce performance.

Hawker fighters, the Hurricane, Typhoon and Tempest, were among the earliest to carry specially installed racks for external stores. For the

Typhoon, hardpoints and pick-up points were designed into the wing undersurface structure to take a bomb rack, and introduced on all production machines as standard, following trials, from mid-1943.

Development and trials work on the Typhoon paved the way for trials with the Tempest; indeed, the fighter-bomber equipment for both aircraft was developed and tested in parallel. In August 1942, the Aeroplane & Armament Experimental Establishment (A&AEE) began trials with a Typhoon (R7646) carrying a 500-pound bomb on faired racks below each wing. The fairings and the carriage of bombs had little effect on the aircraft's handling, and the release of the bombs had scant effect on trim. There was increased buffeting in the dive at over 350mph, which led to a limiting diving speed of 400mph being imposed. At 8,000 feet, without carriers or bombs, the Typhoon could achieve 372mph; with carriers and two 500-pound bombs, it achieved 336mph. The trials were successful and the bomb racks and 500-pound bombs were cleared for service in October 1943, transforming the Typhoon from a fighter into a true fighter-bomber – with notable effects on the course of the air war.

Hawker Aircraft began to fit some production Typhoons with bomb carriers and systems. The first such aircraft were issued to No 181 Squadron in the middle of October 1942. To begin with, production was divided between the Typhoon fighter and bomber variants. From mid-1943, all Typhoons were produced in the fighter-bomber variant.

A fully bombed-up Typhoon weighed 12,250 pounds and was a handful to taxi on the ground, for the tail could lift and skid. Anti-shimmy tailwheel tyres were fitted on units, and became standard in production from March 1943. A Typhoon was not easy to control in the take-off: with 15 degrees of flap and full left trim, full left rudder was needed to kill the forceful swing to the right produced by the Sabre's torque. Fully bombed-up, the aircraft had a tendency to buck on take-off from a grass surface, and it was wise to use an asphalt or concrete runway.

During the spring of 1943, Nos 181, 182 and 183 Squadrons, the first Typhoon fighter-bomber units, began to attack shipping and coastal targets with two 250-pound or 500-pound bombs. The Typhoon attack squadrons, influenced by the tactical teachings of Hugh Dundas and now of Crowley-Milling, flew loose pairs, in twos, fours or sixes. Larger formations of 'Bombphoons' were usually escorted by fighter Typhoons, but sections would operate independently, capable of looking after themselves with their firepower and low-level speed.

A shipping attack flown by four No 181 Squadron Typhoon Mk IBs on 10 February 1943 shows the anti-shipping technique clearly. Crowley-Milling received 'Surfat' (or 'Ramrod') orders to attack enemy shipping off the Dutch coast between The Hook and Ymuiden. At 11.05 hours, he and Flying Officer J. W. H. Wilson (Red Section) with Flight Lieutenant P. S. C. Lovelace and Sergeant D. Green (Blue Section) took off from RAF Ludham.

To achieve maximum surprise they flew well below radar height, at zero feet, skimming a medium swell, in dull sunlight. Wisps of broken cloud floated over the North Sea at 2,000 feet. They flew in two sections, in line abreast, on a course of 124 degrees. It took them twenty-seven minutes to cross the North Sea and hit the Dutch coast. Crowley-Milling turned the Typhoons north.

For seven and half minutes they cruised up the coast at 270mph, about two miles out from the shore. Four pairs of eyes scanned the sea for shipping. Over the Dutch coast, the negligible cloud had given way to dense cloud at 3,000 feet. Visibility was only around four or five miles, but enough. About two miles west of Ymuiden, they sighted an armed trawler of about 500 tons. It was stationary, bows to the shore. Crowley-Milling called the attack.

The formation immediately opened out and climbed to 500 feet. In a well-practised routine, each section banked in a wide turn to get into position to attack. From opposite directions, the two sections made simultaneous beam attacks to try to overwhelm the ship's defences. It was 11.40 hours.

Further to alarm the defenders and to divide their fire and draw it from the Number 2s who would drop the bombs, the section leaders – Crowley-Milling and Lovelace – strafed the ship with their 20mm cannon. From the port beam, Crowley-Milling hosed 120 rounds (half and half ball and tracer) into the vessel and Lovelace, from starboard, twice that number. Their accurate shooting started fires on the bridge and fo'c'sle. The ship's machine-gunners fired back, their tracer whipping ineffectively round the Typhoons.

Now, into this confusion, came the bombers, following behind their leaders, simultaneously, one from either beam. The Number 2s carried two 500-pound general-purpose high-explosive 'iron' bombs each. Attacking at mast-top height, 50 feet, from the trawler's port side, Wilson sighted his target by eye. Judging distance and trajectory as carefully as he could, he released his bombs. They dropped simultaneously. One fell within ten yards of the vessel's starboard side amidships – the other fell five yards further on. Wilson loosed off a hundred rounds of cannon into the vessel as he flew across it, then broke off to his starboard out to sea. Seconds later, his bombs exploded, sending water towering high into the air and hammering the vessel's hull.

Flying at the trawler's starboard beam, Green pressed the bomb release at 50 feet. Only one bomb fell away. It overshot the vessel and fell 30 yards beyond its port beam. The other hung up. Green held his fire as he crossed the vessel, concentrating on the hung-up bomb. He curved out to sea. The bomb freed itself, falling uselessly into the sea 500 yards to port beyond the trawler.

The Typhoons left the ship on fire and listing to port, with a considerable amount of white steam and smoke coming from amidships, and probably sinking. The four Typhoons did not wait in the vicinity, as they might attract enemy fighters. Well pleased with their work, Crowley-Milling led them back to England at low level. They landed at Snailwell at 12.37 hours. The total mission time was 92 minutes. They claimed the armed trawler as damaged, possibly sunk.

There were few offensive sorties flown by Typhoons in early 1943. The poor winter weather prevented many operations. The operations flown were usually 'Rhubarbs', the dreaded low-level armed reconnaissance missions by two or four aircraft, attacking ground targets of opportunity. As had been the case with the Spitfire 'Rhubarbs', losses to flak on such operations were very high, yet they produced little result, mainly just nuisance. However, losses to mechanical failure and accident had by now fallen, as the work done during 1942 took a grip.

From early 1943, Squadron Leader Crowley-Milling's No 181 Squadron was engaged in dive-bombing. On 22 March, six 'Bomphoons' of the squadron were ordered to dive-bomb Alkmaar aerodrome. Denis Crowley-Milling with his wingman, Pilot Officer A. E. S. Vincent (Red Section), Flying Officer J. W. H. Wilson and Sergeant D. S. Green (Blue Section), and Flying Officer L. R. Allen and Sgt R. Guthrie (Yellow Section) took off from Coltishall at 14.12 hours.

Twenty minutes later they crossed the English coast. They spread out in loose line abreast and flew at wave-top height on a course of 102 degrees across the North Sea. Ten miles off the Dutch coast, they climbed hard to attack altitude, 10,000 feet. Crowley-Milling set them up precisely and they arrived over their target in the sun.

There was haze up to 3,000 or 4,000 feet over the target area. The airfield was extremely well camouflaged, and there appeared to be no aeroplanes on it. The attack began at 14.46 hours, the Typhoons diving from 10,000 feet out of the sun. Each of the six pilots dived from 10,000 feet, selected their targets, and released their two 500-pound general-purposes bombs at 4,000 feet and pulled up. There was no flak. The bombs had instantaneous fuses and several bomb bursts were seen on the aerodrome and among huts to its west.

There was still no flak. There was no sign of enemy fighters but visibility was only about three to four miles, so Crowley-Milling formed up the Typhoons and led the formation fast to the coast at 4,000 feet. Just off Egmond, they saw a convoy of fourteen ships, flying barrage balloons. They avoided it, as such convoys could be very well defended and needed specialized attacks. The six Typhoons flew at zero feet until they crossed the English coast at 15.20 hours.

The weather improved in the spring. From April, offensive operations increased considerably and, once the Jabo threat had decreased, became the mainstay of Typhoon units. They flew 'Circus', 'Intruder', 'Ramrod', 'Ranger', 'Rhubarb', 'Roadstead' and 'Rodeo' operations. As the Typhoon's low-level performance and heavy armament made it ideal for anti-shipping strikes, 'Roadsteads' became an important and frequent part of the Typhoon units' operations. Formations of Typhoons hunted along the German-held coast from Brittany to the Scheldt, looking for coastal shipping. With the formation of the Second Tactical Air Force, Typhoon offensive operations began to increase in pace and effect.

During early 1943, several new Typhoon units formed or converted. In March and April, two Hurricane fighter-bomber units converted, No 174 at Gravesend and No 175 at Colerne. By mid-summer, they were operational. During the summer of 1943, preparations were being made for the formation and operation of the Second Tactical Air Force, which would conduct operations against German defences on the Continent in advance of the invasion and would support the invasion forces. Among these preparations was the establishment of a series of Advanced Landing Grounds in the south of England.

These developments mark a critical watershed in fighter warfare in north-west Europe. It is necessary to create a background to the next period of warfare by discussing the Second Tactical Air Force. The British had considerable experience from the Middle East and North Africa of operating ground and air forces in co-operation. Its application to north-western Europe had been reinforced by developments in the United Kingdom and Exercise SPARTAN, the very large-scale Army Co-operation exercise of March 1943.

There were seen to be two crucial factors in the organization of air forces which were to co-operate with ground forces. First, they had to be mobile, able to move at hours' notice from base to base, with minimum break in operations; secondly, there had to be close contact at corresponding Army and Air Force levels for training, planning and conducting operations.

It was clear that the invasion of Europe – projected for 1944 – and subsequent operations on the Continent would require a British supporting air force to be formed at an early date, as a separate entity but using Fighter Command facilities for as long as possible. Hence, on 1 June 1943, the Second Tactical Air Force was formed within Fighter Command, where it was to remain until a Commander-in-Chief Allied Expeditionary Air Force was appointed. The new force replaced Army Co-operation Command, which ceased to exist as of that date.

The Commander-in-Chief was to be none other than Air Chief Marshal Sir Trafford Leigh-Mallory. His experience with fighter warfare was completely appropriate to his task, and he had shown tactical appreciation of the use of flexible force, as in 1941 when commanding Douglas Bader. Moreover, his experience of air-ground co-operation went back twenty-five years to a leading role in the pioneering of tank-aircraft co-operation during the great Amiens offensive of April 1918.

The Second Tactical Air Force comprised three tactical groups, Nos 2, 83 and 84; it would also deploy photo-reconnaissance, spotting and airfield defence formations. No 2 Group, transferred from Bomber Command on 1 June 1943, provided medium/light bombers for interdiction. No 83 Group, formed within Fighter Command on 1 April 1943, and No 84 Group, formed later, provided fighters, fighter-bombers and fighter-reconnaissance aircraft.

No 83 Group was formed for specific tasks. In the pre-invasion phase, it was to assist in the air operations which were necessary to make the invasion of Europe possible. During the landing phase, it was to provide direct air support for the ground forces. When the landing forces had established themselves, its units were to operate alongside the invasion forces on the Continent, providing tactical air support to the land battle which developed.

From its inception, No 83 Group's priority was developing the organization of a tactical air force and practising the techniques required for this type of warfare, including co-operation between Air Force and Army Headquarters. From April 1943, four RAF airfields were put on a permanent basis and allocated to No 83 Group: Middle Wallop, Eastchurch, Stoney Cross and Lasham (Nos 121, 122, 123 and 124 Airfields). In the reshuffle, four Typhoon squadrons were transferred from Fighter Command to No 83 Group: Nos 175 (Squadron Leader J. R. Pennington-Leigh, DFC) and 182 (Squadron Leader T. P. Pugh, DFC) at RAF Appledram, and 245 (Squadron Leader S. S. Hordern) at RAF Selsey, and Squadron Leader Denis Crowley-Milling's No 181 Squadron which was transferred to No 124 Airfield.

No 83 Group undertook operations from the beginning of its existence. These were primarily fighter and fighter-bomber sweeps against German defences, and reconnaissance. At first they developed slowly but their tempo increased weekly as more aircraft and better weapons became available. No 181 Squadron's Typhoons began operations against targets on the Continent, softening up the defences using 500- and 1,000-pound bombs, and rocket projectiles. Carrying these new stores on the Typhoon in 1943 demanded considerable pilot skill.

Rocket projectiles had been used operationally by FAA Swordfish and by RAF Hurricanes since mid-1943. In June 1943, Hawker's fitted a Typhoon (EK497) with Mark I rails, of steel, for eight 3-inch rocket projectiles. The A&AEE and the Air Fighting Development Unit tested the combination over the next few months. By October, the first unit was equipped with the weapon, No 181 Squadron. They transformed the Typhoon's role.

In April 1943, the A&AEE flew a Typhoon (DN340) with two 1,000-pound bombs, one under each wing – an all-up weight of 13,350 pounds! This aeroplane was fitted with a four-bladed propeller which was necessary to give control with such a load, but Squadron Leader Hugh Dundas's No 56 Squadron had found during trials conducted in November 1942 that it badly affected the handling of an unladen Typhoon. However, with a three-bladed propeller and two 1,000-pound bombs, squadron pilots had a hard task taking off. The four-bladed propeller was cleared in early 1944, mainly by fitting a larger tailplane, not only enabling pilots to haul two 1,000-pounders off the ground with greater margin for error, but reducing the Typhoon's airframe vibrations.

In the autumn of 1943, Denis Crowley-Milling was promoted to wing commander, with his own Typhoon Wing. Squadron Leader F. W. M. Jensen, AFC, took over command of No 181 Squadron. Shortly, however, fighter squadrons were transferred from Fighter Command and joined Second Tactical Air Force. The Typhoon wing was replaced at Appledram by three Czech Spitfire squadrons. The Typhoon squadrons moved out, Nos 181 and 182 to RAF New Romney and No 175 to RAF Lydd.

Crowley-Milling had led No 181 Squadron with great distinction, and had developed new operational techniques and explored new weapons. He had also managed to survive many strenuous operations. In late 1943, Typhoon losses were much less than they had been in 1942, and most were to enemy action, few to technical problems. Between September 1942 and October 1943, No 181 Squadron suffered eight losses, all to hostile action. This included a serious loss on 25 October, when four pilots fell to flak over Caen during a 'Ramrod', including the new Commanding Officer, Jensen.

PART VII

CHAPTER 22
Fighter Pilots' Paradise

In mid-July 1942, Air Vice-Marshal Keith Park took over Malta's air defences as Air Officer Commanding from Air Vice-Marshal Hugh Pugh Lloyd. Lloyd had pursued aggressively Malta's offensive role when the circumstances had permitted. Park now brought a desire for offensive fighter action, exploiting the Spitfire Mk V's performance. On this small island, barely seventeen miles long and nine miles wide, there were Spitfire squadrons at Takali, Luqa and Hal Far. Park insisted on a policy of forward air defence, intercepting raids as far out as possible, and introduced offensive fighter sweeps against Sicily. The result was reduced damage to the island and increased morale.

On 5 July 1942, the Malta Blitz had opened again with another assault on Takali, followed by one on Luqa the next day. On 11 July, new Spitfires arrived. From 27 July, there was a lull in the fighting. This was fortunate because Malta's fighters were low on aviation fuel and were depleted and worn. Spitfires were not taxied on the ground – they were manhandled. Another convoy was desperately needed.

During this phase, the enduring lessons of Stan Turner and 'Woodie' Woodhall could be seen. Instead of struggling for height, after inadequate warning, and attacking from disadvantage, a prey to the Bf 109s, the Spitfires attacked from judged tactical positions. To counter a raid, the defence would scramble a section of four, exceptionally a squadron. The fighters, taking ten minutes, climbed to 18,000 feet, ignored the enemy fighters and went for the bombers.

The squadron climb would take too long. It was made in three sections of four. The aircraft in a section were widely spaced, 50 yards between aircraft in a pair, and more between each pair. The three sections were widely spaced, and at different levels. The squadron climbed in a wide spiral, not straight up, so that the sections crossed over every 360 degrees. They were thus able to keep an all-round observation of the sky.

The pilots were constantly searching, methodically scanning the sky, left, right, above, waggling the wings to look down on either side, raising the nose to look below the most vulnerable area, the lower six o'clock. The squadron was completely defended. The Malta pilots had perfected the offensive 'finger-four' into a defensive formation. In a hostile environment, a friendly fighter would always try to formate by flying alongside, some way off.

Malta was a very different environment from France. Over France, strict adherence to a timetable of an operation and rigid formation discipline were essential. The objectives of operations were what mattered, not individual success. Over Malta, there was greater room for individualism. In such a way people like 'Screwball' Beurling flourished, not by fighting lone wars but by flexible use of formations. The Malta formation flown by the fighters left rather more initiative for the pairs in it than was allowed over France. This was largely attributable to the defence situation. Once the fighters went over to the offensive, adherence to the timetable began to become the overriding factor.

Malta's Beaufighters and Spitfires flew a total of 407 sorties over the PEDESTAL ships once they came within range. On 14 August, one of the patrols over *Ohio* was led by 'Screwball' Beurling. Once in harbour, the RAF put up a continuous umbrella of fighters over Valletta Harbour to protect the merchantmen.

When Wing Commander Arthur Donaldson arrived on Malta, he was initially put in charge of ground training. In August, he took over from Stan Grant as the Wing Commander Flying at Takali, comprising Nos 229, 249 and 185 Squadrons. Donaldson had demonstrated great leadership and tactical abilities in command of No 263 Squadron's Whirlwinds, and now he led the Takali Wing with conspicuous skill. He was able to apply all the 'fighting principles' that Bader had taught him. He took the Wing on to the offensive.

Group Captain Walter Churchill, DSO, DFC, a kinsman of the British Prime Minister, led the fighters off *Furious* during PEDESTAL. He was to come to Malta to take command of fighter operations. He had fought in the Battle of Britain, had eight victories and had also served briefly with Bader. Among the others coming in from PEDESTAL was Squadron Leader 'Timber' Woods, who took over command of No 249 Squadron from Squadron Leader 'Mitch' Mitchell. Woods was English but had lived a long time in Canada.

On 20 August 1942, Donaldson led the Malta Spitfires on to the offensive in a two-squadron sweep, but the Axis did not respond. South of Malta, the twenty-four fighters formed up in wing formation: eight at 27,000 feet, eight at 28,500 feet and eight at 30,000 feet. They flew in line abreast, as always on Malta, to clear each other's six o'clocks, two pairs of eyes always looking inwards and two pairs of eyes always looking outwards.

They crossed the Sicilian coast over Cape Scaramia. They did a circuit of the island, over each of the main airfields, Comiso, Biscari and Gela, but the Germans and Italians did not respond. There was no flak either. With an eye on their fuel gauges, the Spitfires swept out to sea again over Cape Scaramia.

On 23 August, another offensive sweep was mounted, with eight Takali Wing Spitfires from No 249 Squadron. Group Captain Walter Churchill led Arthur Donaldson, 'Timber' Woods, 'Screwball' Beurling, John 'Willie the Kid' Williams, Scarlet Shewell, Georgia Wynn and Eric Hetherington. They crossed the Sicilian coast at 18,000 feet, but Donaldson's propeller began to give trouble, so the Spitfires retired, without seeing the enemy. Donaldson managed to glide back to Malta!

On 26 August, Donaldson led another sweep, of eight aircraft from each

AIRFIELDS ON
SICILY AND MALTA, 1942

Catania

Ponteolive ●

Farello ●

Liscata
●   ● Gela

SICILY

Syracuse ●

Cassible ●

Biscari ● ● Comiso

Pachino ●

MALTA CHANNEL

GOZO   **MALTA**

Takali ⊕
⊕ Hal Far
Luqa ⊕

Airfield: ●   RAF ⊕

of the Takali squadrons, Nos 249 and 603. Donaldson led at the head of No 249 Squadron's Flight – himself, Beurling, Hetherington, Williams, Shewell, Bryden and Micky Butler. They passed over Cape Scaramia as dusk began to fall over Sicily. They did a circuit of the island, but nothing stirred. They began to retire. Then Butler shouted over the radio that he had to bale out . . . but he held formation. He repeated his statement, then suddenly the Spitfire dived, vertically. It hit the ground and exploded.

Air Vice-Marshal Park decided that it was time to stop tickling the Axis on Sicily and hit them instead to force the Axis fighters into responding. There were reconnaissance reports of increases in the numbers of bombers on the main Sicilian aerodromes. Park instructed Group Captain Churchill to mount an attack on the airfields.

On 27 August, the three-squadron Wing made a low-level assault on the three Sicilian airfields, each squadron taking one of them. The Wing was led by Arthur Donaldson with Walter Churchill flying as his wingman, Number 2.

The force maintained radio silence on the low-level flight across the Mediterranean, then divided and launched simultaneous attacks on Comiso, Biscari and Gela airfields. The Spitfires took the airfields by surprise. Axis pilots could be seen trying to scramble, but the Spitfires caught three before they could begin to climb.

Donaldson led his Spitfires on the attack on Biscari. The gunners were putting up a heavy barrage of flak. As the Spitfires came in low, cannon firing, the flak made a direct hit on Churchill's Spitfire, which burst into flames and crashed in the middle of Biscari, killing Churchill.

A Dornier bomber was lifting off the airfield and Donaldson and his Number 3, Jim Ballantyne of No 229 Squadron, chased it across the Sicilian countryside. They hit it several times, but could only claim it as probably destroyed, shared.

The pilots' total claim for the raid was reduced by the 'spies' to ten confirmed shot down and twenty-nine destroyed on the ground. The Malta Spitfires lost two of their number, an American from a Hal Far squadron and Churchill.

The Axis response came two days later. A large force of fighters swept in over Malta. The RAF failed to shoot any of them down, although they had two casualties themselves.

Spitfires from Malta now began to fly almost daily sweeps or 'Rhubarb'-type operations. During intervals between sweeps, sections were flying dawn and dusk 'nuisance raids' on Axis bases in Sicily, such as the seaplane base at Syracuse, or the reserve airfield at Pachino, or Cape Scaramia. The Germans were reluctant to meet the sweeps. On 2 September, Donaldson brought down a Macchi MC.202 on a section sweep near Sicily. At night, the Malta Beaufighters started to fly 'Intruders' (night 'Rhubarbs') over Sicily.

In early September, Park altered his tactics. He ordered 'Ramrods'. They comprised a fighter escort to a small force of Hurricane fighter-bombers. The 'Hurribombers' were flown by some of the Fleet Air Arm Swordfish pilots who were unemployed on Malta while waiting for Axis convoys. They were given a swift conversion course in applying their bombing skills to a single-seat aeroplane.

On 11 September, three 'Hurribombers' set out to attack Gela aerodrome, Sicily, escorted by twelve Spitfires from the Takali Wing, including six from No 249 Squadron – Donaldson, Beurling, Bob Seed, Georgia Wynn, Shewell and Giddings. The operation followed the practice of No 11 Group, Fighter Command offensive sweeps. The Spitfires orbited at 8,000 feet over Filfla island to form up in escort formation. With the Hurricanes tucked in safely, they turned for Sicily and began a slow climb to 18,000 feet.

The formation crossed the coast. Donaldson was aware that the Axis radar would have picked them up. As the Hurricanes prepared to attack, Donaldson positioned his Spitfires below a bank of clouds and began an orbit, to give the Hurricanes target and withdrawal cover. The twelve Spitfire pilots scanned the sky, alertly.

Just as the Hurricanes began to dive, two Bf 109s appeared above the Spitfires. As Donaldson held his fighters in position to ward off the Bf 109s, the Hurricanes dive-bombed Gela airfield. Two pilots were on target, and three of their bombs fell on the runway areas, but the third aircraft's bombs overshot and went into the town. The Hurricanes then turned and ran for home at low level and high speed. The Spitfires levelled off on a southerly course, keeping between the Bf 109s and the Hurricanes and watching for interceptors trying to reach the Hurricanes from below. No other German aircraft were seen.

One of the Hurricanes was in difficulties. One of his bombs had hung up and he was manoeuvring frantically to make it fall off before it exploded. Just as they hove in sight of Malta, it fell off, right in the middle of a small fleet of Maltese fishing vessels. It went off, showering the fishermen, but fortunately without serious damage or hurt.

On 19 September, No 249 Squadron lost one of its best pilots on a section sweep over Cape Scaramia. Peter Peters, Hetherington, Georgia Wynn and Beurling were flying in open line abreast, at 20,000 feet. The pilots were scanning the sky carefully, but suddenly, from above, a Macchi MC.202 opened fire on Peters, on the end of the formation. He was killed. The Italian disappeared.

On 24 September, Donaldson led Shewell, Bryden and Beurling on a 'Rhubarb' to Pachino, expecting to find Axis fighters. They found nothing. They turned for home. Just off the coast, Donaldson spotted some small merchant vessels. His formation was too low on fuel to mount an attack so he radioed the sighting to Fighter Control.

Twelve Spitfires were scrambled and navigated impeccably on to the target. They came in for their attack, in pairs, from opposite directions. The vessels were not what they appeared to be. They were flak ships. They opened up with dozens of small- and medium-calibre guns. The Spitfires broke off, fortunately without loss.

Donaldson began to experiment with dropping 250-pound bombs from a Spitfire, fitting bomb-carriers from other aeroplanes and adapting the gunsight as a bombsight. This worked surprisingly well. He took sections of 'Spit-bombers' to bomb Sicilian airfields on a few occasions. This was the first time that Spitfires were used to carry bombs operationally, and they soon became highly successful. However, Donaldson was unable to exploit the new weapon fully.

There was a lull in activity by both sides over a couple of weeks. Sections or Flights flew over Sicily, looking for trouble, but there was little. Meanwhile, British reconnaissance revealed a German build-up for another offensive. The tension on Malta began to mount. A few days into October, the Axis sent across a few fighter sweeps. Showing tactical mastery, they set up their fighter formations over Malta to catch Spitfires on the climb and bounced several seasoned pilots. On one scramble on 3 October, a four-Spitfire section lost two of No 249's most experienced pilots to Bf 109s – Gass and Hogarth.

The final Blitz began on 11 October 1942. The Luftwaffe and Regia Aeronautica had downgraded their offensive against Malta following the PEDESTAL convoy battles. Now, Rommel's need for the free passage of convoys from Italy to North Africa was being threatened by aircraft, and warships from Malta. A new phase of compaigning was about to open in North Africa: the run-up to the battle of El Alamein. Rommel wanted to increase his supplies swiftly to give him the initiative. Again, aircraft, fast warships and submarines from Malta posed the main-threat to the supply convoys from Sicily and Italy to North Africa. And again, the Germans hit the island hard while they sent their convoys.

In late September, the Axis built up their forces on Sicily. Six Gruppen of Ju 88As were established on the island, together with a small unit of He 111H night bombers from Kampfgeschwader 100. In addition, the Regia Aeronautica deployed three Gruppi of Cant Z.1007bis bombers. The Ju 87Ds of II Gruppe of Stukageschwader 3 were also flown in from North Africa to reinforce the Ju 87Bs of the Italian 101° Gruppo.

The Germans and Italians recognized that the defence of Malta was considerably stronger now. The Luftwaffe took the significant step of reinforcing the usual two fighter Gruppen, I Gruppe/Jagdgeschwader 77 and II Gruppe/Jagdeschwader 53 by recalling the latter's I Gruppe from the Russian Front and flying in the crack I Gruppe/Jagdgeschwader 27 from North Africa. They all flew the Bf 109F. The Italians deployed three Gruppi of Macchi MC.202s and one of Reggiane Re.2001 fighters.

Several Malta Spitfire pilots asserted that it was the Bf 109s that would not stay to fight unless they had superiority in numbers and height, but that the Italian fighters were inclined to stay and 'mix it'. The Germans flew open formations, but the Italians more often flew tight formations, which meant that they had to watch their neighbours' wingtips rather than the sky. It is open to argument whether staying to 'mix it' also indicated poor tactics.

When the bombing attacks began again, the defence of Malta now rested on five squadrons of Spitfire Mk Vs – Nos 249, 126, 185, 229 and 1435 – all at full strength and all led by highly experienced wing leaders and squadron commanders, with many Malta veterans among their pilots. Park's squadrons could meet every raid with strong forces, and could break through the protective screen of Bf 109s to hit the bombers. The German and Italian raids were repulsed repeatedly.

On 11 October, Donaldson was airborne, practising bombing over Filfla island, when he spotted eleven Spitfires from No 229 Squadron scrambling. Donaldson joined up in the spare place, and a few minutes later the squadron hit a force of three Ju 88s escorted by nearly thirty Bf 109s. No 229 Squadron went into the formation in a head-on attack, trying to break through to the bombers. Donaldson personally took out one of the Ju 88s, which went down trailing thick smoke.

From 12 October 1942, Donaldson had all the pilots of his wing called at 02.30 hours, and at dispersal just after 03.00 hours. The veterans recognized this as the routine of the July Blitz and all the others before it and knew that they would not be stood down until after sunset.

The policy paid off. They were prepared. On the 12th, the Luftwaffe increased the number of escorts to a raid – it made the formations easy to spot on radar. On the first raid intercepted by Donaldson's wing, eight Ju 88s were escorted by nearly seventy fighters. The Takali Wing caught the formation near Sicily.

The Fighter Controller gave them superb directions and Donaldson was able to set his squadrons up with tactical advantage. The Spitfires attacked in formation, getting in very close to the bombers before opening fire. Donaldson swiftly destroyed a Ju 88 which exploded in flames, and another Ju 88 which dived away steeply, its crew jumping, and their parachutes blossoming. He was fairly sure that he had destroyed another Ju 88, but the fight was so intense that he could not claim a 'definite'. The sky was full of twisting, wheeling fighters and burning aeroplanes. Donaldson fired on a Bf 109 which burst into flames and went straight down, then fired on another which he lost but thought was probably destroyed.

The other pilots of the Wing were also having great success. Another three or four Ju 88s were felled, and perhaps three or four Bf 109s. The enemy formation continued to fly towards Malta and the remaining Ju 88s bombed, causing deaths and damage, but on a much reduced scale.

Next day, 13 October, No 249 Squadron was scrambled at 04.30 hours to meet a raid. The pilots dashed from the readiness room, and within two minutes were retracting their undercarriages.

Fighter Control told them to climb swiftly to 28,000 feet to intercept a formation of fifteen bombers and over eighty fighters – the biggest formation seen for several weeks. The Spitfires had no time to make a perfect interception. They made contact, and broke straight into the fighter screen. Some of the Spitfires made it through to the bombers, but others were enmeshed by Bf 109s and had to break off to stay alive. The Spitfires achieved their objective in large measure. Of the fifteen bombers, only four got through and bombed. Eight enemy bombers and fighters were destroyed.

Later in the day, Donaldson was again in action, against three Ju 88s with a heavy escort. The bombers were forced to jettison their bombs, but the Bf 109s were more successful this time and damaged Donaldson's Spitfire. He was unhurt.

On 14 October, Pilot Officer George Beurling, DFC, DFM, was shot down. He was attacking a Bf 109, but its partner got on his tail and put cannon shells through his cockpit. He was severely wounded and baled out. He was unfit to fly for several months. He had arrived on Malta on 8 June 1942 with a handful of victories from France. Now, he had a total of twenty-eight. His DFC citation, for his work up to 25 September, called him a 'relentless fighter whose determination and will has won the admiration of his colleagues'.

Beurling's ability to shoot accurately at speed at all altitudes and to kill with very few shells was legendary, the product of hard deep study. He was not accepted by many in the RAF because he was rather too individually successful. He ended up in Wing Commander 'Johnnie' Johnson's Kenley Wing, back in No 403 Squadron, RCAF, with whom he had begun his operational career as a sergeant pilot in 1942.

Early on 15 October, the Germans launched another heavy attack. The Luqa Wing had been scrambled to meet it far out, but had failed to make contact. At 06.30 hours, Donaldson led off a section of just four Takali Spitfires, all that were available.

They climbed hard to gain height. The bomber formation had come in close to Malta. Donaldson saw them, still higher. There were eight Ju 88s and over sixty, perhaps seventy, Bf 109s tightly shepherding them. Without hesitation, Donaldson went for the bombers in a head-on attack, lancing through the most vulnerable part of the 'beehive'. The bomber formation broke as the Spitfires went through from front to rear.

Donaldson curved the formation round again as they came out of the back of the enemy gaggle and went in for a full astern attack on the Ju 88s. His Number 2 held on to his wing, but the Numbers 3 and 4, still raw, failed to keep up with his turn or to understand his intentions and lost contact with the section, leaving Donaldson's tail uncovered for the Bf 109s.

Donaldson continued his attack. He sighted on a Ju 88, fired and watched his shells hitting home, flames and smoke issuing from the bomber. But Bf 109s latched on to his uncovered tail. He was still firing when cannon shells came ripping through his cockpit.

His engine stopped. Petrol pumped into his cockpit. He was bleeding badly, he could not tell from where there was so much blood, Two of his fingers were lying in his lap, severed. A cannon shell had hit the side of his cockpit, blowing off the outer two fingers of his left hand as it held the throttle. He was badly hit in the leg and foot. He was in great pain.

With his right hand he turned the Spitfire on its back and dived out of the fight. He was loosing too much blood to bale out, as he would be too weak to stay afloat. He set up a glide towards Takali.

Meanwhile the raid had gone home and had bombed.

Takali was covered with delayed-action bombs and incendiaries. Donaldson's undercarriage refused to respond. He was too weak to delay longer, and came in for a belly-landing. Almost before his aircraft had stopped, the rescue crew had hauled him from the cockpit.

He was rushed to Mtarfa hospital and underwent immediate emergency surgery to save his left hand. But, as he said of the loss of two fingers, they were not 'the important ones!'

A few days later, Keith Park went to visit Donaldson in Mtarfa hospital to tell him that he had been awarded the DSO – like his two brothers before him – for his leadership and fighting flying from Malta. Donaldson had already been awarded a bar to his DFC on Malta. He was a modest man:

> 'Anything I ever learned about leading I picked up from Douglas [Bader]
> in those four weeks at Martlesham in 1940 and 1941. He taught me
> everything I knew.' (Lucas).

Pilots could expect to last about three months maximum on Malta, and would usually be posted at the end of the period. Wing Commander Donaldson had been due to be relieved, within days. Now, Grant took over the Takali Wing.

On 18 October, Kesselring changed tactics. In just seven days, the RAF Spitfire pilots claimed forty-four bombers and twelve fighters 'destroyed', twenty bombers and ten fighters 'probably destroyed' and seventy bombers 'damaged'. The cost to the defenders was high – twenty-seven Spitfires were shot down, and twenty more written off. However, pilot deaths were few.

The bombers could not get through, so the Germans committed fast, low-level single-seaters, attack fighters. I Gruppe, Schlachtgeschwader 2 of Bf 109E fighter-bombers was pulled out of North Africa, where they were desperately needed.

On 19 October, with heavy fighter escort, together with Italian Re.2001s, the Bf 109Es, attacked Malta's airfields. Then, three formations of heavily escorted bombers were sent in, one from the north, one from the east and one from the west, to split and saturate Malta's defences. One Spitfire squadron split up the western attack over the sea, then flew east to repulse the eastern formation. In the dying sun, night fighters were scrambled to tackle the northern formation.

On 20 October, the Bf 109E fighter-bombers made sweeps across Malta. This too was seen to be producing no real results. The Ju 87s were not committed to battle – Stukas could not operate where there was effective fighter opposition. Daylight bomber raids stopped. On 21 October, the Spitfire pilots waited for the scramble call, but the Germans did not come. The day battle was over.

Sporadic night raids by He 111s and Ju 88s began, but the night fighter defences of Malta were strong and effective. These raids too soon ceased. On 26 October, I Gruppe, Jagdgeschwader 27 returned to Africa to aid the Afrika Korps against the Eighth Army's new offensive: then, three days later, HMS *Furious* flew off the last delivery of Spitfires to Malta. The pendulum had swung – and stuck.

Donaldson watched the fighting from his hospital balcony, but he had been too badly wounded to contemplate fighting. He was being sent home. In the early hours of 1 November, he was flown out of Malta on the same Liberator transport flight as George Beurling and several other Malta pilots who were returning to the United Kingdom – 'Rip' Mutch, Al Yates, Hetherington, 'Willie the Kid', Eddie Glazebrook, 'Bye-Bye' Bye and Art Roscoe from Takali, and Spence, Davies, Penny and two Australians and others from Luqa. It was quite a talented party aboard! But the weather closed in and the pilot tried to land at Gibraltar in a violent thunderstorm with cloud at 1,000 feet. Betrayed by the eddies round the rock, the Liberator stalled into the sea from forty feet up. Eight of the civilians aboard and six of the Malta pilots were killed: Glazebrook, who had joined No 603 Squadron during its last days in Malta; Spence and Davies of Luqa; and Mutch, Hetherington and 'Willie the Kid'. The survivors were glad to be survivors and depressed to lose such friends, uncomprehending of such an unkind fate.

☆   ☆   ☆

Malta was still not saved. By mid-November, there would be only a fortnight's supplies of food remaining. Two things signalled the end of the siege: first, the success of Operation SUPERCHARGE; secondly, on 8 November, combined British and American amphibious forces landed in

Algeria to bring a right claw into Rommel's back in a pincer movement. A week later, a convoy from Alexandria arrived in Malta.

In North Africa, General Montgomery had won a great victory at El Alamein. The final stroke was Operation SUPERCHARGE which opened in the dark before dawn on Monday, 2 November. Two days later, the Axis forces were in open retreat, harried by the Desert Air Force. Among Montgomery's chief aims in the follow-up period was the occupation of the Martuba group of airfields on the coast of Cyrenaica just south of Derna. A vital convoy for Malta, whose reserves of food and fuel were again critically low, was due to sail from Alexandria. The Martuba bases were essential to provide day fighter cover as the convoy passed down the narrow sea between Crete and Cyrenaica. By 15 November, the Desert Air Force had occupied the Martuba airfields. On 17 November, a heavy cruiser and destroyer force slipped moorings to escort the convoy of four fast merchantmen from Alexandria to Malta. The Martuba-based fighters covered it on 18 November; when night fell, the convoy had 500 miles in darkness before air cover from Malta began at dawn. On the 20th the four merchantmen entered Valletta.

Roy Marples who had flown with No 616 Squadron of the Tangmere Wing in 1941 and was another Bader pilot who had made senior rank swiftly, was a leading player in an extraordinary operation mounted by the Desert Air Force in the follow-up to SUPERCHARGE. With the First Alamein victory only a week old, Tedder announced that 'the enemy supplies are my main preoccupation'. While heavy bombers attacked the Axis supply ports and shipping, the Axis forces were retreating, and they and their supply lines were harried continually by the Desert Air Force whose mobile squadrons moved forward as the British advanced, to be nearer to their targets and ensure that the advance from Alamein did not waver and did not lose momentum. However, Operation CHOCOLATE took matters a stage further, and had a devastating effect on the morale of the Axis.

Based on an earlier venture by Albacores of the Fleet Air Arm which had used an airstrip 200 miles behind enemy lines on 9 July 1942 to mount a raid on a convoy off Benghazi, Operation CHOCOLATE was swiftly mounted. It was undertaken by No 243 Wing, led by Wing Commander John Darwen, using two of its squadrons, Nos 213 and 238 Squadrons, under Squadron Leaders Olver and Roy Marples respectively. The force deployed thirty-six Hurricane Mk IICs. On 13 November 1942, the Wing flew from its base to Landing Ground 125 – which lay about 140 miles behind the enemy lines. Its task was to harass the retreating Axis forces from their own rear. LG 125 lay about 180 miles due east of Jedabya, while the main Axis forces were to the west of Benghazi.

The squadrons began operations on the afternoon of their arrival at LG 125. For almost three days, the Wing operated without let-up. Panic struck the Axis truck drivers heading for the safety of Agheila as the Hurricanes swarmed out of the desert, many miles beyond the normal reach of British fighters. The Hurricane pilots claimed to have destroyed some 130 motor transports and damaged a further 170, with the 'usual' effects on the soft targets manning the vehicles – killing them, wounding them and certainly helping to demoralize them. Two No 213 Squadron Hurricanes were brought down by anti-aircraft gunfire. Six pilots lost their way on 14 November, and landed in the desert, without damage to their aeroplanes. Fuel was flown out to them the next day, and they flew back to LG 125.

On 13 November, Olver had flown his aeroplane into a telegraph pole, which had damaged the Hurricane's tail. The next day, Olver was strafing an enemy aircraft on the ground. It blew up as he was passing it, and debris from it struck his aeroplane, but again he made it back to base.

In the preceding week, the Luftwaffe had suffered a stunning defeat at the hands of the Desert Air Force, but was still active, and it could not have been long before a counter-air attack was launched on LG 125. It was not until 16 November that the Axis located the Wing's 'advanced' base, which was the day the Wing was ordered to withdraw. Air transport helped to bring back some of the ground crews, and 'Jackie' Darwen withdrew his squadrons to the airfield at Fuka. They claimed fourteen aircraft destroyed in addition to 300 motor transports.

Not only was Malta's future secured by events in north-west Africa following Operation TORCH but, as the Germans were pushed by the Eighth Army from the east and the First Army from the west into ever-shrinking territory, Malta now could play its full offensive role, astride the supply routes to Tunisia. It was the Germans' turn to run the gauntlet.

The effects of Malta on the Axis position can be seen from November 1942, when the offensive phase got into full swing. Spitfire fighters were making frequent sweeps over Sicily, Spit-bombers were proving very successful against targets in Sicily. Spitfires and Beaufighters attacked enemy transport aircraft en route to Tunisia, and Beaufighters, Swordfish and Albacores again began operating freely against Axis shipping. As November closed, the Vichy French forces in Algeria called for a cease-fire. The Allies still had a hard fight ahead to oust the Afrika Korps, but Malta was no longer in real danger. Malta had endured more than 3,340 air raids. The RAF had lost 547 aircraft in air combat and 160 on the ground. In January 1943, work began on Malta to extend, improve and enlarge airfields to operate twenty-six fighter squadrons by mid-summer. A giant aircraft carrier, nourished since 1941, Malta was about to become the stepping stone for the Allies to Europe.

CHAPTER 23
Sicily and Salerno

Hugh Dundas, who had missed going to Malta in 1942, eventually got there in May 1943. Following a restless Staff tour with the North-West African Air Force in Tunisia, Dundas was promoted to wing commander in May 1943. On 11 June, he became Wing Commander Flying of No 324 Wing, No 210 Group, North African Tactical Air Force (NATAF). With long service in the Desert, the Wing was very experienced and was now based at Hal Far for the assault on Sicily. It was commanded by Group Captain 'Sheep' Gilroy (a former Scottish sheep farmer), who had taken command in North Africa in October 1942.

No 324 Wing comprised five squadrons, Nos 43, 72, 93, 111 and 243. Dundas attached himself and his personal Spitfire to No 43 Squadron – appropriately 'The Fighting Cocks'. It was commanded by his friend from the Auxiliaries, Squadron Leader Michael Cook. LACs Lawrenson and Boyd, proudly and enthusiastically, aware of prestige, became Dundas's personal ground crew. The Wing flew the Spitfire Mk VC, although No 72 Squadron had partly re-equipped with Mark IXs in February 1943 to act as top cover for the Wing. In June, four of the Wing's squadrons re-equipped with Spitfire Mk IXs, but No 43 Squadron retained Mark Vs.

The sense of the imminence of great events was sealed when, in June, King George VI flew into Malta and visited Hal Far, but the sense of purpose was apparent in the everyday observation of the number of aircraft crowding on to the airfield for the invasion. In the wake of the Royal visit, and despite this overcrowding with offensive might, Hal Far's Aerodrome Marshal, a flight lieutenant whom Dundas now irreverently titled the 'Marshal of the Royal Aerodrome', insisted on maintaining the dispersal arrangements of the Malta Blitz period. As No 43 Squadron had seventeen aircraft and there were only fourteen blast pens, the Marshal was politely ignored.

The Desert Air Force, which had supported the Eighth Army in the Western Desert, and the British squadrons of the NATAF, which had supported the First Army in Tunisia, had joined forces in Malta in June as the Desert Air Force for the thrust into Europe's 'soft underbelly' – the assault on Sicily and the drive into Italy. Now, the assault escalated rapidly by day and night with heavy, medium and fighter-bombers, and an air superiority battle over Sicily. The first task of the Malta-based aircraft was to attack enemy communications on Sicily in June. Then, from the beginning of July until the sea and airborne landings commenced on 10 July, it was the turn of the airfields and operations intensified. There was little coherent air opposition and the Allies achieved air superiority around and over Sicily.

Dundas was now able to apply the skills he had learnt with the Tangmere Wing in the summer of 1941. No 324 Wing flew in an offensive air superiority role, employing the squadrons flexibly. Nos 72 and 43 Squadrons made their first sweeps over Sicily on 15 and 30 June respectively. No 72 Squadron was also involved in interception scrambles from Malta. Up to three times a day, Dundas led three or four squadrons of No 324 Wing the sixty miles to Sicily, escorting two or three squadrons of light bombers on a sweep intended to bring the enemy into the air where he could be despatched in quantity before the landings. This was a largely successful policy. There was much fighting, and many casualties, but the Wing claimed over sixty victories. Dundas shared in the destruction of a Bf 109 on 4 July 1943. No 43 Squadron spent D-Day Minus One patrolling the convoys heading for the beaches. Significantly, it found no action.

Elements of the Wing took off in the dark to arrive over the beaches at first light on D-Day – 10 July. They encountered a few enemy aircraft. The flexibility of tactical air power and Dundas's leadership abilities were demonstrated repeatedly after the landings, when the Wing was engaged in sweeps, 'Rhubarbs', bomber escorts, and standing patrols over the beach-head. Squadrons, Flights and Sections were used independently. and simultaneously for different tasks. For instance, No 43 Squadron also flew offensive patrols and No 243 Squadron flew mainly heavy bomber escorts. The air superiority battle continued. On 12 July, No 72 Squadron claimed thirteen enemy aircraft and three probables for the loss of two; on the 13th, No 93 Squadron claimed five enemy aircraft, two probables and eight damaged.

On D-Day Plus Two, the Wing landed at Comiso. A bureaucratic error prevented the Wing's ground echelon from reaching Sicily in time. By 16 July, there were six Spitfire squadrons at Comiso, but its concrete runway was needed for bombers, so the Wing moved a fortnight later to the 800-yard dust airstrip at Capo Pachino. There they lived under canvas, a change from Malta's buildings, amid oranges, lemons, olives and olive oil, dust and insects.

Enemy ground resistance was strong but the Allies held air superiority. There was little enemy air activity by day, but more by night. The Wing escorted day bombers on attacks on enemy supply lines north of the battle front, and patrolled the bomb-line to intercept German or Italian bombers. During the consolidation of Sicily, the Desert Air Force operated in close support of the Army. The Axis forces withdrew to the north-east. On 17 August 1943, Sicily fell. The Allies had their springboard to the mainland of Europe.

The Allies believed that they had relentlessly driven the enemy into retreat but the Axis withdrawal had been pre-planned, and was covered by massive anti-aircraft defences. The Allied pilots called the Straits of Messina between Sicily and Italy 'Flak Alley'; the Royal Navy's sane refusal to operate in the dangerous, narrow straits greatly aided the Axis forces. Moreover, Allied air operations concentrated on ports and landing sites, but not the routes to them or evacuation craft. Forty per cent of operations were conducted with heavy bombers, when battlefield operations were needed.

Nevertheless, the Allies learned from Sicily. Developed from the effective air/ground support evolved in the Western Desert, serious co-ordination between land and air forces began to bring air power to bear where it was most needed tactically, while strategic air power and the commanders who wielded it were put in perspective.

Sicily's fall brought Mussolini's downfall. The new Italian Government sued for peace, thoroughly weakening Germany's position. The Allies' air power gave them a decisive advantage in the Mediterranean theatre. The German Luftflotte 2 had been depleted while the Regia Aeronautica, despite some excellent fighters and flashes of brilliance, offered no serious opposition.

After the Sicilian campaign, Wing Commander Hugh Dundas's No 324 Wing was seconded to the 12th Tactical Air Force, US Army Air Forces. The Wing was assigned for day-to-day operations to the US 64th Fighter Wing, commanded by Brigadier General 'Shorty' Hawkins. Preparations began for the invasion of Italy.

No 324 Wing's No 43 Squadron, frequently led by Dundas, began operations against the Italian mainland in August, with an advanced landing ground at Lentone, a method adopted in the Desert to give greater radius of action. Preparatory to supporting the invasion of Italy, No 324 Wing had moved to Panebianco, one of Gerbini's satellites, on 29 August, the first of four moves in a fortnight. It had rained for the first time since May, heavily, rendering Panebianco unserviceable, so the Wing had moved to Catania Main on 30 August, flying from there for two days, moving late on 31 August to Cassala, another Gerbini satellite.

There were two sets of landings mounted on Italy: the first would go in on the 'toe and heel', by the Eighth Army, who would sweep north to link with the second landings in the 'waist' by the Fifth Army. No 324 Wing was not called upon to support the landings in the south of Italy – Operation BAYTOWN. On 3 September, the British Eighth Army landed at Reggio and the next day at Taranto. Desert Air Force wings supported the landings. However, they were relatively straightforward and the ground forces advanced inland swiftly.

Operation AVALANCHE, the landings at Salerno, was expected to be strongly resisted. USAAF P-38s, P-40s, A-36s and RAF Spitfires of the 12th Tactical Air Command, assisted by Seafires from Royal Navy escort carriers, were to support the Fifth Army and British X Corps in crossing the Straits of Messina and landing at Salerno on 9 September. Hugh Dundas would have a leading role in providing air support for the operation. Between 4 and 7 September, No 324 Wing moved to Falcone on Sicily's north coast in preparation for giving air support to the amphibious landings at Salerno. This involved a 350-mile round flight of almost three hours' duration, so the Spitfires were equipped with 80-gallon drop tanks, which ruined handling and made servicing difficult. Even so, the Sicily-based Spitfires could give only brief cover, the Seafires doing most of the work.

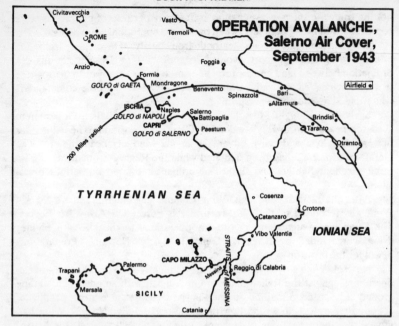

At dawn on D-Day, the twelve Merlin 66s of No 43 Squadron's new Spitfire Mk IXs barked into life, their four-bladed airscrews whirling the fine dust. Dundas led them off Falcone on the first of their 350-mile round trip sorties to the Salerno beachhead, lumbering with their 80-gallon drop tanks. The air over the Tyrrhenian Sea was full of Allied aircraft as the sun rose over Italy. No 43 Squadron relieved the carrier-based Seafires which had been over the beachhead since dawn. Although enemy aircraft were killed or driven off, there was little resistance in the air. On the ground, the invasion forces were encountering far more serious resistance than had been expected. The air umbrella was continuous. At noon, No 43 Squadron flew a second patrol over the beachhead. This squadron alone flew 52 hours on D-Day, 67 on D-Day Plus One, and an average of 40 over the next three days.

From mid-1943, most Spitfire squadrons in the Mediterranean theatre were re-equipped with Marks VIII and IX. Re-equipment was by squadron rather than wing, as aircraft became available. For example, in August, Nos 43 and 93 Squadrons of No 324 Wing partly re-equipped with Marks IX and VIII respectively. The Mark VIII was strengthened and optimized for the tropics but slow development and production had led to the ubiquitous Mark IX being adapted, successfully, to fill the breach. Both used the Merlin 60-series engine. As the Mark IX had greater ceiling than the Mark V, it was used for top cover, which required the Spitfires to be airborne for longer, adding to the burden of a long transit. The Mark IX did not have better range, so drop tanks were necessary, ruining handling.

The Spitfire work involved flying beachhead patrols, fighter sweeps and patrols over the bomb-line covering squadrons giving ground support, usually flying two three-hour sorties a day. It was not exactly the Spitfire's metier. However, the Seafires could cover the beachheads longer than the Spitfires, and from first light until dawn, because their bases, the carriers, were closer to the beachhead.

The Allied troops at Salerno were only just holding the beachhead. They wanted more air support. Allied airfield construction engineers were ordered to build four strips at Salerno in order to permit more extensive close support. In the face of intense German resistance, all the strips were completed by 15 September. The first, at Tusciano, was completed on 11 September, but mainly to boost morale. They could only be used in fair weather and by day.

General Hawkins called on No 324 Wing to establish Spitfires on the Tusciano strip, coded-named 'Roger', which lay parallel to the beach. Two squadrons went in first, led by Dundas, a third squadron following. The ground advance party was waiting, but had had a hectic time getting through. On 9 September, half of No 324 Wing's ground personnel had moved out to embark for Salerno, where they arrived on D-Day Plus Six. The rest of the groundcrew were seriously overstretched and exhausted when the last aircraft left for the advanced landing ground in Italy on 16 September. A vital lesson gained from tactical operations in North Africa had been the need to keep tactical squadrons fully mobile and operational at all times. Moves had to be more thoroughly planned and closely executed. A sea crossing was an added complication.

The advanced landing ground was in a half-circle ringed by hills, and under enemy surveillance and fire. Although the deployment was very much an expedient to raise morale – the Spitfires took off and landed under the constantly firing muzzles of two Royal Horse Artillery, 7th Armoured Division, 25-pounder batteries – most of the Wing crowded on to the strip in the next few days, continuing beachhead patrols against little resistance. The Salerno fighting was intense and the Fifth and Eighth Armies were unable to link up until 16 September; the Germans withdrew. Fighter-bomber and naval gun support had considerably assisted the land forces in holding on.

The Allied forces now pushed on to Naples, twenty miles up the coast. No 324 Wing continued to provide various services. No 243 Squadron continued with its bomber escort role during the invasion and also provided beachhead cover for Naples in September 1943, moving in on D-Day Plus Three, and starting line patrols and strafing. On 24 September 1943, Dundas shared in the destruction of a Ju 88, but the Regia Aeronautica was finished, and the Luftwaffe's fighters were elsewhere. The Kittyhawk and Mustang wings of the Desert Air Force were excelling in close support of Allied ground forces in the geographical nightmare of Italy. Close support and army commands were highly integrated, the former being virtually flying artillery. There was little work for pure fighters. During the push on Naples, No 43 Squadron began flying bomber escorts, as well as beachhead patrols.

The Allied progress in Italy was slow, but Naples fell on 1 October 1943. No 324 Wing was immediately ordered to move on 4 October to one of the two all-weather aerodrome there, Capodochino – 'Capo' – but before they could, non-stop rain began on 3 October. By the 6th, Tusciano was under six feet of water. The Wing did not move until 11 October, once pierced steel planking (PSP) had been laid at Tusciano.

At Capo, for the first time since April, the men moved into billets. The strain and poor environment, however, were telling and between October and December there was much illness, particularly infective hepatitis and venereal disease. In these trying circumstances, one of Hugh Dundas's less warlike qualities became apparent, his ability to care with understanding and intelligence for the men in his charge.

The complex of airfields around the Mount Vesuvius region became vital. On 2/3 October, the Allies landed on the east coast of Italy and secured the Foggia Plain, where another complex of airfields was established, into which the Desert Air Force moved, beginning 'cab-rank' operations in support of the ground forces.

No 324 Wing continued to fly patrols to the bomb-line, and there were some air combat victories in November. However, Luftwaffe resistance by day was scant, and its night operations fell off. As a result, the RAF was able to reduce its presence in Italy, and Spitfire squadrons were sent further abroad. No 324 Wing still operated under the 12th Tactical Air Command on the Fifth Army's front, although it was administratively under the Desert Air Force's control.

In November 1943, 'Sheep' Gilroy completed his tour and was off back to England. His successor was Duncan Smith, who was the Wing Leader of the Desert Air Force's No 244 Wing, based in Italy, Duncan Smith was promoted and appointed group captain in command of No 324 Wing on 29 November (Stan Turner took over No 244 Wing). Dundas remained Wing Commander Flying. No 324 Wing now comprised Nos 43, 72, 93 and 111 Squadrons, commanded by Squadron Leaders Parrott, Daniels, Westenra and Matthews. No 243 Squadron had taken its last air combat victory during the month. From then, it went over entirely to fighter-bomber work, leaving No 324 Wing for Gioia del Colle on the Adriatic coast, and not returning to the Wing until 1944. No 43 Squadron re-equipped completely with Spitfire Mk IXs and went over to armed reconnaissance, attacking targets of opportunity. No 111 Squadron had been among the first units in the Mediterranean to convert to Spitfire Mk VIIIs.

The winter of 1943–44 brought a brief respite in the fighting. No 324 Wing moved to Lago, one mile north of the River Volturno, in mid-January 1944. In the first week of January 1944, just before the Anzio landings, Dundas handed over No 324 Wing to Johnny Loudon; Dundas had been posted to operations staff at Advanced Headquarters Desert Air Force, taking Loudon's place.

Hugh Dundas had led No 324 Wing with great success in fighter and support roles, and he had shown considerable ability and understanding in dealing with the men under very difficult living conditions. Dundas's departure from No 43 Squadron's mess was made memorable. Leaving the mess in the early hours of a moonless morning, he tripped over an unseen fire-extinguisher and landed head first in a thorn thicket!

CHAPTER 24
'Greycap' Leader

By early 1943, the Focke-Wulf Fw 190 was proving so superior to the Spitfire Mk V that penetrations into France had almost ceased. The Fw 190A had entered service in Autumn 1941, with Adolf Galland's elite Jagdgeschwader 26 in France. In 1942, it rapidly regained air superiority over France from Fighter Command, for whom Dieppe had been a shock. The Fw 190 was superior to the Bf 109F and, flown by ace and 'squadron standard' pilots alike, completely outclassed the current Spitfire variant, the Mark V. The Jabo 'tip-and-run' raids by Fw 190s had to be countered by Typhoons.

To overcome the superiority of the Fw 190, the RAF could not wait for the Spitfire Mk VIII with a redesigned airframe and the new, more powerful, two-stage supercharged Merlin 60 series engine. Instead, the Mark IX was pressed into service. It was basically the existing Mark VB airframe re-engined with a Merlin 60 series. Mark V production lines were converted rapidly. The Mark IX was a superb compromise – a Spitfire with the Mark VIII's performance without the delay. Much faster in level flight and in the climb than the Mark V, it had the tactical advantages of a greatly improved ceiling while being visually similar. In most respects it was superior to the Fw 190. The Mark IX invariably had the very effective universal or C type armament, a combination of two 20mm Hispano Mk I or II cannon and four .303-inch Browning machine-guns.

Fighter Command also needed experienced leaders. By March 1943, 'Johnnie' Johnson had been flying operationally for over two years. After a comparatively restful winter, his squadron, No 610, had rejoined the Tangmere Wing in January 1943, flying from Tangmere's satellite, West-hampnett. Shortly afterwards, the squadron lost five pilots in one week to Fw 190s. Although Johnson himself destroyed an Fw 190 on 13 February, they were proving hard for the average squadron pilots in Mark Vs to kill. Morale was falling.

Squadron Leader Johnson was due for a rest, but it was evident that he was invaluable in this crisis. He had some 1,000 flying hours and about a hundred operations on Spitfires. He had also now occasionally led the Tangmere Wing. His tactical abilities had been sharpened by the legendary Bader. He seemed a natural choice to take the new Spitfire into battle. In mid-March 1943, he was promoted to wing commander and posted to command the Kenley Wing, which was re-equipping with the Spitfire Mk IX. It comprised Nos 403 and 416 Squadrons, RCAF. It had been led by Wing

Commander Hodson, DFC.

As Kenley Wing Leader, Johnson selected Mark IX EN398 and had his initials substituted for codes, 'JE-J', a wing leader's privilege. The Intelligence Officer warned him that it would attract the enemy – thereafter, all his Spitfires bore his initials. Some wing leaders' initials were in conspicuous colours, but Johnson's were the standard colour for codes – Sky. At the same time, he chose the call-sign 'Greycap', using it, despite the Intelligence Officer's further counsel to change it periodically for safety, throughout the war.

Changes were taking place in the RAF. New roles were being devised. In early March 1943, Operation SPARTAN was run in southern England in which army co-operation, fighter and medium bomber units had co-operated with ground forces. This provided much useful information for the formation of a tactical air force. Further army co-operation was practised as an increasing part of the squadron's activities, but there was much to be learnt.

On 24 March 1943, two No 403 Squadron pilots, Pilot Officers W. J. Lane (Mark VB EP280) and H. J. Dowding (Mark VB EP114), took off at 12.50 hours on an army co-operation exercise to provide 'fighter cover to troops in an army exercise near Penshurst.' [ORB].

They were back at 14.15 hours, but they were 'not too happy about it for, while they were at the required place at the required time, the troops to be covered didn't seem to be around.' [ORB].

No 403 Squadron was a very successful Canadian unit. On 30 March 1943, it celebrated its anniversary and its continued success, and Johnson – 'who recently took over the wing' [ORB] – was a guest of honour. The arrival of their new Spitfires added vigour to their view of their future!

The Wing met no opposition on the first occasions Johnson led it, until 3 April when it flew 'Ramrod' 49 to the St Omer area, providing cover for the withdrawal of a Typhoon strike from France. The Typhoons were from No 181 Squadron, led by Squadron Leader Denis Crowley-Milling. Their target was the Abbeville airfield, which they successfully dive-bombed. The Kenley Wing Leader had his two squadrons over the coast just south of Le Touquet to cover the fast retiring Typhoons.

Johnson climbed his wing to 24,000–26,000 feet. Using ground-based radar superbly, the fighter controller vectored the Kenley Wing on to an enemy force which climbed towards the Wing. It was less than 5,000 feet below them and five miles ahead. They would meet east of Montreuil. Johnson took the Wing down in a gentle dive. It was 15.05 hours. As the Wing was about to attack, the controller warned of another enemy force behind. Johnson weighed the timing and decided to press the attack. The fight was over quickly, and at 15.10 hours he ordered the Wing home before the second force arrived. For the loss of one Spitfire, the Canadians destroyed six Fw 190s, one of which fell to Johnson's guns. It was a highly inspiring introduction to combat with the new wing leader and the Mark IX.

The Canadians' appreciation of Johnson's tough professional leadership mounted rapidly, as the aggressive wing leader put his tactical experience to the test. Johnson introduced the 'finger-four' and Bader's doctrines to the

Wing with excellent results. Throughout the gruelling summer Johnson's estimation of the tough, pugnacious Canadians' fighting skills grew.

The pace of operations was relentless, but there were many that provoked no Luftwaffe response, or produced no victories. There was much that was routine, and there was much for the pilots to learn. Combat experience was important, and Johnson saw that his Canadians got it. On 16 April 1943, the ORB for No 403 Squadron recorded: 'No combats but plenty of flying to tire the boys.'

In the morning, a Flight of five aircraft was scrambled at 10.35 on an air-sea rescue cover mission. The five returned at 12.20 hours. The mission was flown by Flying Officer J. I. MacKay, Sergeant N. F. Cottrill, Pilot Officer F. C. McWilliams, Pilot Officer H. J. Dowding and Sergeant N. V. Chevers.

In the early afternoon, the Wing set out on a sweep over France at 14.15 hours. Although they saw enemy fighters below and behind the Wing, and turned to engage them, neither No 403 nor No 416 Squadrons could get within range. The squadrons landed back at Kenley at 15.40 hours.

At 17.35 hours, they were off on another sweep – 'Ramrod' 61. Nos 403 and 416 Squadrons acted as Second Fighter Echelon, with Wing Commander Johnson leading at the head of No 403 Squadron. The No 403 Squadron ORB recorded that the Wing flew:

> '. . . out at Beachy Head at zero feet, climbing to 21,000 feet at D'Ailly then to East of Fauville to Caudebec and out north of Le Havre at same height thence due west to 20 miles east of Barfleur at 10,000 feet, doubled back on track to 10 miles off Fecamp at 500' then vector of 340 for 30 miles, seeing an upturned yellow wooden raft 6×4 feet. Returned to Beachy at 2,000 feet. No cloud and nothing else seen. . . .'

Both squadrons were down by 19.00 hours.

It is interesting to note the details of the sections of No 403 Squadron on these sweeps. Johnson took trouble to bring on good leaders. The first sweep was flown by ten pilots. Wing Commander Johnson, who frequently led at the head of No 403 Squadron, was leading the Wing at the head of No 416 Squadron. No 403 Squadron's Commanding Officer, Squadron Leader Syd Ford, was absent, pending his posting. Therefore, No 403 Squadron was led by Flight Lieutenant C. M. Magwood. He normally led Blue Section when Squadron Leader Ford or Wing Commander Johnson led the squadron at the head of Red Section. This was good experience for Magwood, who had shown skill as a leader. No 403 Squadron's sections were:

Blue Section
Flying Officer N. R. Fowlow
Pilot Officer D. H. Dover
Flying Officer J. I. MacKay
Sergeant G. R. Brown

Red Section
Flight Lieutenant C. M. Magwood
Sergeant W. C. Uttley

Yellow Section
Flight Lieutenant H. C. Godefroy
Sergeant W. McGarrigle
Pilot Officer H. J. Dowding
Sergeant D. C. Hamilton

The second sweep was flown by eleven pilots. Johnson led at the head of No 403 Squadron this time, as Red 1, displacing Magwood back to the lead of Blue Section. For this mission, two pilots were replaced and others exchanged sections and positions in sections. Squadron formations were flexible. The fact that the lead section, Red, flew with two men on the first sweep and with three on the second is of note. It was not unusual for Red Section to fly with three men. The outer sections normally flew with four. As Red Section was central and covered by Blue and Yellow Sections, so long as the line-abreast formation was used, complete cover could be ensured.

Blue Section
Flight Lieutenant C. M. Magwood
Pilot Officer D. H. Dover
Flying Officer N. R. Fowlow
Sergeant G. R. Brown

Red Section
Wing Commander J. E. Johnson
Flying Officer F. C. McWilliams
Flying Officer J. I. MacKay

Yellow Section
Flight Lieutenant H. C. Godefroy
Sergeant W. McGarrigle
Pilot Officer H. J. Dowding
Sergeant J. E. Abbotts

The following day, 17 April 1943, the Kenley Wing was detailed to provide escort cover to a squadron of Venturas which were to bomb a railway yard. Wing Commander Johnson led at the head of No 403 Squadron, as Red 1, with Pilot Officer D. H. Dover (Red 2) and Flying Officer G. D. Aitken (Red 3).

It was a beautiful, cloudless afternoon, with bright sun and very little haze. Nos 403 and 416 Squadrons took off at 14.17 hours and set course for the rendezvous over Beachy Head. The twelve Venturas and the Spitfire Mk VBs of No 411 Squadron who were flying close escort were four minutes late for the zero-altitude rendezvous. The two Spitfire Mk IX squadrons positioned themselves over the Venturas and Spitfire Mk VBs. The two marks of Spitfire were being deployed to make best use of the superior fighting ceiling enjoyed by the Mark IX.

As the 'Beehive' flew across the Channel, a Mosquito and a Defiant were spotted following them out. Johnson 'broke R/T silence to send a section [of

No 403 Squadron] to investigate them' (ORB).

As it approached the French coast, the force climbed, crossing the coast at 14.53 hours. The Spitfire Mk Vs and the Venturas were at 13,000 feet. The Spitfire Mk IXs flew cover, stacked up from 15,000 feet.

Johnson set his fighters up in a protective screen for the bombers as they approached the target area five minutes later. As the bombers ran in on the railway yards, a little heavy flak opened up on them, but they bombed successfully and turned for home. The Venturas and No 411 Squadron crossed the French coast between Le Tréport and Cayeux at 10,000 feet at 15.05 hours. Nos 403 and 416 Squadrons were stacked up above them.

So far, no enemy aeroplanes had been seen. When the force was 20 miles across the Channel, the Fighter Controller called up Wing Commander Johnson and told him that the Hornchurch Wing was engaged with enemy aircraft in the Abbeville area.

Johnson left the bombers and close escort and climbed Nos 403 and 416 Squadrons up to 33,000 feet, up-sun. Under Special Control from the Fighter Controller, he was vectored to the Le Tréport area where about fifteen Fw 190s were ripe to be bounced.

Flight Lieutenant H. C. Godefroy (Yellow Leader) was flying at 29,000 feet on the right of No 403 Squadron. He saw three Fw 190s at about 20,000 feet climbing out to sea. The Wing Leader gave him permission to attack them. Godefroy led Yellow Section down (Sergeant D. C. Hamilton, Flying Officer H. D. MacDonald, Pilot Officer P. K. Gray). Godefroy picked the Fw 190 on the right, Gray (Yellow 2) the one on the left.

Godefroy came in from about 10 degrees astern of his Fw 190, opening up at 250 yards with a two-second burst of cannon and machine-gun fire. His fire was accurate, hitting the port wing root and the fuselage in front of the cockpit. The enemy's port cannon magazine exploded. The Fw 190 spun out and down for 2,000 feet and burst into flames. The pilot jumped. Hugh Godefroy turned to port and climbed again.

Gray opened fire on the port Fw 190 at about 200 yards range. The enemy aircraft flicked into a half roll. Gray fired again. The Fw 190 went into a spiral. Smoke poured from it. The pilot jumped, and his parachute opened. The third Fw 190 dived away.

By now the Spitfires were low on fuel, after nearly an hour and a quarter in the air and through flying at altitude. 'Johnnie' Johnson ordered the two squadrons to set course for home. They crossed the French coast near Le Tréport and the English coast near Beachy Head, at only 1,000 feet. All the squadrons' aircraft had landed at base by 15.52 hours.

On 20 April 1943, Flight Lieutenant G. M. Magwood was promoted to squadron leader and became Commanding Officer, after Squadron Leader L. S. Ford had been posted on promotion to wing commander. Flying Officer H. D. MacDonald was promoted to flight lieutenant and took over 'B' Flight.

On the afternoon of 20 April 1943, the Kenley Wing was detailed for 'Ramrod' 67, to provide support for eight 'Bomphoons' which were to bomb Tricqueville aerodrome. No 403 Squadron, led by Wing Commander Johnson, and No 416 Squadron acted as Target Support over the aerodrome.

Taking off at 18.15 hours, the Wing rendezvoused with the Typhoons and crossed the coast at Beachy Head at zero feet. To evade radar contact, they flew over the Channel just above the wave tops. As they approached the French coast, the force climbed rapidly and crossed the coast at 7,000 feet. The Wing flew to the Lillebonne and Tricqueville area. The Typhoons dive-bombed the aerodrome successfully, and then retired, fast.

After the bombing, the Wing climbed to Blangy at 21,000 feet. Soon afterwards, they were taken over by Special Control. Near Dieppe, six Fw 190s rushed head-on at No 416, but the Spitfires shot down one of them and damaged another, without loss. No 403 Squadron's Spitfires held position, but fifteen more Fw 190s were seen bearing in from astern of the Wing, preparing to attack.

Johnson ordered the Wing home, as the Spitfires were near their fuel limits – one of them, Sergeant N. F. Cottrill (Blue 2) had to land at RAF Redhill just south of Kenley as he was so short of petrol. The Wing flew out over Le Tréport heading for Hastings and landed back at Kenley at 19.50 hours.

A mission to escort USAAF Fortresses the following month shows a contrast in escort styles to that of the Venturas on 17 April. During 1943, the US Eighth Air Force began its bomber offensive, first over France, as practice, and extending it to Germany during the summer. Although the Spitfire's short range – even with drop tanks – excluded it from escorting the bombers to Germany, they were able to escort missions over France, which proved the viability of escorted daylight bombing, and they could cover the first and last legs of raids on Germany.

On one occasion that the Kenley Wing escorted B-17 boxes into France, they flew as close escort. The bombers were attacked by enemy fighters, and the Spitfires wove in among the bombers, chasing the enemy. However, the RAF pilots became aware that the B-17 gunners were shooting at any fighter.

Wing Commander Johnson discussed this with the US bomber squadron commanders, urgently. They did not want close escort, like that the RAF flew, as on the 'Circus' operations. To ward off any enemy aircraft that got close, the B-17s relied on the cross-fire from all the guns of the eighteen bombers in their protective boxes. Any fighter that got close was assumed to be hostile. In fact, the Americans were sure that they would be able to blast a way to the target, unescorted. Still, what they would like would be a protective screen around the bomber boxes to keep the enemy fighters breaking into the formations.

On 13 May 1943, the Kenley Wing flew 'Ramrod' 71, detailed to provide an attack, target and withdrawal escort for a Fortress bombing raid into France. Although this was a similar operation to that flown by Johnson on 20 August 1942 with No 610 Squadron, it is instructive to see how he handled it in relation to the tactical guidelines agreed with the USAAF. The weather was 'perfect'. Johnson was leading Red Section, with three aircraft, Pilot Officer Harry Dowding (Red 2) and Pilot Officer R. B. Bowen (Red 3). Wing Commander Johnson's combat report recorded:

'We met the Fortresses over Berck two minutes before the rendezvous and as they set course, I positioned the Wing to cover the rear box of bombers. On the way to the target I saw about 6 desultory attacks by e/a [enemy aircraft] on the leading formation of bombers. Between Amiens and the target I saw a gaggle of at least 50 e/a; these a/c climbed up sun and prepared to attack the bombers in 2's, 4's and 6's. I ordered the Wing to engage and we were successful in holding a considerable force of e/a from attacking the bombers. A general mêlée took place with both 109's and 190's. I saw 4 190's approaching from my port beam and I attacked No 1, closing in to 250 yards from approximately starboard beam to quarter. I saw strikes near the cockpit and e/a went into a steep dive; I broke away and watched this FW.190 crash near the target area. By this time the bombers were well on their way out and I ordered the Wing to cover the rear box of bombers, who were being attacked. We ourselves were subjected to continual nibbling attacks and had to break continually. I asked S/Ldr Bolton (416 Sqdn) to lend a hand, and he replied that he was joining me; he was not seen or heard after this. I ordered my section of 3 a/c into line abreast and directly afterwards an a/c attached itself to my section in No 4 position, line abreast some 300 yards away from me and on my starboard side; so that he was looking into sun. We flew along for some time, when Red 3 (P/O Dowding) called up and said that the a/c was a 109. I instructed him to shoot it down, which order he promptly executed. We reformed in line to see a Fortress disintegrating about 5 miles ahead. We chased several more e/a with inconclusive results but when approx. half way across the Channel I saw 2 190's about 1,000 feet above. I led my section up sun and prepared to attack, but the leader saw us and half rolled and dived vertically downward; No 2 followed and I followed him well out of range. These two e/a continued their vertical dive and No 1 pulled out when very low and made off towards France. No 2 however, was not so fortunate, as he continued his dive and went straight into the sea. We claim this 190 destroyed, shared between Red Section. No one fired.'

The attack on the enemy aircraft took place between 16.30 and 16.48 hours, in the region of Berck and Le Touquet. Johnson claimed one Fw 190 destroyed, the section claimed a third share each in another but, notably, the leader had given the unblooded Dowding his first kill. No 403 Squadron sustained no losses, but No 416 Squadron lost their Commanding Officer, Squadron Leader Foss Bolton, who was shot down and wounded. On 17 May, No 421 (RCAF) 'Red Indian' Squadron replaced No 416, led by Squadron Leader 'Buck' MacNair, who fought in Malta as a Flight Commander.

Such missions into France enabled the Spitfire to fly escort to the B-17s; but the real targets lay inside Germany. And there was still one essential ingredient that the Spitfire Mk IX lacked – the range to take an offensive campaign to the skies over Germany.

On 17 August 1943, two forces of US Eighth Air Force B-17 Fortress bombers set out to bomb the Messerschmitt aircraft factory at Regensburg and the ball-bearing plants at Schweinfurt. These were important targets: ball-bearings were used in many war machines and reduced production would have a knock-on effect throughout the German war industry. The B-17s were escorted as far as the Thunderbolts and Spitfires could take them, and then they were on their own – but the Americans had placed great faith in their bombers' ability to fight their way through with cross cover and good defensive formations – combat boxes. The Regensburg force, led by one of the chief proponents of daylight strategic bombing, General Curtiss LeMay himself, would fly across Europe and land at bases in North Africa. The two combat wings of the Schweinfurt force would fight their way out of Germany and come back to England.

Johnson's Kenley Wing was one of those detailed to escort the force on its way in, as far as the Spitfires could fly. The Spitfires would be flying at maximum range. To extend their radius of action, the Wing took off from Kenley and flew to Bradwell Bay, in Essex, and refuelled before taking off again to rendezvous with the B-17s. The Canadians rendezvoused with the Fortresses over the North Sea. Positioning themselves down-sun and 1,000 feet above the bombers, they took them as far as the Dutch border. Then, with just fuel enough to get back, they headed for home, and the bombers went on with a few P-47 Thunderbolt squadrons for another hundred miles, before the P-47s would have to turn back, and the bombers would be on their own.

The Kenley Wing returned to Bradwell Bay and refuelled. Nearly three hours after landing, they took off to meet the bombers. Four hours after they had left them, they met them over Belgium between Liége and Antwerp. Johnson positioned his wing at 23,000 feet, to act as top cover. The bombers could be seen from over 20 miles away in an intensely blue sky, streaming into the setting sun. Below them on the ground, there were two pyres, marking where the smoke from crashed bombers entwined.

The Fortresses had been subjected to over four hours of flak and fighter attacks. Many of the bombers had been shot down. Others were badly damaged. The two combat wings held together, about ten miles between them. Here and there, bombers which had been damaged and were separated from the defensive boxes, were being picked off by Bf 109s, Bf 110s and Fw 190s.

The USAAF's P-47s had already met the bombers and were fighting over the rear combat wing. The German fighters redoubled their efforts as the Fortresses came within reach of the RAF's Spitfires. The Germans were diving from altitude, condensation trails streaming after them, then they flashed through the bomber boxes, firing.

The Spitfire pilots could only wait until they and the Fortresses converged, helpless to ease their ordeal. Johnson timed his moment, and led his Canadians, hungry for blood, into the defence of the bombers, just as the P-47s, low on fuel, turned for home. The Spitfires were able to make the last leg of the journey safe for the Fortresses.

Johnson firmly held that the Spitfire was the best close-in defensive fighter of all, and that its lack of range was the product of shortsighted Air Ministry policy in the previous two years, and that it left the US bombers unnecessarily exposed over Germany. The Chief of the Air Staff, Portal, refused to have the Spitfire Mk IX developed to take larger internal tanks to enable it to fly to Berlin and back, like the later P-51B Mustang. Many of the

RAF's wing leaders in 1943 felt deeply that they were unable to assist the US Eighth Air Force bombers by escorting them.

Wing Commander Johnson and his Canadians watched with frustration as the air war shifted inexorably to the skies over Germany. The first tangible signs had been the arrival of the P-47 Thunderbolt in England, with 'Gabby' Gabreski. The P-47 was the first effective long-range escort in Allied service, and remained numerically the most important. When the P-47 entered service with the US Eighth Air Force in the United Kingdom in 1943, the fighter pilots' first task was to learn to use its best features – flying high, they swooped on enemy fighters and avoided manoeuvring fights. Within weeks, the P-47 had made a tremendous impact. The first models could take bombers just into Germany; by 1944, models with greater range were escorting them to the Reich's heart.

The P-47 was the first real fighter to take the air war to Germany. Later, in December 1943, when Don Blakeslee took his Anglo-American designed P-51B Mustangs on a 1,000-mile round-trip escort to Kiel, the message for the Reich was plain. It was also plain for the Spitfire pilots: the German skies were the Americans' preserve; the Spitfires would be battlefield weapons.

RAF fighter offensive operations were thus restricted to northern France and the Low Countries, where the Luftwaffe still flew in force. But these were relatively unfruitful areas compared with the skies over the Reich. Summer brought intense fighting, Johnson claimed his twentieth victory on 25 July 1943, the Wing's ninety-ninth. However, the tactical air war was also altering. 'Circuses' and 'Rhubarbs' drew less reaction from the Luftwaffe, although the RAF still lost valuable pilots flying them. The capabilities of the Typhoon fighter-bombers brought new tactics, as they strafed and bombed Luftwaffe airfields and other targets, destroying fighters on the ground or stinging them into the air for the Spitfires which flew above them.

In this kind of fighting Johnson preferred to lead two rather than three squadrons as a wing. A wing leader's task was to bring a concentrated force into action, using pre-mission instructions and the fighter controller's radar-directed instructions. Johnson found that fighters in a larger formation – thirty-six, as flown by the Tangmere and other wings in 1941, rather than twenty-four, as flown by the Kenley Wing – tended to obstruct one another. Johnson retained a reflector sight until after the war, preferring it to the gyroscopic sight which he thought demanded too much attention for safety.

In August 1943, the Kenley Wing became No 127 Wing, No 83 Group, Second Tactical Air Force. The Second Tactical Air Force was to be the air element of the Allied forces, undertaking an interdiction campaign before the invasion and then operating from Continental bases, after the invasion of Europe. In preparation, the Wing operated from a rough field in Kent (127 Airfield, at Headcorn) during August 1943.

Shortly, Johnson handed over command of No 127 Wing to his protégé Hugh Godefroy for, in September, bureaucracy caught up with Johnson, and ordered him out of active combat. He was posted to No 11 Group Headquarters, RAF Uxbridge, as a staff officer. He worked with USAAF officers co-ordinating the fighter escorts for the Eighth and Ninth Air Forces over Europe. The Americans valued the RAF's advice and learnt rapidly, and Johnson found the experience valuable. He also exerted his influence at HQ to have 'Rhubarbs' discontinued.

However, he loathed being grounded and flew with combat units regularly to keep in contact with the tactical situation. He flew with his old wing, which he wrote later was a mistake for any ex-Commanding Officer to do. He flew with other Spitfire Mk IX squadrons. In October 1943, Wing Commander Johnson flew combat sorties in a Spitfire Mk XII with the Tangmere Wing. This mark had really changed tactics.

The Typhoon and the Spitfire Mk IX were not the only solutions to the problem of tackling the Fw 190. Whereas the Spitfire Mk IX countered the Fw 190 at 'fighting' altitudes in the air superiority war over France, the Spitfire Mk XII was built for the low-altitude interception role to combat the low-level Fw 190 intruder raids that began in mid-1942. The Mark XII was a 'panic version' of the Spitfire produced to utilize the power advantage of the newly available Griffon over the Merlin, and the manoeuvrability edge of the basic Merlin-Spitfire airframe over the Fw 190.

The Mark XII was the first production Griffon-engined Spitfire. One hundred were built, using Mark VIII and IX airframes from existing contracts and fitted with stronger longerons and a single-stage supercharger 1,735hp Griffon Mk IIB or III. The Mark XII had the universal or C type armament.

The Mark XII had a fantastic performance low down: its speed at sea-level was high for its day, 346mph, rising to 386mph at 18,000 feet. It had a ceiling of 39,000 feet, but was rarely fought above 20,000 feet. It had an excellent initial rate of climb, 4,750 feet a minute. Its low-altitude role dictated clipped wings, which gave a manoeuvrability edge over the full elliptical wing below 15,000 feet.

Johnson perceived the change in tactics imposed by the new Spitfire and its different powerplant, and decided to fly a sortie in it. The Mark XII fully equipped two squadrons, No 41 from February 1943 until December 1944, and No 91 from April 1943 until March 1944. These formed the Tangmere Wing in 1943. The tactics employed by the wing leader, Ray Harries, were extraordinary.

Johnson flew as wingman to Harries, very uneasy about the tactics. They were flying at just 12,000 feet – a suicidal height, an invitation to be bounced. But that was the idea: Harries's tactic of tempting the Fw 190s down from their best fighting altitude to attack the Mark XII at its best altitude had produced great results, for the Mark XIIs were capable of beating anything at low altitude. It is a clear example of how technical change can affect tactics. The Wing was not bounced on Johnson's flight with it.

It was not only the British who were making technical advances. Continual development of the Fw 190 brought repeated performance improvements. When the RAF countered the Fw 190A with the Spitfire Mks IX and XII, the Luftwaffe matched it with the 'long-nosed' Fw 190D. There were many tough battles ahead.

CHAPTER 25
Offensive Air Support

On 21 November 1943, Stan Turner was again given command of a wing, No 244 Wing, taking over from 'Smithy' Duncan Smith. Turner was an excellent shot, a fine leader in the air and on the ground, and a gifted fighter tactician. However, he had tended to upset senior officers by speaking his mind rather more directly than British decorum could tolerate. In the next six months, his performance in command of No 244 Wing marked him as one of the great fighter leaders.

No 244 Wing was an experienced wing. It had been officially formed by Middle East Air Order No 409 of 2 February 1942 as a 'Mobile Offensive Fighter Wing which will control three fully mobile fighter squadrons at any required location'.

It now comprised four squadrons, Nos 92, 145, 417 (RCAF) and 601. Turner had commanded No 417 Squadron, until his promotion to Acting Wing Commander and posting to Wing HQ as Wing Commander Flying. He was well acquainted with the functioning of the Wing. The Officer Commanding was Group Captain C. B. F. Kingcome, DSO, DFC and Bar, who had been in the post since the post of Officer Commanding a Wing became that of a group captain, rather than a wing commander, in July 1943. The Wing had too many Wing Leaders during early 1943, until Wing Commander D. G. S. Duncan-Smith, DSO, DFC and Bar, arrived on 22 July, on posting as Wing Commander Flying. He had a longer tenure than his predecessors and left on promotion to acting group captain to command No 324 Wing.

Turner's first week in command of No 244 Wing brought some tough fighting, with the British Eighth Army's assault on the German line on the River Sangro in full swing. However, by this stage in November, the Wing's three air defence squadrons, Nos 92, 145 and 417, had destroyed only three enemy aircraft and damaged three. In addition, No 601 Squadron, devoted to ground assault since October, had destroyed an Fw 190 and two SM.79s on 3 November, and damaged an Me 210 on the 7th, all on the ground. On 26 November, Flying Officer Minto of No 145 Squadron added a rare bird to the Wing's bag, an Me 410.

Then, on 28 November, matters changed. No 145 Squadron brought down a Bf 109 and No 92 Squadron destroyed a Bf 109 and an Fw 190 and damaged two Fw 190s (one of which the Wing was quite sure was a kill, but Higher Authority would not allow it).

However, that day was not good for ground targets, as No 601 Squadron only came across worthwhile targets once. In the early afternoon they spotted two 3-tonners with trailers on a road near Popoli. They destroyed one of the lorries and damaged the other and both trailers. They also shot up a staff car in the area. This amounted to: '1 M/T. dest. 4 M/T dam.'

Next day, 29 November 1943, the Allied air offensive continued against the enemy positions around Lanciano. No 244 Wing flew nine patrols over the battle area, but not one enemy aircraft was seen. The only air activity was Allied, in support of the Eighth Army which was forcing the German Sangro line back against 'stubborn but diminishing resistance'.

Wing Commander Turner led one section of No 417 Squadron on a patrol over the battle zone. He reported that British artillery was heavily shelling a ridge north-west of Casoli. The German artillery batteries were putting up no counter-fire, or any resistance.

No 601 Squadron was patrolling over the battlefield throughout the day, waiting for targets. On their last patrol, the squadron had to miss some good targets because of flak. One aircraft was hit and had to land wheels-up at base. There might have been no enemy fighter opposition, but the flak remained effective and seemed to be heavier in some areas than others.

The following day, 30 November, Luftwaffe operations again intensified. The Wing's three air defence squadrons intercepted over forty enemy aircraft. The Spitfires fulfilled their primary objective and prevented almost all the enemy aircraft getting through to their targets, into the bargain destroying four certainly and one probably, and damaging another.

No 92 Squadron was the first in successful action that day. A force of over ten Fw 190s and Bf 109s was seen strafing the road to the west of the Sangro. A section of two aircraft led by Lieutenant Bertie Sachs dived upon them. (Sachs was South African and his brother had joined the Luftwaffe – and now flew Bf 109s in Italy!) Sachs selected his target – an Fw 190 – and bored in on its tail. He closed right up, then pressed the red button on his control column with his thumb – a steady burst. His fire was deadly accurate, and the Fw 190 went out of control and crashed near Guardiagrele.

Sachs, with his wingman still clinging to his wingtip, looked around for another target, but Warhawks had also attacked. Warhawks were ill-disciplined. Sachs watched one Warhawk make an ineffective attack on an Fw 190, then break away. He closed in on the same Fw 190 and fired, hammering cannon shells into its wing roots. But then a Warhawk flew right through his sights . . . Sachs's thumb recoiled from the red button . . . he stopped firing . . . but when the Warhawk was clear, so was his target. By then, the other German fighter-bombers had scattered, and the rest of the No 92 Squadron Spitfires did not get a chance to engage them. There were several such encounters with Warhawks.

After midday, the enemy's opposition increased, with Jabo operations against ground targets. British battle area patrols were increased in response. Wing Commander Turner led sections of No 92 Squadron on a patrol. Turner spotted a formation of twelve Fw 190s, jockeying for position near the Sangro. They were about to bomb one of the bridges across the river. Turner set his Spitfires up, quickly, as there was little time.

If the Fw 190s succeeded in destroying the bridge, they would seriously hamper the British advance. The Focke-Wulfs were pressing their attack with determination in the face of ground defences, but the instant the fighter-bomber pilots saw the Spitfires curving in above them, they panicked. Even before the Spitfires had closed to lethal range, the Fw 190 formation had broken, the pilots jettisoning their bombs and boosting their engines. Turner and several of his pilots fired at the Fw 190s, but such was the confusion, they could make no claims.

Again, the primary objective of the Spitfires had been accomplished – preventing the fighter-bombers bombing. Turner's success in routing this attack was of vital importance to the Sangro battle. This action showed the folly of unescorted fighter-bomber sorties in an area where the enemy held air superiority. It was a basic tenet of the Desert Air Force that the air superiority battle had to be won before the fighters could be turned into fighter-bombers.

At the same time, another section of four Spitfires from No 92 Squadron was on patrol over Casoli. They intercepted eight Fw 190s. The Axis airmen stayed to fight, and shot down Flight Sergeant Brister. He baled out and managed to land behind Allied lines. When shortly he returned to the Wing, he claimed an Fw 190 destroyed, but the claim could not be verified either by eyewitnesses or by wreckage.

No 417 Squadron saw the four No 92 Squadron Spitfires engage the Fw 190s over Casoli, so they climbed to 28,000 feet to seek other prey. At about the same altitude, they saw Fw 190 fighter-bombers approaching from the west. No 417 Squadron turned into the enemy fighter-bombers. As they did so, the enemy aircraft jettisoned their bombs and tried to escape. Warrant Officer Johnson fired on one Fw 190. Smoke poured from it and it slowed. Johnson . . .

> '. . . throttled back and flying alongside it, drew level with the cockpit which was a mass of flames. He then fell back and came in astern for a final attack which sent the 190 into the deck 6 miles South West of Cheiti.' [ORB].

Flying Officer Eastman attacked a second Fw 190 which exploded and crashed into the sea off the mouth of the Sangro. Flying Officer O'Brian attacked another which began to pour out smoke, and tried to return over the German lines. A pyre of smoke east of Guardiagrele suggested that it crashed. O'Brian claimed a probable.

No 92 Squadron flew the last mission of the day. Ground control reported enemy aircraft in their vicinity. A section of two Spitfires, led by Flying Officer 'Curly' Henderson, was detached to deal with them. They caught one Fw 190 and two Bf 109s, diving gently towards the mouth of the River Sangro. Reasoning that the fighters were on a tactical reconnaissance mission, Henderson selected the Fw 190, and closed in. He fired, and the Fw 190 went over on to its back, belching smoke. It crashed north of Fossacesia.

Desert Air Force wings were fully mobile, self-contained, flexible, multi-role organizations, capable of mounting a variety of operations simultaneously, and of responding swiftly to developing air and ground situations.

The squadrons in a wing would be assigned to particular tasks, but often sections would be the most appropriate tactical unit, and a section was always two pairs of fighters – still, in this kind of warfare, the most sensible formation.

For day-to-day operational control, No 244 Wing came under the US 64th Fighter Wing, but was a Desert Air Force formation. It comprised four squadrons. Nos 92, 145 and 417 Squadrons were assigned to air combat roles. While one squadron might be employed patrolling the bomb-line to prevent enemy fighter-bomber attacks, another might be escorting medium bombers, and another might be operating in a freelance role. The Wing's fourth unit was No 601 Squadron which from October operated in the ground-attack role.

At first, No 601 Squadron was engaged in interdiction work, chiefly against road and rail transport. This was a concrete task upon which the unit could gain experience. Later, their expertise extended to battlefield support. During October, its first month of tactical operations, No 601 Squadron had destroyed one locomotive, fifteen railway trucks and forty-one motor transports and had damaged nine locomotives, thirteen wagons and twenty-three motor transports. In addition, it had destroyed two aircraft and damaged a further seven on the ground.

November showed a marked improvement in No 601 Squadron's skills, and the pilots demonstrated the flexibility of high-performance, heavily armed single-seat aeroplanes. On 2 November, the squadron had an excellent anti-railway strike, destroying two locomotives and thirteen wagons. Next day, it attacked a landing ground and destroyed two SM.79s and an Fw 190 and damaged two other aircraft. By the end of the month, the squadron had destroyed a further four locomotives and two wagons, and had damaged eleven locomotives and forty-one wagons. It had also destroyed twenty-eight motor transports and damaged forty. There was great similarity in the use of the Spitfire to that on 'Rhubarbs' over France and Belgium but in Italy their work could be seen to have a cumulative effect on the battlefield.

Although the Allied fighter-bombers were outstandingly successful, the Allied ground offensive had lost its momentum, hampered by the enemy, long supply lines and winter's approach. Bad rain swamped airfields, too. The Allied offensive had been halted by the formidable Gustav Line south of Rome, centred on Monte Cassino, at the end of Autumn 1943. German fighter and fighter-bomber resistance increased in November and Spitfires fought as fighters again, mainly RAF Mark VIIIs and the two USAAF Spitfire groups, inflicting heavy losses on the Germans but notably on the Fw 190 ground-attack Gruppen. As had been established, before successful support operations could take place, the air superiority battle had to be going in the aggressor's favour, if not won outright, before fighter-bombers could succeed. The Germans were not in this position, and their losses were high. The Allies decided to 'leap-frog' and make an amphibious landing at Anzio, north of the Gustav Line.

The winter of 1943–44 brought a brief respite on the east coast, but on the west coast air operations entered their third phase with the landings at Anzio on 22 January 1944 – Operation SHINGLE – intended to leap-frog the

Allies past the Gustav Line and Rome. Most of the Desert Air Force moved to the Naples area in support of the Anzio landings, some 850 fighters, fighter-bombers and bombers assembling. Although Allied air operations prevented any Luftwaffe reconnaissance and SHINGLE effected complete surprise, the Luftwaffe reacted viciously, flying bombers and torpedo-planes from southern France to reinforce the Rome-area air bases. Some of the fiercest air fighting of the Italian campaign took place in this period, with Spitfires heavily involved. Thereafter, Luftwaffe resistance by day was scarce and fell off at night and the Spitfires went increasingly over to fighter-bomber work, beginning to fly the 'cab-ranks', or 'Rover David' missions.

The Fifth Army's January 1944 offensive across the Garigliano to Monte Cassino had petered out, and German resistance remained strong. However, Operation STRANGLE began in March, a full-scale interdiction campaign to cut the German lines of movement and supply – a demonstration of the true use of tactical air power, in which Spitfires played a full part.

Now, the armies and the air forces were co-operating to a uniquely close degree. HQ Desert Air Force, under Air Vice-Marshal Harry Broadhurst, who had pioneered tactical air power in the Desert, and Army Advanced HQ were both based at Vasto on the east coast and were highly integrated. The RAF's fighter-bombers employed the very effective 'cab-rank' tactics, and 'Rover David'. Sections of fighter-bombers circled behind the front in radio contact with forward observation posts. The pilots and ground observers each had copies of a gridded map; the ground controller identified a grid square and features within it to the fighter leader, and pinpointed the target. The aircraft circled the designated target area, located the target – it might be a large house or a concealed mortar emplacement – and attacked. Points of resistance which could hold up ground troops for hours or days could be dealt with in minutes, and aircraft could take out smaller concealed targets that were difficult for artillery.

It was usual for Spitfires to be assigned tasks on a squadron rather than a wing basis, the wing being an administrative body. Different tasks were assigned to squadrons in a wing. This required flexible use of the aircraft available, and the unequal distribution of the Spitfire Mks V, VIII and IX. It needed good management for which wings were ideal. The Spitfires continued with bomb-line patrols in addition to their other tasks.

During the Anzio operations, Wing Commander Stan Turner's No 244 Wing was based at Marcianise and Canne. On 28 January 1944, the Luftwaffe made a considerable effort over Anzio. No 244 Wing had three interceptions. A pair of No 92 Squadron Spitfires had been scrambled to search for a US Navy PT Boat which was carrying a VIP and had reported that it was being attacked by enemy aircraft. The Spitfire pilots did not find the PT Boat. At 11.40 hours, they spotted eight Bf 109 Jabos diving towards Anzio. The Axis pilots spotted the Spitfires, and immediately jettisoned their bombs. Black smoke belched from their exhausts as the Bf 109s accelerated. The Spitfires followed fast, but the Bf 109s pulled away and the Spitfire pilots could not get within gun range.

Shortly before midday, No 417 Squadron was flying a beachhead cover patrol, led by Wing Commander Stan Turner. He spotted six Bf 109s at 16,000 feet approaching the beaches. He turned the Spitfires towards the enemy fighter-bombers, and attacked. Turner fired two bursts into one Bf 109, but saw no results. Flight Lieutenant Everard also fired at a Bf 109 but saw no results. Turner selected another Bf 109 and fired, but again without result. One Bf 109 was seen to crash into the sea and was claimed for the squadron as destroyed.

Meanwhile, Everard latched on to a Bf 109 and chased it to the north. His gunfire blew a panel off the enemy's port wing and it began to pour out black smoke. But he could not finish it off because two Warhawks cut in like starlings, attacking both the Bf 109 and the Spitfire. They fired on Everard and forced him to break off. The Warhawks went after the Bf 109. Everard could only claim a damaged.

This was not the only brush with the Warhawks that the Wing had that day – but it was a one-way game. No 92 Squadron were covering the shipping off Anzio. They located twelve Fw 190 fighter-bombers which were escorted by a cover force of eight Bf 109s. Warhawks were already engaging them, but when the No 244 Wing Spitfires 'tried to pick off the stragglers, the Warhawks cut in every time and edged us out.'

All the Allied fighter wings operating over Anzio that day brought down twenty-one enemy aircraft. No 244 Wing's share of the total was one destroyed and one damaged, despite determined efforts. Yet, again, the main purpose was achieved: protecting the beaches and the shipping, not racking up victories.

During January 1944, the Wing flew 1,909 operational sorties, totalling 2,816.05 hours' flying. By then, the Wing had claimed a total of 348 victories, plus 101 'probables' and 299 'damaged' (including seventy-five, twenty-seven and 107 respectively scored by squadrons no longer with the Wing). Of the remaining victories, No 92 Squadron claimed the lion's share, 103, which it added to its already impressive tally. No 145 Squadron followed with ninety-two victories, and No 601 with sixty-seven. The newest squadron with the Wing, No 417 trailed with eleven. All the squadrons had victories from the period before they had joined the Wing: respectively, 194, 101, 136 and two.

On 6 February 1944, No 244 Wing, flying from Marcianise and Canne, was supporting the Anzio fighting. All four squadrons were engaged in air superiority work, with No 601 Squadron reassigned from ground-attack and interdiction. The weather was poor. It was a frustrating day.

On its way to Anzio, No 145 Squadron heard a report of forty-plus enemy aircraft in the area. By the time they had arrived on the scene, another squadron had dealt with them and they were gone. Other reports came in. They led to nothing. Then vapour trails were spotted at altitude. No 145 Squadron's top section climbed rapidly to intercept them, gained on the enemy aircraft, and identified two Fw 190s, but could not catch them because the section leader's engine began to cut out.

Nos 92 and 601 Squadrons had even less luck. No 92 Squadron escorted an attack by Bostons north of the bomb-line without incident. The Luftwaffe rarely intercepted bombers. Later, No 601 Squadron was detailed to escort a wing of thirty-six Marauders, but the bombers missed their rendezvous with the squadron through bad weather.

The next day, 7 February, the air offensive increased in tempo, and No 244 Wing had greater success. In the morning, No 601 Squadron was on patrol over Anzio when they intercepted twelve to fifteen Fw 190s. 'Curly' Henderson, now a flight lieutenant, caught one which crashed and fired on another which he claimed as damaged.

At about the same time, No 417 Squadron had a strange but not unique experience when they were escorting forty-eight Marauders to Palo. The bombers had just bombed their target and were turning for home. The Spitfire pilots scanned the sky around and above them. An extra aircraft joined Yellow Section:

> 'To general surprise this was seen to be a lone 109, which had tacked itself on to our formation in the sadly mistaken belief that it was among friends.' [ORB].

No 417 Squadron's Commanding Officer, Squadron Leader Houle, 'seized the chance to show the rest of the squadron how a Hun should be shot down.' [ORB].

The German pilot had realized his error and tried to escape. Despite his initial mistake, he showed talent. Houle had quite a task trying to draw a bead on the Bf 109. Finally, he closed in to point-blank range – twenty yards – and fired. The Bf 109 blew up. Houle flew right through the debris, and bits festooned his aeroplane. The German pilot managed to bale out of his disintegrating machine at 300 feet.

In the afternoon, No 601 Squadron was on patrol over Anzio. They spotted twelve Fw 190 fighter-bombers coming in to attack, but the AA gunners also spotted the enemy aircraft. The flak batteries opened up on the aircraft – which made the interception very hazardous for the Spitfires. Despite the black bursts of flak all round, two pilots, Flying Officers Ibbotson and Yarnell, each damaged an Fw 190. Between the Spitfires and the flak, the bombers' attack failed.

The next day, the Luftwaffe was very active over the Anzio beaches, but the Wing did not get its 'full share of the pickings' [ORB]. Two Bf 109s were seen shadowing No 417 Squadron when it flew to Anzio for its first patrol. Squadron Leader Houle ordered the top section to intercept them, but the Bf 109s climbed away into the clouds the instant the section began to climb. A little later, four Bf 109s were seen through a break in the cloud cover, taking 'a tentative peek' [ORB], but they also climbed back as soon as they saw the Spitfires.

No 417 Squadron flew another patrol that day, led by Wing Commander Turner. They broke up an attack by over fifteen Bf 109s. Turner damaged two of the Bf 109s, and Warrant Officer Lapointe damaged another.

The following day, 9 February, the Luftwaffe flew about one hundred sorties over Anzio. Again, the Wing was disappointed. Only No 601 Squadron saw anything – two unidentified aircraft which they failed to engage.

The air operations over Anzio were continuous and very tiring, for the pilots and the ground crews who had to keep aeroplanes serviced, repaired, constantly rearmed and refuelled, and monitored for fatigue. Running a wing was a very demanding task, and although Turner was freed from much of the paper work by the Group Captain, he still had a fair burden to shoulder, and direct responsibility for the welfare of all the nearly two thousand men who comprised the Wing. As Bader had found, placing Stan Turner in a position of responsibility was not a risk – he responded with thorough professionalism, and continued to lead his men from the front, by personal example. On 1 March, the Wing was grouped together at Marcianise. The ORB recorded:

> 'As we have been doing more than the lion's share of operations, 64th Fighter Wing ordered a general release for us today, so that pilots and ground crew could relax.'

The same day, Squadron Leader Neville Duke, who had flown with No 92 Squadron in the Wing, returned as Commanding Officer of No 92 Squadron.

Dominated by air support, the Allied spring offensive opened on all fronts in Italy on 11 May 1944. The interdiction campaign had been highly successful and the Gustav Line was rapidly overrun. Monte Cassino fell on 18 May. German resistance in the air was frequently strong. The chief German aeroplanes encountered were the Bf 109 and the more effective Fw 190. The Germans had learnt how to use the Fw 190 in tactical roles on the Russian Front, where it was used extensively and successfully as a fighter-bomber to remedy the Luftwaffe's deficiency in ground-attack aircraft. The Fw 190F fighter-bomber and Fw 190G ground-support aircraft were developed, the latter largely replacing the Ju 87 Stuka as a battlefield aircraft by late 1943.

The Germans also continued to employ the Fw 190 as a fighter. In North Africa, the Fw 190s had as dramatic effect as they had over France, but were too few to be decisive. Fw 190s were rushed to Tunisia in November 1942 to counter the TORCH invasion, forcing the RAF to fly out Spitfire Mk IXs to take them on. Tropicalized Fw 190s served in the Western Desert in 1943, covering the Afrika Korps. When the Allies had invaded Sicily in July 1943, they had encountered five Gruppen. Fw 190s aggressively defended Salerno. Now, the remaining Fw 190 units fought with determination, if not with tactical success, to break the Allied hold on the Anzio beachhead. Fw 190s fought in dwindling numbers in Italy as fighter-bombers and night fighters until the end of the war.

During May 1944, No 244 Wing flew 2,982 operational sorties, amounting to 3,856.25 flying hours. Such figures were not achieved at the expense of serviceability. Under Turner, No 244 Wing had achieved the best serviceability rate in the field, 99.6 per cent. Total claims amounted to twenty-three enemy aircraft 'destroyed', three 'probably destroyed' and twenty 'damaged', all of them fighters or fighter-bombers.

There was plenty to celebrate at the end of May 1944. On 21 May, to the entire Wing's 'delight and satisfaction' [ORB], Stan Turner was awarded the

DSO to add to his DFC. It was a signal for on 28 May Turner was posted to Advanced HQ Desert Air Force as GTI (Fighters). He took over this post from Wing Commander Hugh Dundas, DSO, DFC, who was posted to No 244 Wing in his place as Wing Commander Flying.

Then, on 31 May, the Wing's records were tallied and the Adjutant confirmed that the Wing had destroyed 400 enemy aircraft in its 28 months' existence. The ORB recorded: 'Operations were outshone today by the Wing party held to celebrate our 400th destroyed. . . . W/C Dundas arrived on posting, just in time for the party, naturally.'

Hugh Dundas had served under Air Vice-Marshal Harry Broadhurst at HQ Desert Air Force, until Broadhurst left in March 1944. The HQ was then at Vasto on the east coast of Italy, co-located with Army Advanced HQ. The two HQs were highly integrated, planning the Italian campaigns on a joint Army-Air basis. The experience of being involved with operation preparation and control was very valuable for Dundas when he returned to operations. In March 1944, Dundas's DSO was gazetted, in recognition of his work in the previous year.

Soon after Dundas took over No 244 Wing, it was redesignated a fighter-bomber wing, which Dundas thought a highly dangerous occupation and not for a fighter pilot or for Spitfires. Dundas had become familiar with tactical operations. He had retained his Spitfire Mk IX at No 239 Wing's base. There he had seen at first hand the operations of No 239 Wing, USAAF, who were based at Vasto with P-51 Mustangs. He felt lucky not to be engaged on fighter-bomber work for it seemed to be a high-risk business, but it was not long before Dundas was engaged in just those direct ground support operations. No 244 Wing worked up in the tactical role for a few weeks, learning by trial and error on simple targets – like bridges and road junctions in central Italy – how to use the gunsight as a bombsight and to judge the angle of dive and pull out and time the bomb's release. Dundas's experience at Desert Air Force HQ came in very useful.

Following the Allied spring offensive in May which broke the Gustav Line, Cassino fell, then Rome fell on 5 June 1944. The Allies linked up with the Anzio bridgehead, and consolidated. Now, No 244 Wing's squadrons moved from Venafro on the Adriatic coast to Littorio, near the captured capital. There, six Seafires joined the Wing. Later in the month, the Wing moved to Fabrica. No 244 Wing, still in No 211 Group and comprising Nos 92, 145, 417 (RCAF) and 601 Squadrons, was largely equipped with Spitfire Mk VIIIs and IXs by the end of Summer 1944.

As USAAF units in Italy were reduced, Desert Air Force work increased, but Luftwaffe resistance fell dramatically following the Normandy invasion on 6 June. Within a month, only a few Italian fighter Gruppi and fewer Luftwaffe reconnaissance and one night ground-attack unit remained in Italy, providing little air superiority work. The Allies had the essential component of success in tactical operations: freedom from interference by enemy aircraft. The Wing's duties centred on fighter-bomber and close-support work, roles to which the Spitfire adapted surprisingly well.

From June, Nos 92, 145 and 601 Squadrons did interdiction work, their

**INTERDICTION IN ITALY
June 1944**

Line of Interdiction, 1st June 1944
Railway System ++++++

Spitfires equipped with single 500-pound bombs and using their guns, on tactical targets, for the advance up and through the Gothic Line, a formidable defensive line on the southern edge of the north Italian plain, behind which the Germans had consolidated. The fighter-bombers' targets were roads, bridges, transport, armour, trains, railways, tunnels, observation posts and gun positions. No 417 Squadron flew patrols and bomber escorts, in support of the Eighth Army, and attacking targets of opportunity on armed reconnaissance. No 92 Squadron also maintained a fighter detachment on the west coast of Italy to intercept Luftwaffe photo-reconnaissance aircraft, until September 1944.

No 244 Wing became operational in the close-support role in July 1944, and moved to Italy's east coast in support of the Eighth Army's attack on the Gothic Line. They attacked targets of opportunity, often only a few hundred yards in front of Allied troops. The German anti-aircraft guns put up intense barrages at all altitudes in and around target areas and the work demanded low-level, fast flying. Casualties were heavy. The Spitfires adopted the tactic of attacking the front and rear vehicles of a convoy, then finishing off the jam.

Dundas had his Spitfire's elliptical wingtips removed – 'clipped' – to improve low-level manoeuvrability and the rate of roll, which he considered essential for survival in this environment, although it reduced the lift for take-off at full load from a short strip and for landing. In Italy the average life-span of a Spitfire and pilot was considered to be just three months. At the end of that time, if the Spitfire had survived enemy ground fire or accidents, it would have been so heavily used that it would often be written off.

No 244 Wing had started out as a three-squadron formation, and had expanded to a four-squadron wing. Now, on 24 July 1944, a fifth squadron was added, No 87 Squadron.

During July, the Wing flew a total of 2,488 sorties amounting to 3,079.35 hours. A great deal of the work was in support of Army operations in the battlefield, and the Wing dropped a total of 1,895 bombs, amounting to 472 US tons. No 145 Squadron destroyed the Wing's first tank on 17 July. Interdiction took a secondary place. Total claims for the month amounted to only two railway wagons destroyed by No 601 Squadron on 22 July, and three motor transports destroyed and eleven damaged throughout the month. Counter-air operations were limited, but No 601 Squadron strafed Rimini landing ground on 8 July, destroying one aircraft. There was only one air-to-air victory during the entire month, on 21 July, when Squadron Leader Cox and Lieutenant Manne of No 92 Squadron claimed a Ju 88 destroyed.

The progressive record from the beginning of October 1943, when No 601 Squadron had gone over to tactical operations, until the end of July 1944 was impressive:

Squadron	Locomotives Dest.	Dam.	Railway Trucks Dest.	Dam.	AFVs Dest.	M/T Dest.	Dam.
No 92	–	–	5	–	–	8	4
No 145	–	5	15	53	1	28	91
No 417	–	1	–	6	–	6	11
No 601	30	34	53	89	–	128	113
TOTALS	30	40	73	148	1	170	219

The solitary victory in July brought the Wing's total claim to 427 'destroyed', 109 'probables' and 364 'damaged' (including the seventy-five, twenty-seven and 107 respectively scored by squadrons no longer with the Wing). In the six months since the end of Janaury 1944, No 145 Squadron had rapidly caught up on No 92 Squadron with twenty-eight victories in six months, against No 92's eighteen. As a result, Nos 92 and 145 Squadrons were now neck and neck with 121 each – although No 92 had twenty-five 'probables' and 117 'damaged' against No 145's twenty-six 'probables' and sixty-seven 'damaged'. No 92 Squadron had scored 194 victories before it joined the Wing, and was already bidding fair for the title of top-scoring RAF squadron of World War Two. No 601 Squadron had claimed eighty-three victories and No 417 Squadron twenty-seven, with the Wing, both having claimed sixteen in the last six months.

Now, the wider political issues of the war began to have serious effects on the conduct of air operations in Italy. Most US units and some RAF units were withdrawn to support the invasion of southern France, but there was little Luftwaffe opposition to the invasion.

No 244 Wing had moved to Perugia on 25 July and remained based there until mid-August. In July, King George VI came to Perugia to thank the Wing for its work. On 17 August, No 601 Squadron escorted Churchill's Dakota on a visit to Marciano and Venafro.

Between 16 and 18 August 1944, Dundas was incapacitated by bronchitis, but on the 19th he was leading his pilots again. That day, the Wing undertook several tactical tasks, flying from Perugia. The weather had been poor but improved enough for the Wing to 'show "Rover David" what we could do, and this was plenty' [ORB]. A section of No 145 Squadron Spitfires carrying bombs was first on the cab-rank. 'Rover David' called the section up and gave them a target: 'four buildings enclosing a quadrangle in which were five lorries' [ORB]. The four Spitfires dive-bombed the target and 'scored four direct hits, smothering the place in smoke and dust' [ORB].

Another section of No 145 Squadron was directed towards another target, six camouflaged gun positions. The four Spitfires scored two hits within the target area.

Wing Commander Dundas was leading a section of No 417 Squadron, carrying bombs. They were given the grid reference for another group of guns, lying south of a house. They identified the house, and peeled off. All their bombs registered in the target area. Another section of No 417 Squadron was not so accurate in bombing another gun site, and all its bombs missed the target.

There were several bridges to be destroyed, to hamper the German withdrawal and re-supply. The Spitfires were directed on to several bridges in rapid succession. Direct hits were scored, and railway tracks were cut in many places. No 417 Squadron made another direct hit on the centre of the Lavezzola bridge.

There were no losses to the Spitfires. It was a most satisfactory day. Hard-bitten 'Rover David' even sent a message to compliment the Wing: 'Very satisfactory and accurate bombing. First bomb of first mission was a direct hit on target.' [ORB].

With the departure of the US 12th Tactical Air Command for France, the Desert Air Force was left to support the assault on the Gothic Line, which was due to open at the end of August. On 15 August, No 145 Squadron of No 244 Wing had also left for the invasion of France. In preparation for the assault on the Gothic Line, the other squadrons of No 244 Wing moved to Loreto during August and all went over to the 'cab-rank Rover David' duties controlled by the Army in close support of the advancing armies and continued the interdiction campaign by attacking railway locomotives and wagons. From an advanced base on the Adriatic coast, the Wing played a vital part in softening up tactical targets, No 92 Squadron alone dropping over 108 tons of bombs in the process.

During August, the Wing destroyed three locomotives, sixteen wagons and twenty-two motor transports, and damaged a further seven locomotives, six wagons and nineteen motor transports. The only aerial victories were three Bf 109s destroyed, which brought the Wing's total score at the end of the month to 429 enemy aircraft destroyed.

The assault on the Gothic Line opened on 26 August 1944. It failed, largely because air power in Italy had been depleted. No 244 Wing moved to Fano on the Adriatic coast in September/October, Nos 601 and 417 Squadrons on 5 September, then No 92 Squadron in October, part of the evolving pattern of the campaign. This was the first time that the Wing had been in billets after thirty-one months under canvas.

After the invasion of southern France was firmly established, the new US 22nd Tactical Air Command was formed in Italy with US tactical units and a Spitfire wing, bolstering air support. With little enemy fighter-bomber or bomber presence, the Desert Air Force was mostly fighter-bomber orientated, and interdiction on the Gothic Line continued.

One day in November, the squadrons flew eighteen missions of 108 sorties. On 19 November, the Wing flew twelve missions of fifty-nine sorties against gun positions – that was the day that Dundas was promoted to group captain and granted a permanent commission. He succeeded Brian King-combe in command of No 244 Wing. Dundas was succeeded as wing leader by Wing Commander W. Lovell, but he took every opportunity to fly, despite his administrative responsibilities. For a pilot who had thought little of the idea of using Spitfires for tactical work, Hugh Dundas had come a long way. He was already a polished fighter tactician and had become a leading exponent of army support operations, and now he was the youngest group captain in the RAF.

No 244 Wing moved to Bellaria during December for the winter, Nos 601 and 417 Squadrons on the 4th, No 92 Squadron just before Christmas. It was a hard winter, bringing a lull to the fighting, torrential rain turning airfields into swamps. Nos 417 and 601 Squadrons moved twice in January, first to Udine, then to Cortina where they made their longest stay of the campaign. No 92 Squadron stayed at Fano. During the winter with lower air resistance, tac-air assets in Italy were further reduced.

The intense close-support activity lasted until the hard Italian winter of 1944–45 forced a lull in the fighting, halting the Allies' advance on the River Senio on the east coast. Often cloud was too low for dive-bombing and air support could frequently be prevented. On one occasion with the cloud-base at 1,000 feet, and support urgently needed, Dundas requested that the artillery put down smoke shells where the support was needed, then took a squadron of Spitfires in and, spotting the smoke and guided by forward observation posts, his twelve Spitfires swept down in line abreast and strafed the area. Dundas was mentioned in despatches in early 1945, and in March his bar to the DSO was gazetted.

Three months of fighter-bomber interdiction activity began, with No 244 Wing engaged in striking road, rail and bridge targets in preparation for the reopening of the assault on the Gothic Line. The assault, supported by massive aerial and artillery bombardment, engaging both the Desert Air Force and US 15th Tactical Air Force, reopened in April. The long interdiction campaign had been fully successful: the German defences, shallow and frameless, fell.

The crossing of the River Senio in April 1945 brought the last battle. A number of Spitfire wings were engaged in ground support, which included strafing the north bank of the narrow Senio with Allied troops on the south bank only twenty yards away. Bombing and strafing operations lasted unabated throughout the daylight hours. Dundas had a special belly-rack fitted to his Spitfire to enable two bombs to be carried side-by-side. The Spitfires claimed dozens of armoured fighting vehicles, thousands of supply vehicles and trailers, and scores of coastal and river craft during the last three weeks of war in Italy. As an indication of the intensity of air-ground operations, during April No 601 Squadron became the first tactical squadron in Italy to exceed one thousand operational hours a month, with 1,082, and it also established a monthly record in destroying motor transport, motor-cycles, barges and horse carts. The Germans were finally driven over the River Po into the Alps.

On 1 May, Dundas was confirmed in the substantive rank of wing commander. During his period with No 244 Wing, Dundas added two more enemy aircraft to his personal air combat score, bringing it to eleven confirmed kills. However, in the last months of war, the Wing had concentrated on ground support and there was little air-fighting. On VE Day, Dundas landed back at Treviso after an operational flight and was informed by signal that the war was over. That night there was a massive thrash in the mess, which was rudely interrupted by a message arriving to demand a dawn patrol to escort mysterious trains through the Alps. Dundas led eleven hung-over pilots on this strange, last mission, without event.

Later in May, No 244 Wing moved to Treviso. There, following the German surrender on 2 May, Nos 601 and 417 Squadrons disbanded in May and July respectively. No 92 Squadron did occupation duties, disbanding on 30 December 1946 at Zeltweg, Austria. Group Captain Hugh Dundas spent several months in the environs of Venice, getting used to peace.

CHAPTER 26
'Top Gun'

I t is perhaps not a coincidence that both the top-scoring Royal Air Force and the top-scoring Fleet Air Arm fighter pilots of World War Two should have been trained by Bader – 'Johnnie' Johnson and Dicky Cork. By the end of 1943, with the war definitely going in favour of the Allies on all fronts, both men were very experienced leaders with high reputations throughout the flying services.

On 25 November 1943, Lieutenant-Commander (A) Richard Cork was appointed Wing Leader No 15 Naval Fighter Wing, comprising Nos 1830 and 1833 Squadrons equipped with the latest Fleet fighter, the Corsair. This was an appointment of great importance. The squadrons were working up to embark in HMS *Illustrious* who was bound for the Pacific theatre to form part of a joint US-British carrier force. The squadrons were currently at RNAS Stretton, Lancashire, and due to go to the 'cross-roads' of the FAA, Machrihanish, before embarking at the end of December. Once again Cork was bound for the Far East.

Cork was pleased with the choice of Squadon Commanding Officers. No 1830's Lieutenant-Commander Brian Fiddes was an old friend of Cork's from No 880 Squadron. He knew Brian's qualities. He had become No 880 Squadron's Senior Pilot after it had disembarked from *Indomitable* in 1942. The other Squadron Commander, No 1833 Squadron's Lieutenant-Commander H. A. Monks, DSM★, was a 25-year-old Regular officer who had fought his way up from Boy Seaman. A disciplined, firm leader, he was already an ace. These were men whom Cork respected.

On 10 December 1943, Cork had his first flight in a Corsair. It was a considerable change from the Merlin-powered aeroplanes he had flown so far. The Corsair Mk I was big, heavy and powerful, even to look at. It weighed just over 12,000 pounds, loaded, and came down on the deck, even an armoured deck, with a heavy crump.

In the air, it was better than any FAA fighter and a match for any land-based fighter. It was powered by a 2,000hp Pratt & Whitney R-2800-8 Double Wasp radial. At 25,000 feet, it could achieve 393mph in level flight, and much more when the pilot put the nose down in a dive. It packed a heavy punch – with 0.5-inch machine-guns. It was manoeuvrable, too. It had already gained a reputation as a pilot-killer, and had won the unlovely epithets 'Bent-Wing Bastard' or 'Hose Nose', after its two most noticeable features, the long nose that made forward vision difficult and the gull wings. Vision was improved with a bubble canopy, but No 15 Wing's first aircraft had the original frame-work canopy.

Cork by now had considerable experience of naval fighters and a deep understanding of the nature of naval air warfare. The Navy had groomed him well. After coming out of *Indomitable* following his exemplary service with No 880 Squadron during PEDESTAL, Cork had served on Nos 759 and 760 Squadrons at RNAS Yeovilton as Chief Flying Instructor from 10 September 1942. From 10 April 1943, he had been Chief Flying Instructor at the newly-formed No 2 Naval Flying School, Henstridge, inculcating new pilots with his lore and honing his own skills. He had also flown Spitfire Mk IXs operationally on attachment to Nos 611 and 165 Squadrons, RAF, and had undergone a course at the Fighter Leaders School, gaining valuable insights into current fighter practices.

Cork was well pleased with getting a Corsair wing. His experience of Merlin-engined fighters and his recent exposure to Air Force Spitfires and Naval Seafires might have led Their Lordships to appoint him to the command of one of the Seafire Mk III squadrons being formed. The Seafire was not a wholly satisfactory naval fighter. When the FAA did receive effective fighters, the Hellcat and Corsair, it was important that they had the best leaders for the squadrons flying them – men like Dicky Cork.

Cork's appointment as Wing Leader on 15 November 1943 was greeted with enthusiasm and pride by the pilots of the Wing. He was famous, a legend throughout the FAA. He had flown at the right wingtip of Bader during the Battle of Britain – that guaranteed him attention. Cork introduced the Wing to the 'finger-four' he had first experienced at Tangmere, and had later learnt to perfect. In the States, where they had been formed, the squadrons had learnt to fly in three sections of three in 'Vics' (with one spare aircraft). Now, each with fourteen Corsairs, Nos 1830 and 1833 Squadrons adopted three flights of four machines each (with two spares), and henceforth flew the pair of pairs formation. Each squadron, with fourteen pilots commanded by Fiddes and Monks and their Senior Pilots Lieutenants Bud Sutton (a Canadian) and Norman Hanson, respectively, was divided up into three Flights, as in No 1833 Squadron:

Red – Lieutenant-Commander H. A. Monks, Red 1; Eric Rogers, Red 2; Johnny Baker, Red 3; Steve Starkey, Red 4

Blue – Lieutenant 'Bash' Munnoch, Blue 1; Stan Buchan, Blue 2; Alan Booth, Blue 3; Joe Vickers, Blue 4

White – Lieutenant Norman Hanson, White 1; Neil Brynildsen, White 2; Gordon Aitken, White 3; Reggie Shaw, White 4

The Wing's embarkation in *Illustrious* was attended by tragedy when No 1830 Squadron's Commanding Officer, Brian Fiddes, crashed over the side and was killed. Such accidents were only too familiar with the Corsair whose oleo legs had a 'built-in bounce'. Lieutenant-Commander Mike Tritton took over No 1830 Squadron. He was an Old Etonian, with a natural reserve and cultivated easy authority. He had been a very early Volunteer Reserve applicant for the Fleet Air Arm. He was already part of a legend. He had been one of the pilots who had fought in Malta when they had only a handful of Gladiators and Hurricanes in 1941. A skilful and safe pilot, he did not approve of flashy flying or 'colonial attitudes'. His Senior Pilot became Lieutenant Percy Cole, RNVR.

For the next few days, No 15 Wing worked up. *Illustrious* also embarked two Fairey Barracuda squadrons, Nos 847 and 810, and wore the Flag of Rear Admiral 'Clem' Moody, fitting her to lead a carrier task force, which gave spice to some of the vague rumours circulating about their deployment. On 30 December 1943, they knew: they were going to the Far East, to join the Americans in the fight against the Japanese. At 21.25 hours, they left the Firth of Clyde. On 2 January 1944, the carriers rendezvoused in mid-Atlantic with the battleships HMS *Valiant* and HMS *Queen Elizabeth* and the battle-cruiser HMS *Renown*. In the early morning of 5 January, the fleet steamed through the Straits of Gibraltar. It was eighteen months since Cork had sailed through aboard HMS *Indomitable* with No 880 Squadron to cover PEDESTAL. Now, the Mediterranean was a far safer place.

No 15 Wing went to work in the Mediterranean. Some of Cork's shine began to rub off on them. He drove his men hard. They flew frequently, practice ADDLs, formations, air gunnery, strafing, tactics, escorts . . . until on 27 March 1944, in the Indian Ocean, *Illustrious* rendezvoused with her American counterpart, the USS *Saratoga*.

Embarked in *Saratoga* was the crack, battle-hardened Air Group 12 with SBD Dauntlesses, TBM Avengers and F6F Hellcats. The Air Group's commander was J. C. 'Jumping Joe' Clifton, who flew a Hellcat. Clifton was as much a legend in the US Naval Air Service as was Cork in the FAA. They were a combination that ought to worry the Japanese. Kenneth Poolman wrote that Cork and Clifton 'came together like left hand and right hand from the start – two great flying sailors, two great and gallant gentlemen, representative, each man, of the very best our two countries can produce.'

After meeting, the force shaped course for Trincomalee. On 31 March, both carriers flew off their aircraft to China Bay, then entered harbour. The two air groups spent the next fortnight getting to know each other and working up as a co-ordinated strike force.

On Friday, 14 April 1944, a dawn exercise was scheduled for *Illustrious*. The Corsairs were to take off before dawn, join up and land at China Bay just after sun-up. The wind was unreliable. The Corsairs waited on deck in the pre-dawn gloom as *Illustrious* manoeuvred. Cork, as Wing Leader, was first in line. *Illustrious* got enough wind over the bow to help the Corsairs off. Cork was waved off. But the breeze fell just as he lifted off. His Corsair stumbled into the air. Only his experience held her there.

The wind was not yet reliable. 'Wings' cancelled flying and called off the operation. Cork continued to circle. He could not land back on. There was no room on the deck, crowded with two dozen Corsairs, prepared for flying-off. Commander Flying instructed him to go to China Bay and land. He radioed a cheerful acknowledgment.

When he arrived over the airfield, a new pilot, Anderson, was on the runway preparing to take off to undertake his deck landing training on *Illustrious*. Cork was given a 'red' on the Aldis lamp by the RAF Controller. He pulled up his undercarriage, veered away and went round again.

He circled, then dropped his undercarriage for a second approach. He was preoccupied with his responsibilities, and anxious to get down. For some reason Cork ignored a repeated 'red' lamp and a red Very signal.

Anderson saw him coming. He could have swung off the runway into the jungle which would have done little damage to his tough Corsair. But he was an inexperienced young man, and he did not know this, for the tailwheel locked in preparation for take-off. He sat in his cockpit and winked his navigation lamps at the oncoming Corsair.

Cork settled down on his approach, touched down and crashed head-on into Anderson's Corsair in the middle of the runway. Both Corsairs burst into flames on impact. They burnt out completely. Both pilots were killed. They were buried at Trincomalee the next day.

Cork's death was a tragic loss. It was not only the pilots of his wing who mourned him. He was regarded almost as a god by younger fighter pilots, and his reputation was invaluable to the FAA both as a role model and for morale. With a final score of at least thirteen victories, Cork remains the highest-scoring FAA fighter pilot.

The two Squadron Commanders, Hanson and the more senior Tritton, now jointly ran No 15 Wing. On 19 April, the two Air Groups made their first strike, against Sabang in Sumatra. The targets were the oil storage tanks, the airfield and the submarine base. On this, the Royal Navy's first Corsair operation in the Far East, Nos 1830 and 1833 Squadrons flew close escort to the Barracudas, and then strafed. No 15 Naval Fighter Wing acquitted itself in exemplary fashion. Dicky Cork had trained his men well.

☆　　　　　　☆　　　　　　☆

In March 1944, Wing Commander James Johnson was posted to command No 144 Airfield, No 83 Group, Second Tactical Air Force. It was an RCAF wing which had been formed on 9 February from Nos 441, 442 and 443 Squadrons at RAF Digby. Early in April, No 144 Wing became operational at Tangmere, flying escorts and sweeps. A month later, it moved to RAF Hurn, near Bournemouth. On 12 May, it became No 144 RCAF (Fighter) Wing, a fighter-bomber wing. The three squadrons' Spitfire Mk IXs were fitted with two improvised underwing bomb racks. This adaptation of the Spitfire's role was necessary as part of the co-ordinated plan to destroy the enemy's communications and radar facilities in preparation for the invasion of Europe.

Tactical air attack capability is essential to all armed forces. A tactical aircraft is tasked with supporting ground forces by reconnaissance, bombing and strafing battlefield targets and with disrupting communications and transport networks and enemy reinforcement operations in support of the objectives of air and ground force commanders within and around a battlefield. In the first phase of an operation, bomber types would be used under the protection of fighters. The objective of the fighters is to secure air superiority. Once that has been attained, by defeating the enemy's fighters, then the fighters themselves will go over to fighter-bomber roles.

Many fighter pilots, including Johnson, were neither enthusiastic about, nor convinced of the wisdom of, using the Spitfire in tactical roles. They felt that the Spitfire was not suitable for such rugged, rather mundane fighting – it was intended for the rather more stylish fighting of fighter-versus-fighter. Later, many fighter pilots recanted, including Johnson. Immediately after the invasion, the wing's primary task would be air superiority, and only after that had been secured would it assist as light bomber, dive-bomber and ground-attack aircraft in isolating the battle areas and in interdiction.

As a fighter-bomber wing, No 144 Wing's Spitfires were equipped with underwing bomb racks. The E wing normally carried two 20mm cannon mounted in the outboard cannon positions and two 0.5-inch machine-guns. Bomb racks were fitted below the outboard cannon mounts, which, on the E wing, was found to cause buckling which could lead to structural failure.

Despite the change in role, Johnson's air combat score increased. On 5 May, Johnson stalked and destroyed an Fw 190 which he found flying low and alone. He claimed another Fw 190 later that month. Its pilot jettisoned the canopy and began to clamber over the side before Johnson fired. Johnson fired. The pilot dropped away, his parachute deploying. As Bader had found in 1941, a claim of 'frightened' was insufficient to gain a victory.

In late May, the Wing moved to RAF Ford, Sussex, in the centre of the invasion build-up area. Tanks and soldiers were everywhere. Invasion stripes were painted on Allied aircraft on 4 June and the next day No 144 Wing was detailed to form part of the force protecting the invasion force's eastern flank from air attack – a fighter pilot's job again. At dawn on D-Day, Johnson led the Wing over the invasion beaches, but for three days the German fighters did not appear.

On the afternoon of 8 June, Johnson took his wing into the first Allied landing ground in France, Croix-sur-Mer. It was near Caen, and had just been finished by the RAF Commandos. Johnson was detailed to carry out a sweep, then land at St Croix. The first Spitfire landed at 13.30 hours. By 14.00 hours, all the Wing's Spitfires had been serviced and refuelled and were taxi-ing for take-off. The Wing carried out a sweep before returning to Ford, thus becoming the first RAF unit to operate from France since June 1940. The stay was temporary because the area had still to be secured. A contemporary news release ran:

> 'The first Spitfire wing to land in France is now giving the Allies close air support from an advanced base. Led by W/C Johnnie Johnson, the planes took off from an English airfield, swept 20 miles inland from the beaches over the Caen area and landed on an airstrip prepared by RAF Commandos. The first Spitfire touched down at 1.30 p.m. on 10 June, within 20 minutes they were fully serviced and refuelled.'

No 144 Wing became the first Canadian wing based in Europe.

Luftwaffe reinforcements had arrived and Allied and German fighters fought daily. The Germans were on the defensive over both Germany and France. Although the Luftwaffe operated in large formations over Germany, over France it operated in small units. The RAF, too, found that large formations were tactically unsuitable in France. Combats were small-scale, and responses had to be rapid. Moreover, the latest aircraft were difficult to keep together effectively in large formations.

In response to this tactical perception, in early July the three Canadian Spitfire wings in France, Nos 126, 127 and 144, which were operating in co-ordination, were re-formed into two wings, Nos 126 and 127, within which squadrons operated separately, affording tactical flexibility. Johnson became wing leader of No 127 Wing – Nos 403, 421 and 442 Squadrons, RCAF. It had formed as No 127 Airfield (RCAF) on 11 July 1943, and now became No 127 (Fighter) Wing, RCAF, on 12 May 1944. It disbanded on 7 July 1945.

When Johnson had been appointed Wing Commander Flying of No 144 Wing in March 1944, he had twenty-five victories. He became the subject of increasing Press interest as his score closed on that of the RAF's top-scoring fighter pilot, 'Sailor' Malan, who was no longer flying operationally. On 16 June, Johnson shot down an Fw 190. One Bf 109 destroyed on 22 June, two on 28 June, and one on 30 June brought their scores level. On 5 July, Johnson destroyed two Bf 109s. The Press feted him. However, he maintained that Malan had fought defensive warfare in small units against heavy odds, but he himself fought offensive warfare, usually in wing strength. The job of a fighter leader – of a section, squadron or wing – was to ensure that his pilots destroyed as many enemy aircraft as possible, not to gain personal victories. Teamwork was essential to ensure maximum offensive and defensive effectiveness, flushing out and stalking the enemy to bring as many guns to bear as possible.

Throughout the campaign in north-east France, the Spitfire units' primary function was to protect the Typhoon fighter-bombers, either by escorting them, or by gaining local air superiority. They also engaged in extensive ground-attack work. Over the Falaise Gap, where the Allies were concentrating their assault, the Germans put up a massive fighter umbrella to cover their withdrawal on the ground, and there was a period of intense and costly fighting.

No 127 Wing was based some 25 miles from Falaise, and fought hard over the area. Johnson destroyed two Fw 190s on 23 August, but his aircraft was also hit for the first time by enemy fire. After the combat, and isolated from the Wing, he had tried to join a formation of six aircraft. He realized too late that they were Bf 109s. He eluded them with difficulty, but not before one had put a cannon shell through a wing root. After landing, he flew another Spitfire into combat immediately – and collected flak shrapnel in the tail.

After the Germans had retreated, the Wing rested for three weeks west of Paris. It moved on 19 September to Le Culot in Belgium to provide support for the fighter-bombers and ground forces during the Arnhem operation. On 27 September, Johnson shot down an Fw 190, his thirty-eighth victory, and his last.

The Fw 190 remained the German equivalent of the Spitfire, used in air combat and tactical roles, and continued to be met by RAF pilots until the last day of the war. The Fw 190 was held in high regard by its pilots and by Allied pilots who fought it. It was superior in performance, firepower, ruggedness, handling and fighting powers to the Bf 109. The Fw 190D was equal to the Spitfire Mk IX and XIV and P-51D Mustang, a fast, manoeuvrable, punishing dogfighter. Allied bomber crews feared it by day and night. It fought the Allied tactical air forces in Normandy through Falaise and into Germany, and in Italy.

However, in late October, when No 144 Wing had moved to airfield B.82 (Grave in Holland), they faced an entirely different proposition. Now, the first Messerschmitt Me 262 fighter-bombers appeared, attacking Second Tactical Air Force bases. The jet-propelled Me 262 completely outclassed the Spitfire. Standing patrols brought little protection. Later, the fighter version began to appear in small numbers. Fortunately for the Allies, their appearance was too late and too minimal to affect the air superiority war. Had they appeared in June 1944, the air battle would have been a very different contest.

The Wing soon moved to B.56 (Evère, near Brussels). In early December 1944, it partly re-equipped with the Spitfire Mk XVI. No 403 Squadron exchanged its Spitfire Mk IXs for the Mark XVI on 4 December. Several pilots were lost flying this mark when the American-built Packard Merlin 266s caught fire in flight because of faulty quality control in the factory, which failed to detect cracks in piston big ends. The Packard Merlins did not have the performance under boost of the Rolls-Royce version, and pilots were almost unanimous in their preference for the British-engined Spitfire variant – the Mark IX.

A member of Johnson's wing, F. W. Town, a young Canadian flying officer who flew with No 403 Squadron, RCAF, between June 1944 and June 1945, had this to say about the Spitfire Mk XVI:

> 'Our work was not of the Battle of Britain nature but mainly air to ground pressing a retreating army. . . . We hated to see the Spitfire Mk IX leave for it was the ultimate in Spitfires with the Rolls-Royce engine and elliptical wings. Now we were given the Mark XVI and, ultimately, it was a wonder it ever got off the ground. We could carry two 500-pound bombs and a slipper tank, but the Packard Merlin did not compare as there were many times when the crankcase and pistons could not handle the boost. Three feet clipped off the wing span and taking off from a grass field or a quickly laid strip certainly did not help the lift at take-off.'

On 1 January 1945, the Luftwaffe launched Operation BODENPLATTE, intended to be a decisive blow against the Second Tactical Air Force. It wrought destruction at Allied bases, destroying scores of aircraft and killing and wounding many airmen. The Allies could quickly replace their losses in aeroplanes and personnel, but the Luftwaffe could not recover. The Germans' losses in aircraft were heavy but they could also be made up. However, they had committed the core of their experienced fighter pilots to the operation, along with many novice pilots – they could not be replaced. The operation had dealt a mortal blow to the German fighter arm. Despite this, and especially after the Allied Rhine crossing, the Luftwaffe fought courageously until the last day of war.

In March 1945, Johnson was promoted to group captain and given the command of No 125 Wing. It comprised three squadrons equipped with the new Spitfire Mk XIVs, powered by the 2,050hp Rolls-Royce Griffon engine. For those used to the Merlin Spitfire, these no longer felt or handled like a Spitfire. They were powerful, fast and hard-hitting, but the propeller rotated in the other direction, and the engine responded differently and produced a lot of torque, which meant that it needed constant trimming, especially when manoeuvring. 'A nice, fast flying machine,' said Johnson after his first flight, 'but it's not a Spitfire anymore.' He flew the new mark in combat several times, but he was not alone in preferring the Rolls-Royce Merlin-powered Spitfire Mk IX.

The post of Commanding Officer of No 125 Wing was essentially an administrative post, but Johnson regularly led the Wing or a squadron. Late in April, he led the Wing over Berlin for the first time, encountering an untidy swarm of Soviet fighters, which contrasted with the tight formation in which Johnson held his wing. Both groups treated each other suspiciously.

The Germans surrendered on 8 May, with No 125 Wing based at Celle, near Hanover. Immediately after the surrender, Johnson took the Wing to Denmark, organizing a flying display to celebrate victory, attended by the Queen of Denmark, in aid of the children of Denmark.

Group Captain Johnson, DSO, DFC, American DFC, finished the war with a score of at least thirty-eight confirmed, two probables and six damaged. This amounts to forty-two victories, because he shared eight of the confirmed victories, counting as halves, including his only twin-engined aerial victim, a Bf 110 destroyed on 17 August 1943; he also shared in destroying a Ju 88 on the ground on 28 March 1944. His score makes him the RAF's official top-scoring fighter pilot of World War Two. However, Johnson's greatness lies not in his own, albeit considerable, individual combat ability, but in his sense of position and timing which gave him the ability to place his squadrons to inflict the maximum damage on the enemy.

PART VIII

CHAPTER 27
Post-War

D ouglas Bader had decided to leave the RAF. He knew that he could not serve for long periods in hot climates; his legs would become raw. That would bar him from rising to the top, as such service was part of the rise. In peacetime, he would not get an 'unrestricted' medical category. Secondly, his mentor, Leigh-Mallory, had been killed in an air crash two years before. Without him, a rise to the top would be harder. Bader was not interested in a restricted, unadventurous Service career. He resolved to leave. Before leaving, he served in two posts which in their different ways served to show that the decision to leave was the right one.

Dick Atcherley, who had served with Bader on No 23 Squadron at Kenley in 1930, was now an air commodore after a brilliant if unorthodox wartime career and was commanding the Central Fighter Establishment (CFE) at Tangmere. In May 1945, he offered Bader the command of the Day Fighter Wing of the CFE, with the rank of group captain. Bader took the post keenly, but it was a mistake.

When Bader arrived back at Tangmere in early June 1945, he had not been operational for nearly four years. Not only had he been non-operational, but he had had no contact with the air war at all. It was not the same as coming back in 1940 after being away in the 1930s. Then change had been slow and he had been in constant contact with aviation and military pilots. The changes during the four years since 1940–41 had been fast, large and wide. Bader had fought a pure, aggressive fighter war, a fluid war. In the intervening years, fighters had become tactical weapons. They had flown in support of the armies in North Africa, Italy, France and Germany, striking at ground targets, often on the battlefield and often under tight control. Bader had had no experience of such operations, and few kinds of operation can be learnt except by flying them. The fighter leaders who had experienced this highly stressful warfare had flown for many months. Bader was keen, but they were spent. These experienced men were unlikely to respond to being driven by a boss whom they considered to be out of date.

The Commander-in-Chief of Fighter Command, Air Vice-Marshal James Robb, quickly posted Bader to command the North Weald Sector – a post to quicken the pulse of 'The Few'. He commanded six fighter stations, with twelve fighter squadrons, including one of Meteor jet fighters. He got his own personal Spitfire, and had his own code painted on it, 'D-B'. But there was no vitality in the job.

On 1 September, No 11 Group HQ instructed Bader to organize the flypast over London to celebrate the fifth anniversary of the Battle of Britain, on 15 September. He had two weeks, but it was a task he could relish. There was a certain irony in forming up and flying three hundred RAF aeroplanes over London at the same time . . .

On several airfields across East Anglia that mid-September morning in 1945, aeroplanes were gathering for the flypast. In the van were to be a dozen of the most celebrated of 'The Few'. They were gathered on the tarmac at North Weald, along with the Commander-in-Chief Fighter Command, Sir James Robb, and Air Vice-Marshal Dermot Boyle, Bader's instructor from his days at Cranwell and now Air Officer Commanding No 11 Group. The 1940 Commander-in-Chief of Fighter Command, Air Chief Marshal Lord Dowding, stood chatting with his pilots.

It was not a good flying day. There was low cloud over south-east England. The timing of the flypast was critical. Three hundred aeroplanes were taking part in it. They all had to form up to make one continuous formation.

As the men talked on the tarmac, the groundcrews made the final checks on the twelve Spitfires. Most of them bore the personal codes of their pilots.

A decision would have to be taken – would they fly or was the weather too poor? Sir James turned to Dermot Boyle: 'I think we must leave it to Group Captain Bader to decide whether to go or call it off.'

Bader replied instantly: 'We're on sir.'

Bader stepped up on to the wing of his aeroplane. He hauled himself into the cockpit. Holding on to the canopy and the windscreen, he pivoted on to the seat and dropped down on to his parachute pack. He pulled his straps on. Quickly, he ran through his cockpit drill. The engine coughed into life immediately the starter banged. Blue-black smoke billowed back in the slipstream, bright blue flames flickered a second in the exhaust pipes, then the Merlin 66 settled to a steady, fast beat, flames licking from the exhausts.

Behind him, eleven Merlins roared and crackled. The rush of air flattened the grass surrounding the tarmac and wound the onlookers' tunics and trouser legs around their bodies, making them bend and shield their eyes and deafening them as they watched the green and grey aeroplanes, shining and smooth, begin to roll.

Bader led the squadron out, bouncing and dipping like ducks across the grass. He looked around behind him at the eleven pilots, hoods back, waiting for his signal. He pointed into wind, and opened the throttle. The others followed. In precise formation, the elite squadron gathered speed, lifted off, wheels folding up smoothly, and gained height. Bader wheeled them round for a quick pass over the airfield and then led them climbing away to the south-east to join the formations that were being created all over East Anglia – a Big Wing with a vengeance.

It was an exhilarating moment. Stan Turner and Denis Crowley-Milling closed up on Bader. There behind him were the other representatives of 'The Few', gently bouncing in the autumn air behind him: Tim Vigors; Keith Lofts; Billy Drake; John Ellis; Bill 'Hawkeye' Wells; Pete Brothers; Roy Bush; Bob

Tuck; and Al Deere.

It was an honour for Bader to lead in such distinguished company. He had vaguely hankered after a crack against the Japanese . . . but . . . and the Air Ministry wanted him back permanently and would give him the seniority he would have had had he served continuously since 1929 . . . but Bader had felt in Colditz that he should leave the Air Force after the war. The past few months had shown him his feelings were right.

The Fighter Leader School at Tangmere still had a job to do, but there was a sense of anti-climax. Pilots were weary. The aeroplanes, the men, and the attitudes, the whole atmosphere, were different. Fighters had become sophisticated multi-role tactical instruments. Command of the North Weald Sector brought twelve fighter squadrons under his control, but where was the enemy? the purpose? the challenges? Demobilization was sending the war-weary pilots back home. Government cuts were running the Air Force down fast.

In March 1946, Bader left the RAF. Shell wanted him back too, and, in July, he returned to Shell's Aviation Department at St Mirren's Court, in the City of London. In order to conduct their worldwide business, they gave Douglas Bader his own light aeroplane . . .

☆   ☆

Douglas Bader was not alone in leaving the RAF after a successful wartime career. Many who had attained senior rank were reverted to their substantive ranks when hostilities ceased. Some were confirmed in their rank, like Dundas who held a regular commission. However, very few of those who had fought in Bader's squadrons and who had survived the war remained in the RAF. Only one of the FAA pilots who had fought with Bader survived the war, Richard Gardner, RNVR, who had been demobilized soon after VJ-Day as the Admiralty hastily disbanded the Reserve. Working in the cosmetics industry, Gardner rose rapidly in the ranks of the Yardley corporation.

Many wartime pilots who left the RAF and RN joined or rejoined the Auxiliary Air Force – including Cocky Dundas – which on 16 December 1947 was granted the prefix 'Royal' in recognition of the Auxiliary squadrons' services. Dundas retired from the RAF on 27 January 1947, with the courtesy rank of group captain, higher than his substantive rank of wing commander, in recognition of his service. Later, in 1947, he joined No 601 (County of London) Squadron, Auxiliary Air Force, as a Flight Commander. The squadron had re-formed at RAF Hendon in June 1946 under an old friend of Dundas, Squadron Leader Max Aitken, DSO, DFC, MP, who had served with the squadron between 1935 and August 1940. It flew Spitfire LF Mk XVIs from December 1946. Aitken relinquished command to Dundas in June 1948. In March 1949 the squadron moved to North Weald in preparation for receiving jet fighters, for which Hendon was too restricted. It became operational on the de Havilland Vampire F.3 that December.

In 1950, Hugh Dundas married and retired from the Royal Auxiliary Air Force. Group Captain Dundas had joined Beaverbrook Newspapers in 1948, becoming *Daily Express* Air Correspondent. Later, in 1961, he joined Redifusion, reaching the board in 1966, and subsequently held portfolios on several Redifusion Group and other company boards, and was awarded a knighthood for his services to broadcasting.

Several other Bader squadron pilots also left to pursue successful careers in 'civvy street'. Among them was Arthur Donaldson. At the end of the war, he was in charge of day fighter operations at the Uxbridge HQ of No 11 Group, Air Defence of Great Britain. He saw no stable future in the RAF. Stan Turner could see little place for himself in the senior ranks of the RAF post-war, and left. Unsurprisingly, he made his mark and rose to command his own corporation in Canada.

Other 'Hostilities Only' pilots decided to remain in the RAF, including James Johnson and Denis Crowley-Milling. For both of them, it was a good decision, for they were given several responsible positions, rose rapidly in rank and had distinguished careers. Both were valuable assets, aside from recruitment publicity: they had the tactical knowledge which the RAF needed.

In 1945, Crowley-Milling was appointed to a post in the Air Ministry Operational Requirements Section for which his vast operational experience made him highly suitable. After the war, Johnson reverted to his substantive rank of wing commander, and was posted to No 124 Wing, Second Tactical Air Force.

In January 1947, Crowley-Milling was also posted to an operational command, No 6 Squadron at RAF Nicosia, Cyprus, in RAF Middle East Command. The squadron was re-equipping with the new Tempest Mk VI, the first to do so. The Mark VI had been developed from the Mark V specifically for the Middle East and was the most popular Tempest among pilots. The ultimate Sabre-engined fighter, it was highly successful in tactical roles in five squadrons of Middle East Command.

A few weeks after No 6 Squadron had relinquished its Tempests, and converted to Vampires, in December 1949, Crowley-Milling was appointed Personal Staff Officer to the Commander-in-Chief Fighter Command. Later in 1950 he returned to an air base, RAF Odiham, as Wing Commander Flying, where he served until 1954.

In 1946, 'Johnnie' Johnson was appointed Officer Commanding Tactics Branch, CFE; then in 1947–48 was sent on a Staff course at Royal Canadian Air Force College, Toronto – appropriately, in view of his long association with Canadian squadrons. An exchange posting to US Tactical Air Command at Langley Field, Virginia, followed. Serving under Lieutenant General Pete Quesada of 'Question Mark' fame, he assisted in organizing air displays. Johnson assumed the USAF rank of colonel for presentation purposes! He flew American aircraft, including the North American F-86A Sabre.

When the Korean War broke out in June 1950, Johnson was posted to the US Far East Air Forces for a three-month tour of active duty. Operating from Japan, he flew Douglas B-26 Invaders over Korea as far as the Yalu River, photographing North Korean-held territory and concentrations by day and night. This was a vital activity as the main USAF effort was directed at fighter-bomber operations and there was little other air activity, the Allies having been driven into the sea.

When Johnson returned to the RAF, with the US Air Medal and Legion of Merit, he was posted as Wing Commander Flying of No 135 Wing in West Germany, which flew the Vampire jet fighter. In 1952, promoted to group captain, he was appointed Commanding Officer of RAF Wildenrath, near the German-Dutch border, when it opened in January 1952. There he oversaw the formation of the RAF's first Sabre fighter wing in 1952–53, No 135 Wing comprising No 67 and 71 Squadrons, operating Sabre F.1s, F.2s and later F.4s. The Wing was part of RAF Germany which descended from the Second Tactical Air Force and was assigned interceptor, strike and tactical attack duties, and support of the British Army of the Rhine.

There was considerable prestige in flying the Sabre, for the F-86 was the major Allied day fighter of the Korean War. Inaugurating the first RAF Sabre wing was a task that required a leader of Johnson's calibre. During the war, he always strove to get his units to the action; in peace, he passed on with clarity his considerable practical and analytical tactical knowledge to his pilots.

Group Captain Johnson held that the Sabre handled as perfectly as a Spitfire. The Sabre represented the first truly successful jet fighter, and it is appropriate that James Johnson should have commanded the first Sabre squadrons, just as Denis Crowley-Milling should have commanded the last of the piston-engined fighters, the Hawker Tempest Mk VI, for he had flown the last of the RAF's biplane fighters, the Gladiator, and then the first of the Hawker monoplane fighters, the Hurricane.

In 1954, Johnson was appointed Deputy Director of Air Operations at the Air Ministry, and in 1957 became Officer Commanding RAF Cottesmore, Rutland, the base of the first V-bomber wing. In June 1957, he was accorded a singular honour when he flew one of the RAF's last two operational Spitfires, PR.19 PS853, from RAF Woodvale to RAF Biggin Hill to found the Battle of Britain Memorial Flight.

In 1960, 'Johnnie' Johnson completed a Staff course at the Imperial Defence College, and, promoted to air commodore, was appointed Senior Air Staff Officer at Bomber Command's No 3 Group HQ, Mildenhall, Suffolk. On 1 January 1963, he was promoted to air vice-marshal and posted to Aden as Air Officer Commanding Air Forces Middle East. In 1956, Johnson published *Wing Leader*, an autobiography and a classic account of fighter wing tactics. *Full Circle* followed in 1964, a tactical history of fighter warfare from 1914 to Korea. He retired from the RAF on 15 March 1966. He later became a director of British, Canadian and South African companies and President of Johnnie Johnson Housing Trust Ltd.

Denis Crowley-Milling spent nearly four years (1954–57) on the Directing Staff of RAF College Bracknell, followed by a post at the Flying College, RAF Manby, in 1957–58. He was a member of the Plans Staff, Fighter Command, in 1958–59, and became Group Captain Operations, CFE, between 1959 and 1962. In 1962–64, he became Station Commander, RAF Leconfield, followed by another overseas posting as Air Officer

Commanding, RAF Hong Kong, between 1964 and 1966.

Crowley-Milling became Director Operational Requirements, Ministry of Defence (Air), in 1966–67, and then the Commander, RAF Staff and Principal Air Attache, Washington, 1967–70. In 1970, he was appointed Air Officer Commanding No 38 Group, with his HQ at Odiham. Throughout 1973, he was Air Officer Commanding No 46 Group, with his HQ at Upavon.

Crowley-Milling had been made a Companion of the British Empire in 1963 and was created a Knight Commander of the Bath in 1973. For over a year, 1974–75, Sir Denis was the United Kingdom Representative on the Permanent Military Deputies Group in the Central Eastern Nations Treaty Organization. At the end of his appointment, Air Marshal Sir Denis Crowley-Milling retired from the RAF. He did not cease his involvement with the Services, and he was Controller of the RAF Benevolent Fund. Honours continued, and he became a Gentleman Usher of the Scarlet Rod and Registrar and Secretary of the Order of the Bath.

SELECT
BIBLIOGRAPHY

APPS, LT-CDR MICHAEL, *The Four Ark Royals* (William Kimber, London, 1976)
— *Send Her Victorious* (William Kimber, London, 1977)
BADER, SIR DOUGLAS, *Fight for the Sky – The Story of the Spitfire and Hurricane* (Sidgwick & Jackson, London, 1973)
BAKER, E. C. R., *The Fighter Aces of the RAF* (William Kimber, London, 1962)
BEAMONT, ROLAND, *Phoenix into Ashes* (William Kimber, London, 1968)
BEEDLE, J., *43 Squadron* (Beaumont Aviation Literature, 1966)
BEURLING, F/O GEORGE & ROBERTS, LESLIE, *Malta Spitfire: The Story of a Fighter Pilot* (Oxford University Press, 1943; Arms & Armour Press, London, 1973)
BOWYER, MICHAEL J. F., *Aircraft for the Royal Air Force* (Faber and Faber, London, 1981)
BRENNAN, P/O PAUL, HESSELYN, P/O RAY & BATESON, HENRY, *Spitfires over Malta* (Jarrolds, London, 1943)
BRICKHILL, PAUL, *Reach for the Sky* (Collins, London, 1954)
BROWN, J. D., *Carrier Operations in World War II* (Ian Allan, Shepperton)
CAMERON, IAN, *Red Duster, White Ensign, The Story of the Malta Convoys* (Frederick Muller, London, 1959)
CHURCHILL, SIR WINSTON S., *The Second World War* Vols I-VI (Cassell, London, 1948–55)
DEERE, AIR CDRE ALAN C., *Nine Lives* (Hodder & Stoughton, London, 1959)

DUNCAN SMITH, GROUP CAPT. W. G. G., *Spitfire Into Battle* (John Murray, London, 1981)
DUNDAS, GROUP CAPT. SIR HUGH S. L., *Flying Start – A Fighter Pilot's War Years* (Stanley Paul, London, 1988)
DOUGLAS HAMILTON, LORD JAMES, MP, *The Air Battle of Malta: The Diaries of a Fighter Pilot* (Mainstream Publishing, Edinburgh, 1981)
EDWARDS, MAJOR A., *Customs and Traditions of the RAF* (circa 1978)
EMBRY, AIR CHIEF MARSHAL SIR BASIL, *Mission Completed* (Methuen, London, 1957)
FRANKS, NORMAN, *Sky Tiger – The Story of 'Sailor' Malan* (William Kimber, London)
— *The Greatest Air Battle: Dieppe 19th August 1942* (William Kimber, London, 1979)
GALLAND, GENERAL ADOLF, *The First and the Last* (Methuen, London, 1955)
GODDARD, AIR MARSHAL SIR VICTOR, *Skies to Dunkirk – A Personal Memoir* (London)
GRETTON, VICE-ADMIRAL SIR PETER, *Convoy Escort Commander* (Cassell, 1964)
HALLEY, JAMES J., *The Squadrons of the Royal Air Force and Commonwealth* (Air-Britain)
HOGAN, G., *Malta: The Triumphant Years* (Robert Hale, London, 1979)
HUNT, LESLIE, *Twenty-One Squadrons: The History of the Royal Auxiliary Air Force 1917–73* (Terence Dalton, 1975)
JACKSON, ROBERT, *The Hawker Hurricane in Action* (Blandford, Poole, 1987)

— *The Hawker Tempest and Sea Fury* (Blandford, London, 1988)

JAMESON, WILLIAM, *Ark Royal, 1939–41* (Rupert Hart Davis)

JOHNSON, AIR VICE-MARSHAL JAMES E., *Wing Leader* (Chatto & Windus, London, 1956)

— *Full Circle* (Chatto & Windus, London, 1964)

KEMP, REAR ADMIRAL PETER, *The Fleet Air Arm* (Herbert Jenkins)

KILLEN, JOHN, *A History of Marine Aviation* (Frederick Muller, London)

KNIGHT, DENNIS, *Harvest of Messerschmitts: The Chronicle of a Village at War, 1940* (Frederick Warner, London, 1987)

LEWIS, PETER, *Squadron Histories RFC, RNAS and RAF since 1912* (Putnam, 1959 and 1968)

LUCAS, P. B. 'LADDIE', *Flying Colours – The Epic Story of Douglas Bader* (Hutchinson, London, 1981)

MASTERS, DAVID, *So Few* (Eyre & Spottiswoode, London, 1941, 1943)

MINISTRY OF INFORMATION, *The Air Battle of Malta* (HMSO, London, 1944)

OWEN, RODERIC, *The Desert Air Force* (Hutchinson, London, 1948)

POOLMAN, KENNETH, *Ark Royal* (William Kimber, London)

— *Illustrious* (William Kimber, London, 1955)

POPHAM, HUGH, *Sea Flight* (William Kimber, London, 1954)

RAWLINGS, JOHN D. R., *Fighter Squadrons of the RAF* (Macdonald, 1969)

ROSKILL, CAPT, RN, STEPHEN W., *The War at Sea: A History of Second World War* (Cassell, London)

RUTTER, OWEN, *Ark Royal* (HMSO, London, 1942)

RUSSELL, SIR HERBERT, *Ark Royal* (John Lane, London)

SHORES, CHRISTOPHER & WILLIAMS, CLIVE, *Aces High: The Fighter Aces of the British and Commonwealth Air Forces of World War Two* (Neville Spearman, London, 1966)

SMITH, PETER C., *'Pedestal': The Malta Convoy of August 1942* (William Kimber, London, 1970)

— *The Battles of the Malta Sailing Forces* (Ian Allan, Shepperton, 1974)

STEWART, ADRIAN (pseudonym), *Hurricane – The War Exploits of the Fighter Aircraft* (William Kimber, London, 1982)

TEDDER, LORD, *Air Power in War* (Hodder & Stoughton, London, 1953)

TERRAINE, JOHN, *The Right of the Line* (Hodder & Stoughton, London, 1985)

TOWNSEND, PETER, *Duel of Eagles* (Weidenfeld & Nicolson, London, 1970)

TURNER, JOHN FRAYN, *The Bader Wing*) Midas Books, Tunbridge Wells, 1981)

WARNER, OLIVER, *The Greatest Sea Battles* (Spring Books)

WINTON, JOHN, *The War at Sea* (Arrow, London)

— *Find, Fix and Strike: The Fleet Air Arm at War 1939–45* (Batsford, London, 1980)

WYKEHAM, AIR VICE-MARSHAL PETER, *Fighter Command* (Putnam, 1960)

PUBLIC RECORD OFFICE

This book could not have been written without this rich repository of documents. In particular, the following were consulted: Air Tactics, under AIR 9 and AIR 10; Squadron and Wing Operational Record Books, under AIR 26 and AIR 27 respectively; Combat Reports, by unit and famous individuals under AIR 50; and HMS *Indomitable*, under ADM1.

INDEX

INDEX